DECOLLECTIVISATION, DESTRUCTION AND DISILLUSIONMENT

Decollectivisation, Destruction and Disillusionment

A community study in Southern Estonia

Edited by

ILKKA ALANEN
JOUKO NIKULA
HELVI PÕDER
REIN RUUTSOO

Routledge
Taylor & Francis Group

LONDON AND NEW YORK

First published 2001 by Ashgate Publishing

Reissued 2018 by Routledge
2 Park Square, Milton Park, Abingdon, Oxon OX14 4RN
711 Third Avenue, New York, NY 10017, USA

Routledge is an imprint of the Taylor & Francis Group, an informa business

Publisher's Note
The publisher has gone to great lengths to ensure the quality of this reprint but points out that some imperfections in the original copies may be apparent.

Disclaimer
The publisher has made every effort to trace copyright holders and welcomes correspondence from those they have been unable to contact.

A Library of Congress record exists under LC control number: 00110698

ISBN 13: 978-1-138-72560-7 (hbk)
ISBN 13: 978-1-138-72557-7 (pbk)
ISBN 13: 978-1-315-19183-6 (ebk)

Contents

v

List of Figures

List of Tables

Contributors

Dr Ilkka Alanen is Professor of Sociology (specialised in the study of rural areas in Russia and Eastern Europe) at the Department of Social Sciences and Philosophy, University of Jyväskylä, Jyväskylä, Finland. He has published extensively on rural sociological theory and agricultural reform in Central and Eastern Europe.

Dr Jouko Nikula is Research Fellow (Academy of Finland) at the Department of Social Sciences and Philosophy, University of Jyväskylä, Jyväskylä, Finland. He has worked on several international projects researching class structure, and most recently new entrepreneurship in post-socialist countries and the formation of labour markets and the worker movement in Russia.

MA Helvi Põder is a long-serving lecturer in psychology and sociology at the Estonian Agricultural University, Tartu, Estonia. She is a veteran sociologist with a long experience in Soviet times and today.

Dr Rein Ruutsoo is Professor of Political Science at the Department of Political Science, University of Tartu, Tartu, Estonia. He has published extensively on the history of ideas and civil society. He is one of the most distinguished debaters on social issues in Estonia.

Dr Mati Tamm is Emeritus Professor at the Estonian Agricultural University, Tartu, Estonia. He was the central designer of the practical implementation of Estonian agricultural reform.

Foreword

The privatisation of Kanepi kolkhoz in the southeastern part of Estonia – like the stories of many other collective farms, we presume – turned out to be a much more dramatic series of events than our research team could have ever imagined. For us, it proved to have all the hallmarks of a drama, full of exciting incidents and unexpected turns. Nevertheless, despite occasional farcical elements, the overall workings of this drama have been profoundly tragic. It has revealed to us a fragment of real life that appears to have forced people to encounter conditions almost as insurmountable as the shipwreck of the passenger ferry Estonia, an event to which many of the interviewees compared the privatisation process.

Not only is the privatisation of the kolkhozes a dramatic series of events that has devastated people's conditions of existence; it is also a challenging subject of interpretation on the level of social theory. What was "real socialism" really like – that is to say, in the light of empirical research – from the viewpoint of agriculture? How did this system finally come to a dead end, and how was it forced to give way to another system in a situation of economic collapse (and in Estonia also under pressure from the nationalist movement)? One should note, however, that the social system that replaced it was not anything new. In actual fact it was a system much older than the state socialist system, and it originated from a world that was economically and technologically at an entirely different level. Estonia regained its independence and was capable of reinstating capitalist social relations that bore a close resemblance to the social relations in the first Estonian republic (1918–1940). However, its attempts at restoring the old peasant society turned out to be a romanticised utopia. Our research shows the social relations of the Soviet era had a fundamental effect on the way the transition from the socialist system to the "new" capitalist system took place. For example, the fact that an agricultural education system of largely high standards produced specialists for large-scale farming, the fact that agricultural machinery and production buildings were geared to large scale production, and the concentration of the former agrarian population in larger population centres make the resurrection of the world as it stood in the past an unattainable goal. Yet, even if this impossible romanticised utopia cannot be replaced by any alternative strategy, the nostalgic ideology still exerts a strong influence over the way social relations are being restructured in the countryside.

Stripped of any comforting illusions, the birth of capitalism is in reality a dramatic process of ownership redistribution and wealth in general; it could never have been the idyll that many in Estonia might have hoped for. Nevertheless, the Estonian people would certainly have gained much if the social changes that took place during the Soviet era (such as the ones mentioned above) had been taken into account more carefully in the implementation of the agricultural reform.

I would like to thank my co-authors Jouko Nikula, Helvi Põder, Rein Ruutsoo and all the other persons involved in the preparation of this book. Without their co-operations this project would not have been possible.

I express my special thanks to Jouko Peltomäki who translated three chapters and was largely responsible for the technical editing of the book. In addition to offering valuable editorial assistance he also helped in improving the language of the entire book and was responsible for liaison with the publisher, the language checkers, and our layout specialist.

This book was created as a result of a research project: "The Privatisation of Agriculture, the Family Farm Ideology and Class Formation in the Newly Independent Baltic Republics". The project has received funding from the Academy of Finland.

Ilkka Alanen
Leader of the Research Project, General Editor

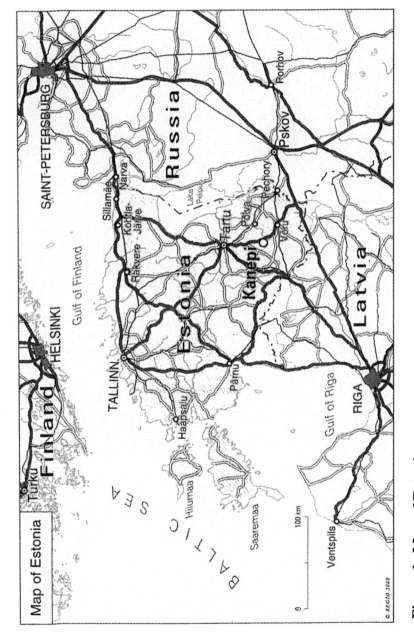

Figure 1 Map of Estonia

1 Introduction

ILKKA ALANEN

Research Background

At the turn of the century the political significance of the agrarian population, and especially the small farmers, was crucial in northern and eastern Europe. They were one of the most important population groups in terms of newly emerging parliamentarism, and also the group on which the new nation states were based. The agrarian question and the independence movement were closely linked, and even after the achievement of independence, peasants were the cornerstone of the nation state. This undoubtedly held true for the Baltic countries also, including Estonia. Estonian national consciousness and its peasant culture were interconnected in a very concrete manner. The country was predominantly agrarian, and land cultivation was in the hands of small farmers. This is the historical heritage that accounts above all for the predominant nostalgic desire to reinstate family farming in post-socialist Eastern Europe.

A strong desire to revive the Estonian countryside destroyed by the Soviet occupiers formed an integral part of the 'Singing Revolution' in Estonia. Yet, for the majority of the genuine agrarian population that desire denoted primarily the restoration of legal rights of ownership of the old family farms, returning the farms to the former owners or to their heirs. Probably only a small percentage of the agrarian population actually wished for the dissolution of all collective farms. The desires of the agrarian population were towards agricultural reform on the basis of two principles: the preservation of large-scale production to some degree and the restoration of private land ownership. However, the political elite did not identify, accommodate or act on the first of these desires.

If the material and intellectual resources for large-scale production cannot be transformed into resources for small-scale production within the agricultural industry, and if there is no reliable support for small-scale farming, a reform setting small-scale production as its target is doomed to failure. In retrospect, it is clear that a reform aiming at small-scale production without adequate planning or support simply destroys the material and mental resources of the old system. In the long run, once market forces have had the opportunity to develop their own logic, a dogmatic peasant ideology has no chance of achieving its ends, since the new market forces will still have at their disposal some of the resources of the old system based on large-scale production. Hence, over time, one can predict that the current family farm project of the Estonian government will possibly, and even probably be transformed into its opposite, a project for large-scale farming – if Estonian agriculture is not totally destroyed in the meantime. Some signs of the new orientation are visible today.

From a theoretical point of view, it is difficult to investigate the transformation using a survey method, since it is next to impossible to collect a sample of data large enough to shed light on aspects such as the concentration of ownership mentioned above; purely financial considerations play a part here. On the other hand, one might expect that our investigation would be able to demonstrate the gradual decline of the old large-scale production system. There are similar problems with the use of public statistics, which are in any case confusing, given the use of various old Soviet legal categories as well as more recent reform-related categories none of which correspond at all well with current realities. Private plot farms and peasant farms are two examples of legal categories denoting land ownership. But in reality, the acreage of land owned is by no means the deciding factor in considering the relation of large-scale to small-scale farming.[1] There are also problems in assessing those private enterprises that use the old collective production plants, or in predicting their future. Some of them are simply dying off, while others have managed to reverse the process and display signs of dynamic growth.[2]

Large-scale farms can be, for simplicity, divided into at least two categories: co-owned and privately owned. However, legal categories such as these are often deceptive. In many cases both real share ownership and the power has been concentrated in the hands of one individual or a small number of people. All those large-scale enterprises owned by a small number of people are now moving in the direction of private capitalistic farms.

---

1   Many active farmers rent farmland at very favourable terms from landowners who do not wish to start cultivating the lands that have recently been restituted to them. At the moment there is plenty of farmland available for rent.

2   Since autumn 1998 these promising agricultural enterprises have also faced enormous difficulties due to the Russian economic crisis and Estonia's ultra-liberal customs policy. These later developments, however, are not covered in this study.

It follows from all this that case studies are needed in order to forecast the future and possibly also to formulate an agricultural policy that would be more rational than the agricultural policy of the Estonian government over the past few years. Our research on the Kanepi case contributes to this specific end. Phenomena that may still be in their embryonic state in the area of a former kolkhoz, such as with our case in Kanepi, probably offer a firmer basis for predicting the future than overall statistics or average values based on a survey. Indeed, true developmental trends can perhaps only be substantiated using certain specific types of field studies. Of course, generalisations do require the support of survey sampling and overall statistics. To serve this purpose, in the Kanepi case research we have made use of survey material gathered in the context of the research project mentioned in the foreword and also the Baltic-Nordic research project.[3] Still, it is clear that the Kanepi project in itself does not meet the need for extensive case studies in Estonia, let alone the other Baltic republics, since the more one looks at cases from the widest possible range of areas, the more accurate will be the picture that emerges of the overall situation. Hence, we will leave final generalisations for a future occasion.

Estonia is a small country in the Baltic region, and on a Europe-wide scale its agricultural production is of negligible importance. Moreover, the area covered by our research is considered remote and peripheral even within Estonia. Despite these facts, a case study such as this does have general significance. The Baltic states were a part of the Soviet Union, and in addition to this, the Soviet agricultural system had spread to nearly all the countries in the Soviet block. And indeed, from the All-Union perspective, the kolkhoz was not particularly peripheral, nor did it have exceptionally adverse natural conditions. Thus, it is likely that an Estonian case study will provide a useful insight into the transition process that the whole of Eastern Europe and Eastern Central Europe is currently undergoing.

The Special Character of Kanepi

The municipality of Kanepi is a rural community of under 4,000 inhabitants, and it is situated in south-eastern Estonia. The eponymous Kanepi kolkhoz was a fairly successful enterprise at the time of the Estonian SSR; at a national level it fared above average, and in Põlva county it was reckoned

---

3   'Social Change in the Baltic and Nordic Countries. A Comparative Study of Estonia, Latvia, Lithuania, Finland, Norway and Sweden,' financed by the Nordic Council.

among the elite. Land reform was not particularly successful in Kanepi, but neither were its results exceptionally poor. However, the peripheral geographical location of the municipality and natural conditions below the Estonian average always meant that great efforts were required for success, and they now cast doubt on future prospects for agricultural production.

The fact that Kanepi had already been the subject of some research was more important than the "typical qualities" of our case – even supposing such "average cases" actually existed in those tumultuous times of transition. It was an advantage that we did not have to start from scratch. Kanepi kolkhoz had also had pioneering status, in the sense that researchers from the Estonian Agricultural University had been closely involved in the planning of the reform in co-operation with the kolkhoz leadership of that time. Thus, our plan to initiate a research project in Kanepi was probably a welcome move, and very interesting from the viewpoint of the Kanepi personnel. The co-operation that evolved on this basis is manifestly evident in this book. One of the writers of the book – Emeritus Professor Mati Tamm – was a member of the group that drew up plans for the reform. Indeed, the choice of Kanepi as the subject of our case study may largely be attributed to the interest shown towards the municipality by Estonian agricultural researchers, although none of them, not even Professor Tamm, participated in the actual gathering and analysis of the new material. The choice of Kanepi has, all in all, provided us with a number of advantages from the point of view of conducting our research and, of course, writing this collection of articles.

Methodological Foundations

The principal method used in gathering the material was snowball sampling. The basic principle used in this method is that the information gathered in an earlier interview plays a great part in the formulation of questions in future interviews, and consequently the choice of the next interviewees. This method may result – an indeed happened – in the need to interview a number of individuals repeatedly.

While we were drawing up our plans for the interviews we were able to find out the legal procedures of decollectivisation, the decision-making procedures of the Soviet agricultural system, and many structural characteristics of the kolkhoz. Furthermore, we also gained some kind of an idea about the history of Kanepi municipality as well as Kanepi kolkhoz, the subject of our research.

Prior to embarking upon our field studies we were further briefed by Professor Asser Murutar of the Estonian Agricultural University, and Director Jüri Ginter of the MAI (*Maaelu Arengu Instituut*, Institute for Rural Development) institute in Tartu. Not only are they pivotal experts in Estonian agriculture and the Estonian countryside but they had personally taken part in the design and execution of the agricultural reform plan in Kanepi kolkhoz. This ensured above all that no relevant individuals or groups were left uninterviewed and unrepresented. Moreover, we improved our knowledge by familiarising ourselves with local and county archives. However, in terms of the outcome of the study, the interviews with the members of Kanepi kolkhoz and other local residents have been the most important source of information; these interviews have been crucial in guiding the selection of new interviewees and also in finding ways to supplement the interview material from other sources.

The research group filed work through various stages and with varied combinations of researchers in the spring and summer of 1995. Subsequently, only relatively minor supplementary interviews (1996, 1998 and 1999) were conducted. In many ways the year 1995 was ideal for gathering all the essential data, since the greatest turmoil of decollectivisation had died down and people had had some time to process the events in their minds – yet the vivid details had not been forgotten. Today, gathering as rich a body of data would no longer be possible.

Working in teams facilitated a quick preliminary evaluation of the information gathered in the interviews, and the division of our activities into several periods spread over a longer time facilitated an unhurried digestion of the information. The interviews were not conducted by the four authors of this volume alone (the work division of responsibility will be detailed later). An important part was played by a large number of researchers from Estonia and the Nordic Countries, who had worked in the Baltic-Nordic project. Although not as deeply involved in this community study as the main project members, they valued the opportunity to get in touch with everyday realities in the newly independent Baltic countries. They added a valuable contribution to the empirical material gathered during the interviews by taking up viewpoints that would perhaps otherwise have been ignored.

Although Estonian and Finnish are closely related languages, and though a Finn soon picks up some basic Estonian phrases, the interviews by the Finnish researchers would not have been possible without interpreters. On many occasions our Estonian colleagues served as interpreters for the Finns as well as for the other visiting researchers, but on several occasions we had to employ dedicated interpreters. Complete simultaneous interpretation would have been impossible in the interview situation, which is why the interviews were recorded in their entirety for subsequent transcription into either Finnish or English.

Generally speaking there were at least two representatives of the project in every interview situation (an interviewer and an interpreter), but there were cases where half a dozen researchers were at a session with a single interviewee. The typical interview sessions were lengthy, often taking several hours, with thirty-minute mini-interviews the exception rather than the rule. The attitude of the interviewees was as a rule very positive, and the positive disposition was usually strengthened rather than weakened during the course of the interview. Some interviewees were very reserved to begin with, but after a while they seemed to relax. Apparently, this was due to the fact that the interview sessions were often experienced as a kind of therapy. We never needed to set any limits to the subject matter of the questions because of the reluctance of the interviewees – not even in the interviews with the key personalities, which, adding up the separate sessions, may have taken more than ten hours per person. We – the researchers – are very grateful for the openness of the interviewees. Thanks to them, the decollectivisation of agriculture was revealed to us as a much more eventful and dramatic process than we could ever have imagined before the interviews.

Ethical Considerations

When we set out to do field work in Kanepi, we made our intentions known in the county newspaper. Consequently, we also decided to be open about our research subject – the community of Kanepi – in this anthology of articles, and not to make any attempts to conceal its identity or location. Even if we had not publicly announced our research plans in the local newspaper, the extensive field work stage and the number of people involved in the project would not have gone unnoticed in such a small community.

Verbatim quotes from the interviewees play an important role in the empirical documentation of our research. When dealing with the decollectivisation process proper, we have decided against using the real names of the individuals in interview excerpts – except in a few instances where it has been absolutely necessary for the purpose of substantiating the subject matter. This policy is sufficient to conceal the identity of the majority of the interviewees, who often described very delicate matters in their interviews. Thus, a milker or a tractor driver will not have to fear that he or she may be subjected to criticism on the basis of what was confided to us in the interview.

In this matter we have, however, encountered a real problem, since profession, place of residence, etc. are often important parts of the argumentation. Hence, we cannot avoid using such expressions as the "former municipal director" or "later kolkhoz chairman," which are instantly recognisable at a local level, and would be identifiable by anybody who was determined enough to find out the names of these individuals. In this matter we have taken the following position: as long as a person holds or has held a public position, such as those mentioned above, he or she also holds public responsibility for his/her actions. Nevertheless, as far as all individuals are concerned – whether public figures or not – we have carefully avoided revealing anything of a distinctly personal nature, for example details that might harm a person's family life. Such delicate issues are generally not dealt with in the articles dealing with the municipality of Kanepi and the developments in local civil society. Hence, we have been able to be more open with the true names of individuals in these particular chapters.

It should be noted that although the privatisation of kolkhozes and sovkhozes – as with privatisation processes everywhere – has included a good many morally, and sometimes legally, reprehensible incidents, it is not our mission to name the culprits, let alone prove anyone's guilt. This does not imply that everything that took place was morally acceptable or even necessary. One must bear in mind that a dramatic process such as this can hardly ever be carried through, even in principle, without moral-legal controversy; there will certainly be conflicts, and probably from a certain point of view, misappropriations. Notice also that at the time of kolkhoz privatisation, morally questionable acts were often not in contradiction with any specific section of the law. And even if a particular act was against a specific law, there may have been another section the law that permitted it. On the other hand, in some cases the law was entirely clear, but apparently it could not be enforced. The rapidity, and the conflicting and unexpected nature of the events made legal control extremely difficult. Some people exploited this situation. The majority of clear breaches of the law will remain hidden for good, largely due to the fragmentary nature and destruction of concrete evidence (apparently some of the evidence has been destroyed deliberately). However, lack of evidence will not prevent the debate on the moral aspects of the events from continuing for years to come.

Our research did indeed bring forward a great number of allegations concerning misappropriations. We have made no attempts to verify whether each individual accusation holds true. Furthermore, it is advisable to consider the colloquial nature of the language used in the interviews in any attempt at interpretation. Thus, when the interviewees state that somebody "stole" and in a few instances admit that they themselves "thieved", these remarks often represent a primarily moral evaluation, not a legal one. Yet all in all, in the light of our study we are thoroughly convinced that there were numerous instances of morally disputable and frequently legally questionable events, some of which are mentioned by the interviewees in this book. These aspects are also extremely important in explaining and understanding all the consequences of the privatisation of agriculture.

The Structure of the Book and the Division of Labour Between the Researchers

This anthology has been compiled as an integrated volume, although it is composed of articles written by several individuals. The conclusion section (Chapter 7), however, is the joint effort of three authors and the article written by *Professor Mati Tamm* (Chapter 8) is another exception to the rule. Although Professor Tamm pays special attention to the kolkhoz of Kanepi, his article is, above all, an account of the background and execution of Estonian agricultural reform as described by the central designer of the practical implementation of the reform.

The writings by the members of the project team can be divided into two thematic areas. The bulk of the book is formed by the articles written by Helvi Põder, Ilkka Alanen and Jouko Nikula, who concentrate on the privatisation (decollectivisation) of the kolkhoz and its immediate consequences. The two articles by Rein Ruutsoo focus on the themes of municipal administration and local civil society. The former articles deal primarily with the privatised kolkhoz of Kanepi and the latter with local civil society, an understanding of both being required in order to grasp the complexity of the overall situation. The analysis of the special characteristics of rural district administration in the Soviet era and the description of the development of the Singing Revolution at a local level make it easier to understand the formation of the opposition, and how it became the vanguard in many of the decisive events in the kolkhoz. On the other hand, both the local administration and local civil society have been dramatically affected by the upheavals in the kolkhoz. Thus these two thematic areas complement one another.

In her description of Kanepi kolkhoz (Chapter 2), *Helvi Põder* concentrates on the historical background of Kanepi and the collective farm, and also describes the collectivisation on the basis of archive material and survey statistics. *Ilkka Alanen* concentrates on the privatisation process of the kolkhoz proper (Chapter 3) as well as its social implications and the new post-socialist agricultural enterprises, while *Jouko Nikula* (Chapter 4) studies local enterprises, especially those operating in manufacturing and service industries. The decision to divide *Rein Ruutsoo's* writings into two separate articles (Chapters 5 and 6) was made on the basis of the fact that social theory typically differentiates between the government and civil society, since their logic is different (although neither can be understood separately from the other). This variety of approaches serves the purpose of readability within the book.

All four writers worked in close co-operation throughout the entire project, and they have benefited enormously from each other's help. Furthermore, the frequent discussions between the researchers throughout the writing process have helped to create a degree of mutual understanding, although we do not attempt to explicate any common theoretical view. Although the views of the researchers do not greatly differ from each other, each researcher in the end bears the responsibility for the content of his or her article.

The Style of the Book

With this book we have attempted to reach as wide as possible an audience of readers interested in agricultural reform and post-socialism. The book is not aimed solely at a scholarly audience. This does not imply that we would in any respect wish to compromise academic principles, but we have, nevertheless, attempted to be as economical as possible with some of the scholarly apparatus typical of academic research. Thus, we have reduced our theoretical argumentation to the minimum. We do retain a basic theoretical methodology, but we intend to save the detailed analysis of concepts, as well as debates on the theories of other researchers for later publications. We have also collected a number of photographs from the kolkhoz and municipality of Kanepi, in the belief that a picture can tell more than words. On a personal level, we have all come to experience the privatisation of Kanepi kolkhoz as a great drama, and we hope to be able to convey to our readers this sense of an unfolding of dramatic – and for many of the participants, tragic – events.

Local and National Levels

This book focuses on the local level, i.e. the events in Kanepi kolkhoz and Kanepi municipality. Of course, the local developments could never be fully understood without an appreciation of the nationwide context of the Soviet Union or Estonia, but often the significance of nationwide developments runs the risk of being overlooked or otherwise hidden behind the sheer multiplicity of detail in local history. To facilitate an understanding of the matter we have set out two chronological tables (Tables 1.1 and 1.2) at the beginning of the book. The first table contains a chronology of the most important general political developments in Estonia and the Soviet Union, while the second table lists all the most important decisions in economic policy and legislation affecting agriculture. Table 1.2 also includes a calendar of the locally important events in Kanepi kolkhoz and municipality.

National economic circumstances set the basic conditions for the way events unfold. For example, it is altogether a different matter to make decisions on the breaking up of a kolkhoz in a situation of hyperinflation with the prices of agricultural produce relatively lagging behind than it would be in more stable conditions; thus the success of the transition can also be evaluated in the light of the figures delineating the development of agricultural production.

Table 1.3 at the beginning of the book presents a set of economic indicators (GDP, Inflation, Government budget, PSE, Volume of gross agricultural output, Agriculture and food trade balance, Share of agriculture in employment, Share of household income spend on food) important to an understanding of the economic background to the developments we describe.

Table 1.1   Chronology of the most important general political developments and selected local events in Kanepi

- 6 August 1940. Estonia loses its independence and is officially annexed to the USSR.
- 1985–1991. Era of Gorbachev's *glasnost* and *perestroika*.
- 23 August 1987. The first political demonstration in Tallinn.
- 12 December 1987. Founding of the Estonian Heritage Society (*Eesti Muinsuskaitse Selts*) in Tallinn.
- 13 April 1988. Founding of the Estonian Popular Front (*Rahvarinne*).

- 10–14 June 1988. 'Night song festivals' in the Tallinn Song Festival Grounds, giving birth to the term 'Singing Revolution'.
- 16 June 1988. The pro-Soviet empire ECP party secretary Karl Vaino is replaced by the reform-minded Vaino Väljas.
- Days of Kanepi organised in the summers of 1988, 1989 and 1990.
- 11 September 1988. 'The Song of Estonia 1988' festival in Tallinn draws 300,000 people.
- 25 September 1988. The reinauguration in Kanepi of the monument commemorating the memory of those who died in the War for Independence.
- 16 November 1988. ESSR Supreme Soviet declares the sovereignty of the ESSR.
- 18 January 1989. The Language Act is approved, declaring that Estonian is the state language.
- February 1989. Formation of Citizens' Committees begins.
- 23 August 1989. Baltic Chain: Baltic Popular Front movements organise a 600-kilometre human chain from Tallinn to Vilnius.
- 10 November 1989. Law on the principles of local government (municipalities).
- 10 December 1989. Local elections (Elections to the Local Councils of People's Deputies).
- 23 February 1990. ESSR Supreme Soviet abolishes the article in the constitution granting the Communist Party a leading role in society.
- 24 February to 1 March 1990. Elections to the Estonian Congress.
- 18 March 1990. Free Elections to the Estonian Supreme Council.
- March 1990. Supreme Soviet declares Soviet annexation of Estonia to have been invalid.
- 3 April 1990. Edgar Savisaar, leader of the Popular Front appointed Prime Minister.
- Spring and Summer 1991. Violent clashes between Soviet troops and pro-independence protestors in Vilnius and Riga. Soviet airborne troops arrive in the Baltic Republics.
- 3 March 1991. Referendum on Independence, 78% say yes.
- 19 August 1991. Failed communist coup attempt in Moscow.
- 20 August 1991. Declaration of Independence.
- 23 January 1992. Prime Minister Edgar Savisaar resigns.
- 20 September 1992. The first post-independence Elections to the Parliament (*Riigikogu*).

- 21 October 1992. Mart Laar, leader of the Estonian Congress movement and Isamaa Party is appointed Prime Minister.
- 17 October 1993. Municipal elections (Elections to Local Government Councils).
- A new municipal director appointed in Kanepi.
- August 1994. Fall of Mart Laar's government.
- 31 August 1994. Last Russian army units withdrawn from Estonia.
- 28 September 1994. Shipwreck of the car ferry 'Estonia' on its way from Tallinn to Stockholm. 852 lives are lost.
- 27 October 1994. Andreas Tarand appointed Prime Minister.
- 5 March 1995. Elections to the Parliament (*Riigikogu*), crushing defeat of the Isamaa Party.
- 7 April 1995. Tiit Vähi appointed Prime Minister.

Table 1.2   Chronology of the most important developments in Estonian agriculture after World War Two and in the decollectivisation of Kanepi kolkhoz

- 1940–1953. The Stalin era: Forced collectivisation of agriculture, 1947–1951; introduction of the quota day system; deportation of *"kulaks"* (wealthier peasants) to Siberia in 1941 and 1949.
- 1953–1964. The Khruschev era: introduction of monetary wages; rapid modernisation of agriculture.
- 1964–1982. The Brezhnev era: large investments in agriculture; nevertheless there were increasingly serious agricultural problems towards the end of the period.
- 1985–1991. The Gorbachev era: the All-Union debate on the further development of Soviet agriculture is initiated; CPSU allows private farms in 1989.
- 26 September 1987. Publication of the Economically Independent Estonia Programme (*IME, Isemajandav Eesti*): a four-man proposal for economic autonomy with the vanguard role projected for the agricultural sector.
- 1989–1990. Researchers from the Estonian Agricultural University carry out a poll in Kanepi to gauge people's attitudes towards kolkhoz reform.
- 6 December 1989. Farm Law passed establishing the rules for creating private farms.

- September 1990. Abolition of state subsidies to milk, meat and fish products and a reduction on subsidies to grain products.
- 20 December 1990. Kolkhoz board presents the first reform plan to the kolkhoz general meeting, but it is subsequently rejected as a result of opposition action.
- 21 February 1991. Meeting of the kolkhoz council of representatives; earlier opposition leader is elected the new chairman of the kolkhoz.
- 13 June 1991. Law on the Principles of Property Reform.
- June 1991. Price controls abolished on all agricultural produce except basic dairy products.
- By the end of 1991 28 private farms were established in the area of the kolkhoz.
- 11 March 1992. Law on Agricultural Reform ordains the reorganisation or liquidation of collective farms.
- 20 June 1992. Introduction of the new national currency, the Estonian kroon (1 kroon equals 1/8 German marks; it equalled 10 Soviet roubles at the time).
- 15 September 1992. Kolkhoz reform committee founded.
- 6 October 1992. New reform plan passed by the kolkhoz general meeting.
- 26 February 1993. The final general meeting of Kanepi kolkhoz.
- 11–23 March 1993. Kolkhoz auction.
- 30 March 1993. Kanepi kolkhoz ceases to exist.
- May 1993. Law on Land Taxation.
- 9 June 1993. The Property Law.
- October 1994. Double customs tariffs imposed by Russia.
- October 1995. Agricultural Market Regulation Law. The law was enacted but it has never been put into effect.

Table 1.3　Estonian economic indicators, 1989–1997

Year	1	2	3	4	5	6	7
1989	8.1	N/A	80	7.5	N/A	12.0	28.2
1990	−6.5	32.8	72	−13.1	N/A	N/A	N/A
1991	−14.0	232.0	57	−4.0	N/A	N/A	36.4
1992	−14.3	1,076.0	−91	−18.6	N/A	N/A	N/A
1993	−8.3	89.8	−30	−7.7	N/A	N/A	N/A
1994	−1.8	41.7	−6	−14.2	N/A	N/A	N/A
1995	4.3	28.9	3	−1.2	−60.0	7.7	33.3
1996	4.0	14.8	8	−3.6	−173.0	7.0	32.7
1997	9.0	12.5	9	−2.0	−255.0	7.0	N/A

1 = Gross Domestic Product (GDP), change in %
2 = Inflation, %
3 = Percentage PSE (percentage of value transfers to agricultural producers)
4 = Volume of gross agricultural output, per cent change from previous year
5 = Agriculture and food trade balance, US$ million
6 = Share of agricultural sector in total employment, %
7 = Average share of household income spent on food, %

Source: Agricultural Policies in Emerging and Transition Economies. Monitoring and Evaluation 1998 (1998), OECD, Paris

2 The Historical Background of the Kolkhoz and the Municipality of Kanepi

HELVI PÕDER

Introduction

In less than eighty years during the 20th century, Estonian agriculture has undergone three basic changes that have deeply influenced ownership relations and the ratio of large and small-scale agricultural production. Soon after Estonia gained its independence, the first of these changes was realised by the radical land reform of 1919 when the large holds of landlords were abolished and the family farm became the dominating form of rural enterprise. This reform put an end to the coexistence of large and small-scale agricultural production in Estonia in favour of the latter.

The second basic change took place in the 1940s when Estonia fell under the occupation of the USSR. It began with the nationalisation of all land and continued through the pre-war years of 1940–1941 and during the post-war land reform from 1944 to 1947. This reform seemed to support small-scale production in rural areas, as the land which was confiscated from large (over 30 hectares) farms, as well as from various organisations, was given to landless people willing to start farming and to peasants who had very little land. The truly Soviet-style reorganisation of agriculture continued as forced collectivisation into the late 1940s with the introduction of socialist large-scale collective farming.

The third period of change began with the disintegration of the Soviet economic system at the end of the 1980s. The changes accelerated after the restoration of Estonian independence in 1991 and became irreversible with the abolishment of the kolkhoz and sovkhoz system in 1992–1993. These changes are still underway.

In this chapter, we analyse the developments in the agricultural system of the Municipality of Kanepi over the last 50 years. There used to be two kolkhozes (collective farms) in the municipality: the Kalev kolkhoz and the Kanepi kolkhoz. This study focuses on the agricultural privatisation process in the Kanepi kolkhoz. It is based on materials from the State Archives of Estonia, statistical records, and the data obtained from several polls.

The Municipality of Kanepi

The Municipality of Kanepi lies in the southeast of Estonia, in the western part of the Põlva county, on the border between the Võru and Valga counties. It covers an area of 233 km^2. A characteristic feature of the municipality is its picturesque, richly varying nature: hills, forests and several lakes. Its soil is not very fertile, and the relief of the municipality does not favour cultivation. The centre of the municipality is the small town of Kanepi, which is near the Tartu-Võru highway.

Historically, the Municipality of Kanepi is a part of Kanepi parish, which was established in 1675. The small town of Kanepi grew out of a church village in the 19th century.

The Municipality of Kanepi was established in 1939 by the government of the first independent Estonian Republic. After the occupation of Estonia by the USSR, the administrative structure of the Estonian Republic (municipalities and counties) initially remained the same. Later, in 1945, the Municipality of Kanepi was divided between three village soviets. In 1950, a new administrative structure was introduced: rural districts (governed by village soviets) and rayons (rayon is the Russian language word for county). Kanepi belonged to the Põlva rayon. In 1954, the three village soviets were amalgamated into one – the Kanepi village soviet – and in 1963, a neighbouring village soviet was joined to it.

The Municipality of Kanepi was restored after Estonia regained its independence.

The Development of Agriculture in the Municipality of Kanepi before 1940

Agriculture in the Municipality of Kanepi in 1939

After the restoration of the Estonian Republic in 1991, the different political movements in Estonia agreed to restore the ownership legislation of 1939. What had been the agricultural situation in the Municipality of Kanepi in

1939? The answer to that question lies in the data of the economic report on agriculture, compiled in that same year.

Table 2.1 The number of farms in 1939

Farm area (ha)	In the Municipality of Kanepi		In Estonia	
	Number	%	Number	%
1–10	198	37.1	45,810	32.7
10–30	286	53.7	65,687	47.0
30–50	46	8.6	21,720	15.5
over 50	3	0.6	6,774	4.8
Totals	533	100	139,991	100

Source: Eesti Statistika, 1939; No. 9

As we can see in Table 2.1, the percentage of small and medium-sized (1–30 hectare) farms was greater (89.8%) in the Municipality of Kanepi than in the whole of Estonia (79.7%).

Table 2.2 Usage of farmland in 1939

Land classification	In the Municipality of Kanepi		In Estonia	
	Area (ha)	Share (%)	Area (ha)	Share (%)
Field and garden	5,883	57.8	1,117,800	35.10
Cultivated grassland	107	1.1	43,048	1.35
Cultivated pasture	68	0.7	12,241	0.40
Natural grassland	1,420	14.7	889,474	27.90
Natural pasture	975	10.1	682,886	21.50
Forest	992	10.3	189,345	5.95
Other	516	5.3	247,652	7.80
Totals	9,661	100	3,182,446	100

Source: Eesti Statistika, 1939; No. 9

As we can see in Table 2.2, the share of field and garden land was noticeably higher in the Municipality of Kanepi in comparison with the whole of Estonia. In the municipality, these figures denoted the small farm fields, some of which remained untilled and overgrown with brushwood in the kolkhoz era unless they became absorbed into greater units in the process of the amelioration of the soil. One tenth of all the land was covered with forests and, as we shall see later, the restorable forest became an important factor in the process of privatisation.

The most important cereals and other field crops cultivated in the fields of Estonia were oat, rye, and flax. There were 708 horses and 1861 cows on 533 farms in the whole municipality. On most farms, horsepower only was used for farm work – there were only 9 tractors. Farm machinery consisted of 21 seeding machines, 61 reaping machines, 134 mowing machines, and 175 horse rakes. There were dwellings on 518 farms out of 533, 97 of which were built after 1930. Out of 513 cowsheds, 120 were built during the same period.

There were signs of newer technology being introduced – 10 farms in the municipality had constructed pig houses and 7 farms had poultry houses. Ensilage was introduced on one farm.

To understand the situation better, we have to go back to 1851, when the Lord of Karste manor sold the first small-farm to a peasant. In the present-day area of the Municipality of Kanepi, 153 family farms had been bought from manors by 1913. The majority of farms were established as a result of the land reform in 1919. Second or third generation owners lived on freehold family farms bought before 1917, and only the first generation lived on the newly established farms. The great dream of the serf, who had had to work hard on the manor fields for hundreds of years, to become the freehold owner of his own land had finally come true. The result was the formation of a rural population that was relatively content with the situation. In the Estonian Republic, agriculture was the main area of state economics and the leaders of rural population-oriented parties held key positions in politics. The government paid attention to the interests of the peasants, especially when shaping the policy of prices and customs during 1930–1940, which aimed at promoting domestic agricultural production. In addition, the popularity of co-operative agricultural enterprises helped to improve the situation. Estonian produced butter and pork was able to compete on the western markets of the time.

Naturally, certain problems existed: the backward state of mechanisation, the lack of fertile soil, debts, and unemployment. However, the two decades of the first Estonian Republic was too short a time for the citizens to fully feel the influence of these negative factors. The terrible impact of the events that followed – the loss of independence, World War II, deportations, forced collectivisation – helped to paint the past in a more idyllic way. The rural family farm of the late 1930s remained in the memory of hundreds of thousands as a time and place of economic success, inspiring bright hopes for the future. (The results of the agricultural census of 1939 show that 625,460 peasants lived on family farms in Estonia, i.e. over 60% of the whole population).

Now, fifty years later, when Estonia has regained its independence, these romantic memories of a rural idyll – the clearer the memory, the less day-to-day farm work the rememberer must have done – influence the choice of strategy in achieving further progress in the agricultural production structure. The most just solution to the problem seems to be the erasure of everything that has happened in the meantime – a return to the past, to the time when everything was in its initial state and to start building the future from there. However, the sad reality is that Estonia has undergone irrevocable changes during these fifty years – and so has the world that forms the background for developments in Estonia. The strategy chosen will bring with it a whole new set of legal, social, psychological, economic, cultural, technological and demographic problems. Thus, a couple of years after the privatisation of agriculture, the situation in the Estonian village is the coexistence of manual based agriculture, a characteristic of an Estonian village in the early 20th century, with agricultural enterprises using the Soviet technology of the 1980s and several enterprises using top level contemporary western technology.

The Agricultural System of the Soviet Era

In accordance with the secret additional protocols of the Molotov-Ribbentrop pact concluded between the USSR and Germany on August 23, 1939, the Estonian Republic came under the sphere of influence of the USSR. In the autumn of that same year, Estonia had to give up certain territories as military bases for the USSR and in 1940, the USSR occupied the territory of Estonia. The election of the new State Council (*Riigivolikogu*) took place on July 15, 1940. Following the tradition of the USSR, only one candidate was set up in every electoral district. The result of this non-democratic election carried out in an atmosphere of oppression and dread was the official result that 92.8% of votes went to the candidates of the Front of the Estonian Working People

(*Eesti Töötava Rahva Väerinne*). The State Council, which was elected by such methods, held its first Session from July 21 to 23, 1940 and passed four major resolutions directly concerning the future of Estonia:

1) Estonia was declared a Soviet Republic.
2) Estonia's application for status as a member state of the USSR was announced.
3) The land in Estonia was declared the common property of all the people.
4) All banks and large-scale industries were declared the property of the state.

Thus, the State Council abolished private estates by assigning them to the state. It annulled all the debts of the peasants. At the same time, it gave the "working peasants" the right of permanent tillage of up to 30 hectares of land. In practice, this innovation meant that some of the land of farms larger than 30 hectares was taken away. In Kanepi, 49 family farms (9.2% of the sum total) suffered from this decision. In the whole of Estonia, the number of farms was 28,494 (20.3% of the sum total). Land belonging to various organisations, towns, and the church was also confiscated and added to state assets (in the Municipality of Kanepi, the church manor land). Together with the land that had been state property before occupation, the total collectivised land formed 24% of all cultivated land in Estonia. Half this land was distributed between landless peasants (*uudismaasaajad*, i.e. new landholders) and family farms of less than 30 hectares. Consequently, the number of private farms increased by about 18% in comparison with 1939. The average area of a farm decreased from 22.7 hectares in 1939 to 16.7 hectares in 1941. To help the new landholders cultivate the land, 25 machine and tractor stations and 250 horse-hiring stations were established.

The influence of the land reform remained short-term as these new landholders and the family farms, which had received additional land, had to give up their newly obtained property before the first crop could even be harvested. In the late summer of 1941, German troops moved into Estonia and the German occupation began. Most of the confiscated land was returned to the previous owners.

The new land reform started in 1944, before the end of the Second World War. Legislation concerning the land reform was approved on September 17, 1944, when a large area of Estonian territory, including Tallinn, was still under German occupation. The new land reform was significantly more fundamental than the reform carried out in 1940–1941. Legislation determined that all the land that had belonged to the "enemies of the people," (who had escaped from Estonia with the Germans) the land of German colonists, the land used by German state institutions during the occupation and all land which had remained unowned, was to be included in the state land fund. The peasants, who were accused of having been in the service of the German occupiers, had to bear the greatest losses in this new wave of confiscation.

The size of such peasant farms was only 5 to 7 hectares and practically all of their livestock and machinery were confiscated. All other farms were allowed up to 30 hectares of land per family and the remainder was added to the state lands. If required, some land on the 30 hectare family farms could also be confiscated – only 20 hectares of every farm was to be left intact.

From the state land reserve, which was made up of confiscated land, every landless peasant received a 12 to 18 hectare plot and additional land was dealt out to small family farms. Land also had to be assigned to sovkhozes for the needs of tractor stations, auxiliary farms (plot farms) and other enterprises or organisations. In land as well as property distribution, priority was given to demobilised Soviet army soldiers, Second World War invalids and the relatives of Soviet army soldiers and the Soviet partisans killed during the war.

On April 30, 1945, the number of applications presented throughout Estonia reached 53,388, among them 2,783 from privileged applicants. The reasons for such a large number of applications were, on the one hand, a most intensive political campaign carried out by the functionaries of the Communist Party and the executive committees in favour of the new land reform and, on the other hand, the cherished hopes of many working people to finally become landowners.

The progress of the land reform in the Kanepi district is described in the so-called "Black Book" (*must raamat*), which gets its name from archivists and the colour of its covers. The contents of the book are also consistent with its name. The book contains 146 separate lists, each of them presenting the minutes of the district executive committee concerning the land reform. As the number of family farms over 30 hectares in Kanepi was less than the general average in Estonian rural districts, the land reform influenced about one quarter of all farms in the district. In 6 cases, the minutes were countermands of earlier decisions, usually based on the decisions by the Land Reform Committee of the Republic (PMA 28/368).

Eighty-nine hectares of land were confiscated from the congregation of the Kanepi Lutheran Church. Eighteen farms were declared ownerless. Five farmers were found guilty of having co-operated with the German occupiers. Over fifty farmers were declared major landowners. Among them, several had farms with areas of less than thirty hectares. There were four cases when a family in possession of two farms simply had to give up one of them. In the course of the land reform, all peasants were given a "certificate for permanent land usage" (*maa põhilise kasutamise akt*). These became worthless pieces of paper in just two years, when the forcible collectivisation process was carried out.

This land reform did not introduce any improvements into the social and economic situation in rural districts, and least of all into human relationships. The reform was carried out in an atmosphere of unrestrained, rough political campaigning that extensively employed sticking various derogatory labels like "enemy of the people," "hireling of the occupiers," "blood-sucking kulak," etc. on various individuals. The land reform, as well as the following collectivisation process, helped to promote the dark sides of human nature: envy, revenge, arrogance, and animosity.

The aim of the agricultural policy of the USSR was definitely not to promote small-scale production in rural districts. In the compilation "Eesti NSV põllumajanduse kollektiviseerimine. Dokumentide ja materjalide kogumik" ["The Collectivisation of the Agriculture of the Estonian SSR. Collected Documents and Materials"] (Tõnurist, 1978), one can find an analysis of the agricultural policy of the Communist Party of Estonia. The analysis explained that " . . . although the main strategic aim of the Party at that time was to reform Estonian agriculture into a system of socialist large-scale farming enterprises, it was impossible to start with its realisation immediately. At that time the Estonian peasant thought about his better future in terms of his own piece of land which on the basis of earlier historical experience was, for him, the proper source of abundance" (ibid.).

In accordance with the archive data, there were 567 family farm owners in Kanepi district in 1947. In 1948, the number was 576. Their fate, however, was already predetermined. In the above-mentioned collection of documents, the necessity of agricultural collectivisation was supported by the explanation that agriculture based on small-scale production was inadequate for producing enough food to feed the population (which was rapidly increasing due to industrialisation in Estonia). It stated that the stabilisation of the economic situation in rural districts was decreasing and the symptoms of the increase in social inequality were already evident. The expressed hopes of reaching an effective state of farming in 1.5 or 2 years of the post-war period could not be taken seriously and it is clear that this was not the real aim of these reorganisations. The actual purpose of the policy was the collectivisation of all agriculture. The land reform was carried out for political reasons – to provide the new legislative establishments with political support from the group of new landholders during the early stages of Soviet occupation.

The plan for the collectivisation of the whole agricultural system was announced in May 1947. The Political Bureau of the Communist (Bolshevik) Party of the Soviet Union gave an order to the Communist Party organisations of the Baltic Republics to start preparations for mass collectivisation. One of the important steps in carrying out this policy was the "elimination of the kulaks as a class". On August 30, 1947, the decree of the Soviet of Ministers of the ESSR on the taxation of private farms was issued. The taxes of so-called kulak farms were increased two or threefold in comparison with the "non-kulak" farms. In the same decree, the criteria for farm "classification" were presented. The main criteria in pronouncing a family farm "kulak" were: the presence of hired workers, lending money to other people, the existence of tenants, items of equipment being leased from the farm, trade activities, and the ownership of enterprises. The district executive committees had to compile lists of kulaks. An official reprimand by the Võru rayon executive committee to the Kanepi district executive committee exists for carelessly compiled and defective lists. The problem of kulak lists evoked a special correspondence between the rayon and the district executive committees. Some names were removed from the list and some were added. In June 1948, there were 14 names on the kulak list of Kanepi district and by then, some of these people had already been arrested (PMA 28/75). The land had been declared the property of the people in 1940. In the meantime, the land was distributed for "free and permanent usage". Now it had to be given up "voluntarily" to the kolkhoz (collective farm). The new landowners and peasants, who had received some additional land, were now in the same situation as the farm owners who had had to relinquish part or all of their land for redistribution. After joining the kolkhoz, the land left for gardening was, as a norm, 0.6 hectares per family. All machinery, cattle, and tools also became common kolkhoz property. As mentioned above, the land reform of 1944–1947 did not succeed in putting an end to economic inequality; but now a very "successful" step had been taken – all the people were equally poor collective farmers (*kolkhozniks*).

The first kolkhoz in the Estonian SSR was established in September 1947. During the first year and a half, the foundation of kolkhozes was very slow. By March 20, 1949, only 8.2% of all farmers in Estonia had joined kolkhozes. The anti-kulak propaganda, the deportation of kulak families, subsidies for voluntary new kolkhoz members and so on, did not bring the desired results, so stronger methods of oppression had to be applied. On March 23, 1949 and in the days that followed, an extensive mass deportation of Estonian people took place. Over 20,000 people (including women, children, and the elderly) were put on freight trains and cattle wagons and sent to Siberia.

The list of people for deportation from Kanepi district included 120 people; the actual number deported was 77, the rest remained in Estonia. The Kanepi district is notable for the relatively long list of people to be deported, as well as for the relatively high percentage of people who escaped deportation (Koit, 1992).

In this atmosphere of fear and hopelessness, the mass deportations were followed immediately by the period of rapid kolkhozation. Only one month later, by April 20, 1949, 61.1% of all private farms had joined kolkhozes. In July 1952, the percentage of kolkhoz member farms was 97.1% of the total number (Tõnurist, 1978).

The Estonian peasant had taken a long step on the road leading downhill. There was still a long way to go to reach the bottom. Using the example of the Kanepi kolkhoz, we shall try to analyse how the bottom was reached and how the tough fight to climb uphill began.

The Termination of Small Production and the First Years of the Kolkhoz System From 1947–1950

The establishment of the kolkhozes and the decline of agriculture   The predecessors of the Kanepi kolkhoz were 12 small kolkhozes (see Figure 2.1). The articles of association of nine of these kolkhozes were all certified at the executive committee of the Võru rayon on April 8, 1949. The resistance of Estonian peasants to the kolkhoz system was broken by violence – by "the deportation of kulaks and other enemies of the people", to use the terminology of those times. As before, during earlier times of repression, the victims of the deportations to Siberia were the most inventive, the most educated, the most independent people of Estonia.

The memories of those days still live on in the minds of the Estonian people. People can still recall those events, even those who at that time were little children and who could not clearly understand what was going on.

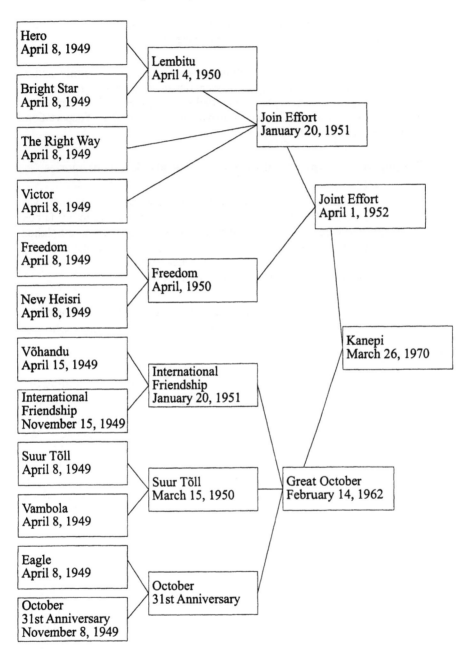

Figure 2.1 The formation of Kanepi kolkhoz from smaller units

> I remember that one day my father came home and told us that my uncle's family had been taken away. (A five-year-old boy at the time)

> I remember my mother and father talking about our neighbour's family having been taken away the previous night. We went out and stood in the farmyard, we could hear big trucks driving along the road some kilometres from our home, taking away the deportees. Our family also lived in constant fear of deportation. (A nine-year-old girl at the time)

The time of the formation of the kolkhoz has also left its memories:

> I remember that there were some weaving-looms in our living room and I was hiding under them. The men, our neighbours, had come to talk to my father. They said that there was no way out and everyone must become a kolkhoz member. I understood that something very bad was going to happen, that is why it has stayed in my memory. Also, the fact that they offered my father, an abstinent man, spirits . . . (A six-year-old boy at the time)

People were very depressed and in great fear of being deported to Siberia. Everybody kept silent. However, there were also the ones who got appointments in kolkhozes.

When the time of mass collectivisation was over, several lone farms had remained untouched by the process. To force these farms into also joining the kolkhozes, sales quotas to the state and agricultural taxes were introduced.

> My father and I were the last ones here to become kolkhoz members. We postponed this moment as long as we could, waiting for the 'white ship' (as the hoped-for help from Western states to re-establish the independence of Estonia was called). We had to pay enormous taxes – 16,000 roubles to the state. We had sold everything we had – our crops, our cattle, and our wood. There was nothing left to do, except to become members of the kolkhoz . . . (A kolkhoz construction worker at the time, now a pensioner trying to rebuild the family farm)

What did the initial position of the new collective farms look like? We can compile a survey of the situation from the appendices to the "voluntary" applications of peasants to become kolkhoz members, where the accounts of the properties and other belongings to be handed over to the kolkhozes can be found. These accounts became enormously important during the liquidation of the kolkhoz system in 1992–1993 because, based on these, the remnants of the collectivised properties were returned or proportional compensation was paid. In the Kanepi kolkhoz, 372 resolutions to compensate the collectivised properties were made. Based on random selection, we undertook an analysis of 182 resolutions. These farms gave up 169 horses, 129 cows, 22 heifers, 134 ploughs, 135 wagons, and 45 hay rakes, 4 sowing machines, 11 cultivators, 2 threshers, and other implements to the kolkhoz. In 74 cases, production buildings were given over to the kolkhoz (PMA 117/784 and 117/785).

The tractors and threshers from more prosperous private farms had earlier been expropriated and given to the machine and tractor stations or horse lending stations. The land had already been collectivised in 1940. Now all the cattle and tools were also taken away. The previous family farm owners became kolkhozniks.

In accordance with the kolkhoz articles of association, each kolkhoznik had to earn his basic income by doing kolkhoz work. The number of obligatory quota days of each kolkhoznik was appointed annually.

Each kolkhoznik had the right to use 0.6 hectares of land for private gardening, to raise one cow, one pig, some sheep, and poultry. The domestic economies (auxiliary farms) of kolkhozniks were not allowed to interfere with kolkhoz work and production enterprises. In a report from a 1951 session of the board of management of one of the "forefathers" of the Kanepi kolkhoz – the Ühisjõud (United Power) kolkhoz – a clear statement can be found setting the conditions for kolkhozniks to pasture their "private" cows:

> The kolkhozniks are allowed to pasture their cows only on land unfit for the kolkhoz herds. The kolkhoz pastureland may be used to feed kolkhozniks' private cows only after the kolkhoz herds have finished feeding there. (PMA 117/88)

The collectivisation of all agricultural machinery resulted in the dependence of the kolkhozniks on their kolkhoz even in cultivating their private plots. At first, a horse from the kolkhoz stables could be used, but later only the tractor drivers could help. In this way, the implements became instruments of power over the kolkhozniks. The punishment for breaking the daily work discipline was the denial of their right to use horses or tractors.

In the beginning there was a kolkhoz in every village. The usefulness of small kolkhozes at that time was explained as a necessity to give the peasants time to get used to the kolkhoz system (Tõnurist, 1978).

In some villages, the first kolkhoz chairmen were local farmers, who tried to find reasonable solutions to agricultural and economic problems in the new situation. However, in many villages the leading posts were given to the "faithful soldiers of the Communist Party" or to people who had not even succeeded in managing their own farms in earlier times.

The search for all kinds of enemies continued. The "kulaks hiding themselves among the kolkhozniks" were exposed, as were the "underminers of the kolkhoz system". Their punishment could be up to 25+5 years' imprisonment with a lifetime deportation from Estonia. As is typical in times of sudden changes in society, all the darker sides of human nature found their outlet in the kolkhoz system: envy, old insults, vindictiveness. Still, the opposite attitude also prevailed – the former owners tried to care for the cattle taken away from them during collectivisation, explaining that speechless animals were not guilty of the events that had taken place. Furthermore, the fields could not be left uncultivated, no matter what the situation in the ownership legislation was like.

> Our family had given up a horse-driven hay mower. My father did all the mowing of the kolkhoz hayfields. He was also the kolkhoz stableman, as all the horses of our kolkhoz were kept in the stable of our farm. To drive the hay mower, my father used two big Ardennes horses that had belonged to our neighbour before the collectivisation. There was very little hay for the kolkhoz horses in winter, so my father fed these horses secretly, using the hay prepared for our own cow. Luckily, [in the accounts] the horse and the cow are considered to feed on different kinds of hay. (A former kolkhoz electrician, now trying to restore his family farm)

The kolkhozes were established by employing methods of violence, and oppressive strategies were used to run them in later times. The dates for starting and finishing any agricultural work in the fields were appointed by high-standing officials who did not take into consideration the local situation or weather conditions. There were many controllers around – representatives of the Committee of the Communist Party, the village soviet officials and employees of the machine and tractor stations.

The years 1951–1957 proved to be the time of a rapid decrease in agricultural production, bringing on a difficult economic situation for the kolkhozes. All produce had to be sold to the state at very low prices. It was impossible to cultivate the fields without using the services of the machine and tractor stations but the work carried out by the tractor drivers was often badly done and in order to arrange payment for the work, a large share of the crops had to be sold to the state. The obligations of the kolkhozes to the state were extensive and the fulfilment of these obligations was of prime importance.

The fund for wages and salaries was calculated based on the surplus crop for the year, so there was little left for the wages of kolkhozniks. At the same time, it was obligatory to work and the meagre wages were paid in kind.

> We worked as hard as we could but at the end of the year we were told that we had not worked hard enough and that we had a debt to pay to the state . . . (A cattle-tender of the first kolkhoz years)

The era of small kolkhozes was short. The process of combining them into large-scale collective farms started within a year. In 1951, the three kolkhozes near the Kanepi township were joined into the Ühisjõud kolkhoz. To get an objective picture of the situation in the kolkhoz, one should become acquainted with the materials presented in the book of the kolkhoz board meeting reports (PMA 117/219 and 117/249).

In accordance with the kolkhoz articles of association, its basic work organisation unit was the work brigade and the key people in the structure were brigade leaders and farm managers. As the work organisation at the time was very difficult, they were often dismissed or they resigned. The real position of brigade leaders is characterised by the following excerpts from the texts of the decrees on organising the spring sowing (PMA 117/27):

> In the event that the spring sowing proves unsuccessful, the brigade-leader must be brought to trial.

> In the event that horses are found idly standing in the stables, a fine of 30 roubles must be paid by the brigade leader and the kolkhoznik responsible for the proper usage of these horses.

Two surveillance methods, approved in a meeting, present two excellent examples of the Stalinist control typical for the era:

> Kolkhozniks are not allowed to work alone in separate fields, they must all work together in a large field . . . The members of the Young Communist League must appoint secret field guards to prevent the removal of corn seed . . .

The brigade leaders had to account for the presence and absence of kolkhozniks every morning and the working day lasted from sunrise to sunset.

The condition of the kolkhoz cattle is best described by a sentence from a report, "Over 20% of cows are unable to get on their feet."

The chairman of the village soviet played an active part at the kolkhoz board meetings, pointing out deficiencies, giving advice, and checking up.

Since the Kanepi kolkhoz had become by far the largest landowner in the Kanepi district, all land applications had to be presented to the kolkhoz. In this way, plots of land were dealt out to the school, and for the gardens of schoolteachers and machine and tractor station workers.

Problems in the relationships between the kolkhozes and local enterprises based on the state budget already existed at that time. For example, the school and the medical centre had applied for the free transport of firewood, but the kolkhoz board's answer to the applications was, "We can give the transport, but for a payment only."

To leave a kolkhoz, a member had to get the approval of the general meeting. The kolkhoz board demanded lists from the brigade leaders of those who had left without permission.

The period from 1951 to 1957 was the most difficult for the kolkhozniks. In comparison with city people, the economic situation was much more difficult for rural inhabitants. They left their country homes at the slightest opportunity. Some went to improve their education (for which the permission of kolkhoz officials was initially necessary). Others used the official enlisting system to answer some All-Union call for builders of a large-scale enterprise or for workers at important industrial enterprises. Some did not return to the home kolkhoz after demobilisation from the Soviet Army. The ones who left were young and enterprising. Often the children departed, leaving behind their parents who found it impossible "to leave their lifelong home."

The situation is aptly characterised in the following account of the kolkhoz Ühisjõud for 1956.

There were 215 families of kolkhoz members – 416 people altogether, of which 236 were able-bodied (147 female, 89 male). During the year, the kolkhoz gained 11 new members and 15 people left. The kolkhoz had 143 cows in 13 cowsheds, 126 horses in 19 stables and 246 pigs in 5 pigsties. Kolkhoz machinery consisted of one 30 horsepower steam engine, 1 tractor, and 4 lorries. The wages for one quota day unit consisted of 0.98 kg of grain, 0.48 kg of potatoes, and 2.38 roubles. The kolkhoz hen house was the only new production building erected during that year. During the first seven years of the kolkhoz, the work was mainly carried out using the buildings and implements that had earlier been relinquished by the self-same people who joined the kolkhoz (PMA 117/244).

The period of stabilisation The period from 1958 to 1964 marked the beginning of the systematic improvement of the economic situation in the kolkhozes. After the death of Joseph V. Stalin, the high state officials realised that the agricultural system in the USSR had developed into a disastrous situation, making it impossible to supply either the population with food or industry with raw materials.

The first substantial changes in economic policy were:

1) 1955: The rise of central purchasing prices; the lowering of the quotas for the obligatory sale of agricultural produce to the state, and the termination of the practice of assigning additional production obligations to more productive agricultural enterprises.
2) 1957: The abolition of the agricultural produce sale obligations of auxiliary households belonging to kolkhozniks, workers, and employees.
3) 1958: The reorganisation of machine and tractor stations into repair depots and the sale of tractors and other machinery to kolkhozes. This prompted specialists from machine and tractor stations to become workers in kolkhozes and sovkhozes. Thus started the formation of their own machine-operator and specialist personnel.
4) 1958–1964: The transition to monetary wages.

During these years, construction began on several new production buildings for the Ühisjõud. In 1957, a new cattle-shed for 300 animals and a grain dryer was completed. The electrification of production started in 1958. In 1961, modern times reached the cowsheds when a system of milking machines was introduced. In 1963, the kolkhoz heating plant in the township of Kanepi was completed.

The use of residences belonging to the kolkhoz became much more active. Some of the houses unused by the kolkhoz were sold to applicants while, at the same time, the kolkhoz bought several households for sale in the kolkhoz area by priority rights. The first two-storied block of flats for cattle-tenders was designed for construction near the cowshed.

The kolkhoz recruited new members: 25 people during 1960, 14 people in 1961 and 20 people in 1962.

About 70% of kolkhozniks took part in general meetings. From the records of these meetings, we can find serious discussions concerning agricultural production problems as well as critical remarks directed at the activities of the board of management for the kolkhoz. The main reproofs were aimed at their carelessness, indifference, incapability, and the resulting lack of organisation in the kolkhoz.

In 1963, the kolkhoz articles of association were modified. From then on, each kolkhoznik family had the right to keep:

1) 1 cow and 1 heifer, up to three months old.
2) 2 pigs (one of which could be a sow). The piglets had to be sold no later than the age of two months.
3) 1 to 2 sheep or goats.
4) Up to 10 heads of poultry and an unlimited number of beehives.

If the number of domestic animals went over the limits set by the articles and if official reprimands were ignored then, according to the articles, the kolkhoz had the right to sell the surplus animals to the state. All expenses incurred had to be covered by the owner of the animals.

This period belonged to the so-called "Khrushchev's Thaw" era. The kolkhoz leadership went on without major changes. This was the time when the CPSU (Communist Party of the Soviet Union) told Estonian farmers to grow Indian corn and to plant potatoes in check rows.

In 1964, the chairman of the kolkhoz Ühisjõud was replaced. This change took place in true Soviet style. On January 15, 1964, a kolkhoz board meeting took place. In addition to the board members, there were 7 members of the CPSU, 5 members of the Young Communist League and 10 representatives of specialists, field, and cattle-shed workers. Three key figures of the executive committee of the rayon were also present. The representative of the rayon committee of the CPSU analysed the situation in the kolkhoz. In addition to the difficulties caused by objective factors, he pointed out the mistakes of the board, e.g. indifference and an escapist mood. In the name of the committee of the CPSU, he recommended replacing the chairman of the kolkhoz board. The former chairman took his leave on January 30, 1964 and the new chairman entered the position that he was to occupy for 26 years (PMA 117/249).

In the next meeting of the board of management (on February 12, 1964), when the new chairman took the chair, he proposed the transition to monetary wages (some Estonian kolkhozes had introduced the transition as early as in 1958, the last ones in 1964).

The new chairman took his leadership quite seriously. He introduced the production meetings for the specialists and production unit leaders every

Monday at seven o'clock in the morning. It was decided to put up a news-stand to display the monthly data for each kolkhoznik (the number of work hours and the wages earned). The brigade leader's range of responsibilities was increased.

An attempt was made to clarify the relationship between the kolkhoz and the auxiliary farms (plot farms) of the kolkhozniks. It was decided that in order to use a tractor to cultivate the land on a private plot, a kolkhoznik had to have his brigade leader's permission. The payment for the work was to be paid to the kolkhoz pay-desk. For example, out of the three roubles paid for ploughing, one rouble was to go to the kolkhoz cash box and two roubles to the tractor driver. Certain useful exchange rates were also introduced: the kolkhozniks who wanted to buy straw for cattle feed from the kolkhoz could now give manure to the kolkhoz as payment. The sizes of the kolkhozniks' auxiliary farms and the adequacy of those farms in meeting the kolkhoz articles of association were checked and the boundary marks set in their proper places. The board gave permission to kolkhozniks to cultivate new grazing grounds and hay-fields and to use a kolkhoz tractor for this purpose.

The rent charges for using kolkhoz residences and other buildings were laid down according to the tenant's wages. The minimum charge was 4.5 kopecks per square metre and the maximum, 10 kopecks. 15 leases were concluded.

From 1965, the kokhozniks' pension system was reformed. From then on, the state paid the pensions instead of the kolkhoz itself. At the end of 1964, 117 names were on the pensioner list of the kolkhoz Ühisjõud.

Building construction continued quite intensively. In 1967, a block of 12 flats and the kindergarten were completed. A pigsty was also built.

The establishment of the Kanepi kolkhoz – progress and stagnation Close to the end of the 1960s, the CPSU once more started amalgamating kolkhozes to create larger economic structure units. In 1970, the Ühisjõud was joined to the neighbouring kolkhoz Suur Oktoober (The Great October). The new economic formation became the Kanepi kolkhoz.

> In 1970, the two kolkhozes were joined together. Ours was much better off – we had more new buildings, we also had a much better inclination to work. The other kolkhoz brought its large debts . . . In the meeting where it was decided to unite these two kolkhozes, many of our people had tears in their eyes; but as the decision had been made on a higher level, it was no use saying anything. We had to obey. (Former kolkhoz chief accountant)

These words are supported by the data from the 1969 reports for both kolkhozes (see Table 2.3).

Table 2.3 Comparative data from the reports of 1969

	Ühisjõud	Suur Oktoober
Number of members	321	400
Members fit for work	121	164
Size (ha)	2,947	4,427
Cows	286	261
Pigs	738	561
Income (per 100 ha, in roubles)	28,735	16,912
Income (per member, in roubles)	2,806	1,196
Income (per one quota day, in roubles)	13.8	5.7
Number of officials and specialists	25	38
Number of tractor drivers	21	24
Number of lorry drivers	9	13
Cowsheds	3	2
Large pigsties	4	2
Living area (m^2)	872	1,709

As we see, in the Ühisjõud, production was much more intensive, whereas the Suur Oktoober owned a notably larger living area.

The process of amalgamating the two kolkhozes slightly slowed down their development but after 1975, the Kanepi kolkhoz was consistently among the five best collective farms in the Põlva rayon.

In the 1970s and the 1980s, the Kanepi kolkhoz developed according to the rules established by the agricultural policy of the USSR. The progress of agricultural production was realised according to the economic development Five-Year Plans, which set the exact rates of the bulk of production, sales obligations to the state, the cost prices, etc. If annual plans and, especially, the Five-Year Plans were fulfilled, the leaders and the most outstanding workers of the successful enterprises were rewarded with Challenge Red Banners, orders and medals. They also got permission to purchase new automobiles, new agricultural machinery, or additional quantities of concentrated cattle feed. The agricultural produce market in the USSR was insatiable. The requirements on quality of produce were very low and on the other hand, the prices of concentrated cattle feed and oil products (petrol, diesel oil, etc.) that had to be imported from other regions of the USSR were also low. The same person occupied the post of the chairman of the Kolkhoz board for over twenty years. During that time, he succeeded in establishing personal relationships and contacts with the heads of other agricultural and industrial enterprises and also with the representatives of the Communist Party and various soviets, so that all possible methods to obtain additional resources for the kolkhoz could be used.

Next, we will discuss the problems this 20-year period caused at the beginning of the 1990s when the termination of the Soviet large-scale collective farm system was implemented.

The main areas of agricultural production in the Kanepi kolkhoz were dairy farming and pig breeding. The kolkhoz also managed the only sheep farm in the district. The Kanepi kolkhoz took an active part in the All-Union cattle raising intensification campaign of the 1970s. One of the fundamental ideas of the campaign was to construct large farm buildings and keep numerous dairy herds or cattle in one place for the mechanisation of cattle feeding and tending procedures. The new large-scale farm buildings were completed in Kanepi (1970), Kooraste (1970), and Karste (1974). In 1979, a modern farm building for pigs was completed. The large herds on large-scale farms needed extensive grazing areas and hay-fields, so an intensive melioration programme was started, which was financed by the state from 1969 onwards. The meliorated land was put to use in all three brigades of the kolkhoz; several irrigation systems were constructed and former farmland was once more cultivated.

The melioration programme caused significant changes in the traditional land cultivation system inherited from the time of separate family farms; some of the old farm fields were left uncultivated under brushwood. This policy caused a lot of problems later, when the fields of former family farms returned to their previous owners. Beside well-cultivated fields, there were plots of land unfit for cultivation – areas growing brushwood; the tilling of which was not within the reinstituted owners' means.

> As the farm owners are not capable of managing the cultivation of their land, they often propose that we keep their land under our management. However, we also meet different attitudes. For example, we recently received an angry letter from a landowner living in Tallinn. He demanded to know why his two-hectare plot of land, situated in the middle of our large farm field, had been cultivated

and sowed. The right attitude, in his opinion, would have been to leave his property untilled. (A chairman of an agricultural co-operative)

The redistribution of the collective farmland between several previous owners is bound to usher in a whole set of problems connected with the cultivation of meliorated lands, as their maintenance assumes certain co-operation among the owners of the area.

The big cattle-sheds necessitated an increased number of agricultural specialists and so, from the 1970s, detached houses were constructed in Karste and in Kooraste. The design of the new households, pastures, and hay-fields was carried out on the assumption that all the land would remain the property of the kolkhoz forever. At the time, it meant nothing to the designers and constructors to which previous farm the building sites belonged. Only some old people, having dwelt in the neighbourhood all their lives, could still remember the original land disposition between the farms.

The situation caused another set of problems when the process of land restoration to hereditary owners started.

I would have been glad to get back my own farm, but there was no land left. The large farm buildings, roads, new houses – all of these had been built on our land. (A young owner of a big cattle-shed)

Due to the establishment of large-scale farming, the need arose to build a number of flats for farm workers. This process also complicated human relationships. Some of the workers had arrived at the kolkhoz from else-where, among them several "rootless persons", who drifted from one kolkhoz to another like "migratory birds". When the kolkhozes were liquidated, some of them fell into the category of "unwelcome guests" especially if they had problems with alcohol, and they accordingly lost their jobs.

One of the means of the policy of the Communist Party to decrease the differences between rural and town lifestyles was to create the set of well-planned central settlements – the so-called "agrotowns". The Kanepi kolkhoz already had the Kanepi township as its centre; the kolkhoz had built several new houses there. All agricultural machinery and tractors were also concen-trated in Kanepi. As oil products were cheap at the time, it was considered effective, from the economic point of view, to locate all machinery as well as workers in Kanepi from where they went in brigades to their working places every morning. A new garage was constructed in Kanepi in 1973, facilities for the repair shop workers were built in 1978, and in 1980, the workshop itself was thoroughly repaired and the pesticide warehouse was completed.

During the kolkhoz era, many new flats were built. At the time of its liquidation, the Kanepi kolkhoz had 96 flats in Kanepi, 20–30 flats some distance from the central settlement, and 18 detached houses. The heating plant was built in Kanepi in 1980 and it was renovated in 1987. As mentioned above, in accordance with legislation, the kolkhoz had the priority rights to buy the houses for sale in the kolkhoz. The kolkhoz often used these priority rights. Some of the houses obtained this way were used as rented lodgings, but some of them were sold to the members of the kolkhoz. All these transactions resulted in another set of difficult problems when the process of returning properties to their previous owners began. A new bona fide proprietor could own the buildings on the land and at the same time, the land could be the property of another person. We have to remember that there were many ways buildings could become the kolkhoz property. Many of the buildings were from the kulak farms, confiscated from people deported to Siberia or those repressed in some other way. Some people had simply moved away and they or their heirs had sold their buildings to the kolkhoz.

All the construction work could be carried out because of the relatively successful economic management of the kolkhoz in the economic conditions of the time. The most successful areas were dairy farming and pig breeding. In 1972, the average milk yield per cow was 3,179 kg, in 1980, 3,652 kg, and in 1988, 4,019 kg. The average milk yield per cow, tended by the two best milkers of the kolkhoz, was over 5,000 kg per cow in 1988. The profit of the kolkhoz in 1989 was 1,385,000 roubles. However, if we considered these characteristics in terms of a market economy oriented society, the production system would be estimated as being ineffective, causing environmental pollution and being unnecessarily expensive. To give an objective estimation to the kolkhoz system we have to consider it in its historical time and place. In the new economic situation, many, perhaps even most of the structures built under socialist rule have proved useless. At present, many buildings have already been destroyed or fallen down. From the human point of view, it is quite understandable how some people involved in the process thought:

> How can you not understand that these buildings did not come into being by themselves, either? They are the result of the hard work of many honest working people. The wages in our kolkhoz were at the average level because of the construction work performed here. Nowadays it seems like we were guilty of some crime . . . In our kolkhoz, the tractor driver who left the edges of the field unploughed was punished for carelessness. Nowadays, we see how large fields near highways are used to 'cultivate' thistles . . . (A pensioner, former member of the kolkhoz board of management)

In 1970–1980, several changes took place in the demographic and professional structure of the labour force in the Kanepi kolkhoz, as well as in the whole of Estonia.

The decrease in population in rural areas was constant. In 1972, there were 479 families in the kolkhoz, in 1980, 449 families and in 1985, 432. The number of able-bodied adult kolkhozniks also decreased correspondingly – there were 319 of them in 1972 and 284 in 1980. In the middle of the 1980s, the number of kolkhozniks began to increase slowly – there were 307 of them in 1985 and 329 in 1989.

The ratio of men and women was unbalanced. There were more men than women in the kolkhoz and the difference widened continuously. In 1972, there were 173 men and 146 women in the kolkhoz, 199 men and 105 women in 1980, and 204 men and 103 women in 1985.

Amongst pensioners, the imbalance was vice versa – there were more women than there were men due to the shorter life expectancy of men in Estonia. The greater number of men able to work was characteristic for the whole district. This disproportion was one of the probable reasons for the cases of asocial behaviour, especially excessive drinking. As the drunkards among tractor and lorry drivers were usually punished by losing their driver's licences and being appointed to work in the repair workshop or in the cattle-shed, those were the places where certain merry groups would gather. Several women, who had to raise their children alone after their former husbands had become drunkards, also mentioned the negative influence of the "friends" of their ex-husbands. Certain problems with alcohol also existed amongst construction workers.

For such workers, the kolkhoz had to perform the role of a social maintenance organisation as well as the roles of ward, keeper, and judge. The wages paid to such workers were, as a rule, disproportionate to the actual work they performed. The money paid to them was usually a welfare benefit paid under the name of wages. From the 1960s, the Comradely Court operated in the kolkhoz. Later, the so-called pedagogic council was formed with the aim of helping to direct the workers in the right way of living. When the kolkhoz was liquidated, these former pseudo-workers formed a major part of the people in the district who needed help with managing their lives in some way.

Female workers were needed in the kolkhoz to develop cattle breeding. The kolkhoz gave the new workers flats in good condition. In the 1970s, the average wages of the kolkhozniks were higher than the wages of industrial workers or white-collar office workers living in larger towns. Thus, many divorced women, single mothers, and asocial women were attracted to the kolkhozes from towns as well as from other districts. As indicated above, the people who continuously drifted from one enterprise to another in search of easier living conditions formed the category of so-called "migratory birds". When Estonia regained its independence, this category of people formed a significant percentage of the people unable to adapt to the new situation.

By the 1970s, a new generation had grown up without previous experience of work on family farms. Their attitude to work was that of wage earners. People of the generation that had survived through the hardest times of kolkhoz life (1950–1961) had reached the age of retirement. The difficulties that had been borne together had helped to consolidate the people, to create the feeling of unity among them, especially on smaller sovkhozes and kolkhozes. In addition, the attitude of the older generation towards the kolkhoz leaders was much more positive as they had fought many hardships and gained certain success by working together. During the reforms of the 1990s, this attitude of unity was manifest in their judgement of the people who had left their family farms in the hard times and now they or their heirs had decided to return to reclaim their property.

> Where were they at the time we were working here without pay? It is the result of our work that there is anything left from older times . . . And now they all dare to come back and demand their share . . . (A pensioner, former cattle-tender)

When several kolkhozes were joined together, this feeling of unity amongst the workers decreased. In the 1970s, meetings of their representatives substituted the general meetings of all kolkhozniks. The tendency of the period was to give the workers selected information only. The inevitable result was the widening breach between the management and workers of the kolkhoz. The right to make any decisions concerning the welfare of the kolkhoz was concentrated in the hands of the members of the kolkhoz board of management and the leading specialists. The number of people partaking in decision-making decreased continuously. Those who had occupied leading positions in rural economic enterprises for years had gathered around them a number of faithful colleagues with similar views on the development of the enterprises. Thus, the closed circle of "trustworthy comrades" was formed which made all the decisions concerning the development of the enterprise.

Over the years, the level of education of farm workers increased notably. The older people who had had fewer possibilities of going to school in their youth became pensioners. As the majority of younger people had received secondary school education, the official obligatory education in the USSR, the change of generations created the rise of the average education level of workers.

The number of people graduating from secondary schools or universities increased from year to year. The results of the poll, performed in the days of the reform in the Kanepi kolkhoz, showed that about 30% of kolkhozniks had graduated from secondary schools and 9% of them had a college or university degree. The rise of the average level of education and of the number of specialists evoked two kinds of problems in the period of the restoration of independence and the transition to a market economy.

In secondary schools and universities, specialists had been trained in over detailed specialities necessary for large-scale production enterprises. In the post-Soviet economic situation, the older specialists in particular, who had worked at an enterprise for decades, had great difficulties in finding new jobs and in attending the necessary further education courses. If a specialist was also near retirement age, then he definitely belonged to one of the risk groups for whom the probability of losing his job was very high.

The second problem related to the traditional system used in the USSR of assigning young specialists to their first places of work. Namely, in the former Soviet Union secondary school and university graduates were appointed to their first jobs by the decree of the State Assignment Commission. They were obliged to serve at the appointed workplace for two years as a minimum. In return, the employers of these young specialists had to provide the new employees with accommodation. At the end of the 1970s and especially in the 1980s, the living conditions and wages offered by the kolkhozes were the most powerful means to make young talented specialists take up jobs in their collective enterprises. The days when the State Assignment Commission dealt out assignments to the graduates often resembled an auction where the best graduates of the year were up for sale. Consequently, the young specialists often set up their new homes far from their home kolkhozes. When the restitution of the farms to their previous owners started, the specialists often found that their houses were situated on someone else's land. Still, higher education in agricultural specialities provided younger specialists with a good investment, which enables them to survive in the new market economy conditions. Many positive examples of this can be pointed out, based on our studies carried out in the Kanepi district. The former agricultural specialists play an important role, even in the new local administration.

Living conditions and wages in kolkhozes were at the same level as in town. Furthermore, it was possible for a kolkhoznik to get additional income from his plot farm and to buy food from the kolkhoz at lower prices. According to the sociological polls carried out at the time, the possibilities of obtaining consumer goods in the country or in town did not differ significantly in Estonia. The number of personal cars was even higher in rural areas (Hion et al., 1988). The kolkhozes were also allowed to support the cultural interests of their members: free visits to theatre performances, holiday trips and partial or full payment for passes to sanatoriums. The kolkhoz also performed several functions in the area of social services: additional payments to state pensions, welfare benefits for families with many children, payment for the school dinners of the kolkhozniks' children, care of the aged. The USSR needed agricultural produce in large quantities. Thus, agriculture was held in high regard during the Soviet era and the mass media paid great attention to the harvest and other aspects of agricultural production.

The Disintegration of the Kanepi Kolkhoz

With the 1987 mass protest movement against the construction of a phosphorite mine devised by Moscow, Estonia proceeded into the era of the "singing revolution". This culminated with the restoration of independence in 1991. As can be seen from the article by Rein Ruutsoo, the inhabitants of the Kanepi district vigorously took part in all the mass activities. The influence of these societal processes on the economic operations of the Kanepi kolkhoz was initially rather weak. The time of change started there in 1990.

The kolkhoz persisted among the five most successful collective farms in the Põlva rayon. The profit in 1988 was 1,369,000 roubles and profitability 43.2% (PMA 117/725).

In September 1987, the plan for economic independence for Estonia was presented in the media – the concept of a so-called Estonian Self-Management (IME, i.e. *Isemajandav Eesti*). Discussion followed all over Estonia on the possibilities for self-management. One aspect of economic independence was the support for the legislature permitting private farming, the propagation for forming smaller production units by dividing large collective farms, and the recognition of the family farm as a production unit. The re-formation of private farms was legalised by the 1989 Farm Law.

The IME programme also came under discussion in the Kanepi kolkhoz. At the session of the kolkhoz board, the main tasks for the economic year 1989 were deemed the intensification of production, the reduction of expenses, and setting wages into a greater dependence on the results of work. The implementation of the IME programme was also prepared for within the kolkhoz by the establishment of the first family farms, by supporting the formation of firms, companies, co-operative enterprises, and by the further inculcation of collective employment.

At the session dealing with the problems concerning self-management, the chairman had to admit that there had been more talk about self-management rather than its actual implementation into daily work. The workers' indifference and the passivity of the leaders were raised as the greatest obstacles. The main factors disturbing daily work after 40 years of the kolkhoz were still the very ones that had constantly been fought without avail: the excessive consumption of alcohol, negligence, indifference, recklessness, and the lack of young and skilled employees.

In 1989, land was allocated for three family farms. In the same year, 14 new members joined the kolkhoz.

The kolkhoz continued its activities in social welfare, also discussed at the meeting of the kolkhoz board of management. The kolkhoz paid additional pensions to 123 people. Pensioners were also given 6 m^3 of timber free of charge. Funeral subsidies were increased. Kolkhoznik families with four or more children under the age of 16 were also paid special benefits (PMA 117/741).

In 1990, the topics of the board meetings altered: the problems concerning reforms now gained primary importance. In February 1990, it was decided to compensate the collectivised assets either to the person who had relinquished them to the kolkhoz or to their heirs. At the same session, the chief agronomist announced that another four families were preparing applications for private farms. It was agreed that the farmers would need help from the kolkhozes in purchasing machinery, as well as in the cultivation of land. The chief agronomist gives his forecast in the minutes as follows: "The transition will be hard. In my opinion, the collective farms cannot be closed down in the next ten years" (PMA 117/742).

The results of the poll of 1990 By the end of the 1980s, it was evident that major changes were under way. In order to study the aspirations, interests and expectations of the rural population in the context of the development of pluralism in ownership and production modes, a poll with the questionnaire entitled *"Mina ja meie muutuvas maaelus"* ("Me and Us in the Changing Rural Life") was carried out in 1988. It was the joint project of the Economics Institute of the Estonian Academy of Sciences and sociologists from the Estonian Agricultural University, under the supervision of Professor Asser Murutar. In spring 1990, another poll was undertaken in the Kanepi kolkhoz with the questionnaire *"Maaelu ja Eesti muutuvad olud"* ("Rural Life and Changing Circumstances in Estonia") that contained the same 200 questions as in the previous questionnaire. The results of the research are provided in a publication titled *"Eesti põllumajanduse tööjõupotentsiaali sotsiaalne areng 1977–93"* ("The Social Development of the Labour Force Potential in Estonian Agriculture 1977–1993"); the MSc thesis by Arno Lõo, a member of the research group (Lõo, 1997), and finally in the report on the studies submitted to the Economics Institute of the Estonian Academy of Sciences under the name *"Maaelu ja Eesti muutuvad olud. Võrdleva kordusuurimuse tulemused"* ("Rural Life and the Changing Circumstances in Estonia. The Results of a Comparative Repeated Study") by Lõo (1990). The choice of the Kanepi kolkhoz as the site of research was prompted by the management of the collective farm. It wished to learn about the employees' opinions before the beginning of rearrangements.

In order to guarantee the comprehensibility of the poll results, it must be stressed that the research was carried out in spring 1990. At that moment Estonia was on the road to independence but still held membership in the Soviet Union. The Farm Law had been passed, facilitating the establishment of single family farms. The economic decline had started and the value of the rouble was dropping rapidly.

Here are the characteristics of the sample: every third person out of the 300 permanent workers of the Kolkhoz was interviewed; in addition, some of the former employees and retired people were also questioned – 126 persons in all. Of those interviewed, 66.7% were men and 33.3% were women; the sex ratio of the sample was accurate. As for education: 9.5% of the sample had higher education; 30.2% had vocational secondary and 23.8%, secondary education.

Occupation wise, the respondents fell into five categories:

a) Pensioners – 13.5%;
b) cattle tenders and milkers – 16.7%;
c) field, garden, and forest workers – 13.3%;
d) machine operators – 35.9%;
e) head managers, specialists – 20.6%.

One third (32.5%) of those who responded had been living in the area since their birth and 22.2% had lived there for most of their lives. To these should be added those who had resided in the district for more than 10 years, thus constituting 70.6% of those interviewed.

The estimation, which the respondents gave to the collectivisation of agriculture, was prevalently negative: 65.1% of the respondents found that it caused the decline of Estonian farming and rural culture. 18.3% asserted that the establishment of the kolkhozes was, indeed, forced upon the country people but that it nevertheless guaranteed the continuity of agricultural production.

The evaluation by the people of the current state of agriculture is presented in Figure 2.2:

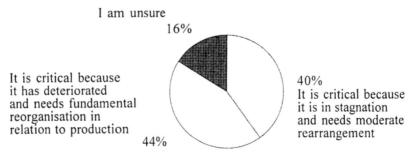

I am unsure
16%

It is critical because
it has deteriorated
and needs fundamental
reorganisation in
relation to production
44%

40%
It is critical because
it is in stagnation
and needs moderate
rearrangement

Figure 2.2 The current state of agriculture

The attitude towards the anticipated land reform is positive; however, thorough preparation is expected (see Figure 2.3):

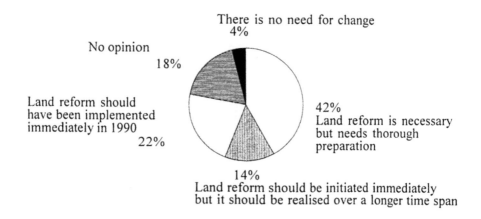

There is no need for change
4%

No opinion
18%

Land reform should
have been implemented
immediately in 1990
22%

42%
Land reform is necessary
but needs thorough
preparation

14%
Land reform should be initiated immediately
but it should be realised over a longer time span

Figure 2.3 Attitudes concerning the land reform

At the time of the poll, in spring 1990, one of the most important concerns was the way in which the land should be distributed to those willing to establish private farms. The idea of restitution, the return to the ownership terms of 1939, was not at that time on the agenda. It was only agreed upon after Estonia regained independence in 1991.

The opinions on the ways of handing the land over to an individual owner can be divided into the following (Figure 2.4):

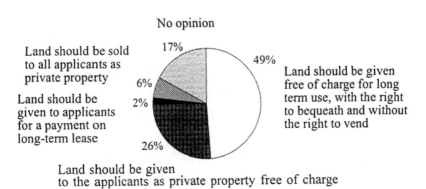

Figure 2.4 Opinions on how to hand over land to individual owners

In terms of returning land to former family farm owners, opinions are divided as follows (Figure 2.5):

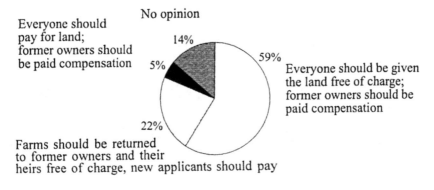

Figure 2.5 Returning land to former owners of family farms

The attitude of the people towards different forms of management is indicated by the responses to the question regarding which forms of production would be compatible with the future of Estonian agriculture and with the interests of the rural population:

Table 2.4 Which forms of production would be compatible with the future of Estonian agriculture and with the interests of the rural population?

	Yes	No
Hereditary family farm	64.3%	4.0%
Family labour (e.g. single-family cowshed)	64.3%	5.6%
Co-operative founded by the owners of separate private farms	59.5%	2.4%
Contracts with sole producers (growing green fodder, vegetables)	59.5%	1.5%
Termination or reduction of collective farms	54.8%	9.6%
Economically independent departments or other units	50.0%	10.3%
Joint-stock company as an intermediary stage for the construction of private farms	43.7%	4.0%
Current kolkhozes	21.5%	33.4%
Current sovkhozes	2.4%	63.5%

The responses indicate the plurality of opinions. The most negative attitude is towards the forms of management hitherto existing, i.e. kolkhozes and especially sovkhozes.

At the time of the poll, the possibility of becoming a private farm owner had only existed for quite a short time. The leadership of the kolkhoz did not display any particular sympathy for it either, as was also noted by the respondents: 47% felt that the establishment of new farms is not supported in their kolkhoz.

The division of responses to the following question, "Would you like to become a private farm owner?" shows the readiness of the respondents themselves to take advantage of the possibility.

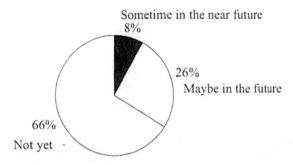

Figure 2.6 I should like to become a family farm owner

The relation between wishes and possibilities is mirrored by the responses to the question; "Does your family intend to become private farm owners?" (Figure 2.7).

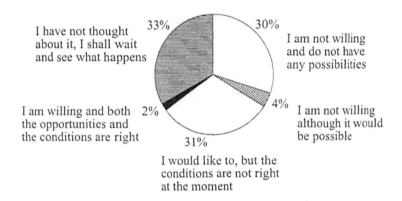

Figure 2.7 Intention to become a family farm owner

Thus, in spring 1990, two thirds of the respondents were still hesitating.

The questionnaire also presented a list of 25 qualities necessary for running a private farm and asked for an estimation of the most vital ones. Being materially-technically equipped turned out to be the most crucial factor; the personal traits and knowledge of family members went into second place. The lack of experience in a market economy is indicated by the fact that the distance of a market was 7th from last in the list of importance. At the same time, being provided with concentrated cattle feed was rated 8th in importance as people were used to buying cheap cattle feed imported from the other Republics of the Soviet Union.

61.1% of the respondents kept animals: mostly pigs (46.0%), young stock (38.1%) and cattle (33.3%). The level of technical equipment was low: only 6.3% owned a milking machine and only one respondent had a milk cooler.

In spring 1990, the discussion on running a private farm was purely theoretical; in their everyday lives, the respondents were still tied to the kolkhoz. How did they estimate their own Kanepi kolkhoz? The respondents judged their collective farm, in comparison to other kolkhozes, from 26 different aspects, on a three-point scale:

1) The kolkhoz is among the worst
2) The kolkhoz is at an average level
3) The kolkhoz is among the best

The analysis brought out five basic areas in which the collective farm could be characterised:

a) The economic success of the kolkhoz
b) The conditions of employees
c) The competence of the leadership
d) Working relationships
e) The care of the kolkhoz for its employees

In comparison to research carried out in 1988 on the collective farms nearby, the employees of the Kanepi kolkhoz gave a better estimation of their economic success and workers' conditions. The activities of the leadership were also viewed positively. The drawbacks, as compared to other collective farms, were injustice in the payment of wages, poor healthcare for the workers, and the negative attitude towards the emergence of family farms.

The collation of the estimations, as compiled by professional groups, reveals that machine operators were the most critical in terms of the leadership: 64% found that the organisation of work was bad and 47% protested against injustice in payment of wages. Specialists, managers and office workers were more critical than average in terms of the low commitment of employees to their daily work.

The results of the research pinpointed the most critical group, the machine operators, which was to constitute the opposition to the leadership.

The kolkhozniks' share of decision-making in the developmental agendas and plans of the kolkhoz, was estimated by them in the following way:

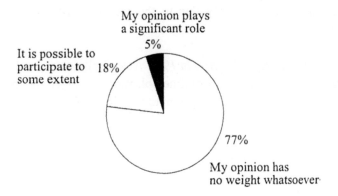

Figure 2.8 The roles played by former kolkhozniks in development decisions

Willingness to participate was indicated by the responses to the question: "Would you like to have more opportunities in deciding the course of events on your collective farm as a whole?"

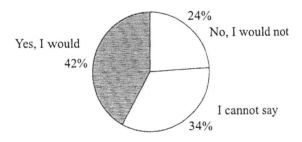

Figure 2.9 Willingness of former kolkhozniks to participate in making development decisions

As can be seen, the kolkhozniks had become estranged from their kolkhoz: three quarters of them felt that decisions were made by others – by the leaders whom they could not influence. Only about a quarter, nevertheless, had completely given up hope.

A year after the poll, the leaders started to reform the kolkhoz. Their venture failed, however, partly due to the lack of trust and the lack of information.

The failure of the attempted reform in 1991 At the kolkhoz council session in June 1990, the results of the springtime poll were presented by some of the scientists from Tartu. The reports prompted the following conclusions to be entered into the minutes of the session (PMA 117/741):

1) The kolkhozes have to reorganise their production because smaller units are more productive due to lower management costs. Large collective farms are facing bankruptcy.
2) As the assets of the kolkhoz are common property, the share of each member should be calculated. The basis for the calculations could be the earned wage as a measure for work done.
3) The springtime poll indicated the support for small-scale production and private farms.

In June, the kolkhoz bank account had a balance of 850,000 roubles. In accordance with the decision made in February, the sum of 300,000 roubles was calculated to be the value of collectivised assets, 148,000 roubles of which had already been paid out to owners or their heirs. It was also decided to start calculating the quota day shares, taking into account that in earlier times, work in the kolkhoz had been measured in different ways: before 1963, the quota day was the basis of calculation and from 1964 monetary wages were paid.

The last session of the kolkhoz council of 1990 took place in September and proved most significant in terms of the logic of the following events. The council members were informed that the shares up to 1963 had been calculated. Summaries had also been made of the years 1964–1969 and 1970–1990. These shares, however, were as yet incompletely calculated as it was not known what should serve as the basis for calculation: the time spent at work or the contribution which was measured by the wages paid.

The minutes characterised the economic situation in the following manner. After the wages and bonuses were paid out, 800,000 roubles were left in the kolkhoz bank account. According to the new Tax Law, valid from the New Year, the income tax for an income of more than one million would be 70%. Therefore, the quest for new forms of production and the division of the collective farm into smaller departments was inevitable.

It was realised that the pace of reorganisation needed to be stepped up, as it had to take place before the implementation of the new Income Tax Law in 1990. The leadership substantiated the planned alterations by also using the results of the springtime poll. Furthermore, it was decided that representatives of the scientists of Tartu should be called to take part in the general meeting.

The general meeting was held on December 20, 1990. All the members of the kolkhoz were given the right to participate – even those who had relinquished their assets during nationalisation, as well as former workers who had left the kolkhoz but who had worked there for at least five years. The aims of the session were the approval of the plan for the reorganisation and deciding on the principles for calculating the shares. However, the session failed because of the following factors:

1) The insufficient preparations made by the leadership of the collective farm. The practice, hitherto employed, where a narrow circle of people made crucial decisions, and the kolkhoz members were just informed of them and expected to give their approval, did not work. The decisions made were to influence the destiny of all the kolkhozniks, so different groups underlined their different interests.
2) The lack of trust in the leadership who were suspected of pursuing their individual gain.
3) The successful action of the opposition. The opposition supporting the continuance of the kolkhoz took advantage of the kolkhozniks' uncertainty and the lack of information. The backbone of the opposition consisted of tractor and lorry drivers whose opportunities for work would be considerably reduced by the re-organisation of the kolkhoz. As mentioned above, the questionnaire had also revealed this group as the most critical about the leadership.

The kolkhozniks did not approve the reform plan presented by the leadership and the session was closed after the decision to summon another one. The chairman, who had been taken ill, chose to withdraw.

The last two years of the Kanepi kolkhoz 1991–1992 The next meeting of the kolkhoz council was held on February 21, 1991. The vice-chairman of the kolkhoz delivered the summary of the previous year, 1990, as the chairman himself was still ill. The profit of 1990 was 1,324,000 roubles and profitability 39.4%. Meat and dairy production had decreased, production expenses had increased, cattle feed prices had risen, and so had wages. In his speech, a lecturer from the Estonian Agricultural University advised continuing the calculating of shares, keeping in mind the imminent inevitable rearrangements in the kolkhoz.

The most important issue at that session was the election of a new leadership and, along with it, a new chairman, as the authorisation of the incumbent ones had terminated. The hitherto chairman refrained from standing for the position because of poor health. The candidature for the position of chairman was put up by the leader of the opposition that had taken shape by the previous session; he was elected by 38 votes with 4 votes against him. A "little revolution" had taken place. Presenting his programme, the new chairman declared himself as a supporter of the kolkhoz system and of establishing private family farms. He assumed that if the kolkhoz were still preserved and prospered, many people would give up their private farms. He considered land cultivation to be the most important matter. The new chairman introduced his eight candidates for the board of management, promising to develop the spirit of co-operation among them. On February 26, 1991, the former chairman yielded his office to his successor.

The next session of the kolkhoz council was held on June 27, 1991. That was the last one before Estonia regained its independence. In August 1991, it was noted that applications had been delivered for the official registration of 27 private farms. The problems concerning work were no longer discussed at the meetings. On December 20, 1991, the minutes of the council session consisted of land extractions for 32 private farms.

On March 31, 1992, the session analysed the work results of 1991. The chief agronomist gave the presentation. He noted that the results could not be compared with previous years because of the considerable increases in prices. Just a year earlier, hopes had been expressed that the kolkhoz would last for a good while longer; however, it was now evident that it would not. The chief agronomist underlined the basic problems: the decrease in sowing land, the lack of means for plant protection, the increase in the number of sick cows, the decrease in the quality of milk, and the difficulties in finding a market for potatoes.

The course was set for the liquidation of the Kanepi collective farm (PMA 117/755).

The Liquidation of the Kanepi Kolkhoz

The Activities of the Reform Committee

A significant step towards the liquidation of the kolkhozes was the establishment of the reform committee. The one in the Kanepi kolkhoz started its activities on September 15, 1992 with a session in the council house. The committee consisted of seven members: the chief agronomist, another agronomist, the secretary from the kolkhoz, the chairman of the municipal council, the municipal land surveyor, a state representative and the chairman of the committee (PMA 117/798).

The entitled subjects of the agricultural reform were defined as:

a) The previous owners of the collectivised assets and their legal successors.
b) The current members and permanent workers of the collective farm.
c) The people who had retired from the collective farm.
d) Those members and employees of the collective farm who had worked on the farm for at least five years.
e) The private farm owners who were former members and permanent workers of the collective farm, with the farm as their last place of work.
f) The former permanent workers of the collective farm, or their heirs in case they had proceeded or would proceed to run a private farm.

According to the reform committee, workshares could also be given to the heirs living in the area of the collective farm.

By October 20, 1992, the committee asked the kolkhoz to submit:

a) A list of integral property: an inventory and buildings according to their location and value.
b) A list of collectivised assets.
c) A list of recipients of the workshares.

After the establishment of the reform committee, operations using the kolkhoz assets could only be undertaken in accordance with the decree of the committee. The minutes that followed did include several decrees of that nature. Kanepi municipal council was offered the district heating plant and the council itself applied to the kolkhoz for the Kanepi kindergarten and a sauna, a couple of buses and cars, a lorry, two tractors and other objects. It was decided the application should be presented to the general meeting.

At the December session, the reform committee had to admit that integral assets had indeed been sold in the kolkhoz after the validation of the sales ban. Stored building materials and working clothes had been sold without the permission of the reform committee.

In compensation for the demolished parsonage, the vicar was provided with a flat free of charge. Consequently, the congregation withdrew its pretensions against the kolkhoz.

The reform plan of the Kanepi kolkhoz was endorsed on February 23, 1993. The date of the next general meeting had earlier been agreed upon as February 26, 1993.

In 1992, the Estonian kroon (crown, EEK) became the currency of the republic. Kroons replaced roubles at a rate of 10:1.

The Decisive Sessions

Only the general meeting could pass the resolution on reforms in the kolkhoz. The session was held on October 6, 1992, with 192 employees participating. The chairman of the kolkhoz reported on the economic situation. The profits were EEK 1,952,836 and the losses, EEK 1,467,334. EEK 468,317 had been given out as wages; EEK 313,930 had been taken in various taxes (PMA 117/776). The profit was small and expenses large. The kolkhoz did not have enough fuel for the autumn ploughing. As it was impossible to continue in the same manner, the leadership of the kolkhoz endorsed the reform plan, which was subsequently presented to the general meeting. The latter in their turn accepted the proposal to carry out the reforms in two stages:

1) The reorganisation of the kolkhoz into smaller units.
2) The liquidation of the kolkhoz.

The last general meeting of the Kanepi kolkhoz took place at 10 o'clock on February 26, 1993 in the assembly hall of the secondary school. There were 323 employees present. The former kolkhoz chairman of 26 years was elected chairman of the meeting by 242 votes.

The chief accountant had previously given an account of the property situation in the kolkhoz on February 1, 1993. The kolkhoz had integral assets worth EEK 2,700,000; working capital worth EEK 1,300,000, which included 582 cows, 850 heads of young stock, 1027 pigs, 115 sheep and 9 horses. The kolkhoz had no debts to pay. Other institutions and individuals owed the kolkhoz EEK 394,000. On top of that, the kolkhoz still controlled EEK 1,200,000 of collectivised property.

At the meeting, the order of calculating and allocating the workshares was explained. The last sentence of the respective minutes states, "The higher the purchase prices for the kolkhoz assets at the auction are, the greater [value of] the workshare will be." I wonder to what extent this concept affected human behaviour in the context of the auction.

Concerning the privatisation of flats and detached houses, the session raised the problem of those flat-owners who, in spite of a very brief working time in the kolkhoz, were able to take possession of very good flats and houses. The following solution was voted upon: on the privatisation of housing, compensation for the collectivised assets and the shares of the flat-owner and his family members will be calculated with a coefficient of 1. If this proved insufficient for the privatisation, shares with the coefficient of 3 would be calculated for the remainder. The documents in the archives did not reveal whether the decision was actually implemented later. It might well have been that it was not felt necessary. Whereas the prices of houses and flats were calculated by January 1, 1993, the price of a quota day nearly quadrupled during the auction. The families of a young economist and the chairman of the kolkhoz respectively owned the most expensive detached houses, costing more than EEK 9,700. The session also resolved that nobody should be given any priority rights for buying assets at the auction.

The concern of the people for the future is also reflected in the minutes: there is little information, it is hard to make decisions, the liquidation of the kolkhoz will be followed by unemployment, and the cultivation of the land is made impossible by the lack of equipment. No solutions to these problems were provided in the last general meeting.

The session also fixed the time schedule of the auction:

March 11, 1993: the auction of integral assets. Permission to participate was given to the workshare recipients of the Kanepi kolkhoz, as well as to the owners of collectivised assets who did not have any debts or inventory to return to the kolkhoz.

March 15 – 17, 1993: the bidding of cars, tractors, trailing implements and production assets (machines, minor implements, and cattle feed). Permission to participate was given to the purchasers of the integral assets, private farm owners, and private farm applicants based on the municipal council certificate.

March 18 – 19, 1993: the machine and minor implement auction for all the share recipients who lived in the kolkhoz.

March 22 – 23, 1993: the bidding of unsold assets for everyone who was interested, with all payments in cash.

March 25, 1993: the official registration for the privatisation of houses and flats.

On March 4 and 5, prior to the auction, it was possible for the applicants, who owned a household in the Kanepi kolkhoz, or had become private farm owners, or were restoring their family farm, to get animals for the return of the collectivised assets. One could get back as many cattle, sheep, pigs, and horses as the kolkhoz had. One could not get a cow instead of a collectivised horse but only a calf or a young bull.

For the buildings that had been used by the kolkhoz, a symbolic compensation of EEK 1,000 or 500 per household was promised.

The time of the final liquidation of the kolkhoz was also fixed in the minutes. The kolkhoz would end its activities when all the assets had found new owners, and when deliveries and the obligations of payment had been officially completed. According to the calculations, the kolkhoz had to be liquidated by April 30, 1993 at the latest.

The Distribution of the Kolkhoz Assets

The last meeting of the reform committee of the Kanepi kolkhoz took place March 10, 1994, a year after the first auction. The results in figures of the reform are fixed in the minutes (PMA 117/798).

The kolkhoz had collectivised assets worth EEK 1,395,560 of which, in 1990: was paid out EEK 191,172, compensated in kind: EEK 52,830, remaining to be compensated: EEK 1,151,830, invested in production units: EEK 256,391. The remainder was deposited into the Savings and Loan Association.

On the day of the final general meeting, the kolkhoz owned property worth EEK 4,000,000 (in book value), of which EEK 1,200,000 stood for collectivised assets. The remainder, therefore, was worth approximately EEK 2,800,000. This sum was divided into workshares of 3,337,678 quota days among a total of 1,224 voucher recipients. The book value of kolkhoz property eventually rose to EEK 7,717,904 during the auction. The value of the vouchers also soared, but soon it transpired that the buyers only had vouchers that totalled slightly over four million kroons to cover the purchase of these assets. The creation of a deficit of over two million kroons was possible due to the lack of adequate regulation at the auction event, which enabled buyers to make bids they could not cover (for a detailed examination of the auction procedure see Alanen, Chapter 3).

The auction list of integral assets contained 62 distinct lots at a starting price totalling EEK 2,778,557. During the auction, the price of these buildings rose to EEK 4,528,930 (included in the grand total of EEK 7,717,904). The new pigsty, including the animals, held the highest starting price of EEK 370,066. The Karste cowshed, including the animals, was next at EEK 289,301 and then the Kooraste cowshed at EEK 208,790. These prices did not increase in the auction. The cheapest lot was a lakeside barn in Kooraste, which started at EEK 180 and went for the same price.

In comparison with the starting price, the wood-processing complex made the biggest increase in value from EEK 60,289 to EEK 625,000. The complex consisted of a timber workshop with a drier, a storehouse for building materials (materials included), and a saw-frame. It was to prove itself a most useful investment for the future.

The majority of the integral assets, 23 separate lots, were bought at the auction by the newly founded Kanepi co-operative. The bidding on buildings was very active and prices rose considerably. Thus, half of the recreation building of the workshop cost the co-operative EEK 670,000 instead of 221,148, and the petrol depot, complete with equipment, cost EEK 155,000 instead of 13,521.

The members of the joint-stock company MTJ made their purchases in concord, buying objects connected with the technical support of the machinery.

One of the larger items of integral assets, the administration building, is also worth mentioning – with a starting price of EEK 77,086, it later sold for EEK 302,000.

According to the minutes, the Kanepi sewage treatment plant (EEK 9,341) and the district heating plant (EEK 94,429) became part of the common property of the municipality. The rest of the objects passed into new ownership, some of them quite by accident. It is mentioned in interviews that an old fellow surprised his family by purchasing a cowshed, animals, and storage buildings at a total cost of EEK 79,793.

There was much more excitement at the auction of machinery and assets. Three 15-year-old draught-horses were put up for bidding at the prices of EEK 22.60, 49.40, and 42.30 respectively. At these prices, they did find new owners, two of whom already had private stables. In a way, the ridiculously low prices of the horses symbolise the depth and irreversibility of the changes which technology has undergone and also the necessity for the political-economic analysis of the distribution of the kolkhoz assets at such extremely low prices after the recalculation into kroons.

Tools were the most desired minor implements. During the auction, the price of a Husqvarna chainsaw rose from EEK 239 to 17,000, a Partner brush saw went for EEK 3,300 from a starting price of EEK 84. The prices of building materials rose tenfold. Some of the high bids are also an indication of the carnival mood that prevailed at the auction. The cashier's briefcase (for carrying the wages and salaries), worth EEK 1.40 sold for 200 and a 5 cent rubber stamp went for EEK 100.

The participants at the auction were mainly interested in land cultivation equipment, especially tractors. These were vital for private farm owners as well as for the new co-operatives and farms based on integral properties. The auction list included 68 tractors: 19 were bought by the Kanepi co-operative, Karste Dairy (Karste Piim) bought 14, and the Liivasaare farm 7. They needed the machines to produce green fodder for the purchased animals and furthermore to provide cultivation services for the employees who had invested their shares into a co-operative. In the course of the bidding, prices soared. Kanepi co-operative purchased a Belarus tractor for EEK 92,000 from a starting price of 1,090. Naturally, in bidding of that kind, many of the private farm owners fell short with their shares, and in principle, the supply of tractors could not meet the demand at all.

There were nine combine harvesters at the auction. The oldest (a 1983 model) was the only one to be sold at its starting price of EEK 1,315. The Kanepi co-operative bought three of them, Karste Dairy bought two, and the Liivasaare farm bought one. The remaining three went to individual buyers.

Analysing the auction list of the combine harvesters obviates the processes of price formation. A deeper analysis of the prices also renders the developments in Estonian agriculture more comprehensible. Of the four most modern combine harvesters of the type Don 1500, one was purchased in 1990 for EEK 4,183. The respective prices of the ones bought in 1991 were EEK 4,391 and 4,499. A Don 1500 obtained in 1992 cost as much as EEK 40,225. The auction prices of other combine harvesters were in the same class, i.e. EEK 40,000.

The rest of the land cultivation equipment also proved insufficient and unable to meet the interests of the private farm owners in either quality or quantity. Nevertheless, everything was bought up, partly due to the joy of bidding and partly in the hope that an efficient household might be established.

Unfortunately, some of the purchased technology was abandoned within the next couple of years because the principal decisions concerning the development of agriculture in the Estonian Republic were, at that time, still to be made.

Kanepi kolkhoz ceased to exist in March 1993, 44 years after the beginning of the collectivisation era. In an interview from 1998, the former chairman of the kolkhoz board of management stated that the order to liquidate the kolkhoz was faxed to the board. There was no direct legislative act in existence to support this order. However, everyone knew the deadline date of April 1, 1993.

The authors of this study started to interview former kolkhozniks in the Municipality of Kanepi for the first time in summer 1995. The aim of these interviews was to learn what real changes had taken place in the situation during the years from 1993 to 1995.

During the course of the agricultural reform, all kolkhoz properties were assessed very cheaply. The value of the entire assets of the Kanepi kolkhoz was set for EEK 4,000,000. This sum was achieved by setting the exchange rate at the course of the monetary reform in Estonia – 10 roubles equal 1 Estonian kroon. At that time, the rate of inflation had been rising for some while already, but the major part of kolkhoz stock had been obtained in the 1980s, when inflation had not weakened the Soviet monetary system much. At the same time, expert opinions, published in newspapers of the period, pointed out that to establish a contemporary productive family farm would take up to EEK 4,000,000. Therefore, in accordance with the monetary policy of the period, the value of all the movable and immovable assets of the whole of Kanepi kolkhoz would barely have been enough to establish one new private farm. Due to the underestimation of the total value of kolkhoz assets, the shares of most former kolkhozniks and other legal subjects were unreasonably small. These shares did not reach the order of magnitude necessary for providing the capital to establish a private farm. As the prices of movable and immovable assets were low, people, or certain groups in key positions, could lay their hands on the most valuable property. Nearly two-thirds of the basic property of the kolkhoz consisted of various buildings. It was physically impossible to portion out shares of them. Many of these buildings were left standing empty and soon, they started to fall apart. At the same time, the prices of new contemporary agricultural machinery had risen substantially.

Even the lucky few, who had succeeded in buying tractors and other machines in the kolkhoz auction, had their problems. Some of them were prepared to cultivate land for other family farmers. However, although they had obtained the machinery very cheaply, the prices for gasoline and lubricants quickly rose to world market levels. Then, the prices for such services also had to rise so high that there were no customers able to pay.

The prices of agricultural products remained low and the situation became so desperate that the agricultural producers were not paid for their products that passed on to processing enterprises even at these low prices. So the agricultural enterprises, struggling against poverty themselves, were forced into giving interest free loans to processing enterprises and commerce, where the turnover is much faster. It took months to get paid for milk delivered to dairies, some of which went bankrupt, thus leaving dairy producers unpaid for their produce. As we know, cows cannot be switched off – they were milked, and the milk was processed and produced; only the milk producers were left penniless.

A new attitude towards country people has gradually been developing in Estonia. In the days of "The Singing Revolution," people talked with respect about peasants being the preservers of Estonian lifestyle. Since then, the attitude towards country people has changed into considering them as a conservative group that demands unfounded special privileges. The opinion has already been expressed that agricultural production in Estonia is ineffective and, therefore, unnecessary anyway. One of the people interviewed in Kanepi expressed his feelings concerning this attitude in the following way: "It is maybe a brutal way of expressing my thoughts but, sometimes, I have the feeling that it is inevitable to have a war [and shortage of food] once more, just to resurrect a clear understanding. There is no future without country people."

The number of unemployed country people rose quickly. In 1991, when the municipal development plan was worked out, there were four unemployed people in the municipality. In 1995, there were over 100 people receiving regular welfare benefits. The small incomes of a significant percentage of country people caused the income decreases in communal services and commercial enterprises. Increasing numbers of people were suffering from depression and the number of drunkards started to increase. The Municipality of Kanepi, once an average level municipality in the Põlva county, has started to descend into an economic crisis with the rest of the southeast region of Estonia.

References

Hion, E., Lauristin, M. and Vihalemm, P. (1988), *Changing Life-Style in Contemporary Estonia*, Perioodika, Tallinn.

Koit, 'Märtsiküüditamine Põlvamaal [The March Deportation in Põlva County],' Koit newspaper, no. 79/1992.

Lõo, A. (1990), *Maaelu ja Eesti muutuvad olud. Võrdleva kordusuurimise tulemused* [Rural Life and the Changing Circumstances in Estonia. The Results of a Comparative Repeated Study], unpublished manuscript, University of Tartu.

Lõo, A. (1997), *Eesti põllumajanduse tööjõupotentsiaali sotsiaalne areng 1977–1993* [The Social Development of the Labour Force Potential in Estonian Agriculture 1977–1993], Master of Sciences thesis, University of Tartu.

Põlva maakonnaarhiivi fondid [Põlva County Archives], file no. 28: Kanepi vald 1944–1950 [Kanepi district 1944–1950], dossier no. 75: Kulaklikud majapidamised [The Kulak Homesteads].

Põlva maakonnaarhiivi fondid [Põlva County Archives], file no. 28: Kanepi vald 1944–1950 [Kanepi district 1944–1950], dossier no. 368: Maareform [Land Reform].

Põlva maakonnaarhiivi fondid [Põlva County Archives], file no. 117: Kanepi kolhoos [Kanepi kolkhoz], dossier no. 27: Ühisjõe kolhoosi juhatuse koosolekute protokolliraamat 1951 [Minutes of the Ühisjõud Kolkhoz Board Meetings for the Year 1951].

Põlva maakonnaarhiivi fondid [Põlva County Archives], file no. 117: Kanepi kolhoos [Kanepi kolkhoz], dossier no. 57: Ühisjõu kolhoosi üldkoosolekute protokolliraamat 1955 [Minutes of the Ühisjõud Kolkhoz General Meetings for the Year 1955].

Põlva maakonnaarhiivi fondid [Põlva County Archives], file no. 117: Kanepi kolhoos [Kanepi kolkhoz], dossier no. 88: Ühisjõu kolhoosi üldkoosolekute protokolliraamat 1951–1952 [Minutes of the Ühisjõud Kolkhoz General Meetings for the Years 1951–1952].

Põlva maakonnaarhiivi fondid [Põlva County Archives], file no. 117: Kanepi kolhoos [Kanepi kolkhoz], dossier no. 125: Üldkoosolekute ja juhatuse koosolekute protokolliraamat 1960 [Minutes of the Kolkhoz General Meetings and Kolkhoz Board Meetings for the Year 1960].

Põlva maakonnaarhiivi fondid [Põlva County Archives], file no. 117: Kanepi kolhoos [Kanepi kolkhoz], dossier no. 194: Ühisjõu kolhoosi 1969. aasta aruanne [Annual Report of the Ühisjõud Kolkhoz for the Year 1969].

Põlva maakonnaarhiivi fondid [Põlva County Archives], file no. 117: Kanepi kolhoos [Kanepi kolkhoz], dossier no. 219: Ühisjõu kolhoosi juhatuse koosolekute protokolliraamat 1951–1952 [Minutes of the Ühisjõud Kolkhoz Board Meetings for the Years 1951–1952].

Põlva maakonnaarhiivi fondid [Põlva County Archives], file no. 117: Kanepi kolhoos [Kanepi kolkhoz], dossier no. 244: Ühisjõu kolhoosi 1956. aasta aruanne [Annual Report of the Ühisjõud Kolkhoz for the Year 1956].

Põlva maakonnaarhiivi fondid [Põlva County Archives], file no. 117: Kanepi kolhoos [Kanepi kolkhoz], dossier no. 249: Ühisjõu kolhoosi 1957. aasta üldkoosolekute protokolliraamat [Minutes of the Ühisjõud Kolkhoz General Meetings for the Year 1957].

Põlva maakonnaarhiivi fondid [Põlva County Archives], file no. 117: Kanepi kolhoos [Kanepi kolkhoz], dossier no. 389: Kolhoosi Suur Oktoober 1969. aasta aruanne [Annual report of the Great October Kolkhoz for the Year 1969].

Põlva maakonnaarhiivi fondid [Põlva County Archives], file no. 117: Kanepi kolhoos [Kanepi kolkhoz], dossier no. 725: Volinike koosolekute protokollid 1989 [Minutes of the Kolkhoz Council Meetings for the Year 1989].

Põlva maakonnaarhiivi fondid [Põlva County Archives], file no. 117: Kanepi kolhoos [Kanepi kolkhoz], dossier no. 741: Volinike koosolekute protokollid 1990 [Minutes of the Kolkhoz Council Meetings for the Year 1990].

Põlva maakonnaarhiivi fondid [Põlva County Archives], file no. 117: Kanepi kolhoos [Kanepi kolkhoz], dossier no. 742: Juhatuse koosolekute protokollid 1990 [Minutes of the Kolkhoz Board Meetings for the Year 1990].

Põlva maakonnaarhiivi fondid [Põlva County Archives], file no. 117: Kanepi kolhoos [Kanepi kolkhoz], dossier no. 755: Volinike koosolekute protokollid 1991 [Minutes of the Kolkhoz Council Meetings for the Year 1991].

Põlva maakonnaarhiivi fondid [Põlva County Archives], file no. 117: Kanepi kolhoos [Kanepi kolkhoz], dossier no. 767: Volinike koosolekute protokollid 1992 [Minutes of the Kolkhoz Council Meetings for the Year 1992].

Põlva maakonnaarhiivi fondid [Põlva County Archives], file no. 117: Kanepi kolhoos [Kanepi kolkhoz], dossier no. 776: Üldkoosolekute protokollid 1992–1993 [Minutes of the Kolkhoz General Meetings for the Years 1992–1993].

Põlva maakonnaarhiivi fondid [Põlva County Archives], file no. 117: Kanepi kolhoos [Kanepi kolkhoz], dossier no. 781: Tervikvara oksjon Kanepi kolhoosis 11.–15.03. 1993. Kanepi kolhoosis [Auction of Integral Property in Kanepi Kolkhoz on March 11–15, 1993].

Põlva maakonnaarhiivi fondid [Põlva County Archives], file no. 117: Kanepi kolhoos [Kanepi kolkhoz], dossier no. 782: Tehnika oksjon. Põhi- ja väikevahendid 22.–24. 03. 1993 [Auction of Technical Equipment on March 22–24, 1993].

Põlva maakonnaarhiivi fondid [Põlva County Archives], file no. 117: Kanepi kolhoos [Kanepi kolkhoz], dossier no. 784: Ühistatud vara kompenseerimise otsused [Resolutions on the Compensation of Nationalised Property].

Põlva maakonnaarhiivi fondid [Põlva County Archives], file no. 117: Kanepi kolhoos [Kanepi kolkhoz], dossier no. 785: Ühistatud vara kompenseerimise otsused [Resolutions on the Compensation of Nationalised Property].

Põlva maakonnaarhiivi fondid [Põlva County Archives], file no. 117: Kanepi kolhoos [Kanepi kolkhoz], dossier no. 786: Ühistatud vara kompenseerimise otsused 1992 [Resolutions on the Compensation of Nationalised Property 1992].

Põlva maakonnaarhiivi fondid [Põlva County Archives], file no. 117: Kanepi kolhoos [Kanepi kolkhoz], dossier no. 798: Reformikomisjoni koosolekute protokollid 1992–1994 [Minutes of the Reform Committee Meetings for the Years 1992–1994].

Tõnurist, E. (1978), *Eesti NSV põllumajanduse kollektiviseerimine. Dokumentide ja materjalide kogumik* [Collectivisation of the Agricultural System of the ESSR. Collected Documents and Materials], EKP KK Partei Ajaloo Instituut, Eesti Raamat, Tallinn.

3 The Dissolution of Kanepi Kolkhoz

ILKKA ALANEN

The Structure of the Former Kolkhoz-centric System

Kanepi Kolkhoz as a Part of the Soviet System

Kolkhozes and sovkhozes were a part of the All-Union agro-industrial complex and hence a part of the Soviet economy. All sectors of the economy were tied together by a plan, which was legally binding on all the different parties to the division of labour within the production system. Each party was committed to a quota, which was allocated by the plan quantitatively, i.e. by defining increases in production of so and so many tons of milk, meat, etc. However, as the true values of different products were not determined by the market, quantitative comparisons between various products lacked a common denominator. For instance, the price relation between the milk to be sold and the cattle feed to be bought in a transaction was determined by mechanisms other than the market value these products would have had outside the Soviet Union.

The Soviet system was basically a variant of a barter economy: exchange, investments in production, etc. were the result of a complicated negotiation system rather than of a straightforward command structure. Production goals were nevertheless assigned from the very top (the Politburo and central planning ministries) down to the bottom (production plants) (Clarke, 1993). Intermediate levels could only decide on the division of tasks between production units. The highest level of the hierarchy was the All-Union level, which was followed by the republic, then the rayon (for details on the Administrative System in the Estonian SSR, see Figure 5.1), which corresponds to the county level within the present republic of Estonia, with the kolkhoz at the bottom.

The further the technical knowledge of the Soviet system developed, the less likely it became that there would be totally arbitrary and irrational campaigns, such as the drive for maize during the Khrushchev period, to say nothing of the absurdities and excesses of the Stalinist era.

Agriculture in the Soviet Republic of Estonia – as in the other Baltic republics – specialised in animal husbandry, especially milk production and pig rearing, to such an extent that the former Minister of Agriculture, Harald Männik, is rumoured to have described Estonia as "the piggery of the Soviet Union." A considerable part of the cattle feed and machinery was brought in from other Soviet republics, and correspondingly, Estonians exported dairy and meat products to other parts of the Union.

The administration of the Estonian republic thus acted as an intermediary in relationships with the Soviet system as a whole.

> Our local administration, the Ministry of Agriculture, was a kind of purchasing department and they knew how to do business with Moscow, so that we received enough feed, etc. (Former chairman of the kolkhoz)

At rayon level the Soviet-wide plan was adapted to local circumstances and its execution was supervised.

> Each year we had the annual meeting of the production board, where the annual reports were presented, at the rayon. The kolkhoz specialists [and] the main accountant took part in it, and then [people] talked things over. If everything balanced, matters were in order, if they did not balance, [we] sometimes had to do [the accounts] all over again. Every year an inspector came around and checked the report, and a senior clerk made sure that it was in line with legislation. (Former chairman of the kolkhoz)

Nevertheless, the command structure was not entirely unidirectional, since every level, including the kolkhozes, had some degree of independence in determining production.

> And then we calculated how much grain we would get from the fields and how much more we could buy from the state. Then we could plan the meat production based on these [figures]. In the best years we had 5,500 or more pigs in the kolkhoz. (Former chairman of the kolkhoz)

The planning and negotiation system of Soviet agriculture was an entity divided both horizontally and vertically. At the core of this entity were administrative units (the state, the republics, the rayons, the kolkhozes and sovkhozes) and productive units (farms, producers of farming inputs, food processing plants).

And if various kolkhoz units required additional resources, such as machines, fertilisers, or labour, to meet their quotas, the system required complicated deliberations with different parties. At the local level, the conciliation of conflicting interests often took the following form.

> Disagreements were settled in a Finnish sauna, the men gathered there, we chatted as long as we could and settled our differences. (Later chairman of the kolkhoz)

In the Soviet system, production and administration were not clearly separated from each other; however, aspects such as the social functions of a kolkhoz, especially at the level of the local community, included a large number of administrative, executive, and even military elements. Soviet farms were an integral part of the Soviet defence system, and various types of military equipment, such as clothes, blankets, etc., were stored in farms.[1] A large part of this property too came up for sale later on.

In addition, the Soviet agricultural system also incorporated parts of the educational system.

> Further education for the chairmen of kolkhozes and sovkhozes was organised in Tartu, and it lasted 2–3 months every five years. (Former chairman of the kolkhoz)

Higher education not only brought students closer to each other but also linked them up with important scientists and the directors of institutes of higher education. Our research has not shown to what extent some of the top faculty members in the agricultural colleges may be regarded as a part of the agro-industrial elite. Nevertheless, the personal acquaintance of the former chairman of Kanepi kolkhoz with the university staff drawing up the reform explains why it was this particular kolkhoz that became a pioneer in agricultural reform, and why the decollectivisation of Kanepi kolkhoz displayed some special features.

On a larger scale, the Soviet agro-industrial complex contained interdependencies which led naturally to the development of internal social

---

1 Kolkhozes and sovkhozes were also required to store fuel for the armed forces. The nature of this close co-operation was aptly described by a senior county agricultural official, who said that the largest tractors had in the first place been designed to tow missile launchers. Even the sauna, where the kolkhoz leadership often entertained distinguished visitors with a view to securing vital resources, was a part of a military control centre constructed in the basement of a sturdy stone house for use during wartime.

groupings, and to an elite network whose branches to some extent reached beyond the sphere of agriculture.

The chairmen of the kolkhozes and sovkhozes were at the core of the agro-industrial complex, but in some cases their role was much more important than that. The chairmen of the largest and most wealthy collective farms in the Soviet Republic of Estonia were public figures of national renown, while other successful and recognised leaders – such as the former chairmen of the two kolkhozes in Kanepi municipality (Kanepi and Kalev) – were well known figures in the provinces.

Kanepi was the more successful of the two kolkhozes in the municipality. Both Kanepi and Kalev were wealthier than the average Estonian collective farm, but Kanepi kolkhoz in particular was counted among the undisputed elite in south-eastern Estonia. It had reached this status in spite of the limitations imposed by a relatively scattered farm structure (the largest field parcels were 20–25 hectares at most, the majority being 3–5) and poor soil quality. These restrictive conditions had an effect on the reform plans of the kolkhoz management during the transition, though the dissolution itself was "a fact of life" they could not influence. Still, natural limitations always set limitations on the future development of the area.

The Dependence of Village Soviets on the Kolkhozes

The Soviet large farm system was not a variety of feudalism; nevertheless it connected and personalised many social relationships and functions in a way analogous to feudalism. In this respect Kanepi kolkhoz was a typical Soviet farm, a centre of economical, political, social and even military power. One of the relationships that clearly displayed these characteristics was its power over the local administrative organ, the village soviet (see Figure 5.1). Admittedly, the village soviet was not even formally an autonomous body, but rather an executive organ, whose appropriations were decided upon in the Põlva rayon, i.e. at county level. It was not until 1991 that a new law restored the autonomous local administrations (including municipal councils and their right to levy a tax) that had thrived in the first Estonian republic. During the Soviet era the duties of the village soviet included matters such as education, cultural activities, limited social services, the upkeep of roads, the police authorities and the organisation of voluntary defence. For these activities there were state-owned facilities, such as schools and cultural centres.

In practice, the village soviets depended on the kolkhozes in many ways. The long-serving chairman of Kanepi village soviet did not lack views and ideas on the future development of the municipality. In many respects he was a strong, even a feared personality, who frequently wrote newspaper columns. Yet, because the village soviet lacked vital financial resources, "he was not taken seriously." This at least was how a fervent opponent of the village soviet chairman, the last chairman of one of the kolkhoz, described the situation. According to him, the chairman of the village soviet became "a sort of a clown" in the eyes of the people of Kanepi, and "everybody made fun of the village soviet." Whatever the local soviet wanted to do, even if they just wanted to do routine maintenance on a dirt road, they had to contact the chairman of the kolkhoz for the execution of the task. This view bears a close resemblance to the truth, though it is an exaggeration; but even in its exaggeration it is indicative of the conflicts that characterised the strained relationships between kolkhozes and village soviets within the Soviet negotiation system, conflicts that came to a head during the reform.

It is true that, as the chairman of the village soviet said, "in many instances the soviet and the kolkhoz were considered synonymous." Nevertheless, only half of the population of Kanepi were members of the kolkhoz. This fact provided the village soviet with some independence, and also legal control. The village soviet played an initiating role as a collector of farming products from the plots (milk, meat, root crops) as well as natural products (berries, etc.), and as a distributor of cattle feed and other farming inputs. It was thus important in helping the villagers to get their produce sold, although the kolkhoz did in most cases act as an intermediary in marketing the goods. The village soviet (as apparently all over the USSR) also distributed some essential consumer goods to the villagers.

> [The village soviet] was never feared, but [it] did have some power. When we had the coupons [after WW II], for example, and times were hard; that was when we put our trust in the village soviet, we believed they could help us. [The coupons] were distributed by the village soviet. If you needed a larger article, the village soviet had a list of names, a waiting list. That was a part of the job of the chairman and the secretary of the village soviet. (A librarian)

In any case, the operation of the Kanepi village soviet was heavily dependent on the resources and interests of the kolkhoz. The village soviet itself did not have the economic resources, the equipment or the organisation to attend to all its obligations. For instance, there was a cultural centre, but the rayon did not allocate the village soviet enough money to arrange a large cultural event, nor did the soviet have the organisation necessary for such an event. Formally, kolkhozes were not under any obligation to cover the costs of such cultural events, but in practice they supported them, one way or another. When the village soviet paid for services provided by the kolkhoz, such as maintaining the surface of a dirt road, the payment only covered of the wage of the employee; it certainly did not go into the funds of kolkhoz, but rather into the pocket of the individual employee who performed the job with a kolkhoz tractor. All the other expenses entailed by the use of a tractor, including fuel and wear and tear, fell to the kolkhoz. And of course it sometimes happened that the soviet needed a tractor for road maintenance at exactly the same time as the tractor and its driver were urgently needed by the kolkhoz. Thus the kolkhoz chairmen must generally have felt that "the kolkhoz was burdened by everybody" (later chairman of the kolkhoz).

Outside requests that consumed kolkhoz resources and interfered with its operation caused continuous strife between the kolkhozes and the village soviet.

> There were a lot of conflicts. One [possible] solution was that the kolkhoz [would] make the decisions. At times we gave each other the silent treatment. (Long-serving chairman of the village soviet and former municipal director)

In these disputes the village soviet was distinctly the weaker party.

> [The former chairman of the kolkhoz] was quite a stubborn chief; he was not on good terms with the others. And at that time the kolkhoz had extensive rights and plenty of money. He did not acknowledge the municipality, [instead] he dictated his own terms to the municipality; the municipality had authority vested in it by the state, but it was powerless in the face of the kolkhoz. On the whole, the relationships were poor. (Later chairman of the kolkhoz)

The dominance of the kolkhoz was also secured by political means: 60–70% of the village soviet membership had to be members of the kolkhoz; and the Communist Party, nicknamed "the party of the kolkhoz" by the former chairman of the village soviet, always checked the backgrounds of all persons put up for the village soviet.

Kolkhoz Chairmen: Personifications of Local Power

The expression, "the party of the kolkhoz," arose from the fact that the kolkhozes were at the core of party activity. One of the vice-chairmen of the kolkhoz had to be a member of the Communist Party, a kind of party representative right at the core of the kolkhoz. Only party organisations within the kolkhozes could afford to employ full-time party secretaries.

Although there were other party organisations in the municipality, their activity was hampered by a lack of full-time employees. However, the party representative who held the most power in the end was the chairman of the kolkhoz, especially in such successful production units as Kanepi kolkhoz. Even the (Estonian nationalist) opposition in the kolkhoz later admitted that the chairman was the only person who in fact acted in the name of the party. Sometimes he "put a little pressure [on someone]," but "only at the meetings, not in everyday life" (later chairman of the kolkhoz). On the other hand, it could be argued that even in conflict situations he acted with the best interests of the kolkhoz in mind.

Although the Communist Party had its own organisation independent of the kolkhoz, and although in principle its members also played a key role at local level, an experienced and distinguished kolkhoz chairman could in real life take command of the party.

> The kolkhozes were everything, . . . and it also was the case that . . . [party] politics were decisive. If the chairman [of the kolkhoz] was determined enough, he could direct the activities of the village soviet either through the party commission [at the local level] or through the party committee [at the rayon level]. (Later chairman of the kolkhoz)

The desire to utilise the party for the good of the kolkhoz is better understood if we take into consideration the fact that the position of the chairman and his authority in the Soviet hierarchy were based on his ability to contribute to the economic success of the kolkhoz.

All in all, the large size of the kolkhozes and their central role at local level reinforced the status of the chairmen. A Kanepi-born amateur historian characterised the chairmen of the two kolkhozes as "the two local chiefs." The central position of kolkhoz chairmen in the negotiation system thus also indicates a *personification of local power.*

> Relationships [between negotiation parties] . . . were on a personal level. If you needed something, let us say, the kolkhoz did not [contact] EPT [*Eesti Põllu-majandustehnika*, the sole supplier of agricultural machinery in Estonia during the Soviet era], instead, Mr. X [phoned] Mr. Z or somebody else. And they wanted to pull a fast one . . . Such and such a price was agreed upon, if it was in somebody's personal interest. (Later chairman of the kolkhoz)

Thus, the important factors were not just the structures of the kolkhozes or how wealthy they were, but also what kind of individuals the chairmen were.

For example, the long-serving former chairman of Kanepi kolkhoz "was a man with an economical way of thinking . . . He did not spend money thoughtlessly," according to one member of the board. That was what others thought of him too, supporters and opponents alike. The former chief accountant, whose dual role also involved acting as watchdog for the interests of the Soviet-state in the financial affairs of the kolkhoz and signing all decisions of economic importance, respected, even admired the former kolkhoz chairman.

> I was supposed to present a cattle breeding report to the rayon [Põlva rayon, today known as Põlva county] once a month, but he demanded it from me every week. [He] was very particular about the annual report too. The milk report had to be completed every week [too]. He demanded analyses, reports about construction sites, etc. from the economic experts. He formed a picture of the real situation from the status reports. If any of the figures were incorrect, he noticed them immediately. (Former chief accountant)

The economy of the kolkhoz improved while the former chairman was in office. This was despite the fact that it became a larger unit when the neighbouring, and poorer, Suur Oktoober kolkhoz was merged into the successful Ühisjõud kolkhoz, which operated in the centre of the town of Kanepi. After the merger the united kolkhoz adopted the name "Kanepi kolkhoz" (see Chapter 2 for details on kolkhoz mergers). "Work ethic was low [in Suur Oktoober]," commented the former chairman himself. The merits of the former chairman can be seen from the fact that Ühisjõud itself had previously been poor. According to a local amateur historian this was due to the fact that "the first board of the kolkhoz consisted of people who were alcoholics and had therefore lost their [own] farms."

> [Although] our soil and production conditions have always been the worst in the district, . . . [we managed to get the production going in these poor fields] so that every year we got more, [and finally] we were among the best in the district. (Former chairman of the kolkhoz)

There were some matters in which the solutions adopted by kolkhozes differed greatly from each other. Considering the subsequent dissolution it is worth noting that Kanepi kolkhoz had decided to concentrate all its agricultural machinery in the centre of the town, because most of the people working with the machines already lived there. (Kanepi had been a small market town at the time of the first independence of Estonia). This decision led of course to house construction, and to further centralisation, the alternative to which would have been the setting up of machine stations in the villages, i.e. machine brigades. Housing construction in turn made it possible for an increasing proportion of the labour force to move to Kanepi from outside the boundaries of the district. In terms of the subsequent restitution of former property, this movement of population would signify a decrease in the proportion of local kolkhoz members entitled to restitution.

Another good example of local initiative was the exceptionally efficient construction team set up in Kanepi kolkhoz.

> We built detached houses, there were about 25 of them or more; and we built them much more economically, [our construction costs were] about one third lower than those of the KEK [*Kolhooside Ehituskontor*, the joint construction company of the kolkhozes] for example. (Former chairman of the kolkhoz)

In addition to detached housing, the kolkhoz chairman also decided to build several blocks of flats. Some of the flats had already been sold at favourable prices and long terms of payment before the actual privatisation of housing began, especially if the prospective buyer had been working in the kolkhoz for a long time. Nevertheless, many people preferred to rent a flat. Rented flats were needed especially for labourers moving into Kanepi from outside the municipality. Blocks of flats were built not just in the centre of the town, but also in the two other brigade centres of Kanepi kolkhoz. These brigade centres were the villages of Karste and Kooraste. Since they had all been constructed by the kolkhoz, these rented flats and flats that had only been paid for in part formed a large part of kolkhoz property overall. According to the later chairman, the kolkhoz still possessed about 100 flats prior to privatisation. Various interests related to housing in general and to detached houses in particular also had an effect on the privatisation of agriculture.

Besides being a good economist, the former chairman of Kanepi kolkhoz was also a controversial personality. Many people attributed this to his childhood background.

> He came from an orphanage, [he] had no parents, [and clearly] he suffered from many complexes. (A local amateur historian)

Many things were different in Kalev, the other kolkhoz in the municipality of Kanepi. It was not quite as wealthy as Kanepi kolkhoz, but its former chairman was strongly in favour of high culture.

> Mr. Y [chairman of the Kalev kolkhoz] . . . grew up on a farm, [and he] married a girl from a large farm. His wife came from E as well. There was a lot of cultural spirit [in the town of E]. There were [during the first independence of Estonia] a lot of societies, a household society, a bull co-operative, a machine co-operative. They even had a submarine relief association in E; they collected money for Estonian submarines [prior to World War II]. (A local amateur historian)

If the cultural manager of the municipality came up with a plan for an arts event or festival, the former chairman of Kanepi kolkhoz often ignored the request for financing included in the proposal, whereas the chairman of Kalev kolkhoz looked favourably on cultural events, although he might have remarked that "the chief accountant won't like this." All in all, the personality of the chairman of Kalev kolkhoz was manifest in the wide variety of cultural offerings for the people of Kanepi, while the personality of his colleague was reflected in the supply of housing and the development of the school system.

The kolkhozes not only covered the costs of some aspects of local administration and formed part of the national defence structure, they also provided a commercial outlet (the kolkhoz grocery store), utilities (electricity works) and welfare services, such as rented flats. Kolkhozes also maintained kindergartens (though the school system was otherwise taken care of by the state through village soviets) and provided canteen facilities for all its workers. The kolkhoz also provided elderly people with firewood for the winter, and aided single parents, giving them the right to buy foodstuffs from the kolkhoz shop at half price.

Efforts to reduce alcoholism were particularly emphasised in Kanepi, since the kolkhoz chairman was a teetotaller. Although drinking was common among kolkhoz employees, both during and outside working hours, attempts were made to control the problem through frank discussions at meetings and workplaces. These discussions were not simply a matter of the foremen laying down the law: ordinary fellow workers also took part. It is characteristic of the socialist system that the worst alcoholics were moved to a hospital for compulsory therapy, while the workshy were sent to prison if matters reached the point where their absenteeism was connected to other clearly asocial activities.

Technocratisation of Agriculture

The Communist Party directed and controlled the agro-industrial complex from kolkhozes to rayons, and from the Soviet Republic of Estonia to the farthest reaches of the giant Soviet Union. Both the Communist Party and the agricultural sector itself had their own vertical decision-making hierarchies, with authority exercised from top to bottom. The decision-making hierarchy for agriculture was in principle subordinated to party control at all levels of activity, both by means of administrative regulations (for example the vice-chairman of the kolkhoz had to be a member of the Communist Party) and personal relationships, such as the high proportion of party members in rayon administration. In each kolkhoz a certain percentage of the labour force had to be members of the party, and as a rule all the persons who held leading positions had to be party members. Some researchers have claimed that the proportion of party members remained the same throughout the Soviet era (Laird, 1997, 472–473), but our data does not support this point of view.

Kolkhozes and sovkhozes went through a gradual process of techno-cratisation. Thus, key members of the management could – after some half-hearted pressure by local party officials – refuse party membership, even though the chairman did not have this option. One of those who refused party membership commented: "Luckily for us, we had ordinary people as party officials." An explanation for this development could be traced to the rise of an agricultural technocracy among the people responsible for party affairs, i.e. the vice-chairman of the kolkhoz and the secretary of the party organisa-tion within the kolkhoz. More and more often these people shared the same agricultural education (agricultural university or intermediate education at an agricultural college) with other members of the kolkhoz board of manage-ment, in addition to their specialised party indoctrination.

> In general, party officials had a good understanding of the people and their desires, at least here [in Kanepi]. They understood the problems of agriculture, etc. (A member of the previous board of management, who had refused party membership)

Another explanation for the rise of a technocracy in agriculture is the economic power of the kolkhozes, an in the case of Kanepi with regard to the strong position of the successful chairman of Kanepi kolkhoz in relation to party officials as a fellow party member. Thanks to his position and merits he also had much support outside the kolkhoz, in particular due to his personal relationships with Põlva rayon officials. "[The former chairman] had good relationships with the bosses of the rayon . . . He got support from there" (a local amateur historian). Thus the kolkhoz was able to gain more economic autonomy as a result of technocratisation. This also reflected the importance of close personal relationships between actors in the agro-industrial complex.

Mutual trust between key individuals was of greater importance within this system than any formal factors, such as party membership. This did not of course affect the essential features of a command economy. However, educated party officials in the rayon could no longer be compared to lords of the manor, who lived away from their farm, and who set, for example, the day for harvesting without any knowledge of local circumstances. Party ideology had to give way to practical needs.

According to the fiercely nationalistic and anti-Communist chairman of the last phase, the local main organiser of the party understood "his presence in a very Estonian way" and in meetings he often simply stated that "this is politics, but life is quite another thing." (Another party organiser actively helped the later chairman in the efforts of the strongly nationalist Estonian Heritage Society (*Eesti Muinsuskaitse Selts*), but this is not directly connected to the kolkhoz (see Ruutsoo, Chapter 6).

It is possible that by the 1980s at the latest there had begun a development which in practice integrated the kolkhoz party executive with the kolkhoz and its chairman – even partly subordinated the party, as described above. Even if the chairman also happened to be a member of the party, his real mission, and the one his standing depended upon was primarily economic.

Towards the end of the Soviet era the activities of the party withered away. At first people's attitude became practical. The party organised meetings at many levels (workplace, rural district, rayon, republic, etc.), where the participants gave talks in a ritualistic manner designed to please the powers in Moscow, but the actual decision-making was accomplished very pragmatically: the local leaders made as sensible decisions as they possibly could. Finally, at the very end of the Soviet era all that remained was a kind of propaganda organisation, before it finally disappeared almost unnoticed from people's everyday life. Many party leaders had already resigned prior to the declaration of independence, and it was said that "only a couple of men of principle" were left in Kanepi. The speed of the withering of the party no doubt varied depending on the municipality and kolkhoz, but the vice-chairman of Kanepi kolkhoz (who had refused party membership, but participated in its meetings) believed that "in our kolkhoz the party did not have such an important role that a decrease in its membership would have affected people's lives."

Yet, on a wider scale, the Communist Party did have great significance almost up to the time of independence. For instance it exercised a kind of right of veto as late as the 1980s. When people wanted to set up a distillery in Kanepi kolkhoz, the party thwarted the plans. Before independence the elite of the entire kolkhoz system turned to the party for support when they were defending their position against increasing criticism (see Tamm, Chapter 8). And the KGB – at least at the level of the Soviet Republic of Estonia – was apparently more or less in co-operation with the Estonian Communist Party, though as an organisation independent of the party.

In the end, the system of kolkhozes and sovkhozes leaned on the Communist Party. Nevertheless, the destruction of the Communist Party and the ruin of the Soviet-type large-scale production system were not two sides of the same coin. The decline in the significance of the party was only evident in the technocratisation of agriculture, i.e. as a gradual shift in emphasis within everyday life from one vertically structured organisation (the Communist Party) to another (agricultural administration). This development is in itself easily understandable. As soon as the Soviet system was able to create a sufficient technological basis for its agricultural large-scale production system, to educate an adequate labour force, and to imprint a corresponding way of life on these people, political domineering became unnecessary, or downright harmful. The technocratisation of the kolkhozes actually displays a tendency towards overcoming the basic weakness of the Soviet system – according to Talcott Parsons (1971) in his classic modernisation theory – namely the subordination of economic institutions to political institutions.

The system of large-scale agricultural production developed a legitimacy of its own among the agrarian population. This was partly due to wage-work as such, since a workforce developed within the kolkhoz which was dependent on wage-work and the internal division of labour in large-scale agricultural production; moreover, this workforce increasingly lacked any roots in the municipalities, with fewer and fewer having any personal experience of the small-scale agricultural production that existed before World War II. Gradually the system developed a way of life of its own, with its canteens, weekly days-off, kindergartens, cultural activities, summer holidays, etc. This sense of legitimacy was also strengthened by the small-scale private farming allowed in the kolkhozes.

The Symbiosis of Large-scale and Small-scale Production in Kanepi

Soviet agriculture was not based only on large-scale farms; alongside the large farms there were various types of petty production on private plots and gardens. Three more or less contradictory interpretations of the position of petty production in this system have been presented in post-socialism debate. The first (e.g. Vasary, 1990, 12–13) considers large-scale production to involve notions of exploitation and subordination, and to some degree compares it to serfdom (Raig, 1989). In the second interpretation "this dual structure deprived the state sector of efficient labour and the private sector of efficient technology" (World Development Report, 1996, 58) i.e. parallel forms of production existed to the detriment of both (Laird, 1997, 472). The survey of Kanepi, however, clearly supports a third interpretation according to which Soviet agriculture was primarily a symbiosis of large-scale mechanised production and unmechanised petty production (see e.g. Alanen, 1996). Nevertheless, the early kolkhoz system bore some resemblance to feudalism, especially in the Stalinist era (see Chapter 2), and there were some elements that decreased productivity within the symbiosis too, in accordance with the second interpretation.

During the Stalinist era, private production and collective large-scale farming were in opposition. "Quota days" determined, in a manner analogous to feudalism, the labour input due to the collective farm; however, people's livelihoods, in fact their survival, were crucially dependent on their private plots, although they did get a modest wage paid in kind for working on the collective farms (see Chapter 2). Quota days supplied the farm with the necessary labour force, and the availability of labour was facilitated (in addition to political goals) by restricting the amount of private production. Since it was in the people's interest to maximise the amount of work on private households and minimise the working hours given to the kolkhoz, the relationship could obviously not be described as a symbiosis. The situation changed in the mid-1960s as the system of quota days was abandoned, and monetary wages were paid for work done on the collective farms. So, the changeover from quota days to monetary wages was really dramatic.

> In Suur Oktoober [a kolkhoz subsequently annexed to Kanepi] . . . there was a field brigade . . . which was not able to carry out its duties, not even planting a field with potatoes and lifting them in the autumn. So in the spring we transported people from Kanepi to plant the potatoes and again in the autumn [we] sent people to lift them. Then [in that year] wages were already being paid in money, and they [the potato lifters] made so much that they had never before earned such a sum of money. And people left their own chores there and then and rushed to work for the kolkhoz, to lift potatoes. (Former chairman of the kolkhoz)

The members of the kolkhoz produced a large amount of vegetables, etc. on private plots and gardens. Nearly all the families in the kolkhoz had 0.6 hectares of arable land or meadow land, while non-members tilled 0.15–0.20

hectares. Although the attitude towards private plot farming varied over the years (see Chapter 2), the restrictions imposed on small-scale production were gradually relaxed. The acreage cultivated by private households could be increased step by step, sometimes within the framework of old legislation.

> My mother had 0.6 hectares and we had 0.4 hectares, which is about 1 hectare altogether. At the time the yard, building land, and the garden were not included in the calculation of private plot areas. (A man who later got his parents' farm by restitution)

Plot farmers could also make use of other pieces of land within the bounds of the kolkhoz. Since the kolkhoz of Kanepi had "a lot of hilly ground and lake shore, there were plenty of meadows that could only be cut by hand. Their cultivation was given over to the people," said the former chairman of the kolkhoz. The assignment of these meadows for the use of private households was of course not a problem as such, since the kolkhoz itself was unable to cultivate them. Private households also arranged for kolkhoz machines to be used on their private plots, but "the kolkhoz did not charge anything for their use, the customer only paid the worker in cash for the work he had done" (ibid.), although one would think that it would be a problem that "the use of the tractor was to be paid by the kolkhoz" (ibid.). But in the 1980s, when the kolkhoz and private households were already regarded as a composite unit by the Soviet authorities, everything "disappeared into one great pot" (ibid.). Thus one could claim that "there was no rivalry or clash [between large-scale and small-scale production]. There were no problems in marketing either; all the meat and milk [that was produced] sold instantly." All the quotes above originate from the former chairman of the kolkhoz. From a historical standpoint his views are hardly applicable to earlier times, but only to the period after kolkhoz members had started receiving their wages in cash. It might in the end be a question of a necessity, which was gradually realised to be a virtue.

However, from the interview material we can draw the indirect conclusion that the symbiosis was not flawless. "The [people's] attitude was never completely honest . . . in the kolkhoz, somebody was always pinching something," stated the former chairman. Part of this "pinching" was of course the use of machines for the benefit of private households and tractor drivers at the expense of the kolkhoz. The interests of private households lowered the quality of production in the kolkhozes, reduced the work contribution, etc. in many ways. Paradoxically, the same problem is still visible today in the now capitalistically-organised large-scale production. According to a present-day agricultural entrepreneur in Kanepi, "the first condition for the milkers employed by us was that they did not have their own cows at home; the other condition was that when they took milk home [a permitted perk of the job], the milk should be taken from the common tank [not high quality milk especially set aside for their personal use]." Furthermore, "a tractor driver should not have more than two hectares [of arable land for his personal use]." From this it would appear that the cultivation of one's own plot might sometimes be restricted in present-day Estonia on the same grounds as in the Stalinist Soviet Union.

The free right to use kolkhoz machinery was probably never based on any new theory of the symbiosis of private plot and large-scale production. The use of kolkhoz machines, not to mention all other forms of thieving, did not rest upon any written agreement: rather, kolkhozes [and sovkhozes] had to adapt to it as an undeniable fact which followed from the renunciation of Stalinist methods. Agricultural work is by nature decentralised, carried on in various holdings and performed in various stages; in Kanepi private plots were dispersed around the municipality, next to the buildings of former peasant farms, often in the middle of a forest. Thus the symbiosis was originally more of a historically developed fact than the result of a deliberate plan. The unlawful use of machines, a minor form of thieving by private households, became a virtue as it turned out that the practice increased overall agricultural production.

The role of the Kanepi village soviet as an organiser and intermediary also shows that people were interested in carrying on private and garden farming independently of the kolkhoz – although they were still making use of all the resources of the kolkhoz. The farming organised by the village soviet and the production plans of the kolkhoz did not have the product range that the private producers could achieve. As far as those other parts of the product range were concerned, the kolkhoz could only benefit from them indirectly, to the extent that private farming improved the workers' living standards and overall satisfaction. But later on the symbiosis of small-scale and large-scale production had become such a crucial element in the *legitimate basis* of Soviet agriculture that a great part of rural population wanted to preserve it, although people were also interested in the restitution of their old family farms (see Figure 3.2).

As soon as the additional economic benefits of the symbiosis had been realised, it was adopted as a method of increasing production efficiency in workplaces where there were a lot of stages requiring manual work and continuous attention. It should also be remembered that the need for labour varied seasonally in large-scale production. Full-time kolkhoz workers frequently spent days working on their own plots in off-peak seasons.

In the Soviet bloc, a systematic pioneer in the application of this policy was Hungary. Other socialist countries had the possibility of following Hungary's example if they wished. In the Soviet Union, agricultural production by private households was specifically encouraged during the 1980s. Kolkhozes gave people calves and bought them back after they had been raised; they also sold small-scale dairy farmers the cattle feed they needed and bought the milk they produced. And, significantly, all the work done by kolkhoz members in their private gardens, plots and small cowsheds was included in the working years of the kolkhoz. The system used in cultivating fodder beet and sugar beet was as follows: the kolkhoz sowed the beets, fertilised the field and performed the first mechanical weed control, but from that point onwards private households were in charge of the cultivation. For that purpose open beet fields were then divided into smaller lots, and the kolkhoz contracted itself to buy the crop.

In the middle of the 1980s the state made an attempt to promote petty production by integrating it into large-scale production in kolkhoz bookkeeping. A 50% bonus was paid at the end of the year for the proportion of production that exceeded the results of the previous five-year period. "Now the kolkhoz too was interested in including the meat and milk produced by private [households] in the statistics of the kolkhoz," commented the former chairman of the kolkhoz regarding these developments. This encouraged many people to expand their domestic production. "No longer did they just have one or two cows at home, but more, and . . . pedigree cattle." (Ibid.)

The extent of petty production was of course also dependent on the availability of labour, that is family size and structure. Families that had a large number of children or included family members who had retired in good physical condition, had the greatest opportunities.

Nevertheless, All-Union legislation on private households and petty farming was sometimes in direct conflict with the interests of the kolkhoz, as indicated by the following example concerning "the bulls of Kössog."

Then there were the so-called 'bulls of Kössog.' They [the state through rayon officials] paid the plot farmers, not the kolkhozes, a 50% bonus if they [the bulls] weighed over 420 kilos and a 35% bonus if [the bulls weighed] over 375 kilos. [But] the kolkhozes had an agricultural policy of their own. They sold the people [private cattle breeders] hardly any bull calves, but cows [instead]. (Former chairman of the kolkhoz)

The conflict arose from the fact that raising bulls for beef was very profitable for the kolkhozes too. Kanepi kolkhoz even had a specially constructed bullshed for this purpose only. However, this type of conflict of interest between the state and the large-scale farms was probably more the exception than the rule, since the focal point in policy making – up until the end of the 1980s – was always the kolkhoz.

In Estonia, the level of the kolkhozes (and of the food supply in general) clearly surpassed that of Russia. Consequently, private plot farmers in eastern Estonia could easily market their produce directly to the public in the kolkhoz markets of Pskov, Novgorod and Leningrad. Food processing plants in these areas also became their customers. Both kolkhoz specialists and private plot farmers agreed that this type of trade was of great importance, although there is no quantitative information about its economic significance for individual households. According to the leading agronomist of Kanepi kolkhoz, "practically all our production went there." Not only did they export dairy and meat products, their area of responsibility in the All-Union plan, but also garden produce.

> There were no difficulties whatsoever with any variety, whether it was beetroot, cabbage or carrot, everything was good enough. [In Russia, the food supply was] many times poorer, when we used to go there freely [before Estonian independence]. Every year we went and sold our potatoes and at that time if you earned 1,000, 1,500 or 2,000 roubles, it was a very large sum of money. Even then, there was nothing in the shops [in Russia] except tinned fish. We also exported meat from here.

Thus, agricultural production in eastern Estonia was based both on the All-Union division of labour and on autonomous direct marketing to Russia. The fact that the cultivators of private plots and gardens lived next to an inexhaustible market probably improved people's standard of living in Kanepi. In fact, the living standards in traditionally poor eastern Estonia at this time did not greatly differ from those in other parts of the republic where the kolkhozes were wealthier.

But could this symbiotic relationship be characterised by such terms as "exploitation" and "subordination"? These expressions are in any case at odds with the fact that the Estonian rural population had a relatively high standard of living; in fact it was higher than that of the urban population (Palm, 1992). Nor could the rural population actually be forced into small-scale production, since there was a serious shortage of labour in the rural areas.

However, mutually advantageous symbiosis between small-scale and large-scale farming does not in itself provide an adequate explanation for the large part played by small-scale production in the countryside. The inferiority of the food distribution system was another factor.

> During Soviet times there were only cucumbers and tomatoes in the shops, and there were no potatoes for sale in the countryside . . . Spices, onions, dill, etc. had to be grown on [one's own] plot. (A female official from Kanepi)

The Estonian agrarian population kept up the ancient tradition of self-sufficient production and processing of foodstuffs. This tradition did not simply survive Soviet times; it also developed in its own particular way. It was a matter of honour for a housewife to have a neat kitchen garden and an abundant assortment of home-made jams and juices.

> A housewife prepares all these jams and juices herself, because conserves made by hand are better. They are also too expensive in the shops. It is the duty of an Estonian housewife to make everything herself, otherwise she is [considered] lazy and bad. (A female official from Kanepi)

Thus, thriving plot production in rural Estonia was not entirely attributable to the symbiosis between small-farmers and kolkhozes or sovkhozes – a symbiosis which did not come into being until recent decades.

Nevertheless, taken as a whole, within the agricultural system of Kanepi, the dominant aspect was indeed a symbiosis between small-scale and large-scale production. This relationship, however, was not without its contradictions. Although petty production leaned on kolkhoz resources, a sizeable part of the production on private plots had no direct connection whatsoever with the economic objectives of the kolkhoz.

The Patrimonial Character of the Kolkhoz System

The community of Kanepi was characterised by the supremacy of the kolkhozes over the village soviet, and the kolkhoz chairman's ability to make use of the powers of the Communist Party for the benefit of the kolkhoz. Thus the personal characteristics of the two kolkhoz chairmen in Kanepi made a lasting impression on the lives of the inhabitants of the district as well as on the workers of both kolkhozes. At the level of the local community they represented the absolute core of the Soviet nomenklatura. It was typical of the first critics at the end of the 1980s to characterise kolkhoz leaders as "red barons" (see Tamm, Chapter 8). The expression has some descriptive utility, but there were nevertheless plenty of facts that distinguished them from feudal lords. The kolkhoz leaders were more a sort of bureaucratic authority, whose personal and Gemeinschaft-like (Weber) characteristics formed an additional legitimate basis of the kolkhoz system.

The chairmen of the kolkhozes did not inherit their position; rather they attained it by educating themselves and by merit. Although the chairmen had for thirty years been expected to be members of the Communist Party, as the time of the dissolution of the agricultural collectives gradually drew closer, the chairmen increasingly tended to become technocrats. They had achieved their position on the basis of education and professional capability, not by arbitrary political appointments, as many did during the Stalinist era.

The former chairman of Kanepi kolkhoz had received the intermediate education of a cattle technician, and he had worked in Kanepi for several years, initially as a cattle-breeding technician. "He was an energetic worker even then," was how he was described by a person who had been a prominent figure in the kolkhoz administration in those days. Subsequently he proved his competence at work. His appointment as chairman in the mid-1960s, during the rule of Khrushchev, was preceded by twelve months of managerial training. Yet it is true that the chairmen did take on certain "baronesque" features, in so far as the agricultural elite may have been developing in the direction of an "estate" (a Weberian status group). The educational careers of their children, too, displayed signs of preparing them to step into their parents' shoes. In the interviews we occasionally heard claims that the children of the chairman would have shortcuts into educational establishments based on personal connections; however, there is no other research data to support this argument. Whatever the case, at the core of the agro-industrial complex the chairmen of the kolkhozes and sovkhozes formed a close-knit social network, and they appeared to be able to react collectively by appealing to the state or the party, in a way typical of an estate group (see Tamm, Chapter 8).

The closest associates of the director were the members of the kolkhoz board of management, who were mostly department managers and specialists representing various occupational groups. As the size of the kolkhozes and sovkhozes grew, the number of well-educated people increased and their specialisation grew deeper; and quite often the younger the person was, the higher the level of his education. In the last years of the kolkhoz the majority of specialists already had a university degree (see Põder, Chapter 2).

In spite of these changes, the board of management of the kolkhoz remained a closed circle; this was the result of a process going back over many years.

> [The board was] a kind of a circle of friends from the early days of the kolkhoz. This is how it was in almost every kolkhoz. Others had no entry to that inner circle. (Later chairman of the kolkhoz)

The chairman was the undisputed head of the board and he had influence over all its decisions. He could also control admission to the board, although formally the power of decision on such matters was held by the council of the kolkhoz.

> The board of management was elected at a council meeting . . . [the appointments were] dictated by the chairman, [even the nomination] was made by the chairman or somebody else [close to him]. (Ibid.)

Members of the board thus had a close and confidential relationship with the chairman. According to a prominent figure in the opposition which had grown within the kolkhoz, there was a member of the board who

> was as slippery as a fish. He was a loyal fellow, everything he heard anywhere, he passed on to the chairman. The former chief accountant and the others were all the same. (Ibid.)

In terms of the practical exercise of power, co-operation between the chairman and the chief accountant was of especial importance, because

> the chairman and the chief accountant could do anything they wanted. [Only those] two signatures were required [by law]. (Ibid.)

Thus, the people with whom the chairmen of the kolkhozes discussed the most important decisions were within their personal sphere of influence. The importance of personal chemistries is aptly described in an observation made by faculty members at the agricultural university. They had come to the only half-joking conclusion that kolkhoz board members "strongly resemble their leaders in outward appearance." If personal chemistries were incompatible, there were of course problems.

I was a good boy, too, to begin with. [But] there were conflicts when I joined the board of management, and I was not re-elected to the next board. (Later chairman of the kolkhoz)

A work brigade leader in Kanepi kolkhoz who had been dismissed disclosed that he had had "difficulties with people." He had found it "difficult to talk things over [with the kolkhoz chairman], [it was difficult] to do business with him on a personal level." But his brother, who had even crashed a kolkhoz-owned car, had been treated kindly by the chairman. He had simply been told that "such a thing could happen to anybody."

Another prominent personality, the man who later replaced his superior as the chairman of the kolkhoz, had also been dismissed from a managerial function. He admits that he "made a few mistakes," but according to his own interpretation, the first and foremost reason for his dismissal was probably a disagreement over raising cattle. The significance of the offences of the two men cannot be fully determined from the interview material, since there were other interviewees who claimed that the reasons were not trivial in either case. In the former case the direct cause of the dismissal is fairly unambiguous, since the former brigade leader disclosed it to us himself.

We had a big fight [with the former chairman of the kolkhoz], because I was drinking on the job. [Then] he transferred me to the sawmill.

The former chairman was known for his vigorously negative attitude towards everything related to alcohol and its consumption. Indeed, that may have been why he disapproved of festivities organised in the municipality.

Both of the dismissals mentioned above are especially noteworthy in terms of the authority structure of the kolkhoz, since they concerned persons in managerial functions. Likewise, it was interesting to notice that those individuals were not dismissed from the kolkhoz outright; instead they were allowed to stay on the kolkhoz payroll as common workmen. Understandably, they felt resentment towards the chairman, and under normal circumstances this would hardly have had any particular effect on the life of the kolkhoz. But thanks to the political and economic transition that Estonia was going through, these people and others like them gravitated to each other and formed a significant core of opposition. Later the opposition managed to take over the kolkhoz administration.

The people we interviewed usually emphasised that the former kolkhoz chairman treated everyone with equal respect, and an agronomist stressed his high regard for the chairman, who had always shown understanding to a young specialist like himself, although he had to admit that the chairman was occasionally somewhat temperamental. The opinions of the interviewees were on the whole respectful, even though some people were wary of the chairman. "He kept [everybody] under tight discipline," commented a milker, "he was a bit of a conservative, authoritative man." It was his old-fashioned "commanding tone of voice" that the young and the well-educated disliked, and it was one of the matters that later contributed to the development and support of the kolkhoz opposition. Nevertheless, the people "stood by him," said a member of the former board of management. The inconsistent personality of the chairman, however, added a discordant note to the respect in which he was held.

> Some people held him in high respect, but he was also feared. Or it would be more correct to say that he was respected, but he was not well-liked. (A younger person in the kolkhoz)

From the viewpoint of the rising opposition he appeared in the following light:

> Everything he said had to be done. He forbids, commands, hangs and shoots [people]. (A former brigade leader, quoting the traditional Estonian phrase *'keelab, käseb, poob ja laseb'*)

In addition to the phrase "red barons," plenty of other epithets have also been applied to kolkhoz chairmen, for example derivatives of such terms as totalitarianism, dictatorship and command economy. It was not just western social scientists and journalists who used these terms: within Estonia these epithets were used by the right wing of the rising nationalist movement, that is, the Estonian Congress (*Eesti Kongress*). Nor were these terms foreign to the kolkhoz of Kanepi, for they came up in local speech even during our study. All this was symptomatic of an atmosphere that had aided the developing opposition to gain power in Kanepi kolkhoz, as elsewhere.

All in all, however, although Soviet society did have violent characteristics, which were also evident in Kanepi, it seems as if kolkhoz life could after all be best described by Weber's (1978, 231–232) ideal types of patrimonial bureaucracy and officialdom (Maslowski, 1996, 304).

The people in Kanepi had a clear mental picture of their kolkhoz chairman, and the statistics for Kanepi kolkhoz, which were above average for the republic, were regarded as a personal merit for its long-serving chairman. Work meant everything to him, to the extent that he regarded all other spheres of social interaction, such as the festivals organised in town, from the viewpoint of their effect on work.

> He [the former chairman] complained that tractor drivers were not fit for work after the celebration. [He criticised us, asking] why we had to drink alcohol at that party. His [only] desire was that people would work, that the kolkhoz would make progress, and that people would get a decent wage. (A teacher in Kanepi)

It would, in fact, be wrong to label the former chairman as hostile to culture. The kolkhoz maintained libraries, cultural centres, donated money to cultural societies, etc. But he only supported local cultural activities from his own, narrow outlook; in other respects he was rather stingy. According to the cultural manager of Kanepi municipality, the chairman far too often "politely" refused even the smallest financial support to the cultural centre; alternatively he could stifle its initiatives by passing over matters in silence.

The former chairman was perhaps considered too short-tempered ("bad nerves"), but for all his faults people emphasised his fairness. Except for during the "revolutionary period," which will be detailed later on, and the few persons involved in it, there was no deep hatred or grudge. Moreover, those people (a minority) who stubbornly opposed the system of collective farms, even after decades had passed, did not usually turn their anger towards the chairman.

The chairman and his board of management were themselves representatives of expert officialdom; in addition to them, many special duties were taken care of by experts, the majority of whom had graduated from institutions of higher education. There were agronomists, veterinarians, engineers, economists and other specialists. The chairman, however, exerted personal influence on a great number of matters. A member of the opposition, the man who became the last chairman, described the type of situation in which a person responsible for a job was "not relied on" with the result that "the job was taken care of by the chairman, whether it was in a field or in a cowshed." The chairman kept continually moving on from one project to another.

> He had a car, which he used for moving around. At the end of each month he visited every production unit with the specialists to check up on the situation. He could be found at the office only in the morning or late in the evening. [He just] checked the post and was off again. (Former chief accountant)

The leaders of departments and brigades formed the part of administrative hierarchy that was closest to the executive level. However, this structure too varied from one kolkhoz to another. In Kanepi there were plenty of specialised departments: cowshed, piggery, garden, forestry, sawmill, etc., and the cultivated fields were divided into several brigades: Kanepi town centre, Karste and Kooraste.

> [The division into departments] was an internal affair in each economy [kolkhoz]. The chairman of the kolkhoz was the boss of bosses, and if any of the departments came into collision with him, then the future of employees in that department was in doubt. (A former brigade leader)

The leaders of departments and brigades could be portrayed as the extended arms of the chairman, reaching out to the various workplaces around the kolkhoz.

> Foremen made people work. Anyone who lazed around was thrown out of the kolkhoz. He was punished, [and any] extra wages [he might have been eligible for] were taken away. (Former chief accountant)

The behaviour of the former chairman certainly had many authoritarian features, some of which could be traced back to his personal character, and others that could be contributed to his standing in the Soviet system. Even so, our data does not point to the conclusion that internal order in Kanepi kolkhoz would have been the mere giving of orders; rather it was a matter of the direct presence of the chairman.

> Everything depended on the personality of the kolkhoz leader and [his relations with] the party. (Former brigade leader)

Rather than there being a strictly unilateral wielding of power, people could debate problems such as drinking, work, etc., quite freely in open meetings.

> During kolkhoz times [alcoholics] were reprimanded in front of everybody at workplaces, at kolkhoz meetings, and at the meetings of the party. (An interviewee from Kanepi)

Rather than being a direct command economy, kolkhozes and sovkhozes were capable of self-regulation on several levels.

> If people in the years of the kolkhoz noticed that things were getting worse, the people [themselves] talked the matter over, and came up with possible solutions to the problem. (A senior official at county level, former chairman of another kolkhoz)

This is again one of the reasons why the personal authority of the chairman, with his hand-picked board of management, had to be based first and foremost on professional knowledge.

> The chairman promised to bring the hay to the cowshed. As it was raining outdoors, he wanted to dry the hay with a fan. I was against it. We had a fight. I threw him out [of the cowshed] and locked the doors. The next day the chairman came here [and behaved] as if nothing had happened. He understood that he had been wrong. He had already been the head of the kolkhoz for a long time, and his nerves were not what they used to be. (A former technician)

This is an illustration of how, as in Weber's traditional organisation, personal authority always has its normative limits. In the case of the kolkhoz the limit was set by professional capabilities.

"The Dictatorship of Milkers or Tractor Drivers"

Although the kolkhoz system was capable of self-regulation by various means – showing approval, public reproach and so forth – it also tolerated many negative phenomena surprisingly well. The partial tolerance of social problems was due to the fact that the community knew its members on such a personal footing that the disadvantages of applying general norms would have become immediately evident (cf. Weber: the Gemeinschaft-like nature of relationships). It was as clear as day to fellow kolkhoz members that a certain person would have done what he did in spite of punishment, or that any punishment would only have made things worse. On the other hand, we are also dealing with another significant issue, a major structural weakness of the system. In a way typical of Soviet society in general (Clarke et al., 1993), kolkhozes suffered from a chronic shortage of labour, and that was why they had to tolerate all kinds of negative phenomena, from every variety of work-shyness and drinking problems to small-scale thieving.

A shortage of labour also explains a special group of workers, called "migrating birds" by the people in Kanepi. A number of people, whose professional skills and work motivation were low, travelled around the Estonian countryside looking for work. In many cases their background involved social problems from the larger cities, and they hoped to find a solution for their problems in the country. In fact, there were only a few of these rootless people in Kanepi. They were not much respected, yet the shortage of labour was such that apartment buildings were constructed especially for them. They did not, however, always receive "a permanent job" according to the manager in charge of recruitment and housing.

The shortage of labour created unavoidable needs at "ground floor" level and on the whole provided autonomy and encouragement to those who worked in "blue-collar" occupations, such as milkers and tractor drivers. Many of these workers expressed their opinions very energetically and were not afraid of clashing with the chairman, if necessary; but these conflicts did not shake the hierarchical authority structure personified in the chairman. The chairman of the kolkhoz as well as the other managers had to be in personal contact with ordinary people, they had to get along with everybody. Although a manager might push people about and now and then even lose his temper, mere commands would not have had any effect. If a brigade leader did not get along with people, he had to be transferred to other duties. For the same reason, tractor drivers, the best ones in particular, could do odd jobs on private plots for their own benefit. A kind of "dictatorship of milkers and tractor drivers" prevailed in the kolkhoz, as our Estonian colleagues put it during our stay in Kanepi.

The two factors described above, the personal character of relationships and the great shortage of labour, in actual fact had to accommodate many problems inside the work community, such as the low level of education, feeble-mindedness and mental illness. In a capitalist society these problems would have been transferred outside the work organisation and they would then have manifested themselves in terms of unemployment, sheltered work-shops and dedicated welfare institutions.

> There is clearly a marginalised group of people who had work during the Soviet times, but now they just can't get along. (Later chairman of the kolkhoz)

At some point the limits of tolerance were exceeded, even in a kolkhoz: an alcoholic was taken to compulsory care and an extremely work-shy person to prison. From a wider viewpoint, these ways of reacting are more in line with the special patrimonial concept of authority than with theories of totalitarianism.

This kind of patrimonial bureaucratic officialdom probably had its origins in two sources. First, there was the All-Union planning system, in which the execution of production targets (commands) was essentially based on a mechanism of negotiation. The chairman of the kolkhoz, the board of management and the foremen were held personally responsible for fulfilling the commands. The other source of the patrimonial bureaucratic officialdom was the floor-level autonomy largely brought about by the shortage of labour, which brought a negotiation mechanism into the organising of the internal work of the kolkhoz, and gave officialdom a personal character arising from the chairman of the kolkhoz. This typical feature of Soviet enterprises was emphasised by the generally personal character of social relationships in rural areas, and the difficulty of transferring the types of control typical of industrial organisations (Taylorism) to large-scale agricultural production. Although the division of labour was advanced, the various specialised tasks did not form a self-adjusting organic mechanism, similar to an industrial organisation. The non-industrial character of agricultural organisation is particularly evident in crop husbandry.

Floor-level Prosperity and an Indifferent Attitude towards Work

"On the whole, people lacked the ability to think for themselves. They were used to obeying orders from above," stated an entrepreneur from Kanepi. Things were quite different during the first Estonian republic.

> I have also seen [some of the] people who had worked during the Republic of Estonia. They were paid good wages, and their work was of top quality, too. Unfortunately, this generation is dead now. (Manager of a large enterprise)

However, memories tend to grow sweeter with time, and in Estonia the era of previous independence is often highly romanticised. Many of the negative features perceived today in socialism are in fact characteristic of wage–work in general within Tayloristic organisations, and are thus present in the capitalistic West, too. In Finland, for instance, it has been discovered that an entrepreneurial spirit is less common in counties traditionally dominated by large-scale industry (south-eastern Finland) than in counties where the entrepreneurial tradition is strong. One of the people we interviewed, a man who had become a fairly successful shopkeeper by Kanepi standards, commented on the situation as follows.

> I think the main problem is that [during Soviet times] we were all wage-workers, and now everyone has to take care of oneself. [But] they just can't do it. (Former manager of the kolkhoz construction team)

The claims made by our Estonian interviewees attributing the lack of entrepreneurial spirit entirely to Soviet influence should be taken with a pinch of salt. Great shocks and extremely difficult circumstances have a discouraging effect on all people, and of course most of all on ordinary workers, who lack the strategic knowledge required for successful individual activity. (The apathy and stress caused by such great changes will be discussed in more detail later on.) The views of the new business managers should be treated with caution. Nevertheless, we cannot pass over the following description of a work-related problem, since similar views were expressed by several interviewees.

> But we had problems with the local craftsmen. There were ten suitable men in the kolkhoz, but when we asked them [to work], they refused [to work] because of their drinking problems. They said a little hunger is better than hard work. (Manager of a large enterprise established on the foundation of a kolkhoz department).

Despite the caveats mentioned above, some of the problems might still be attributed to the special characteristics of Soviet society and agriculture. The direction of influence in the hierarchies of labour and in other communal activities was from top to bottom.

> I do not believe the people who claim that everything was worse at the time of the collective farm. The only thing that was wrong was that I did not know who I was working for, who I was ultimately employed by. We were never informed about anything. (A qualified technician at the time of the kolkhoz)

> During the kolkhoz years the situation was the same [as now], an [ordinary] worker had no idea of the salaries of the board of management and where it [the money] came from. That's the way it was, and we didn't know anything. (A former bulltender)

Although the traditional Tayloristic factory hierarchy is clearly directed from top to bottom in capitalist societies too, the difference between Soviet society and a capitalist society was, at least as far as farms are concerned, the patrimonial nature of the administration. As a general rule the affairs of the common people were always taken care of by someone else, ultimately by the kolkhoz chairman. On account of this, the people never learned to look after their own affairs; instead, as the former kolkhoz chairman put it from his patrimonial viewpoint, they remained where they were and in a way "demanded" that someone above them should act on their behalf during the kolkhoz reform.

> It was surprising – gosh, I've been thinking about this a lot – how the people were not at all accustomed to thinking, instead they were much more experienced at demanding. If a person works, he must get paid, but the question of where and how the money originates did not matter to people in the past. And now people should suddenly have been thinking about their own future survival. (The wife of the former kolkhoz chairman in a joint interview with her husband)

The individualistic "Lone Rider" philosophy of life was foreign to Soviet society.

> In the past we used to examine a person's references [if] he was coming from outside [Kanepi]. People moved from one place to another looking for better jobs in those days too. At that time we believed [that] a person who had changed his residence and job five or six times was evidently the type that would not stay for long anywhere, and [consequently] he would not be an able workman. People who had worked at the same workplace for twenty-five years were respected. This criterion of evaluation has got to be changed [in today's society]. (A municipal councillor)

A calculating, individualistic type of control over one's own life calls for a desire and real determination to acquire information about existing opportunity structures, as well as the ability to make use of them. But developing such abilities takes a long time. The experiences of a senior county official related below are easily understandable during the transitional stage, given the time delay involved.

> In some respects it could be due to the lack of information, on the other hand people [in general] are not used to doing business with administrative bodies and other civil service departments. You can't just walk into an office at nine, and expect to be met with open arms. There are also other people [to be served], [but] people just don't have the patience. They don't know how to transact business; they are not used to it. During Soviet times most matters were decided elsewhere, people didn't have to get up and attend to the matters themselves. We are talking about a generation who had their affairs decided by others.

Small businesses are the schools of the new attitude to life. In small businesses the flow of information from below is much more important than in the traditional (universal) Tayloristic factory organisation. This is one way of interpreting the workplace changes experienced by an electrician in Kanepi.

In the kolkhoz you would never give instructions to a boss. But now bosses are willing to listen to your suggestions. I've got thirty years of experience as an electrician [in the kolkhoz]. I know my work. I can give instructions and the bosses are [now] willing to listen to me. They think the matter over, and then we'll do whatever suits them best.

The position of ordinary agricultural workers in Kanepi was autonomous. Like workers all across the Soviet Union, they could not be coerced by threatening them with dismissal. The employees were therefore free to work independently. Yet irrespective of their autonomy they were unable to affect most of the terms of their own work, let alone have any active say in decision-making (Clarke et al., 1993). Nor were there any structures characteristic of a civil society, which would have provided room for other types of independent social initiative. The functioning of the Soviet social system was something that people had simply learned to adjust to (Ruutsoo, Chapter 6). The thrill of exerting one's civil influence through the Estonian Popular Front (*Eesti Rahvarinne*) in the early 1990s was a totally new experience for the people who took part in those activities, as one of the contributors to this book, Rein Ruutsoo, has pointed out in person-to-person discussions.

Patriarchal care by kolkhoz and sovkhoz directors created a sense of overall social security, and the All-Union subvention system for agriculture provided a relatively high standard of living for the rural population, especially in Estonia.

Towards the end of the kolkhozes, people led a better life in the countryside than in the cities. Kolkhoz workers could buy meat, etc. more readily than people in towns could. We did not pay [as much] taxes on our wages. It was also possible to take something from the fields in secret and take it home. During the last years of the kolkhozes, a kolkhoz member was better off than a state official. (A local amateur historian)

Taking into account the fact that the Soviet Union was underdeveloped as a consumer society, we can better understand the mentality of Soviet citizens, which is generally described in the following terms by the most educated and most prosperous.

Under Russia [i.e. the Soviet Union] people were stuck in the mind-set that if you had a car, a house, and a little money, you [had made it, that you] didn't need anything else. (Former kolkhoz manager, present entrepreneur)

Consequently, in spite of its prosperity and secured position, the Soviet agricultural system ultimately produced a socially passive type of human, especially at grassroots level, among the most uneducated people. This judgement, however, refers only to the workplace and to civil activity in general. By western standards, many of the arts such as theatre, literature, classical music, and so on, were highly developed in the countryside (see Ruutsoo, Chapter 6).

The Development of Capitalist Production Relations, as Viewed from Kanepi

The So-called Original Accumulation and Agriculture

Production modes in Soviet society differed in many ways from those of a capitalist society. Above all, the differences manifested themselves in the fact that the appropriation of social resources in socialist countries was not determined by the market; instead it was based on a plan (commands). The preconditions for a capitalist market economy are private ownership of the means of production and a mass of individually free wage-workers, who are not in possession of those means, as Karl Marx in his day argued. Nearly all the means of production of any importance in the Soviet Union were state-owned, and although the kolkhozes in particular were in principle owned by their members, the significance of this nominally co-operative ownership was relatively minute, since kolkhozes were subordinate to the same "command economy" as the state enterprises.

The non-capitalist character of Soviet society compared to capitalism could be seen in the status of a wage-worker. Although the overwhelming majority of people at first glance made their living from wage-work, just as they do in capitalist countries, the Soviet Union had no labour market typical of a capitalist society. In a capitalist labour market, a mass of unemployed wage-workers always appears at least at the stage of the economic cycle characterised by a crisis of overproduction. Soviet society was by contrast characterised by a chronic shortage of labour. In Kanepi this manifested itself in the form of problems in work discipline and a bureaucratic patrimonial hierarchy of power.

The process that created the structural basis of capitalist society, the absolute private ownership of the means of production, and an army of wage-workers, has been termed *"the so-called original accumulation"* (Marx,

1954). That is basically the question when we are talking about the de-collectivisation of agriculture also, although the Estonian government did not by any means attempt to establish a system of capitalistically organised large farms based on wage-work, but aimed rather at smaller family farms. The creation of family-owned small enterprises is of course not in conflict with the principles of capitalism as such (Alanen, 1991), although the large production buildings and machines of the kolkhozes and sovkhozes, as well as the purpose-designed infrastructure (e.g. road networks, housing) and the specialised educational system, were better suited to large-scale agriculture. Notice also that capitalism does not in itself require any specific form of ownership (ibid.); alongside individual ownership there may be ownership through shares, co-operatives, and even forms of completely impersonal institutional ownership.

The process of transforming Estonian agriculture into a capitalist branch of commerce has involved a complicated interaction between government policies and unofficial practices. The government has had to make choices in two dimensions: first, between two types of production, small-scale and large-scale production, and second, between two strategies of privatisation, the restitution of earlier ownership and other forms of privatisation, most of which have been based on workshares.

Restitution meant above all the restitution of pre-war land ownership, since as a rule all other means of production – with the possible exception of cattle –had ceased to exist long ago, and in any case they had belonged to another technological era. Still, even if the strategy of restitution had been carried through to its extreme conclusion, it would not necessarily have led to the abolition of large-scale production. As Mati Tamm writes in his article (Chapter 8), all the property of the kolkhozes could in theory have been interpreted as profit accumulated to the collectivised assets. This approach would only have replaced the chairmen of the kolkhozes with private owners, but the large production complexes could have been preserved or they could have been divided into smaller units by the owners' common consent. The most significant problems with this strategy were, however, the practical conditions surrounding the implementation of restitution. If officials had emphasised the rights of the legal heirs, the land would have been divided into sections through a statutory apportionment, without any restrictions on the size of acreage. This restitution strategy might have been applied down to the level of cousins: land would have been returned to former owner families with no regard to their current situation, whether they worked on the farm or even in the municipality. The preservation of large farms would thus have become more problematic. Most probably, many of the former owners and their families would not have been at all interested in maintaining large-scale agricultural production; most of them lived in the cities or had at least moved away from the municipality, and they would have preferred a rapid realisation of their assets as cash. Concerns of this type made it difficult to develop a strategy to preserve large-scale farms, bearing in mind the technical problems (the large number of owners) and the political problems (e.g. restrictions on selling).

The restitution of agricultural assets only to those who worked in agriculture or at least lived in the municipality would have significantly increased the chances of preserving large-scale production. Perhaps the most suitable method for achieving this end would have been a strategy of workshares, where the share of each individual in kolkhoz ownership depended on the amount of work done over the years. But this strategy would not necessarily have led to the automatic preservation of large complexes, since many of the former workers had retired or were about to reach the age of retirement, or in some cases had moved to other occupations. A strategy that effectively protected large-scale production would have required a number of restrictions, giving priority to present kolkhoz employees, and forms of restitution that would have facilitated the continued cultivation of large-scale farms whose ownership was being broken up. Furthermore, privatisation would have had to be regulated to prevent the splitting up of economically optimal units, such as the specialised cowshed complexes.

On the other hand, there were many more or less feasible ways of implementing a strategy aiming at small-scale production. The most radical forms of realising a strategy of small-scale production would have required the destruction of large-scale production and the transfer of kolkhoz resources to small farms that met the requirements for modern family farming (e.g. sufficient acreage and a convenient location from today's point of view). The most ineffective ways would have involved splitting up landed property and a mechanical restitution of land according to pre-collectivisation borders, with no regard to the changes in the use of land (e.g. afforestation) and infrastructure (buildings, roads, utility lines, etc.) and with usable resources drifting from large-scale agricultural production to other areas of the economy, or simply being destroyed.

As I shall demonstrate later, the decollectivisation of Estonian agriculture was not realised according to either of the two major alternatives above. Instead it was a compromise solution between these strategies. This was particularly apparent in privatisation, which was implemented as a compromise between restitution and a system of workshares. The privatisation of the kolkhozes coincided with a shift of emphasis in government policy on corporate structure, from a policy favourable to large-scale production (the early stage of the Estonian Popular Front) to a policy more favourable to small-scale production (the period of the Estonian Congress). In practice, though, the policy of the new government led to both the splitting up of property and its transfer outside agriculture, and even to the extensive destruction of property.

The dissolution of the collective farms was not only confined to the restructuring of agriculture, since the kolkhozes and sovkhozes were also involved in other activities, and it was possible to transfer the wealth gathered in agriculture to other more profitable activities. In the end, the dissolution took place in a very anarchic fashion.

> The break-up of the kolkhoz resembled the shipwreck of the [passenger ferry] Estonia.[2] Everybody tried stay afloat, everybody grabbed whatever he could, because that period [of time] was terrible. Many earlier agreements were broken of course. There were quarrels over machines that had already been distributed to people, excessive prices were offered, fist-fights were common and drunkenness prevailed. (Later chairman of the kolkhoz)

The sense of anarchy was intensified by the fact that the Estonian government had not been able to create a sufficiently functional legislative mechanism and controlling system for the process. This was the reason why the manifestations of the so-called original accumulation in Kanepi (and according to the specialists we interviewed, also elsewhere in Estonia) did not usually, in any fundamental way, differ from those in 15th to 19th century England and Scotland: they were "anything but idyllic" (Marx, 1954, Chapter 24).

> When we are talking about the dissolution of the kolkhoz, not all things in every instance fell within the letter of the law. That's the way capitalism has created big riches all over the world. Nobody can never be sure whether the first dollar was earned by fair means [or not]. (A municipal councillor)

A very few individuals have made a fortune, some have been able to maintain a moderate standard of living, but for the majority of people the

---

2   The passenger ferry Estonia capsized on the Baltic Sea en route from Tallinn to Stockholm on September 28, 1994, taking the lives of 852 passengers and crew members. The Estonia ferry disaster was the largest single catastrophe to befall Estonian citizens after the re-establishment of the nation's independence.

process has been more or less tragic. Local people commonly compared the dissolution to the forced collectivisation and repression of the Soviet times: "As a son of a kulak I have the right to say that the dissolution of Kanepi kolkhoz was a more repressive measure than the forced collectivisation after the war," concluded a former leading kolkhoz specialist his interview.

The property of the kolkhozes ranged from various production and administrative buildings, many types of machinery, equipment, spare parts, complete production units, shops and kindergartens, entertainment and recreation facilities (e.g. a song festival stage), detached houses and blocks of flats, all kinds of consumer durables (e.g. cars), to masses of small objects (e.g. tableware and clothing). The property was thus both extremely varied in its contents and great in value. According to the former chairman, the warehouses alone contained goods valued at three million roubles (see Põder, Chapter 2).

The Influence of Other Forms of So-called Original Accumulation on the Dissolution of the Collective Farms

The so-called original accumulations outside (see Nikula, Chapter 4) and inside the kolkhozes and sovkhozes had an effect on each other. At one stage, fortunes were made by smuggling semi-precious metals to the West from other parts of the Soviet Union; then the businessmen started brokering used cars acquired from Finland and Germany (the Zhiguli stock of Estonia was rapidly exhausted) to Russia. Business was also done in spirits, and quite often agricultural machines that had been donated from abroad for distribution to struggling farmers were grabbed by one of the middlemen for himself.

> Mr A started [his dubious activities] after 1988. At that time he was the chairman of the Farmers' Union in X [county]. He managed to help himself to the machinery sent here from Finland and Sweden. He took too many of the donated agricultural machines for himself, and that's why he had to give up the office of chairman of the union. (An agricultural specialist and municipal councillor)

The events described above are not exceptional; similar occurrences have been exposed all over the country. All these ways of accumulating wealth were more or less connected with the grey, or in fact illegal, economy. Many sources of income at the early stage, such as transactions in semi-precious metals, soon withered away. At the time of our field studies (1995–1996) according to the manager of the development and information department of Põlva county administration, the most important sector for a profit-seeking business was the timber trade. Indeed, the timber business is practised to such an extent in the grey zone that it is often described as "stealing" (see Nikula, Chapter 4).

> If a forest is not yet ready for felling, the farmer cannot cut the area. That permission is granted by the forestry officials. If a person wants to fell some trees, he must also have the authorisation of the municipality. Stealing the timber is by far the easiest way; you get your money without delay. You also need permission for the transport [of timber], but in spite of that it is possible to steal. (A senior official at county level)

The money earned in this way could then be invested in kolkhoz property, which offered good value, especially in the first years of privatisation. All in all, the boundary between honest and dishonest business activity is by no means unambiguous, simply because of the inadequacy of legislation. A municipal councillor told us that "tax legislation is very much undeveloped, and all enterprises conceal some of their income." Thus the distinction between the formal and the informal economy became a line drawn on water.

In addition to this, the existing legislation was, and still is, often such a complete failure that honest business was next to impossible in many fields, e.g. in forestry. But it must not be forgotten that many people earned money in honest business activities, too. (For more details about entrepreneurship, see Nikula, Chapter 4). The ability to make even the smallest investment at the right time was sometimes the decisive factor for future success. Modest foreign earnings or a small amount of Western currency received from relatives living abroad in the rouble era often gave the crucial positive impetus to new emerging enterprises during the transitional period. At that time one could, for example, purchase a tractor from the kolkhoz at a highly favourable book value, comparable – according to a senior county official – to "the price of a sandwich." One entrepreneur was happy to comment that "I had been [a trainee] in Germany [for four months in 1991], [so] I had cash and I could buy for cash."

Many people had small funds such as this, but one had to be able to foresee the future in order to turn these minor savings into productive investments instead of wasting them on personal consumption. On the other hand, personal consumption often turned out to be a clever choice considering the effects of the monetary reform of June 20, 1992. One Estonian kroon replaced ten Soviet roubles. The exchange rate of the kroon was fixed to the German mark (EEK 8 equals DEM 1). The reform enabled Estonia as a nation to better adapt itself to the world economy, but both private persons and enterprises lost their savings and available funds in this devaluation.

Farms Set Up According to the Farm Law of 1989

The farms set up before the independence of Estonia, or during the rouble era at the latest had a privileged position in the process. On the basis of a special Farm Law (1989), land was taken from sovkhozes and kolkhozes, and placed at the farmers' disposal (see Tamm, Chapter 8). These farmers also received machines that were usable, but written off in book value by the kolkhozes, as well as help at harvest time, etc. The state granted them loans on favourable terms, and these loans were soon eroded by inflation. Furthermore, the state granted them tax exemption for a period of five years, and built the infrastructural framework required for peasant farms (roads, wells and electricity lines). The rebirth of small farming aroused great enthusiasm among the rural population of Estonia's western neighbours. Subsequently, a generous amount of serviceable second-hand machinery was got together and repaired in Scandinavia for the use of independent farmers in Estonia.

The earlier the farm had been set up, the greater was the purchasing power of its agricultural income. But since the workers of kolkhozes and sovkhozes were still well paid, private farmers typically continued working on the collective farm, from which their own farm had been split. In this way they could use their wages for the construction of buildings on their own farm. Those who were most successful in anticipating the future could at that time buy cattle, building materials, as well as agricultural machines, at a very low price. Many prepared themselves for the future by buying equipment and materials which they expected to become more expensive, and which they knew they would themselves need later.

> As I took up farming, I had planned [made lists of] the things I would need. That's the reason why I raised a loan in roubles. Then I bought the things I needed, as well as some [pieces of equipment] for the future. I bought five tractors to ensure the supply of spare parts, because only one [of the tractors] was new. I also bought building materials with the money I borrowed. If I had not taken up a loan in roubles, I could not have bought anything. [But now] I could have bought twenty cars with that money. (A successful private farmer)

In the area of Kanepi kolkhoz just a few farms were set up on the basis of the Farm Law. This was in part due to the fact that the locations of farms people sought to establish were often in conflict with the effective farming of the kolkhoz. According to the law, kolkhozes had the right to refuse requests they found unsuitable, or alternatively they could offer land from a different location (see Tamm, Chapter 8). For instance, an heir whose family had fought to the bitter end against the kolkhoz tried to reclaim his family farm, but unfortunately his lands were situated right next to the kolkhoz centre.

> The kolkhoz did not want to give the farm back . . . The chairman of the kolkhoz didn't give his permission. I only got the meadowland. The other fields were in very good shape, that's the reason why the chairman didn't return those fields to me. The kolkhoz director did not want to break up the kolkhoz, [that was why] he opposed the restitution of [family] farms. (A farmer whose farm was later restored in the restitution)

The heir, frustrated in his hopes, was well aware of the significance of the delay caused by this. "The people who took a farm based on the Farm Law had better opportunities to steal machines, etc. So, they had good possibilities to set up farms." (Ibid.) The word 'steal' in this context refers primarily to purchasing at favourable book values (cf. Põder, Chapter 2). This type of usage is illustrative of many kolkhoz members' attitude: machinery and cattle would also have been available for some people without payment as compensation for forcedly collectivised property, but as Tamm (Chapter 8) describes, many kolkhoz workers were opposed to the use of this procedure.

There were also many who were not particularly anxious to have their farm back. In the area of Kanepi kolkhoz, there were six restituted farms at most. And the owners did not usually think of them as private farms completely independent of the collective farm. For instance, some of them did not use all the land that the kolkhoz would have given to them. Because of this and other connections maintained with the kolkhoz, we cannot say that the Farm Law actually brought about any change in the system, but rather a modification of the earlier symbiosis.

It is true that there were those striving for independence, and who cherished other great hopes as well. However, a number of these individuals have now given up their farms, or are about to give them up.

> There were 5–6 farms at that time [1989]. There has been no change. There is X's farm in the neighbourhood, it was bought by a man whose parents lived here. He himself was working in the town of V as technician, but he came with his mother to live here. But I don't know how they are getting along. They have a limited company, they sell milk and other things to people. They wanted to build a hotel, too. Now they want to sell the farm to the municipality. (A member of the former board of management)

Thus, in this case production has been reduced to direct sales, and the people would like to give up. Yet the farms of the rouble era in particular include the ones which are doing best, since this was the most favourable time for establishing a farm. Before the period of restitution and privatisation, these farms had a clear advantage over others. It was not only a question of very remarkable economic benefits, but also of the experience the owners had gained of managing a private farm. This gave them the knowledge of what was required: on the basis of their experience they could adopt a more rational attitude towards the stage of restitution and decollectivisation.

There was, however, an exception in this group, namely the individuals who got their land from an area which later became an object of restitution. "Among those people there were some who took their farm from the lands belonging to other people [i.e. owned during the earlier independence of Estonia]," said a farmer whose farm was restored by the restitution. True, the situation of these farms became uncertain only as regards the fields, as they were allowed to keep the buildings and equipment. In Estonia at present, the primary condition for carrying on agriculture is not personal land ownership, but the ownership of other means of production.

The Assets Received in Compensation

From the outset in the politics of Estonia, the idea of establishing private farms had a central position. Nevertheless, the problem was initially approached on a fairly pragmatic basis: instead of applying strict doctrine the aim was to solve the problems of agriculture by reforming large-scale agriculture and by developing different types of small-scale production. Soon after independence (August 20, 1991) a significant change occurred in the politics of Estonia, with the new political trend represented by the Estonian Congress (the government of Mart Laar 1992–1994) reversing the political trend represented by the former Popular Front (the government of Edgar Savisaar 1990–1992). At the beginning of the reform the principle of agricultural policy had been "to give land to the ploughman," i.e. to transfer the resources of production to agricultural people. But in 1992 a legalistic principle of restitution became dominant. There was a desire to return to the land ownership according to original farm boundaries preceding Soviet occupation, and this was to happen completely independently of the present and partly the future occupation of the owner, his place of residence, even of his country, distance of relationship, etc. (see Tamm, Chapter 8). The abolition of the agricultural collectives was of secondary importance in comparison with this event. The deadline laid down for the legal abolition of the kolkhozes and sovkhozes was the end of 1993.

The restitution of agricultural land has proved to be a very slow process, for both technical and political reasons (see Chapter 8); compensation and the restoration of other assets in kind has been much easier. The basic unit of restoration became a cow, which the government (in 1993) determined by law should be valued at EEK 700; everything else (horses, sheep, horse-drawn machines, etc.) was valued in proportion. It is true that the restoration started in some farms already before the official "cow unit," and possibly at a lower price per cow. Prior to this law individual kolkhozes and sovkhozes had applied extremely heterogeneous methods in evaluating cows and other assets. Yet the actual date of the restoration was probably much more important than the monetary value of the cow unit, since the purchasing power of money began to fall heavily in the middle of 1991. In the kolkhoz of Kanepi, the restoration of collectivised assets was carried out a long time before the deadline adopted by the government.

> In 1989 we paid for the assets given to the kolkhoz – cows, horses, etc. – compensation of 300,000–400,000 roubles, at the time when roubles still had some value. At that time we only gave money, but later on [in 1992] those who wanted to have a cow also got a cow. (Former chairman of the kolkhoz)

Other types of confiscated assets were also compensated for, e.g. factory buildings, and the proceeds could also be invested in agriculture. This survey has not determined how the people of Kanepi spent their money. It does, however, appear that it was mainly used in consumption, since the true privatisation of the kolkhozes was yet to come. There were only a few farms set up on the basis of the Farm Law, and the thought of starting an enterprise of one's own was undoubtedly a novel idea to most of the rural population. A minority might buy out their dwelling in the kolkhoz, but the money was primarily used for everyday necessities, and apparently also for consumer durables, especially cars. This could partly explain why there were surprisingly many Western cars in the economically hard-hit areas of rural Estonia. Those who later on (in 1992) wanted to have compensation could also be paid in kind, in cows for instance (see Põder, Chapter 2).

But a cow is not a uniform unit of exchange like money, since there were huge differences between individual cows. According to one interviewee, it would have happened like this for him, too. A farmer who got his farm back in the restitution said that "it would have been possible to have the cows back for instance, but they were in bad condition, sick, they would die soon." The cows of the interviewee's friend had died, because of this the interviewee decided to take the compensation as shares instead of cows. There is no systematic study on the extent of this, but it is evident that the right to a cow did not automatically guarantee the quality of the animal.

The Right of Restitution of Land in the Form of Compensation

The restitution of land is legally a complicated process, with compensation as one alternative to it: this compensation is in the form of land elsewhere, not as a cash payment by the state. In the municipality of Kanepi, one third of the land areas that were the object of restitution (i.e. of the two thirds already dealt with) had resulted in restoration by the time our data were gathered in autumn 1995.

In addition to the acreage, the basis for calculating the compensation is the quality of soil and the "price of the growing forest" if the land contains forest. This price is not, however, paid in money but in EVP vouchers (*erastamisväärtpaperid*, privatisation bonds). Calculated in bonds, the average price of a hectare of agricultural land in the year of the survey (1995) was EEK 4,000. With the compensation vouchers it was possible to buy land elsewhere. The tendency, however, is for the value of money to decrease as a result of inflation and for the price of non-agricultural land to rise. On the other hand, if these vouchers are not used in agriculture, but rather to buy land for other purposes, e.g. for a building site, the price of the site is on average considerably higher – even ten times higher according to a local surveyor. Consequently, the value of vouchers received as compensation for land decreases rapidly, and their significance for buying land other than for agriculture is minor. Thus, the compensation for arable land does not create any notable capital reserves, but has nevertheless stimulated the transfer of land ownership from one municipality to another. This is worth noticing especially in cases where a person entitled to restitution might want to start farming.

For many people, the question of whether to seek the restoration of one's land or compensation is far from simple. Even if the land has deteriorated as agricultural land, e.g. because it has become overgrown with bushes, or if one is not interested in farming, land tax may nevertheless be due on it, and the payment may be significant in terms of levels of income in Estonia. And if one does not quickly convert the compensation vouchers by finding a suitable investment, the vouchers will lose their value through inflation. Thus, one person who was entitled to 16 hectares of land confronted the following problem. The land had become overgrown and had value neither as forest nor as arable land. To clear it for fields would be expensive, and in any case people are not interested in renting fields. If one receives land, taxes will be due on it. The other alternative is to receive land as compensation somewhere else, but if one does not have any use for land, the "Blue Card" might as well "be hung on the wall of the toilet." The individual concerned solved the problem by doing nothing i.e. he neither realised his right to restitution of his land nor applied for compensation.

Any land area that is compensated for in the restitution will be resold. If a family lives on the area in question, it has an option on the land at the price of the land tax. The payment can be made either by vouchers or in money. Failing this, the land will be sold by auction. The system tends to maintain old plot farms (cultivated previously by the owners of the residences) though to some extent it also promotes new family farms. In no case does it develop significant accumulations of wealth, since the possibilities for market speculation on land are minor. This is essentially due to the fact that if the land is not transferred to the former owner, or the owner who lives on the holding, the option on the land is transferred to the municipality (as is usual in connection with the sale of landed estates). The option of the municipality prevents speculations in land, since land cannot be sold to speculators at less than the current price, given the possibility of intervention by the municipality.

Previously, the Law on the Principles of Property Reform enabled people to take only the forest and to be compensated for the field. "And people who lived in town, took the forest back and left the field" (a senior official at county level). As a consequence of this, a good deal of wealth has been flowing from the countryside to the cities and from agriculture to other industries. As a result, some "new farmers don't have timber at all, and if necessary, they have to buy it" (ibid.). The law has since been changed, but what is done cannot be undone.

The Privatisation of the Kolkhoz

Once the restituted property and debts of an enterprise had been deducted from the property of kolkhozes and sovkhozes, the remainder was valued, and that value was then distributed to the former employees. Neither the method of valuing the assets nor the method of distributing them was stated in the law; these matters were decided at a general meeting of the kolkhoz by all the members of the kolkhoz, and all those workers who had worked at least five years at the kolkhoz.

Various assets could be sold at book value or by auction. It was also possible to sell different items of the assets in larger units, and to arrange separate auctions for different kinds of assets. The voucher of the worker could be calculated according to either working days or wage, and both the working days and the wage could be calculated in a number of different ways. For instance, fees could be added to the actual wage, or calculations could be made more complicated by introducing weightings for different types of employment typical of the various stages of the kolkhoz: for example, there could be adjustments for the starting period of the kolkhoz, when the quota day model predominated, and only a small fee was paid in kind.

It should also be noted that although the work vouchers were the only legal means of payment for kolkhoz assets, it would have been possible to regulate in various ways the market that came about for exchanging vouchers to cash. Similarly, it would have been possible to require some kind of security from the buyer to ensure that he had funds to meet the purchase offer. But whatever strategy was chosen, it was always more compatible with the interests of one group than another.

Above all, information was essential. The situation was unprecedented for Estonians, and rational decision-making would have required time for discussion and information to be provided systematically. The amount of information clearly had a relationship with the benefits one could receive: the more one knew, the more one could make use of the opportunities available. For this reason, acquiring and concealing information was bound to become a means of furthering one's own interests.

In the kolkhoz of Kanepi, the restituted share of the kolkhoz at the beginning of 1993 accounted for a third. The remainder was to be privatised by other means (see Põder, Chapter 2). In addition to those who had received restitution in vouchers, people (the "subjects") entitled to a part in the next phase, i.e. privatisation, were all those who had worked for the kolkhoz for the minimum of five years and/or were members of the kolkhoz (see Põder, Chapter 2).

The share of an individual subject would depend on how the shares were calculated. As we shall see later in this chapter, a stormy general meeting of Kanepi kolkhoz eventually decided that this share should depend only on working days, not at all on wages or the stage of kolkhoz history (cf. the period of quota days). This meant that after the value of the assets to be privatised had been estimated, there would be a calculation on the basis of working days of how large a share each person was entitled to, and thence of the value of the share in kroons. The value in kroons, however, depended on the real value of the assets to be privatised, not on the book value. This real value could only be determined by the markets, and thus the book value was more or less fictional. In general, however, one could say that for machines, buildings and many other sorts of assets the book value was lower than the market value. For instance, a machine could have lost its entire book value according to the write-off system, but since it still was usable, it would still have a value in kroons on the market. By the book evaluation, the price of one working day was set before the subsequent auction at 60 Estonian cents (EEK 0.6).

Savings And Loan Associations as a Solution for Unrealised Vouchers

Each individual Savings and Loan Association applied the mode of procedure drafted by Professor Mati Tamm (see Chapter 8). This mode of procedure was the principal solution to the problem that all persons (subjects) entitled to a share from the privatisation of the kolkhozes and sovkhozes were not able or willing to share with each other the items to be privatised, though they had the possibility to form alliances for this purpose e.g. to buy a complete cowshed and the cattle belonging to it. In practice this meant that someone who did not invest his share (or part of it) in some concrete item could deposit his share in a Savings and Loan Association, and someone who bought an object larger in value than his or his alliance's workshares could borrow the deposited workshares. The conditions under which the Savings and Loan Associations lent the workshares valued in kroons could be decided by the kolkhoz or sovkhoz. In Kanepi kolkhoz the annual interest was laid down as 1%; the loan period for machines was set at five years, but for cattle and buildings at ten years.

Although the period for the estate and cattle loans was short, given the low annual rate of interest the loan had every prospect of being very profitable, at least in principle, since the Estonian inflation rate was at this stage very high (1993 90%, 1994 42% and 1995 29%, for more details see Table 1.3).

The book value of a working day was based on a kind of gentleman's agreement, the aim being to divide the items to be privatised between the subjects at the lowest feasible nominal price. In reality, however, it resulted in an auction which significantly raised the nominal value of a working day in kroons, and thus also the nominal values of savings and credits.

The Privatisation of Residences

A proportion of the residences of Kanepi were totally or partly in the possession of Kanepi kolkhoz. In principle, the residents of all rented apartments – assuming that the residence was not among assets to be restituted – had priority rights to buy both the residence and the site. The tenants were able to use both the common privatisation vouchers (based on working days) given by the state – to all citizens – and the privatisation vouchers of their workplaces. But if the owner of the rental residence was a kolkhoz there arose a problem. The law allowed these residences to be combined with production units (e.g. cowshed complexes) to be sold at auction and at same time gave the residents rights to buy them.

> The tenant had priority. The misfortune of the agricultural reform was that it was carried out before anything else, and those who got their hands on something were winners, nothing was taken back. (A senior official at county level)

This conflict led to a collision of interests, which contained, from the viewpoint of the so-called original accumulation, a theoretically interesting special aspect, since the possibility to develop the agricultural units as capitalistically organised units was partly dependent on the ability of the employer to control the existing residences. The privatisation of residences seems to have been (at least in the countryside) the most significant form of egalitarian division of assets. Many employees of the kolkhozes and sovkhozes were able to secure a residence for themselves and also for their children living in the municipality or in town. (The children, too, did have an option, but because of their age they did not have enough working years to be eligible for the privatisation of kolkhoz residences.)

As the privatisation of residences was relatively straightforward, problems arose regarding the mobility of labour. In the countryside people had residences, whether dating back many years or resulting from privatisation, but the privatisation of agriculture deprived many people of their jobs. At the same time, there arose a shortage of moderately priced rented flats in the towns, and it was not possible to buy a flat in town with the money received from selling one's residence in the countryside. As a result of this, a substantial relative excess population (Marx, 1954) accumulated in the countryside. For the next few decades, this will be significant in terms of preserving the plot farming system of Estonian agriculture. These two aspects of the residency issue will be later examined as determining variables for social relations within agriculture.

The Need for Decentralised Decision-Making and the Problems it Entailed

The former kolkhoz chairman emphasised the efficiency of the old control system.

> Previously in the Soviet times there was 'people's control' (*'rahvakontroll'*) [supposed 'control by citizens' in socialist countries], it was possible to get around it. The second [level of control] was the procurator. He made 2–3 rounds each year [in the kolkhoz] . . . In the early days the procurator was quite strict, everything was examined in detail.

The situation changed radically after independence.

> After the independence of Estonia was declared, the control system disappeared completely, and even today there is no authority that would keep a close watch on the situation.

However, this did not hold absolutely true, since the kolkhoz was, according to the later chairman, even after independence subjected to "a very close auditing of the accounts." Yet this kind of detailed audit was only connected with taxation, not with the reform itself. As regards the agricultural reform, it was controlled by the municipality, and there an auditor was engaged for it. However, the same auditor was employed for several municipalities, and he was "usually . . . old enough and near the age of retirement; he was not interested in things, [he] usually signed everything" (former municipal director). Moreover, "in the local [village] soviet there were the bosses of the kolkhoz, and those who had their own interests voted for the decision" (ibid.). Yet, illegalities were, according to the former chairman of the kolkhoz, already "so widespread" that "if one started to check up on things now, nobody would be able to do it at all."

All this was possible because of the book-keeping system of the kolkhoz itself. For instance, machines and other items could be listed in the books, but it was not always possible to identify the real machine purely from the "book" machine. This meant that the resources of the kolkhoz could be transferred to private ownership simply by book-keeping tricks.

One common problem in privatisation was that the process had to be very much decentralised. This was because Estonia lacked the necessary central authority mechanisms, i.e. the device itself together with the officials needed for it. The need for decentralisation also came from the widely varying local conditions, and the fact that the most competent specialists were precisely those within the kolkhozes and the sovkhozes (see Tamm, Chapter 8). Undoubtedly, those who were in the best position to exert control were also those who had the best opportunities to move resources to themselves illegally, and if necessary enter into alliances with each other for this purpose.

The Crisis in the Kolkhoz System and the General Outlines of the Reform

The First Two Phases of the Reform Policy

One fundamental aspect of the Singing Revolution of Estonia was the memory of earlier independence, together with a nostalgic picture of Estonia as a peasant society. The dream of restoring independence was at an early stage linked to the idea that agriculture – with the Estonian peasant cultivating a farm of his own – would become the driving force of the future economy (Lieven, 1993, 355; Liepins, 1993). This was evident as early as 1987 in the IME economic programme (Palm, 1992), although a simple legal transformation involving the changing of collective farms to joint-stock companies had also been proposed as a way of converting them to a (socialist) market economy (Tamm, Chapter 8).

The first phase of the Estonian agricultural reform, approval for the expansion of private agriculture and the establishment of a small number of family farms alongside the collective farms, largely arose from this ideology, which could be expressed openly with the arrival of Perestroika. This ideology did not touch Estonia alone; it gained ground in all the Baltic countries and in their nationalist movements. The kolkhoz system of the Soviet Union as a whole was in a state of crisis, the basic reasons for which were 1) the excessive size of the kolkhozes and the transport and management problems resulting from this (Tamm, Chapter 8), and 2) the weak work motivation of the employees. Poor motivation became a particular factor as agriculture became more technocratised and as the economic incentives given to the workers became less effective (due to the lack of any possibilities for increased consumption). As a result of wasteful spending and general inefficiency, the productivity gained from new investments was relatively less than it had been some years earlier. Even so, the standard of living reached by the agricultural population in the Soviet Union was high compared to other segments of the population, mainly because of large subventions by the state

(Selden, 1994). The various devices used to encourage people to set up or to expand small-scale private auxiliary farms raised the standard even further. This generalisation also applies to Estonia, bearing in mind that its agricultural sector was one of the most efficient in the Soviet Union. Even more than in other parts of the Soviet Union, the Estonian rural population may have been at a clear advantage compared to the population in the cities, in terms of standard of living (Palm, 1992, 289).

The agricultural officials of the Soviet Union and the Soviet Republic of Estonia were not unaware of these problems, and in Estonia the management of the kolkhozes could see the problems of the whole kolkhoz system. "The kolkhozes could no longer continue in the same way," and renovation (or dissolution) "was bound to happen" said the former chairman of the kolkhoz in an interview with his wife. Thus, the need for agricultural reform was obvious to specialists. But how could it be accomplished so that the material losses caused by the transition would not grow too large, agricultural production would not collapse, the living standard of the agricultural population would not be endangered, and the agricultural population itself would be convinced of the need for such a strategy? The agricultural experts certainly deliberated on the problem of production resources, and on production itself. However, they did not have a clear enough picture of the views of the different groups within the rural population.

The article by Mati Tamm (Chapter 8) relates how these reforms progressed. In the first phase, from the year 1987 onwards, peasant farms were established on kolkhoz lands without any special agricultural legislation; later on (1989) this policy was confirmed by the Farm Law and supported by the state. However, the establishment of a new farm was in principle only possible if it was unanimously supported by all members of the kolkhoz, and in practice it was largely dependent on the will of the kolkhoz management. Moreover, the new farms did not sell their produce on a free market in the Western sense of the word, since the preconditions for production within the heavily subsidised Soviet economy were very profitable (Tamm, Chapter 8).

> It was easier to get a loan in those days, since not that many people kept a farm, fewer than now. Besides, the kolkhozes and the sovkhozes still existed, and those who kept a farm didn't have so many problems in acquiring machinery. Kolkhozes and sovkhozes helped them with the farming, and the acreage used to be smaller in those days. People still worked for the kolkhozes and the sovkhozes, too. It made things much easier. Another matter that helped in that situation was that with the inputs – such as petrol, electricity, cattle feed and

such – [if one thinks of] the costs compared to the prices paid for the produce, that ratio was still reasonable. [Agricultural] production really paid off [in those days]. (Chairman of the Põlva County Farmers' Union)

Nevertheless, few among the agricultural population were willing to set up a small farm and the basic structure of the system remained unchanged (see Figure 3.2).

In the second phase the emphasis shifted to the issue of the future of large-scale production. In March 1990 the Supreme Council of Estonia declared the collectivisation carried out after annexation to the Soviet Union illegal, which meant that the principle of restitution of former ownership came to the fore in practical agricultural policy. In direct terms, this meant that the tenure rights of the existing large-scale production enterprises became dependent on individuals who had rights to the land by restitution. Most of the assets of the collectives had, however, been acquired only after collectivisation. Thus, the second phase did not automatically mean the destruction of existing large-scale production units to make way for small-scale enterprises; it remained possible for the segment excluded from the restitution to be transferred to the ownership of the existing workers. This meant that some of the reformers could take as their starting point the principle of the old land reform (1919) implemented in Estonia's first period of independence, according to which the land would belong to the worker ("land to the ploughman"). The reform experiment of Kanepi was based on this ideology, promulgated by some who had personal relationships with this kolkhoz (Tamm, Chapter 8). Indeed, the management of Kanepi kolkhoz assumed that the fate of the experiment would decide the fate of the entire large-scale farming system.

Even back then Mati Tamm said that it was the last chance. If that did not work, it would result in the dissolution of the kolkhoz. (Former chairman of the kolkhoz)

The basis for the experiment was laid out following a study carried out by the agricultural university. The results were used – admittedly, rather one-sidedly – to promote the reform in meetings and in local newspapers (Põder, Chapter 2). According to the general idea of the reform plan, the kolkhozes (and sovkhozes) were to be divided into a handful of smaller production units. The former chairman of the kolkhoz put the starting point of the reform as follows: "We thought the main thing would be that with every production unit functioning separately, calculating its own income and expenses, it would be able to operate more economically." The smaller economic units would also have been legally independent of each other. As a result, one large kolkhoz would have been divided into a number of independent enterprises. The division would partly have been based on territory (by villages), and partly on a division of labour, with a separation of agricultural and non-agricultural units. The issue of ownership was open in the reform plan, but it was assumed that the managers and specialists of the kolkhoz would undertake the business management. These reform tendencies, however, soon collided both with an unfavourable ideological environment and with conflicting interests, and this in part explains the transition to the third phase. But what exactly was the nature of this ideological environment?

Conflicting Utopias and the Background of the Transition into the Third Phase of the Reform

The dream of the Singing Revolution to re-establish family farming was more a desire of an intelligentsia dreaming of independence than a goal of the agricultural population. Relatively small numbers of the rural population were interested in setting up a farm of their own during the most favourable phase before independence (Pajo, Tamm and Teinberg, 1994, 13). Nevertheless, the romantic family farm ideology of the Singing Revolution with its dreams of restituting the old peasant farms to the former owners did not leave the rural population entirely cold. The idea gained ground in particular among the rightist section of the nationalist movement, the Estonian Congress (*Eesti Kongress*). According to one of the Kanepi leaders (an executive) this influence was not direct, but rather of a "political-psychological" nature. People became more critical of their leaders, and yet their reforming zeal seemed to be limited to modifications within the existing kolkhoz structure.

In effect they wanted (according to both chairmen) simultaneously to establish independent farms and to preserve the kolkhoz.

> Many people said that this is the good life now, you get what you need from the kolkhoz and have a farm of your own, as well. But this lasted only for a couple of years. (Later chairman of the kolkhoz)

This somewhat romanticised view of things held sway in the years 1988 and 1989. The utopian dream of the ordinary kolkhoznik was to combine small-scale production with large-scale production in a novel way, but no one seemed to be interested in evolving a societal reform plan on this basis.

As a matter of fact, this would not have been such an unusual starting point. It has deep roots in the history of Western thought, in different kinds of co-operative system ideologies. Many political thinkers – small production ideologists such as Oppenheimer and David in Germany, Tönnies among the classics of sociology, and perhaps also Engels and Lenin – toyed with the idea that it would be possible to build co-operative societies as systems of collaboration in basic agricultural production. These societies would supposedly resolve many of the problems typical of small-scale production and yet preserve the characteristic features of the traditional way of life.

It is also possible that the most important idea in the minds of the Estonian rural population was really no more than just the democratisation of the kolkhozes and sovkhozes, by means of privatisation of the land above all. However, it would seem that the political leaders in Estonia, as well as in the other former socialist countries, did not consider the possibility of this type of social development at all. It did not really fit into their picture: the kolkhozes were regarded as bastions of communism, the formation of the kolkhozes had been imposed on an unwilling population in the first place. Thus, preservation of the kolkhoz system was never going to find much favour among the new political leadership.

A large proportion of the dwelling houses that still were inhabited were owned by a former farmer or his heir. He and his family knew well the history of the farm and the land area; even at the time of the kolkhoz he observed it from the viewpoint of his own farm.

> My papa bought this farm. This is my home, how could I leave this land. Now I have the courage to go to the bushes and drive away these migrating birds [workers of the former kolkhoz, who had moved to the village from elsewhere], if they try to cut down my forest. (Farmer of a traditional family farm)

> I didn't like that around our house, right beside the garden, there were the cows of the kolkhoz. It was eight kilometres to the grazing land [where the private economies were allowed to make hay]. At the same time the best hayfields were right next to us, but they were reserved for the use of the kolkhoz. (Farmer's wife on the farm mentioned above)

Still, even those individuals – with some exceptions – wanted to preserve the collective farm, although not quite in its present form. The mistress of the farm mentioned above had lost her job when a large cowshed (formerly belonging to the kolkhoz) cut down its operations. She remained at the family farm to tend a small herd of four cows. When she was asked whether the decision to leave wage labour was "pleasant" or "compulsory," she answered as follows.

> It is not pleasant, here at the farm you have to work really hard and this doesn't pay. If there was a chance, I would go out to work, I would be paid, [and] I would get the chance to earn a pension. The future looks gloomy. Most of the work has to be done by hand.

This should be of course be interpreted in the context of poor current technical and economic conditions for small-scale production, but other factors are also involved, e.g. a pension. Other family farms are confronted with similar technical, economic and social problems. Many of those individuals who have started to cultivate the traditional peasant farms have personal memories of working on their own farm, but in fact they are now at the age of retirement. The general view of these people is that when one starts small-scale production one is faced not only with poor economic and technical conditions, but also the fact that the younger generation is not interested in continuing farming.

Nevertheless, people were interested in plot farming in connection with the kolkhozes, and they even expanded that farming whenever the chance arose. It should be noted that many of those who were not from the district of the kolkhoz also had a plot of land by virtue of being a worker at the collective farm.

During the first and second phase of the reform the area of the plot could reach several hectares.

> I myself received three hectares of land from the kolkhoz, and some people had even more. I was the first to ask, and three hectares was given; at that time [1988], you were allowed to have three hectares at most. (A kolkhoz worker who had started small-scale farming)

The orientation towards plot farming was for long time an economically profitable alternative from the perspective of the kolkhoz. The cultivators of these plots had two visions simultaneously: that they would be "the owners [of their private farms], and that there [would be] the kolkhoz as well [to provide support and a job]." These views were regarded as totally conflicting by the later chairman, who took part in carrying out the reform.

Although the former and the later chairman were representatives of utterly different political views, the former chairman pointed out the same contradiction.

What we would have wanted was what the first private farmers voiced too. [But] it could not have been carried out in reality, private farms inside the kolkhoz. All the benefits offered by the kolkhoz just as before! How many [farms] could have been established that way, maybe 10–15 farms? But it was not possible in practice. If I repossess my land [for example], there will be my farm, [but] where would the kolkhoz be then? (Wife of the former kolkhoz chairman in a joint interview with her husband)

Thus, the wishes of ordinary people were considered totally unrealistic. This kind of estimation was typical of both the kolkhoz managers and the intelligentsia of the village. It was difficult for them to connect in their minds the restitution of land and large-scale production as elements within a uniform reform plan. However, the management of the kolkhoz and the educated specialists, together with the intelligentsia of the village, may have been looking at the issue in a one-sided way, adopting purely the viewpoint of large-scale production. They lacked any concept of a symbiosis of two forms of production, simply because they did not carry out much economically significant production on their own private plots.

The viewpoint of the other employees was different, since for them the double system had been familiar for many years. Their way of thinking no doubt contained utopian elements, since the advantages of uniting small-scale and large-scale production during the Soviet times were partly artificial – as became more and more obvious during the first and second phases of the reform policy.

Still, their utopias were hardly more unrealistic than were those of the kolkhoz managers supporting large-scale production, or those of the Estonian Congress supporting small-scale production. To combine large-scale and small-scale production within the same system would not have been impossible. In the developed capitalist countries, most agricultural enterprises consist of semi-proletarian economies, with workers who earn part of their living by wage-work outside the farm – e.g. on large farms. In any case, practices from the earlier symbiosis of small-scale and large-scale production could perhaps been adapted to new market-economic conditions on the basis of farming contracts.

The Estonian Congress, which in October 1992 had developed into a power competing with the ruling Popular Front of Estonia, had a radical restitution ideology. It wanted to replace the kolkhozes with private small-scale production units. They had a rosy picture of family farms, mainly modernised, but set up on the basis of the old peasant farms. The dominating group within the Estonian Congress principally constituted of urban intellectuals; later these formed the kernel of the ultra-nationalist Isamaa Party. It is true that the Estonian Congress also contained people from the countryside, but the rural members had no influence in terms of agricultural policy.

> I discussed things with X [who was one of the leaders of the Isamaa Party]. We now belong to the same party. [As we talked I found out that] they don't actually know what is going on here in the countryside. (Later chairman of the kolkhoz)

The breaking up of the kolkhozes by the Estonian Congress and their replacement by small restituted farms did not at all coincide with the perspective of the rural population. The Estonian Congress conceived of a different kind of utopia, and therefore its message "remained remote and strange [for the people]" (later chairman of the kolkhoz). The third phase did not, however, begin during the office of the government of the Estonian Congress (led by Mart Laar's Isamaa Party); it was already under way before this, but the Laar government radicalised it.

The Third Phase of the Reform Policy

In the background of the third phase of the reform policy there was a gradual movement in Estonian politics to the right. But there were also other factors not dependent on the government, connected with the dissolution of the Soviet Union and the independence of Estonia.

In June 1990 Estonia abandoned agricultural subsidies, and shortly before independence, in the summer of 1991, price control was also abolished (with the exception of the most important dairy products). The new government of Estonia (led by Laar's Isamaa Party) exchanged roubles for crowns (June 1992) in the proportion of ten for one, and abandoned the remaining subventions and import duties. The government also imposed a high income tax on the kolkhozes and sovkhozes. This high tax was seen as directed at the kolkhoz system in particular.

> From the year 1992 the kolkhoz had to pay entrepreneurial tax. When the kolkhozes were set up [after World War II], things were done exactly in the same way: those who didn't join the kolkhoz were punished with high taxes. (Later chairman of the kolkhoz)

The abolition of price control in Russia (summer 1992) led gradually to the dissolution of all pan-Soviet networks, including agricultural networks (Hirschhausen and Hui, 1995, 425). This accelerated inflation considerably, but at the same time producer prices fell behind the prices of production inputs. The overall picture was that the demand for foodstuffs decreased rapidly along with consumption in general.

As a result of this, the food processing industry got into financial difficulties: they could no longer manufacture their products and pay firms for the materials already bought (Tamm, Chapter 8). The first two years of independence – 1991 and 1992 – were the most difficult, and particularly after the Estonian kroon was introduced in 1992. Hardships continued in 1993 and 1994 until the national economy stabilised and even recovered in 1995–1997 (see Table 1.3). Thus, the decollectivisation of agriculture, commenced on the basis of the Law on Agricultural Reform enacted in March 1992 was executed in extremely difficult economic circumstances.

As a result of these economic factors and political shifts, funds built up earlier by the kolkhozes soon dwindled away; in Kanepi too all the money had gone and general operating conditions had changed radically for the worse. The kolkhoz had to sell its property, to end the most unprofitable parts of its activities and to give notice to some of its employees. The government too gave a push to this process: it set a deadline for drawing up plans for the abolition of kolkhozes and sovkhozes as legal entities by the end of 1993. Even before this, the restoration of collectivised land property had begun and the end of the year 1992 had been fixed as the deadline for applications. However, the date was postponed for six months. Although the restitution of agricultural land began before the official closing down of the kolkhozes and sovkhozes, it had become an extremely complicated process for legal reasons. Thus, the restitution of agricultural land fell behind the decollectivisation of other branches of agriculture, which is why it was impossible to synchronise it with the dissolution of the collective farms as part of a uniform process.

Taken as a whole, the changes in the external conditions and the measures directed especially at agriculture involved a transition to the third phase of agricultural reform. Much as in the golden age of peasant populism at the turn of the century, there was a tendency to 'prove' (through 'scientific experiments') the higher productivity of small-scale private plots as compared to large-scale production (kolkhozes and sovkhozes); though in fact the theoretical basis for this was just as weak as at the beginning of the 20th century (regarding peasant fundamentalism, see Alanen 1991; regarding the myth of prosperous family farming as in Estonia, cf. Tamm, Chapter 8).

The government of Mart Laar pushed agricultural policy more and more in the direction of family farm fundamentalism. According to the way of thinking of the government, the legitimate basis of all ownership could be based only on the time preceding the Soviet occupation, with all the legal complications which this involved. The earlier restrictions on minimum acreage were abolished and the rights of other rural residents to buy land around their house were expanded. The aim was to emphasise the position in the transition of petty producers in the transition as compared to large-scale production.

This dogma was tied in with an ultra-liberal economic doctrine. Prime Minister Laar and his party stressed that agriculture "should operate under the same market conditions as other branches without any state interference" (Loko, 1993, 7). The basis of agricultural policy was no longer the existing agricultural sector and the population (with all its problems) which was working in it. The final result was that not only large-scale farms, but also those who would have been willing to establish small-scale production units, became adversely affected.

All in all, the leaders of the Estonian Congress understood the kolkhozes and sovkhozes to be the fortresses of communism "with their red barons" (see Tamm, Chapter 8). For this reason, the government of Mart Laar wanted to develop a petty production system, with collective farms regarded more or less as transient resources for the small farms. However, only part of the resources of large-scale production could be transferred. In addition to these resources, it would have been necessary for the state to direct considerable additional resources to the small farms, protecting them from foreign competition (at least while they were being formed) and creating conditions adequate to small-scale production and the necessary regulation by the state. But such a concrete programme, as required by the restitution ideology and emphasised by the Estonian Congress, would have required a great deal of government money. As the government was neither willing nor (for economic reasons) able to contribute these resources, the programme originally envisaged was replaced during the government of the Estonian Congress (Mart Laar and the Isamaa Party) by a belief in the omnipotence of a neo-liberal economic policy. Thus the Laar government offered very little concrete support for the restructuring of agriculture, even in a situation where the old large-scale agriculture had fallen into a spiral of decline and many workers had lost their jobs. All in all, the process had by now taken a strongly anarchic direction.

Overall, the ideologies of the majority of the agricultural population and the leadership of the Estonian Congress not only conflicted in their starting points but also involved the application of totally different additional resources. The desire of the ordinary people to get their land back and still maintain their wage-work way of life would hardly have been possible without the continuation of some kind of large-scale production system. It might have been possible to realise this desire at the second phase of the agricultural reform, for which quite pragmatic reform proposals were drafted, independently of the government (Tamm, Chapter 8).

Drafting the Reform Plan

The researchers of the Estonian Agricultural University developed their reform plan unofficially and without financing. Their intention was first to determine the share due for each subject and then give the subject, his/her family or heirs the possibility to separate off their part from the collective property and turn it into private property. Reducing the acreage of the inefficient large farms was fundamental in the plan, but it also contained the idea of selling new agricultural and non-agricultural units to members of the kolkhoz on the basis of workshares. The intention was not to demolish large agricultural complexes to make way for peasant small farms or family farms, since even the new farms would have been so large that it would not have been possible for one person to take it over as a farm without large loans. Thus, the most likely owners would be alliances of several persons, and the basis would be wage-work rather than family work. The reform plan relied on the managers and specialists of the kolkhozes and sovkhozes to get these new units under way. It was thought that from this managerial segment there would develop a new class – one which would further advance the agricultural reform.

The father of one member of the group of researchers from the agricultural university was the former chairman of Kanepi kolkhoz, so the group received direct feedback from him. This was also the reason why Kanepi kolkhoz was chosen as a venue for trying out the ideas of the scientists (Tamm, Chapter 8). Kanepi was also a favourable venue in the sense that the chairman of that time was convinced that the existing system had come to its end. The group prepared the reform by carrying out a sociological attitude survey among the members and workers of Kanepi kolkhoz (Põder, Chapter 2). The results contained a certain amount of data critical of the kolkhoz. The results were, however, contradictory, and also presaged the opposition to the reform, which in due course arose. This group of academics would later on participate quite directly in the reform of Kanepi. However, the group did not directly link itself to any party; instead it mainly acted in the role of observer, also giving advice and technical assistance. This seems to have been the common view among the interviewees, who otherwise represented very different viewpoints.

The Kanepi board of management started concrete preparations for the reform. This was not easy, either socially or technically. Socially there were difficulties simply because "part of the management was against it" (former chairman of the kolkhoz). Fears then spread from this group to others, to the tractor drivers and other machine operators in particular. Both these groups were afraid of losing their jobs after the reform. But there were also social difficulties in the method by which the privatisation shares (recorded in vouchers) (with which the members and workers could buy the assets of the kolkhoz) were calculated. There were no unambiguous solutions to this problem in the legislation; instead it was left for a decision by kolkhoz members and those entitled to privatisation shares. One problem was that working days for the kolkhoz were different at different stages of the kolkhoz. At the early stage, people got modest wages, if any, but during the 1960s there was a change to monetary wages. An attempt was made to solve the problem by adding in special factors, but the calculations became technically so complicated that subsequently they were abandoned (former chairman of the kolkhoz). Another difficulty involved the question of whether the basis of the calculations would be wages or working days. If wage were chosen, this had the advantage that it "was directly related to the amount of work [a person had done]," as the wife of the former kolkhoz chairman put it in a joint interview with her husband.

> A tractor driver who had worked hard earned perhaps 500–1,000 roubles a month, another got 120 roubles and counted them to be sure he wouldn't get one rouble too much – so that wouldn't be left without [the social] support money for the children. (Ibid.)

If working days alone were the basis, "those who worked hard in difficult conditions, [and] earned much, but also lost their health, would suffer the most. Mainly those who worked on a farm or as tractor drivers would be the ones on the losing side" (ibid.).

At the time of the former chairman the workshares were calculated and presented for acceptance by the general meeting in the following manner.

> [The calculations would be] made in four steps. Older people got quota days with a certain coefficient, which was taken as the basis, then came the second stage with a lower coefficient, then came the stage where the coefficient was

one, and at last, as the wages grew higher, it [the coefficient] was set at 0.8. And in that manner we hoped to achieve fairness, or how should I put it, to the extent that justice is possible. (Ibid.)

It should be noted that having shares linked to wages would have favoured people who had a better education and were in a leading position. In general, this principle would perhaps have been less egalitarian for the division of resources. In Soviet collective farms the wage difference in favour of the leadership was not, however, as straightforward as that: some of the best tractor drivers, for example, made higher wages than the chairman. The principle of wages was unfair in another way, since wages could also include extra fees, and these in turn were possible only for managers and specialists. The proposal made by the management of the kolkhoz was based on wages, with the inclusion of fees as well.

In the privatisation of the assets of the kolkhoz, land and other property were placed in a separate category. All the landed property owned by the kolkhoz would be returned in due course to the former owners, and the kolkhoz had no power to decide in this matter. Instead, the kolkhoz had to estimate the value of the assets that would *not* be restituted (the land remained unrestituted, but a large part of the assets had already been paid out in money). At the same time, the assets had to be divided into units to be privatised, in the way that would be best from a technical and economic point of view.

We wanted to divide it [the kolkhoz] into ten units, agriculture separately, cattle husbandry separately and forestry separately. They [the production units] would have then become autonomous. (Ibid.)

The most important production buildings of the kolkhoz were situated in three places, the municipal centre of Kanepi and in the larger villages of Karste and Kooraste. In each village the cultivation of land was entrusted to an organised brigade. However, in terms of being natural territorial fixed points of large-scale agricultural production units, the villages were in a different position compared to the centre village. Machine halls, repair workshops, warehouses and many other activities were all centred in Kanepi. This led to problems in dividing the resources, and people in Karste and Kooraste were afraid of being left behind.

The Reception given to the Reform Plan

No particular effort was made to keep the reform plan secret, and many people besides the kolkhoz chairman and the board of management participated in preparing it. Nevertheless, the people of the kolkhoz worried about their future and began to speculate about the possible hidden interests involved – about the winners and losers. They were particularly suspicious of the real motives of those persons in the kolkhoz administration who were responsible for the details of the reform proposal that was to be submitted to the general meeting (i.e. the members of the board of management, in particular). In fact, some people were inclined to see not only the reform plan, but also certain other decisions made in the kolkhoz as covert attempts to protect the private interests of board members. The improvements made to the cowshed of Keramägi, while the plan was still in preparation, are good examples. The shed was thoroughly refurbished and an entire heard of high-quality pedigree cattle was purchased and placed there.

It is quite understandable that people were sceptical, since the future concealed, together with new prospects, many threats. Everything that was related to the kolkhoz was becoming more and more uncertain. Eventually, people started to elaborate their own survival strategies – as well as to consider, with a degree of suspicion, those of others. It was only natural to suspect those persons, most of all, who belonged to the influential inner circle of the kolkhoz management. As mentioned above, even the researchers from the Estonian Agricultural University in Tartu had based their vision on the idea that the leaders of the future units, together with professionals and specialists, would hold a key position in starting new enterprises. If these were the general expectations, why assume that the board members were any less concerned about planning their future or protecting their own interests than everyone else – being also better qualified to do so?

Those employees of the kolkhoz with a better education (professionals, specialists, etc.) also had the best opportunity to analyse different options and to consider alternative solutions. Many of them actually took part in drafting the reform plan–but without being at the centre of power, i.e. on the board.

> Mr X, he was interested in knowing how the workshares were calculated, because he had worked as an agronomist for a long time, and he feared that I myself would buy the cowshed at Keramägi. We knew very well what it takes to buy [and run] a cowshed and that it would have ruined our health. But with all that he actually managed to get one group convinced [that we aimed at taking over the cowshed]. (Former chairman of the kolkhoz)

> I saw myself how X made his [own] calculations [of workshares]. [He] drew his own conclusions, then he went to the store and voiced what he thought about the matter. And when a [malicious] rumour once gets started, there's no way to put an end to it. He didn't trust the accountant any more. He took [just] the wages and considered it a share, as if it had been an individual's share. It wasn't a share, it was wages, and should have been calculated according to the coefficient, later on. (Wife of the former kolkhoz chairman in a joint interview with her husband)

The doubts and misinterpretations of the specialist were understandable because of the secretiveness of the board and the uncertainty of the overall situation. Even so, without additional financing or loan, a workshare based on a chairman's salary would not have been enough to cover the price of an entire cowshed, not even if prices had stayed at their intended level, near the book values, which were on the low side. The wife of the former chairman argues the matter as follows.

> By what we figured, your shares [the former chairman's] for all this time in this kolkhoz would have amounted to something like 20,000. Because he had worked in the early days, his salary remained at about 170 roubles for a very long time. With that 20,000 and those real prices you couldn't have bought much, maybe one working place [small cowshed, piggery or other such building, machinery not included] from the centre; a working place of your own you could have bought. That would have been all for a lifetime of service. (Wife in a joint interview with her husband)

It seems clear that the ill health of both the chairman and his wife – and also the way in which the actual situation started to develop – were hardly consistent with some of the popular speculations mentioned above. It is uncertain to what extent people were actually aware of the chairman's state of health or that of his wife, or the plans that these two might have had for their children, for instance. As has been noted, their son took part in preparing the reform plan, which probably contributed to people's suspicions.

Another difficult question concerns the sources from which the people of the kolkhoz, those who did not belong to the inner circle of the board, got their information about the economic alliances of the board members, their ability to obtain shares from other people, etc. However, we have no reason to suspect that the then chairman and his wife were not being sincere.

> We never considered such an idea, and what possible use could we have had for a big cowshed, anyhow? We knew very well that we were not fit for such a thing.

One must have good health. (Wife of the former kolkhoz chairman in a joint interview with her husband)

As regards the acquisition of pedigree cattle and the repairs made at the Keramägi cowshed, both investments can be explained, in retrospect, on the grounds of the economic situation. The kolkhoz had considerable cash funds, and it was important to invest them in solid property, since the rate of inflation was already increasing. "I don't believe that [he] had any personal interests at stake," concluded one of the members of the former board on the subject, since "he [the former chairman] was the kind of a guy who told you at once, if something was wrong." Similar opinions were not unusual among the people of the kolkhoz at large.

Before the details of the reform plan became a matter of contention, the former chairman was generally regarded as honest and straightforward. But in the prevailing circumstances people often found it difficult to trust their own former impressions of a given person, and all kinds of rumours continued to circulate.

I have heard from other people that he built himself a house during the times of the kolkhoz, but didn't get to keep it. Not that I could tell you much about that, though, because I don't know anything for sure. (A milker at the kolkhoz)

Because the reform plan was based on the old, long-established patterns of leadership, the managerial posts were distributed according to the existing power structures.

The board [of the kolkhoz] distributed the units between its members. It was these board members who would have become the directors of the smaller units; and they would have divided the kolkhoz between themselves, so to speak. But there were others who felt that those managers had anything but clean hands. (Agronomist X)

As a matter of fact, the board of management was likely to lose its direct power of decision-making as soon as the kolkhoz property had been shared. It would, nevertheless, remain the most important centre of power within the kolkhoz, because it would still have access to the most accurate information available, and could also use its indirect influence.

So the one subject that people continued to speculate about was the role of the board and its members in the reform process. They were "at the core of power," or as the Estonian interviewees frequently expressed it: "*pumba juures*" (standing right beside the pump). The people who were most dissatisfied showed a strong tendency to associate the objects of privatisation with particular persons, the *beneficiaries*.

> There was also this domestic engineer B, he was supposed to have that complex of buildings over there for himself; and then there's a warehouse next to the repair shop, Y was supposed to have it. He's the chief of a forestry works and has sons in Tallinn. [They planned] to bring a forest harvester here together with Finnish businessmen, and it was sort of public knowledge . . . They were good friends, and that's the way assets were divided up [within that closed circle of friends]. The chairman gave an order and if that bunch had decided that a certain person couldn't get wood, or that some other person wouldn't be allowed to cut trees, then it was agreed [by that select group]. (A former machine operator)

As the reform process advanced, the conflicting interests and the different attitudes of people towards the reform became more obvious. Apart from contradictions related to the kolkhoz power structure, there were also some other matters in which these conflicts came to a head – such as the method of calculating the workshares. Perhaps the most fundamental dimension in which the conflict took shape was the controversy between the "progressives," who preferred large complexes, and the "conservatives," who wanted small peasant farms to replace the kolkhoz system (the terms above come from an electrician at the kolkhoz). The entire professional background of managers and specialists as well as many machine operators and technicians was based on the division of labour that was typical of large kolkhozes. It was these groups that had formed the top of the old kolkhoz hierarchy, and now felt particularly threatened (Tamm, Chapter 8).

What is more, an ever-increasing proportion of the kolkhoz workers and employees had moved to the area from other parts of the country. For this reason they could not expect to get any land, at least in the municipality of Kanepi, on the basis of the restitution. Old age and poor health also limited the possibilities of many people to set up a farm of their own – although a large number of those who actually did take up farming were quite elderly people who already had some experience of the old peasant economy. All the same, many people aimed at establishing a private farm on the lands gained in the restitution, and quite a number of people had already done so on the basis of the Farm Law.

The number of people who appeared at the kolkhoz general meeting on 20 December 1990, when the reform proposal was officially announced to the public, exceeded all expectations. There were about 350 workers in the kolkhoz at that time, and about 400 people arrived for the meeting. There were not enough seats for everybody, so that some people had to stay in the corridors. It is true that the number of those who were, in principle, entitled to participate was quite large (comprising all the kolkhoz members as well as all those people who had, over the years, worked in the kolkhoz for at least five years). But if one considers that at most meetings no more than one member of any family would attend – for domestic reasons if nothing else – the "mobilisation" must have been almost complete. This indicates the great emotional charge attached to the issue. In order to better understand the general atmosphere of this meeting, one should also be familiar with the carefully planned measures which the opposition took against the board.

Opposition and the Wreck of the First Reform Plan

A number of people with various positions within the kolkhoz formed the opposition. Most of them seem to have had some sort of previous disagreement with the kolkhoz management, while the former chairman was still in office. They obviously had other reasons for their discontent besides the reform itself. To this group belonged also the future chairman. He worked at the kolkhoz machine station, which had become one of the focal points of dissatisfaction. In addition to plant and machine operators, a good number of skilled workers from other occupational branches took part in the discussions (see Middle class in Figure 3.1). The keynote of their critique appears to have been their concern about the uncertain future.

> Nobody knew what a person was supposed to do after the kolkhoz was split up. (A kolkhoz building worker)

The necessity of the whole process was called into question.

> But the tractor drivers and other men kicked up a fuss. Why must we destroy the economy [of the kolkhoz], why couldn't we just continue working as it is [in the kolkhoz]. (Former chief accountant)

Although the opposition did not present any open accusations against the management, it had started questioning the motives of the board.

> And I took part in that opposition myself. They [the management] had shared the best parts of the kolkhoz between themselves; the woodworking establishment . . . and there was this one cowshed of Keramägi, which was renovated

during the cold spell in winter. They even replaced the windows, which was never done normally, and it was so phoney and so transparent that one could only assume that it was being prepared for somebody . . . And before that, the cattle were also thoroughly examined and then replaced, the whole lot of them. And the cows that were sick were moved into the main cowshed of the kolkhoz. (A kolkhoz machine operator)

Most of the participants in the assembly knew about these suspicions. It seems, however, that the group of scientists from the Estonian Agricultural University were unaware of the general feelings of people. One of them was elected chairman of the meeting preparing the reform plan.

A couple of speakers – one of whom was the future chairman of the kolkhoz – first demonstrated their expertise in the legal aspects of the reform, and then counted on the various conflicting interests to get support.

That meeting on the 20th, Z [from the group of researchers] started in the chair, and in the opposition there were C and me, who was the car driver of the kolkhoz. He was a qualified engineer from the Agricultural University, but he had some mental problems . . . We sat next to each other and waited to see what would happen. We also had a plan of our own. We'd been working on it for several weeks, looking for the weak points where the course of the meeting could be changed. And we did bring it to a dead end, right from the beginning, there was no turning back, not with those fellows [the former chairman and his supporters], no way. (Later chairman of the kolkhoz)

First, C (the car driver from the opposition) had confronted the chairman of the meeting regarding the reform policy, and about the related issue concerning the workshares. He managed to get the chairman totally upset, so that the latter proceeded in a manner which was probably unwise, considering the feelings of those who were present.

D [the chairman of the meeting] interrupted him and asked him what kind of education he might have, and he answered the same as yourself . . . They exchanged a couple of pointed remarks, and people got carried away, and D lost control of the meeting. (Later chairman of the kolkhoz)

Something quite similar happened to the former chairman of the kolkhoz.

[The former chairman] brought up many examples of shares that had already been calculated. It came close to a quarrel, about it not having been calculated right. Part of the shares was recalculated; there were big scenes as a result. (Former chief accountant)

This was an unexpected turn of events, and the chairman of the kolkhoz consulted people from the Estonian Agricultural University. At any rate, that was how some of the participants of the meeting interpreted his reaction.

> When it became clear that nothing would go according to his plans, he turned his back on people. This made them furious. People took it as an insult. After all, he represented the people. He should have co-operated with the workers, not with lawyers and scientists. (A member of the kolkhoz)

> They made themselves ridiculous, people refused to listen [to the former chairman]; or [to] the scientists, for that matter. People didn't give them any chance to speak. The people from Tartu [the scientists] were a little taken aback. (Later chairman of the kolkhoz)

In this atmosphere of public indignation the opposition had an excellent opportunity to set forth their most important argument.

> I then proposed that we should calculate the shares once more, on the basis of working days; a worker would get as much as a chairman, because they've [the management] already had their share [in the higher salaries], and people accepted that . . . So we took a vote. It was decided [to recalculate the privatisation shares], on the basis of workdays. There were one or two stray opposing opinions, but they [the supporters of the reform] didn't dare to go against the people. The place was in such chaos that they wouldn't have been able to get out, they would have taken a good beating. Even the pensioners started shouting aloud; and they usually keep quiet. (Later chairman of the kolkhoz)

The opposition had planned a successful strategy to get the majority of the people on their side. One of the milkers of the kolkhoz stated in her interview that the former chairman was at this point, "in the general opinion, unreliable."

The dispute over the manner in which the workshares should be calculated united a number of different interest groups in the opposition: elderly people, kolkhozniks from the quota workday period, people with a low income and those who had no connections with the management of the kolkhoz (see Figure 3.1). It might have been possible to produce some reasons to justify the calculatory method proposed by the former chairman, but this would have required wider general discussions in the preliminary meetings. Perhaps the haste, perhaps the fatigue of the former chairman contributed, at least in some respect, to the fact that such preparatory measures were neglected.

Force of habit might also have been partly to blame. The kolkhoz management may have grown accustomed to having their motions passed. Their proposals had never been rejected before. Moreover, consciousness of the fact that people were, after all, extremely reluctant and even frightened to give up the kolkhoz system probably discouraged the management from undertaking any further efforts to clarify their point. The group of researchers from the Estonian Agricultural University were openly astonished at the whole situation, both during and after the meeting.

Insufficient preparations on the part of those who supported the reform might also explain why the strategy of the opposition not only worked, but triggered off such an extreme emotional response – "a downright mass psychosis," as one electrician of the kolkhoz expressed it. The fears and the hopes that people had for their future were another important factor. "People strove for a better life and (the later chairman of the kolkhoz) took advantage of that" (ibid.). In addition, the younger population, tired of the former chairman's surly-old-man's paternalistic style of management, wanted a change.

> I think that the real reason was that [the former chairman] was rather stern with people, and they got tired of that. (A resident of Kanepi)

So, one of the fundamental reasons for dissatisfaction appears to have been the kolkhoz management, although it was the dispute about the calculation of the workshares that finally wrecked the reform experiment.

Because the assembly agreed to reject the initial reform proposal, a new one had to be worked out, and a new draft committee composed. It was decided that the committee would convene within a month, but the course of events took a new turn when the former chairman fell seriously ill. In consequence, the proposed second kolkhoz general meeting was cancelled. This started up a process, which resulted in a transfer of power within the kolkhoz.

The Question of the Fate of the Kolkhoz

After the former chairman had been taken ill, it became uncertain whether he could keep his post in the kolkhoz management. Since the question was left more or less open, the opposition still continued to pursue its activities. The kolkhoz machine station became a pocket of resistance. The tractor and car drivers who formed the core of the organised opposition called a meeting right at the start of the following year (1991). The meeting was well attended: 82 persons were present. Once again, it was their worry about the forthcoming dissolution of the kolkhoz that determined their perspective on the issues.

> I was the recording secretary, then, and one car driver was the chairman, and we talked about all that might happen if everything were sold, and with people living here in those big blocks of flats, what could they possibly start to do if the big tractors were sold to outsiders. And the workshare vouchers, that was something that no one had expected; and the auction, too, it was something that Soviet people hadn't got used to. (Later chairman of the kolkhoz)

The tractor drivers and other plant and machine operators were afraid of losing their jobs if they lost their right to use the kolkhoz vehicles, machinery and equipment. Apparently they also weighed up the possibility of buying these vehicles with their workshares. The meeting revealed how problematic the situation of this specific group might become if the kolkhoz were dissolved. At the previous general meeting, the dispute over the workshares had united the interests of this occupational group with the interests of family farm keepers and farm founders. Both parties wanted to make sure that they would obtain as large a proportion of the workshares as possible. They were hoping that this would enable them to buy some of the tools and technical implements they needed in order to ensure their future opportunities of employment.

Yet there is another, parallel topic which probably illustrates the general feelings of the meeting even better. People were dissatisfied, and severely criticised the manner in which kolkhoz affairs were being looked after – and the former chairman, in particular. He was accused not only of an attempt to break up the kolkhoz, but also of mismanagement, possible malpractice.

> And then we decided to move a vote of censure against the former chairman, and to make it public that he traded timber with a Finnish company; and that money has not been received today, [those] 23,000 Finnish marks [are currently in a bank account] in the Foreign Trade Bank in Moscow. (Later chairman of the kolkhoz)

However, it is difficult to estimate how reliable or well-founded all these allegations really were. Perhaps an Estonian executive no longer had much control over these types of transactions, which were handled through Moscow.

The opposition had already decided in advance that the vote of censure should be passed in black and white. Both the actual document and the names on it were acquired by fraudulent means, in the following manner.

> We used a little bit of cunning, too, for history's sake. Not all of the men would have signed that no-confidence note. But we did it . . . I can't remember where the idea actually came from; so that those who arrived would write their names on a paper, to say that they were present at the meeting, and a signature; and then we wrote down the text there as well, and had the signatures ready. (Later chairman of the kolkhoz)

Soon after the meeting, while the former chairman was still in hospital, his wife found the resolution of the meeting attached to the garage wall. She had been told in the centre of Kanepi village, "Go and read the writing on the wall."

> There were these totally inessential items, like why the chairman had not intervened in the use of the greenhouses, or why hadn't their functioning been analysed, and then a couple of other trifling matters. (Wife of the former kolkhoz chairman in a joint interview with her husband)

As we can see, the criticism was mostly based on economic arguments and concerned, above all, the management of kolkhoz finances. On the other hand, the interviews consistently portray the former chairman as a hard-working, economically oriented person – to the point of emphasising these features. As indicated by the following part of the interview with the chairman's wife, the crux of the matter was in essence the fate of the kolkhoz.

> So I went to a *dispetser* [a specialist], because I had some business there, because of my work, and there was this *dispetser*, one bus driver and one car driver. And I asked them, almost yelled: Hey you men, what on earth have you done? And the bus driver said 'Why do you want to close down the kolkhoz, then?' That is so unbelievable, it shows how people understood the whole affair. It was something so awful that I couldn't go back to work, for two days, I think.

It was not only the staff of the machine station who shared this general outlook on the subject. A milker working in one of the more remote villages of the kolkhoz also approaches the question in a very similar manner.

> [The former chairman] suggested the dissolution, dividing the kolkhoz into four parts, but people didn't agree. [The later chairman] promised to keep the whole

thing intact, he stood up for it, to continue with the kolkhoz. And other people wanted to preserve the kolkhoz too.

Thus, the people of the kolkhoz were impelled to associate the reform plan with the idea of abolishing the kolkhoz, whereas the kolkhoz management saw it rather as a last resort to renovate the kolkhoz system.

> People just couldn't get it in their heads that what we needed now was a new way of thinking, that we should figure out how to continue. (Wife of the former kolkhoz chairman in a joint interview with her husband)

It might be useful to clarify certain aspects of this issue and distinguish between the organised opposition, aiming at a transfer of power, and the majority of the people of the kolkhoz, who had pinned their hopes on the possibility of keeping the kolkhoz intact. It remains unclear what other plans, apart from an aspiration to power, the opposition might have had for the future of the kolkhoz. The situation came to a head in a legitimacy crisis, which gave the opposition a chance to start promoting a rival candidate for the next chairmanship.

The Rise to Power of the Opposition

A leading figure in the opposition, who was to become the next chairman of the kolkhoz, was known as an active member of the Estonian nationalist movement. He was certainly one of its bravest and most devoted adherents (see Ruutsoo, Chapter 6).

> Already before the Singing Revolution, he helped to restore the monument commemorating the first period of Estonian independence, and so on. Sometimes we were a bit nervous, for his sake. We feared for our own safety, too. In 1991 the tanks arrived; we were scared, because the name of my father's brother was on that monument as well. (A kolkhoznik who had regained his family estate in the restitution)

In addition to symbolic capital (Bourdieu), the future chairman had organisational capital. He was one of the local leaders of the rightist Estonian Congress and "fairly active in *Kaitseliit*" (former chairman). The latter was a paramilitary organisation which, as the former chairman put it, "intimidated some people; but then there were also those who respected him for that." The people of the kolkhoz usually described him as "enterprising," "energetic" and "ambitious." The interviews with him also betray his decidedly antago-nistic attitude towards the former chairman.

Given the nature of the debates preceding the elections, the later chair-man had, in practice, committed himself to maintaining the kolkhoz as a whole. The vote was to take place at a board meeting scheduled for 21 February 1991, i.e. in a representative body instead of a general assembly. However, the principle of representation was still exercised only in theory. In reality, the list of candidates for the kolkhoz council had been compiled by the former chairman and the board of management. One vacancy which had to be filled was the chairmanship; the future chairman had, as a member of the Rayon Soviet, discussed alternative candidates for the post of chairman with the vice-chairman of the Rayon Soviet: "It's not that hard . . . [why don't you] take the post yourself," he had said. "So I gave my consent, just among ourselves" (later chairman of the kolkhoz).

The opposition started negotiations with the members of the council over his candidacy for the chairmanship. At that time, he was just a common worker in the machine depot repair shop, but one of the 45 kolkhoz council members was the director of the machine station. He informed the future chairman of the number of votes canvassed in his support so far, and told him that the others did not have any other alternative but to vote him onto the chair. And "just like in the Kremlin," "it was decided who would propose me for chairmanship." (Later chairman of the kolkhoz)

As people were assembling for the meeting, it was still uncertain whether the former chairman would also come forward as a candidate. One council member, the former vice-chairman, asked him to stand at the last minute.

> I went to ask him back, but he refused for medical reasons. It was nobody's fault that he didn't take a step . . . He didn't put up a fight [for the leadership] at all.

In fact, the former chairman had evidently already made up his mind about his retirement some time before, and he does not seem to have regarded the confrontation as such a significant matter as it appeared to the opposition. Nevertheless, he does seem to have favoured someone for the post.

> The person that the people would probably have chosen didn't stand for election and the former chairman said no, absolutely, owing to his poor health. [A senior agricultural official at county level] visited us and he said better [a chairman coming from the opposition] than nobody at all. (Wife of the former kolkhoz chairman in a joint interview with her husband)

Despite the circumstances of the meeting as described above, there was nevertheless a certain sense of drama in the atmosphere of the meeting. The opposition was unsure of itself, but was looking for the vote to take on a political character, with the hope of gaining a victory this way.

> The chief agronomist presided over the meeting and he was scared too. At that time we didn't know what direction matters would take, because the meeting had been called by the board of management and the old chairman was still in office. We didn't know much about the general feeling in the assembly hall, either, and there was the hope that the matter would take on a political character. We had agreed on the man who was supposed to nominate me as a candidate and the chief agronomist conducting the meeting put the question again and again, but that fellow didn't have the courage to speak out. I stood up myself and said that I'd come forward as a candidate myself. If I hadn't opened my mouth, the matter would have been dropped. That would have been the end of it. (Later chairman of the kolkhoz)

The future chairman had thus personally nominated himself, which would have been highly inappropriate in Soviet society. However, the matter was put to a vote by secret ballot. Even then he won by a large majority, and according to his own estimate, those present "mainly" voted for him. All the same, the future chairman says that he made just a couple of changes in the list of names for the new board, and that all the specialists were allowed to keep their seats. From the standpoint of the superseded kolkhoz management, however, the affair took on a different aspect.

> During the elections for the new board, it was said that if a person were a supporter [of the former chairman], then he wouldn't be elected to the board of management. (A member of the former board)

Paradoxically, only a small number of changes followed. It should be noted that the opposition had accused the board of having shared the profits of the reform among themselves. Yet some of these people were still sitting on the new board. Even if the claim were well founded, the only action that would be taken (in the cynics' view) would be a further redistribution of profits for the benefit of the new board. This could perhaps explain the cynical attitude that agronomist X, for instance, adopted towards the new chairman, even at that time.

Another paradox related to these events was that the central figure was also an active member of the rightist nationalist movement, the Estonian Congress, and a leading figure in the Isamaa Party as well.

> I am, even now, a member of Isamaa, and its right-wing faction. (Later chairman of the kolkhoz)

Both of these movements, the Estonian Congress and the Isamaa Party, adopted a hostile attitude towards the large farms of the Soviet era and strove to break them into smaller farms, based on the ownership during the years preceding the Second World War.

As the essential contents of his political stand the new chairman mentioned (in an interview in 1995) the restitution of collectivised assets and low taxation, but equally his view that: "What comes first is that every item should belong to its master." (Ibid.)

Still, the essential factor, from the viewpoint of the majority of kolkhoz workers, was that the plans of the new chairman had been presented in public, and that they understood the main point to be a commitment to the preservation of the kolkhoz as a whole. The new chairman had repeatedly, in public and in writing (see Põder, Chapter 2) committed himself to preserving the kolkhoz.

> The people were furious, and in Estonia public opinion was not yet ready for the breaking up of the kolkhozes. Kanepi was one of the first where people from the [Estonian Agricultural] University made an attempt [to break up the kolkhoz], by way of an experiment, but it didn't work out. [The former chairman] very nearly broke up the kolkhoz; I was elected to preserve it. (Later chairman of the kolkhoz)

This "little revolution" was, according to agronomist X and the judgement of the kolkhozniks themselves, conservative. All in all, it could be characterised as a counter-revolution.

The Reform and Its Execution

Attempts at Modernising the Existing Kolkhoz Structure

The transfer of power combined deeply personal motives with other interest-based factors. The later chairman held a grudge against his predecessor, particularly because the former chairman had dismissed him from the board of management and then from his office as the head of a department, finally demoting him to the rank of a common worker.

I made a couple of mistakes, too, and he [the former chairman] asked me then –
that's a historic moment for a person – called me into his office and said: 'Will
you submit your resignation yourself, or leave [your post, as head of the
department]?' I told him that I'd submit my resignation. And it was exactly the
same day, six years later, that the old chairman opened the door again when I
replaced him [as chairman of the kolkhoz], the 26th of February. That day the
tables were turned. (Later chairman of the kolkhoz)

From the viewpoint of interests it was also a question of a "little
revolution" though from a social point of view it was rather a counter-
revolution. Data supplied by the interviewees confirms the suspicion voiced
by Emeritus Professor Mati Tamm. Tamm has suggested that at the bottom of
the transfer of power there was first and foremost fear on the part of the
specialists and the machine operators (the "progressives") about what would
happen to them if the kolkhoz were broken up. Moreover, the kolkhoz council
meeting that elected the board of management was attended by a select group:
"There were none [or only a few] of the ordinary workers," stressed the
former chief accountant in an interview. All in all, it appears that unskilled
employees – let alone pensioners – had no part in the immediate displacement
of the former chairman and the board of management. Indeed, the very
existence of such intentions never became public knowledge.

Those people who lived further away from the centre [in the villages of Karste
and Kooraste, for instance] were totally unaware of that meeting. Some people
knew hardly anything at all about the replacement of the chairman at that
meeting. (Former brigade leader from another village)

In the events that unfolded the kolkhoz employees were divided into
three status groups (see Figure 3.1). These were 1) the board of management,
with the chairman and his trustees at its core; 2) the "middle class," which
consisted of specialists and skilled workers; and 3) the "rest," mainly consisting of ordinary workers and pensioners.

The "little revolution" was in the first place a "middle class" project.
The machine drivers and specialists formed the nuclear group that entertained
fears with regard to the splitting up of the kolkhoz into smaller units.
Nevertheless, in the controversy over workshares they appealed to the interests of a large majority of the kolkhoz workers and members – or rather a
group of those specialists did, those who were openly in opposition. Their
strategy might seem strange, since the option they proposed was apparently in
conflict with the interests of the specialists (their chance to gain an extra

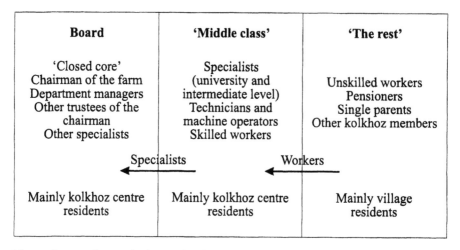

Board	'Middle class'	'The rest'
'Closed core' Chairman of the farm Department managers Other trustees of the chairman Other specialists	Specialists (university and intermediate level) Technicians and machine operators Skilled workers	Unskilled workers Pensioners Single parents Other kolkhoz members
Mainly kolkhoz centre residents	Mainly kolkhoz centre residents	Mainly village residents

Note: Arrows denote the increasing importance of education and professional skills in the status structure.

Figure 3.1 The status structure within collective farms

premium) as well as the interests of the best machine operators (the elite of the kolkhoz in terms of wages). But this was one way of expanding the social support of the "revolution." It was perhaps the price they had to pay, in the end, in order to gain power. For even though the "people" (a term which appears frequently in the interviews and refers either to all the kolkhoz members as a whole, or to employees of the kolkhoz in a stricter sense) were absent from the council, the mood gaining ground, which subsequently turned into an upsurge of heated feelings in the general assembly, constituted an important sounding board for the strategy adopted by the opposition.

The revolution brought about the displacement of that part of the former board which was known for its loyalty to the former kolkhoz management, but "all the specialists kept their posts" (agronomist X). Furthermore, attempts were made to isolate the core of the old management; however, the people of the kolkhoz continued to place their trust in the former chairman, even during this later turns of events. Although his role remained marginal, this might be an indication of the somewhat shallow social foundation of the shift of power. To a large extent the shift was based on populist pretences (as in the characterisation of the conflict, see above), trickery (as in the manipulated vote of no-confidence), slander (accusing the former chairman of having frozen kolkhoz funds in a Moscow bank account) and an appeal to general political sympathies (in keeping with right-wing public aspirations in

Estonia, unfavourable to the kolkhoz management). Above all, the populist approach was an attempt to unify the status groups of the "middle class" and "the rest".

It would be wrong to assume that defending the unity of the kolkhoz was altogether an objectionable idea to the "people", even though a large majority also had some interest in the restitution of assets that had been nationalised in the past. Combining the interests of the "progressives" (specialists and machinists) and the rest of the "people" would not have been an impossible task, although it was undoubtedly difficult. The relatively good results obtained in a couple of Estonian kolkhozes and sovkhozes testifies to the validity of efforts to maintain the kolkhozes – if the idea enjoyed widespread support. One of these kolkhozes was situated in the neighbouring municipality, in the rayon capital of Põlva.

> In 1991, when the reform started, the situation was not easy, and our attitude towards wanting to continue as a unit was highly sceptical. And the food processing plants, the machine station complex and the greenhouse complex became independent first and there was only farm production left . . . We were the first to complete the agricultural reform in our county, in 1992. And we had 860 dairy cows in the days of the kolkhoz, and now we have 940. Our livestock comes to 1,700 head in all, 800 of which are young stock. Before, there were 7,700 pigs altogether, now there are 3,600–3,800. During the kolkhoz era there we had 546 workers, now we have 182. We still have 71 tractors left and 33 cars, and 9 combine harvesters. We intend to produce milk and meat . . . We have increased the number of our cattle and the milk production per cow. We have renewed our stock of cattle. During the kolkhoz, our production was 4,500 litres per cow per year, after it 5,500 litres, and we aim at 6,000. Milk production is profitable if one gets the highest [quality standard] price. [Because] there's so much foreign meat on the Estonian market, which is why our own production is unable to compete, and that's also why we have cut down on the amount of pigs. But we have a very good stock of pedigree pigs from Finland; they have a low fat content, and [therefore] also potential marketing prospects. (Director of a large-scale agricultural co-operative in Põlva in 1995)

Perhaps this particular alternative would also have fitted best with the hopes of the "progressives" in Kanepi. The formation of the large farm company described in the citation above was the result of a hard struggle in which a youthful management team had a central role. Such a case has not been typical in Estonia, although it is not unique (cf. below). No such aspirations actually surfaced in Kanepi. This could have been due to the fact that the fields there were broken up into parcels which were too small for a large estate, as the former chairman pointed out.

A co-operative was finally established in the township of Kanepi, too, but this happened more as a result of middle-class aspirations than as a result of the reform plan. But let us now return to the situation where the new kolkhoz leadership had just taken power.

The new kolkhoz management started off by making a number of improvements that can be described as the *modernisation of the existing kolkhoz* and that seems to have pleased the specialists and skilled workers, in particular. The most noteworthy change was probably the democratisation of managerial practices by way of delegating decision-making procedures to the specialists.

> As soon as the chairman had been elected, the life of the kolkhoz assumed its course under the leadership of the new board [of management] and the new chairman. At the first meeting I addressed all the specialists and emphasised the fact that they were experts in their own field, [that they] had been given a post and entrusted with a task for which they were responsible. For these people it meant a tremendous release from mental terror. In the days of the old chairman specialists weren't allowed to make their own decisions freely, everything depended on the chairman. Not even the head of a work group dared to follow the instructions of the agronomist, if the chairman didn't approve of it. The two professions he didn't give advice to were the electricians and veterinarians. In every other field he was a great expert. (Later chairman of the kolkhoz)

Furthermore, the relationship between a machinist and his machine was made much closer. They were no longer required always to return the machine(s) to the kolkhoz headquarters at the end of the day. "People started keeping them at their homes and held on to them as if they were their own." (Later chairman of the kolkhoz)

In addition to this, a number of material improvements were made, such as the acquisition of computers for bookkeeping and the construction of centres for cultural activities pertaining to the kolkhoz (a song-festival stage); plans were made to construct a Finnish sauna for the employees, and investments were made once again in a manner typical of the old days, but with great urgency, owing to the fact that the currency had already started to lose its value. Improvements were made in the basic technology of production with the purchase of two old lorries and three new combine harvesters. Later the kolkhoz also purchased a great quantity of spare parts for agricultural machinery (see Põder, Chapter 2). In the most important decisions (such as those concerning investments in machines) the procedural legitimacy was consolidated by arranging occasions where people could voice their opinions.

For the most part, people were pleased with this new practice, but some felt that investments in cultural and recreational facilities, and even computers were simply a waste of money. From the standpoint of the "people," the kolkhoz seemed to be progressing, but some of the interviewees saw the line adopted by the new chairman as too specialist-oriented. As a milker remarked in an interview: "He got along just fine with the specialists and the board [of management], but not [so well] with the common worker."

In these interviews with the "ordinary people" the new chairman stands in contrast to the former chairman, who had won their respect in spite of his authoritarian style of management. The later chairman did not adopt the overtly patrimonial style of management of the former chairman. In this light the reforms carried out by the new chairman were interpreted by some as "putting on an act" (milker) or even "petty Stalinism" (technician). Since personal contact was such a typical part of the patrimonial leadership of his predecessor, the fact that the new chairman kept a distance from his employees may have created the impression of an outsider. Nevertheless, the portrait that the interviews paint of the new chairman probably bears the imprint of the events that were to follow, above all his subsequent role as the "liquidator" of the kolkhoz.

All in all, the activities of the new leadership did not bring about any dramatic changes in the everyday life of the kolkhoz.

> That spring we completed the spring jobs by the second of May [1991]. The work was done; I didn't have much to do with it, [I] just got the latest news from the chief agronomist every morning, attended the meetings and if something was needed, money for instance, we settled the matter then. During the spring working there was a lot of competition [between the workers] as there always was in kolkhoz times, and then there were extra payments. And all the work was done, no problems with that. People could decide for themselves what to do. (Later chairman of the kolkhoz)

The early days of the new management did not consist solely of the modernisation of the existing kolkhoz structure. At the national level, there was increasingly systematic preparation for the replacement of the kolkhoz system with something totally different. The group of researchers that had prepared the rejected reform plan kept in touch with the new leadership and cautioned that the circumstances favourable for collective farming were going to change. This prospect affected kolkhoz life from the start of the new administration, hanging over the kolkhoz like the Sword of Damocles.

Return to the Reform Plan of the Former Chairman

The new chairman of the kolkhoz had committed himself, both in his own mind and among the kolkhoz people, to the preservation of the kolkhoz by means of the "little revolution." It would of course have been impossible to preserve the kolkhoz in its previous legally constituted form, since the kolkhozes and the sovkhozes were in principle illegal and ordained to be abolished by the Supreme Court declaration of 30 March 1990. The State Land Board was appointed to draft the land reform and the restitution of collectivised assets. Although these decisions had been made right at the beginning of the rule of the Savisaar government, his Popular Front government displayed a highly pragmatic disposition towards ownership arrangements in agriculture, and hence the goal of the Savisaar government was not by any means the eradication of large-scale production.

However, as regards keeping the Kanepi kolkhoz agricultural unit as intact as possible, the later chairman did not come to the same conclusion as the chairman of the Põlva kolkhoz described above. It appears somewhat strange that the interviews show no sign of this option having ever been seriously considered. The everyday life of the kolkhoz seems to have assumed its normal course, but in the meantime valuable time was wasted, as external conditions grew increasingly unfavourable for agricultural enterprises. The reform that resulted in the creation of the large joint stock company of Põlva had already started in 1991, which despite its political intensity was economically still a relatively tranquil year.

Although agricultural subventions had been abandoned in September 1990, producer prices remained relatively favourable in the first half of 1991 (see PSE data in Table 1.3). Estonia became independent in the late summer of that year and price control was immediately deregulated. The following year the government of Mart Laar (strongly antagonistic towards kolkhozes) came into office, the Estonian kroon was brought into circulation and price control was abandoned across the border in Russia, as well. All this meant a huge increase in the costs of farming inputs, while producer prices decreased. The PSE% indicator plummeted from +57% in 1990 to –91% in 1991 (see Table 1.3). Simultaneously, Estonian agricultural producers were facing serious marketing problems both at home and abroad in Russia, difficulties in obtaining raw materials from Russia, a tightening of the taxation position of the kolkhozes and sovkhozes, and a rapid depletion of kolkhoz financial resources. In Kanepi kolkhoz these resources had been considerable during the time of the former chairman.

The value of money dropped, and it dropped fast. We were still able to plough the land, but not able to harvest it. (Later chairman of the kolkhoz)

The rate of inflation speaks for itself. In 1991, which was still a good year, the rate of inflation rose as high as 232%; the actual hyperinflation of the following year reached 1076%. Furthermore, the introduction of the Estonian kroon in the summer of 1992 depleted the cash reserves of Kanepi kolkhoz.

It had become apparent that the kolkhoz could not continue operating as before under these circumstances (cf. Põder, Chapter 2). In the course of 1992 it became necessary to close some of the less profitable production units, one bullshed for instance, and a large number of workers were temporarily laid off, although this was due to internal as well external factors.

The political situation had also changed by this time. Estonia had regained independence, the pragmatic Popular Front government had fallen in January 1992, and parliamentary elections on 20 September 1992 brought the conservative Estonian Congress coalition to power under the leadership of Mart Laar of the Isamaa Party (the later chairman of Kanepi kolkhoz was also a member of Isamaa). The new government adopted an ultra-liberal economic policy.

In these circumstances the kolkhoz management returned, paradoxically enough, to the very same reform policy which it had criticised – and which had provided it, through opposition, with the opportunity to gain power. Nevertheless, the policy adopted in the quarrel concerning the workshares held good until the end, and the shares were calculated purely on the basis of workdays. Even before that, a special committee had already been established for the calculation and distribution of kolkhoz assets.

[Special] lists were stuck to the wall, [indicating] the share due to everybody, and people were summoned to a new meeting in [6] October 1992 at the end of the autumn work . . . At that October meeting we also elected a chairman . . . to the reform committee; the committee itself was appointed by the municipality . . . By that time that land reform had already become law . . . We did not want to break things up in such a way that everything . . . [the speaker left the sentence unfinished] . . . Cars, tractors and combine harvesters had been divided into four lots [according to location]. Kanepi was the largest, [items from it were further] divided into two lots, then came the Kooraste and Karste lots, like the old small kolkhozes from 1949-50. (Later chairman of the kolkhoz)

The return to the former chairman's reform plan was apparently a big surprise and it seems it was approved only because people were unprepared for such a move.

> To begin with, [the later chairman] promised that everything would go on as before, but soon all sort of things started to happen. First of all, they stopped raising bulls – it wasn't profitable anymore, or so they claimed. And other changes of the same sort followed . . . up until the [final] meeting. (A keeper of a bullshed)

As a result of the increasingly unfavourable economic environment, plus the disappearance and destruction of kolkhoz resources, there was soon a large number of unemployed people.

> My father had been without a job for one and a half years. (An interviewee from Kooraste)

Not only the agricultural units, but also other kolkhoz departments were cutting down on their workforce.

> When I was on holiday I received a letter saying that due to the dissolution of the collective farm I was dismissed from that day on. (Former manager of the kolkhoz construction team)

A kolkhoz worker summed up the situation: "Car drivers, tractor drivers, [those] pensioners who were still working, etc., were being laid off." In this manner, many people were temporarily dismissed and eventually ended up unemployed. But even those workers who kept their posts felt the imminent threat in a very concrete form. A milker said that the kolkhoz "had almost nothing [left]. Not even [enough] money to pay the wages [of the workers]."

The first new enterprises had already provided employment for their workers, too many of them, in fact. It was unrealistic to expect that the unemployed would find work in Kanepi.

The pensioners, too, felt that they were being ignored in the process. They felt that collective property was being passed into someone else's hands. Many of them had previously had part-time jobs in the kolkhoz and supplemented their income by farming a plot, both of which activities were dependent on the kolkhoz. In various ways they had enjoyed services and facilities, such as the delivery of firewood, provided under the system of patrimonial care. From the prospective new units they could not expect to gain anything, indeed they would lose their present benefits. As the former chairman put it:

> The biggest problem was that people felt uncertain of how they would manage. Take a tractor driver who gets a tractor and he can continue cultivating his [own] fields. But then there are these elderly people who have nothing to get by on.

All in all, old people together with other pensioners and unemployed persons made up the groups with the gloomiest prospects. Thus, first and foremost, the ordinary people were afraid, due to the accelerating economic decline of the kolkhoz economy.

> Everyone expected something from that meeting; nobody knew what was going to happen, if farm production would continue. People wanted this matter to be clarified. There were many people who hadn't had a job during the past year. At that time . . . you had to make it on your own, the state didn't give you much support . . . Most people were a bit afraid, because they didn't know what was going to happen: would you get a job or not. (Specialist with an intermediate education)

Rather than providing any concrete answers to these questions, the reform plan actually created further confusion. This is not surprising, since the situation left the specialists and even the government of the country equally perplexed.

> The professors were here several times. They had no recipe, they couldn't figure it out any better, and [matters were] not so clear to the government for that matter. They said that something should be done, and that as soon as the money stopped coming in we would certainly understand. [That] 'we must find the money.' It was so nicely formulated. (Former vice-chairman of the kolkhoz)

If the former kolkhoz vice-chairman had difficulties in understanding the situation, matters must have been all the more perplexing to the ordinary worker, who had nowhere to turn except the kolkhoz. A local amateur historian summed the matter up: "Up until that point the kolkhoz had been the single most important thing in providing people with work and bread."

The scientists from Tartu Agricultural University understood the overall economic situation and therefore tried to hasten the execution of the reform. It is difficult to estimate how much the appointment of the kolkhoz-hostile Laar government affected the scientists, the kolkhoz leadership and common people, but it is certain that the change in government did not further the preservation of the kolkhoz as an integral unit.

There seemed to be no alternative, except to betray this most important thing at the kolkhoz general meeting of 6 October 1992.

> And people accepted that at the meeting, but afterwards they were downhearted and despondent. There was no work left in the kolkhoz. It was the end ... It had become a habit [for us] to have a drink after a meeting, but this time everyone went straight home, and everyone was dead silent. (Later chairman of the kolkhoz)

As has been pointed out, the later chairman had pledged to preserve the kolkhoz by way of carrying out a modernising reform. Giving up the main objective of the "little revolution" in front of those very people to whom it had been proposed less than a year ago must have been a very painful experience. Visibly moved and with tears in his eyes, the later chairman summarised the general atmosphere and undoubtedly also his own impression of the meeting as follows:

> It was so awful it still brings tears to my eyes, [even] now [as we speak].

Thus, after the meeting was closed people isolated themselves from each other. Their reaction might partly reflect their low spirits but also, at a more general level, the helplessness that people felt.

> People had to face the fact that one era had come to an end, but what would take its place – not a word about that issue was spoken. (A local amateur historian)

As the social basis of community life collapsed, not only the kolkhoz economy but also many of the norms that had regulated people's lives broke down with it. In this situation it is no wonder that people's depression was connected to a process of demoralisation.

> After that nothing got done in the kolkhoz anymore, the fields were not ploughed. And since that autumn [there has been] widespread disappearance of materials, in other words: stealing. (Later chairman of the kolkhoz)

The depressing atmosphere and the swift collapse was in itself significant, since the reform plan had, so far, been accepted only on paper. When it came to the actual execution of the reform plan, a number of further practical problems arose. The reform plan was supposed to be put into practice through a series of meetings, to be held in each village. We shall look at what transpired in the following section.

The Reform Committee, Plans for Privatisation according to Book Values and the Rise of a New Opposition to the Reform Plans

The foundation of the *reform committee* on 15 September 1992 would at first glance seem like an important event in the rivalry of the various parties involved in reform politics. According to law the reform committee would consist of three representatives of the kolkhoz, three representatives of the municipality, three private farmers and 1–2 representatives of the state. All the parties were to pick their own representatives, but members of the kolkhoz board of management were forbidden to stand as kolkhoz representatives. The fact that the Kanepi kolkhoz reform committee was made up of only seven members (see Põder, Chapter 2) remains unexplained.

It must be remembered, however, that the reform plan was not drawn up by the reform committee but by the kolkhoz leadership; and after that it had been submitted to the kolkhoz general meeting (see Tamm, Chapter 8). The real executive authority of the committee was not distributed to the parties involved according to the original line-up; in Kanepi (as was mostly the case elsewhere) the executive authority appears to have slipped to the kolkhoz representatives. The former municipal director was not alone in this view:

> But what actually happened was that . . . the decision making shifted entirely to the kolkhoz and its members. (Former municipal director)

This shift of decision-making powers is largely explained by the expert knowledge of the kolkhoz representatives – the same reason why the kolkhoz leadership drew up the reform plan. Still, the identity of the chairman of the committee was not insignificant, since the kolkhoz chairman and the reform committee chairman would become very close working partners.

> [During the reform process, which ended at the dissolution of the kolkhoz,] everything was managed by the reform committee and the kolkhoz chairman – two men. In the end the two of us sat at our tables opposite each other and the secretary took down all our decisions and the orders were executed there and then. The two of us made all the decisions, whilst the reform committee was mostly made up of ill-informed people. The two of us made the decisions. (Later chairman of the kolkhoz)

The chairman of the reform committee in Kanepi was also a kolkhoz member; in fact, he was the kolkhoz warehouse manager. By education he was an agronomist and a teacher of physics. There appear to have been no significant conflicts between the two chairmen, so we may assume that the chairman of the reform committee and the kolkhoz board of management formed a relatively uniform power group. This was quite natural in view of his education, his work experience at the kolkhoz and the fact that in all likelihood the kolkhoz leadership supported him. All conflicts of interests and matters of principle (more about these later) were undoubtedly solved largely to the benefit of the kolkhoz leadership. By law the municipality bore the duty for the regulation of the reform, but in practice it was unable to exert any control.

> The local council once or twice participated at the meetings and they had the right to do so . . . [but] they were ignored. Conflicts arose and in the end they had to give up. (Former municipal director)

All concrete decisions by the reform committee also had to be passed by the municipal council. But the kolkhoz leadership had established a strong representation on the municipal council in the local elections.

> The kolkhoz bosses were members of the local council. They had their own interests [to look after] and they voted in favour of the decisions [they had themselves prepared at the reform committee]. There was no real control. The [actions of the] reform committee were approved. (Former municipal director)

There appear to have been very few hitches in the process of automatic approval. One of the problematic issues (and one which supports the view voiced by the former municipal director concerning the structural causes of the inadequate regulation by the municipal council) will be presented later. We did not study the internal dynamics of the reform committee and its relationship to the municipality in more detail. The principal rule was that the reform committees – as a former kolkhoz chairman summarised the matter – "did not do any good nor any harm for that matter to my personal plans."

A closer examination of the issue might bring forward some more interesting aspects. In this study we have focused on the decisions made within the kolkhoz, and on the basis of the factors described above we believe they were of greater significance than the activities of the reform committee.

The first local meetings dealing with the execution of the reform were held in Kooraste and Karste. The intention was to privatise the property apportioned to integral production units in the villages according to their book values.

Both villages, situated less than ten kilometres from the centre of Kanepi, are typical Estonian rural villages. The gently rolling landscape of Karste is characterised by islets of forest and patches of open field. In the centre of the village one can still see a nineteenth century manor house, and here and there one sees the old buildings typical of Estonian peasant farms, with attractive farmyards dominated by magnificent old ash trees. At the kolkhoz centre of Karste, as well as in the old estates of the German barons, large-scale farming was being practised in large cowshed complexes containing cowsheds, warehouses and other buildings dating from the Soviet period. The architecture and landscape of Kooraste is similar, but it does not show such clear evidence of ancient manorial traditions. Both of these villages, along with the complex in Kaagvere village, were relatively independent production units, with farming entrusted to separate work brigades.

Since the need for manpower in these villages exceeded the supply of labour that local families could offer, terraced houses and detached houses were constructed for workers who moved in from other areas. To a certain extent these newcomers led a separate life from the traditional inhabitants of the village, partly because they did not have their roots there, and partly because they were not even interested in becoming rooted there. The local population and the kolkhoz management called these people "migratory birds". They kept moving from one place to another and according to the opinion of the local population, their work ethics – and indeed their general moral outlook – left much to be desired.

To many of the villagers, and not least to the "migratory birds", it was very important to preserve the kolkhozes, or at least to keep the large-scale farming complexes as undivided as possible. This option was one of the starting points in both the former and the later chairman's reform policy. The problem for Karste and Kooraste was that many of the technical functions and premises were situated in the centre of Kanepi.

> Everything was in Kanepi: grain dryers, workshops, repair shops. If they don't start constructing [such amenities] here, then every single machine . . . must be taken to Kanepi for repair, and that costs money. Here we only had the production buildings, and we had to pay for the use of the grain dryer, the same as for everything else. Other brigades, except for Kanepi, had [absolutely] nothing. Everything had to be taken to Kanepi and we were billed for it. (Former bulltender in Karste)

People in the village centres were particularly concerned about the preservation of the cowshed complexes, but also about the machinery necessary for plot farming – to say nothing of those farmers who planned to cultivate their family estates. On the other hand, for many tractor and lorry drivers the only conceivable "meal ticket" in the future was to procure the machines for themselves. Integrating all these elements into a coherent reform plan must have been a demanding task. The chairman and the board of management were hoping to solve this equation, at least in part, by forming a number of co-operatives.

> As soon as we had finished allotting the machines, we began arranging meetings in the villages to find out who would be ready to set up a machine co-operative in that [particular] village, with such and such machines, and who would take charge of it. (Later chairman of the kolkhoz)

The first place where this matter was brought under consideration was the village of Kooraste.

> We started from Kooraste, got the negotiations over with, but the people didn't get it – that there was no kolkhoz any more – and what [to do] next, and how. (Ibid.)

The locals were confused, which was only natural in the situation, since the advice the chairman offered them on the basic issues remained vague and general in nature.

> There were many [open] questions to which I couldn't give any answers myself. I told them to take the machines home and to share them out among themselves [see above]. A common worker didn't understand that from that day on he could take that combine harvester and take it home with him, or what to do with it. They just couldn't comprehend it. (Ibid.)

The kolkhoz management could have done more to facilitate the execution of the plan, although building up a co-operative on the basis of the workshares must have been a demanding task. It was not, however, altogether impossible, at least in principle. Similar arrangements had been made in other parts of Estonia, and in fact one co-operative was about to be formed in the centre of Kanepi. People's reluctance may be explained by the direction the debate took at the Kooraste meeting.

> The first thing people wanted to settle [was] where to find horses. (Ibid.)

The chairman provided us with a logical explanation for this. Plot farmers and the future owners of small farms had no real interest in large machines, which were designed to be used for farming on an altogether different scale.

> At the end [of the kolkhoz era] those kolkhoz tractors were huge, they weighed many tonnes and were meant to be used on very large fields, and they consumed a lot of fuel. (Ibid.)

It is true that much of the kolkhoz technology was unsuitable for plot and small farming. But it seems that there were additional reasons why the distribution of machinery would have needed more precise "rules". There were fewer machines than people needing them; thus the acquisition of a machine was possible for only a few of the prospective buyers (Põder, Chapter 2). Furthermore, the moral implications of the question were problematic, too, since the machines had already been "earmarked", in a way, for the people who drove them. Some had even taken them home and regarded them as their own private property. To a certain extent these proprietary rights were recognised by outsiders as well. For instance, an electrician from Karste, who had come into possession of a small farm in the restitution, brought up the following argument in explaining why he chose not to take part in the kolkhoz auction, which was the next step of the reform:

> I didn't take part in the auction as a matter of principle. My point was that these tractors had been given to the tractor drivers; for them [they] were tools, they could find work in one [of the] co-operatives, and later on, offer their services [to us]. I didn't think I had any right, economically, to purchase a big tractor for a relatively small farm.

Apparently the machines in question had been handed over to their users at advantageous book values – even if the transaction took place only on paper for the time being. It is highly unlikely that everyone agreed to this, but trying to dispute the widely accepted principle in public would not have been easy either.

Under these circumstances a redistribution of kolkhoz resources would have been a destructive social process, both technically and in terms of being ethically inappropriate to the existing situation. The general disinclination towards dismantling the kolkhoz structure had already manifested itself during the reign of the former chairman, and it must always have been an important underlying factor. This is evident in numerous statements given by the kolkhozniks after the dissolution proper. A person from Kooraste who had later bought all the cowsheds of the village as his private possession, and who still belonged, despite his present hardships, to that part of the population that gained the most in the privatisation process, made the following statement:

> It may [well] be that the kolkhozes should have been left as they were, undivided. We should have remodelled the kolkhoz structure [there was too much wasteful spending, etc.]. We should have adapted the kolkhozes to the needs of modern people and modern production. Breaking them up was imposed on us; it was a command. It wasn't the will of the people.

The importance attached to the few remaining horses of the kolkhoz fits the picture. These horses would have been useful in small-scale, technically undeveloped farming. Moreover, giving away a horse would not have harmed the integrity of the kolkhoz in any way. But due to the mechanisation of production only a handful of horses remained at the kolkhoz and the later chairman remarked that they had already been "given away to people for use in their gardens [or plot farms]."

The newly launched attempt of the chairman to carry out the reform met with increasingly severe opposition in the villages.

> In Kooraste [the meeting] was dissolved, the issue was left open, and within a couple of days, we had [another] meeting in Karste . . . People were [well] prepared there, right at the beginning people took up the issue of the horses. They wanted to know where they were; the tractors didn't interest anybody. They were good for nothing. Then there was an argument; some people accused me of having sent [too] many old horses to the collective meat combine. People didn't [want to] calm down there, [and] it was dark already. I told them that this was neither the first nor the last meeting, that we should meet again. Nothing was resolved. There was some talk about forming a collective [co-operative], though, but what kind of a collective, with horses or machines, no one could tell.

The following meeting took place in the township of Kanepi, the population centre of the municipality. According to the initial plan the agricultural activities of Kanepi kolkhoz which were located in the municipal centre were to be divided into two, i.e., between two separate co-operatives. The village meetings had activated people, and now they had an opportunity to discuss the matter and think it over. In addition, the senior agricultural government official in the rayon and also the press had been summoned to the meeting.

At that point, people were [more] prepared, and the first question that came up in the meeting was who had given me the right to give away those machines as I did. The former head of the agricultural department of the rayon government . . . also shared the opinion that I shouldn't have promised those machines to anyone. I told that I hadn't, that I took no sides, that I had [people in] committees for that, [and that they were] all specialists. But what gives me the right to name one man for this or that? I told them that it's not me who names anybody, but [it is] the people [who choose machines]. But it didn't amount to anything, and there were plenty of accusations. So, it was decided that we must organise a general meeting where a new reform plan would be drafted for the division of the kolkhoz assets. And the crowd scattered, shouting [and] yelling, and that was it. (Later chairman of the kolkhoz)

At this meeting there was no general consensus. The problematic question concerning the machines became the central topic of the debate. People found a new common enemy: the new chairman, whose reform plan was now rejected. The meeting actually became a vote of no confidence in the new chairman, and perhaps also in the reform committee, which was responsible for the draft of the plan. But the general distrust of the chairman was the most important factor. Again, a date was set for a new meeting.

It was decided that I must arrange a new meeting on the 26th of February [1993]. It was settled [there], so [it was to be] within a couple of months. (Ibid.)

In their addresses to the meeting several speakers expressed their lack of confidence in the moral character of the chairman, together with the whole kolkhoz management.

It ended up with shouting and the screaming of accusations. People went crazy. Some of us [in the board of management] had already put small amounts of kolkhoz funds aside, and I was accused of having done that myself. At that time I hadn't taken anything, but later on others did, so I didn't just stand by and watch, either. (Ibid.)

As mentioned above, the large-scale theft of kolkhoz assets had already begun after the meeting of October 1992, since the unofficial minutes of the reform committee meeting in December include a comment on thieving (see Põder, Chapter 2). This phenomenon must also have been one of the reasons why the reform plan received such a cold welcome – all the more so, as it became evident that some individuals in the kolkhoz management were involved in this. Thus, it is necessary to examine more closely this phenomenon of widespread thieving, which started well before the actual reform took place.

Public Thieving and the Moral Bankruptcy of the Board of Management

The future of Estonian collective agriculture had already been called into question in the late 1980s, when the first new peasant farms were established and legislation was passed to allow the expansion of the traditional plot farms. The general principle was that the new farms would get a considerable amount of material as well as other types of support from the collective farms.

A substantial part of this support consisted of serviceable machines, often acquired for "the price of a sandwich", since they had already lost most of or all their book value. According to an expert cited earlier, most of them are still in active use "today" (cf. Põder, Chapter 2).

Since the proprietors of these private holdings were, for the most part, kolkhoz and sovkhoz workers, they probably took advantage of other collective resources in the same manner as the traditional plot farmers. In other words, the symbiosis that had gradually developed between large-scale and small-scale production was extended to embrace small farms much larger in acreage than previously. Certain aspects of this development could have, within the former socialist camp, parallels with the Hungarian model (Alanen, 1996). Even though the establishment and expansion of the family farms took place within the limits of the collective farm system, the process to a certain extent exceeded these limits, and eventually a conflict arose between the two systems (see Figure 3.2).

It is quite understandable that the customary "stealing" (this expression was used by both the new private farmers and the former chairman) of collective property should assume larger proportions and gradually turn into stealing in the proper sense of the word. This phenomenon is likely to have gained more and more ground as the new small producers learned how to do business within the framework provided by the old system. The interviews themselves give no direct proof of an increased transfer of collective resources into private hands. Nevertheless, there are two factors that attest to this possibility. Firstly, the executives of Taluliit (Estonian Farmers' Federation) seem to have contributed to the success of their own estates in this manner. They transferred to themselves some of the machinery that their colleagues in neighbouring countries had donated to Estonia.

Everything [I have at my place] is foreign [Western] technology, except the tractors. (A modern family farmer)

This phenomenon is common knowledge in Estonia, and it kept coming up in the interviews.

Of course there are also those kinds of farms, but only a few are profitable. Those [farmers] are . . . big bosses in Taluliit, who've managed to get a lot of machinery. (A Kanepi entrepreneur whose area of operation extends beyond the borders of the municipality)

If one were not a member of the Taluliit leadership, acquiring a piece of equipment donated by farmers in the Nordic countries to the Taluliit organisation often proved difficult.

One time the Danes sent us [free] ploughs, and they [the Danes] also took care of the [transportation and] unloading of the cargo at the port; but once the ploughs had been two days on Estonian soil their asking price had risen to 800 kroons. (A family farmer)

Secondly, some kolkhoz employees started active preparations for the post-collective period. This is described by a person who, in total secrecy, started to build up a business for himself.

It was as clear as daylight that the collectives would break up [one day] . . . There had been a turnover in the chairmanship . . . and nobody took [any real] interest in anything, and there were signs of everybody starting to cast sullen glances at each other. We had no specific conversations about the breaking up of the collective farms, [there were] just those [general] signs. I was on holiday and after that I took unpaid personal leave and refurbished this shop so that no one in the house even knew what I was doing there.

Another kolkhoz employee and his friend had discovered that they were gradually able to buy less and less of various kinds of materials with their wages, so they decided to invest in these materials.

We had money, because already at the last stage of socialism, as we were building that garage, one could tell that something was about to happen. And so we didn't take money wages for our work [with the kolkhoz construction service], but started to bring in timber [instead]. I had great piles of planks beside my house. After the monetary reform [in the summer of 1992] no one had

> money anymore . . . We managed to sell the timber . . . and that's how we got some money. (An owner of a car repair shop)

What is noteworthy in this example is that the materials were not purchased directly for the needs of a future enterprise – for the repair of a building or as raw materials for a carpenter's workshop – but rather as an investment, where the goods not only retained their value but also yielded a profit. The capital that was raised in this manner could then be reinvested as the initial capital of a new enterprise. One can assume that a great deal of the property obtained from the kolkhoz was converted into cash and reinvested or spent. In a third case, an individual was planning to re-establish an old family farm.

> I studied in Tartu for three or four years. Then I worked for six years as a mechanic in a collective farm. Then came the period during which you had to take up something [new], or else your relatively high [university level agricultural engineer] education would soon be of no value. It was clear to me that the collective farm would break up . . . During [the last years of] the collective farm my grandparents had [set up a family] estate of 40 hectares. I planned that when the collective farm would be dissolved I'd become a farmer. I had three tractors and a couple of other machines, which I had bought during the Soviet era. (Current shopkeeper)

Our fourth example, a person who belonged to the top management of the kolkhoz, was establishing his own shop.

> There was a time during which you could take objects into your own possession. If you let it [the opportunity] slip from your hands, you never got the same opportunity again. (Kolkhoz mechanic, who started setting up a retail shop six months prior to the dissolution of the kolkhoz)

It was possible for everybody to prepare for the future, but no one, not even the kolkhoz management, could have any certainty as to what the future would bring.

> It wasn't like that, the way some people say that all the executives took the best parts, the better stuff for themselves . . . They had the opportunity to steal and they were human like everybody else, they were anxious about the future. Perhaps they got more assets for themselves than an ordinary worker, but it wasn't that bad. A couple of years before the breaking up of the kolkhoz they had the chance to buy cheap machines and equipment. They set up a business. They used their connections and bought all that equipment with the money they'd earned. [As the reform advanced] they already had something set aside.

> In principle, everybody had the [same] opportunity to buy machines from the depot, or elsewhere, from the factories. At that time they were a bargain. For example, a T-25 tractor would cost 3,000 to 4,000 roubles in those days. Now it is priced at 40,000 Estonian kroons. (Present owner of a large farm)

Preparations were made all across Kanepi to set up both agricultural and other types of enterprises, but evidently under conditions of great uncertainty. The examples above principally illustrate the period, which began before the discouraging meeting of October 1992. The interviews do not always reveal the sources from which these people had obtained their assets. During this period it was, nevertheless, possible to buy from the kolkhoz all sorts of material at book values, including tractors. In addition to this one may assume that the people of the kolkhoz also practised their customary less-than-strict ways with kolkhoz property.

In the light of our overall interview data it seems that the fourth interviewee cited above has underestimated the role of the top executives in the appropriation of collective resources especially after the meeting of October 1992. The interviews with both the kolkhoz management and the ordinary employees consistently bear evidence to that. As far as blatant theft is concerned it was not the managers collectively, but a select group among them – namely the board – which were in the most advantageous position.

> There were 350 workers [in the kolkhoz], and only ten of them had any chance of getting their hands on the funds. The group was small enough so that if they planned something among themselves, it didn't leak to outsiders. (Agronomist X)

The collapse in morals appears to have been closely linked with a sense of the imminent dissolution of the kolkhoz. Increased thieving had first been observed as far back as 1990 (Põder, Chapter 2) when the romantic debate calling for the re-establishment of peasant farms had started at national level. In Kanepi the thieving became systematic during the period when the two reform plans were drawn up.

However, as the last two chairmen agree, "the biggest collapse in general morals took place after that meeting, when those who held office, [the ones who were] in the management, and after that everyone else took for themselves what they could get" (former chairman). During the course of the village meetings "some people had already put aside kolkhoz funds" (later chairman). In other words, it was a question of the core of the board making large-scale preparations for the break-up of the kolkhoz, as many of the interviewees attest. It was this core group that presided over the kolkhoz development office.

> They had information, they had power. There were plenty of grey areas in which there were no clear definitions or ownership relations. At the kolkhoz development office they had the chance to speculate, to take something from collective resources for instance. Whoever got there became a big boss. Ordinary people didn't have a clue about all that. A common procedure was to invalidate certain resources, to cancel their very existence. (A long-serving municipal official)

Underlying these events was the collapse of the previous control system, already described in detail above.

> There were stocks worth about three million [roubles in warehouses], but later on the accounts got so tangled that no one could tell the overall picture any more, and that provided ample opportunities for misappropriation. (Former chairman of the kolkhoz)

Many interviewees shared the opinion that new computer software facilitated the deliberate mixing up of the books.

> With the machines there was plenty of room for manoeuvres, there were machines which were withdrawn [from use], machines which were registered and those which were not, until it got so completely confused that there was no making sense of it any longer. And when the books were transferred to the computer, in the final days of the kolkhoz, those diskettes had a tendency to disappear, to get mixed up, etc. The old accountants retired or just left, and then all kinds of things started happening. (Former chairman of the kolkhoz)

The future chairman of Kanepi co-operative was referring to one such occurrence in the following statement.

> I didn't have a clue as to all the things that might have been in the bookkeepers' accounts, we didn't get all those things that should have come to us, they'd gone elsewhere, and nobody exactly knew where they went. For example, we bought the spare parts warehouse, and there should have been a list [of all the items] in the warehouse, but it [either the computer or a diskette] had broken down, so we had no way of finding out what kinds of things were supposed to be in store there. (Agronomist X, then chairman of the new co-operative established in connection with the privatisation of Kanepi kolkhoz)

This observation draws attention to the systematic actions of the kolkhoz board of management, or rather some of its members. In early 1992 the kolkhoz had made a conspicuously large bulk purchase of spare parts. The sum of money spent on acquiring spare parts amounted to 71% of the gross kolkhoz wages for the first nine months of 1992 (Põder, Chapter 2). It is plausible that at this point the inevitability of kolkhoz dissolution was recognised by the board and that they availed themselves of the opportunity – spare parts were easily movable and they might get "displaced" (stolen) and they constituted a kind of liquid assets.

Before the major auctions, which we will discuss later, there were a number of minor auctions putting up for sale all sorts of items, things such as kolkhoz tableware, clothing, etc.

> There was some intrigue going on. No one knew exactly how much money there was. Things were moved from one auction to another. There were rumours that such and such things had already been sold. There were auctions with only two men present. (Municipal councillor)

Bedclothes, for instance, were sold in the following manner:

> There was this lady in charge of the privatisation of the kolkhoz organisation's bedcovers . . . They were sold at bargain prices. Sheets for a couple of kroons, bedcovers for six [kroons]. Those things had been bought during the rouble era. (A local amateur historian)

The basic rule was simple:

> Whoever had an opportunity [i.e., who belonged to the management], took it. Bought cheaper than the others. (Vice-chairman of the kolkhoz during the previous board of management)

Ordinary kolkhozniks made their own observations and were able to describe many concrete examples in convincing detail in the course of the interviews.

> Yes, it was quite common for the bosses to take the articles they wanted, even before the auction. Take the feed distributor from our cowshed, the machine sent to an auction just disappeared. Who else could have taken [all] those machines but the old bosses? They shared many things among themselves . . . [Then] there was this case with the milking machines, which was much the same. The chief cattle-breeding technician ordered them to be moved from Karste to the central warehouse in Kanepi. Shortly after that they simply disappeared from there . . . I was the one who actually transported these machines to the centre of Kanepi

because I'd been told that they would be auctioned. But when the time came for the auctions those machines had gone. How? Where? (A milker from Karste)

On the whole:

> The board had every chance and the workers none. They [the board of management] took everything for themselves. Whereas the ordinary people didn't get anything. (A milker from Kanepi)

Although the misappropriations carried out by the board were undoubtedly large, this is not to say that they would have been the only group involved, as one can clearly see from the interviews cited above. The logic of thieving was quite simple. The board of management had by far the most power, but also the specialists had far better opportunities than the ordinary employees to witness the measures taken at the centre of power, and closer contacts at a personal level.

> A person who takes [steals] himself won't blame another and say: 'Why did you take that?' (Former chairman of the kolkhoz)

The advantageous position of the specialists lay in their connections with the board and the knowledge gained in their profession. That is why thieving inevitably spread beyond the actual nucleus of power. Yet not everyone participated in it, and from certain people the possibility was blocked altogether.

> As for me, personally, I'd worked here since the early days of the kolkhoz, but I didn't get a thing in the distribution of the kolkhoz assets. I couldn't tell [for sure], but I suppose one had to have friends in high places. The kolkhoz chairman, for example. If you were in good terms with him, you had many opportunities to acquire and start up a business. (A former member of the kolkhoz management, removed from the board for being loyal to the former chairman)

To a certain extent ordinary people, too, participated in the thieving. However, their thieving was confined to smaller objects, such as spare parts or tyres.

> At that time there was plenty of traffic going on . . . in things which were then traded. For a bottle of liquor you could get a tyre for example. (Later chairman of the kolkhoz)

Some of the ordinary employees from Kanepi appear to have sold semi-precious metals that might have been stolen from the kolkhoz on their own account. A Kanepi interviewee who was in the semi-precious metals business was able to obtain large amounts of these materials from the local markets. He also bought a lot of metal from Russia. Although the value of many individual items was not in itself comparable to the value of tractors, other types of machinery, or entire consignments of stored material, their overall contribution to the collapse of the technical system might have been equally significant.

It has to be borne in mind that although in the countryside many of the items traded or sold came from the kolkhozes, many could have originated from an industrial collective. The source of an item did not necessarily lie with the local kolkhoz at all. Many different types of commercial activities and markets developed on the basis of goods that had been "bought" (at book values) and goods that were downright stolen.

> [Property] had been taken everywhere. What the shops could sell was sold, what they couldn't was passed to another co-operative [enterprise], another man [somewhere] down the line, who then took the truckload of bale string or whatever you have. There were many different options, but [of course I have] no definite details [on the trading of stolen goods]. Still, tractors and cultivating machines mostly stayed within the agricultural branch. (Former chairman of the kolkhoz)

The amount of property transferred from the kolkhoz into private hands must have been considerable even at this "pre-privatisation" stage, although for bookkeeping reasons alone it is highly unlikely that anyone will ever be able to come up with exact figures.

However, there appears to have been at least one partially documented case. The municipality had purchased the district heating plant from the kolkhoz and after this acquisition the then municipal director noticed that the accounts on the use of heating oil had been falsified. Later he told us that he believed the missing heating oil had been used for the heating of detached houses acquired by kolkhoz board members.

Some of the beneficiaries at this stage used these assets to prepare for starting up a private business; others used what they had gained on personal consumption. It is likely that a number of cars were purchased this way. Perhaps the later chairman, as he claims, did not take part in the thieving when it started. Nevertheless, the entire board of management fell into disrepute because of this moral issue.

The very same board members [as before the 'little revolution' which had led to the dismissal of the former chairman] were renamed managers of [kolkhoz] departments. They were in favour of privatisation, and were seeking to take what they could from the others for their own benefit. They had shared the kolkhoz out among themselves, so to speak. Other people felt that all those managers were not [the types of] people that would act with clean hands. (An agronomist)

Essentially, the chairman himself and the whole attempt of reform had fallen into disgrace. In a way it was a question of a natural conflict between two ideals: the section within the Estonian Congress now aiming at the breaking up of large-scale farms had, paradoxically enough, gained power with a programme of maintaining the general structure of the kolkhoz. The Estonian Congress contained not only defenders of the heritage of the first Estonian republic but also people advocating an ultra-liberal economic policy. After the village meeting in Kanepi, the one that had set a date for the following meeting, which was to take place on 26 February 1993, the position of the later chairman became extremely difficult.

I had already lost my popularity by then. [The former chairman] broke the kolkhoz apart, I was elected to save it, and there I was, breaking it into pieces. (Later chairman of the kolkhoz)

The former municipal director suggested that the abandonment of the programme aiming at the preservation of the kolkhoz as an integral unit marked the start of a series of "wet parties" arranged by the kolkhoz board of management for themselves. No compromises were made on the quantity and quality of the alcohol served, and some people drew the conclusion that this was one way of disposing of the remaining kolkhoz funds.

The growing unpopularity of the later chairman became manifest in a most striking manner in the nomination of the chairman for the future reform meeting: the former kolkhoz chairman was chosen for the post. This is not to say that all the kolkhozniks were against the later chairman and the board. On the contrary, many people who were looking forward to the restitution of small farms saw him as an ideological ally.

[The later chairman] was in favour of restitution. (A pensioner who had got his family farm back in the restitution)

Furthermore, he also had some supporters among those specialists who did not belong to the core of power.

It was not [the later chairman's] fault that the kolkhoz got broken into pieces. (Owner of a large-scale farm)

A great deal of the thieving took place within the limits of the law, in the sense that even in those cases where law was clearly being violated, no attempts were made to take legal action against the offender. When the ordinary workers were asked in the interviews to give an explanation for their silence on these matters, their answers reveal that their position during the breaking up of the kolkhoz was just as powerless and peripheral as it had been during the kolkhoz period.

It was not a subject for open discussion . . . But people had fears of some sort. It's hard to say. [The reason] might be [that they were depressed]. Nobody knew in what manner the kolkhoz was to be dissolved. And then came feelings of depression, because a private person couldn't get anything for himself. Nobody cared about [these] resources anymore: they didn't belong to the kolkhoz any longer, and they didn't belong to me. So it didn't make any difference what happened next. (A keeper of the kolkhoz bullshed)

We'd been brought up in a different way during the socialist era, and then there was fear. At home you could say what you liked, but not anywhere else. And on the other hand, no one wanted to take any responsibility for that mess. A lawsuit would have taken quite a lot of [one's] time; I would have lost my nerves, my family and me. And what's more, I [really] don't think that it would have made much difference [anyway], if I'd reported an offence. (A kolkhoz electrician)

But the course of events during the dissolution did in fact change slightly due to the counter-reaction to the thieving by the management. The idea behind the reform attempts of both chairmen had been to divide the kolkhoz into three or four village-based co-operatives by privatising the remaining assets at book values. The alternative of privatisation through auction was now brought up, but in order to fully understand the outcome, it is necessary to make a closer analysis of the formation of interest groups among the kolkhoz members. At the same time one has to keep in mind the national economic situation, which was becoming increasingly unfavourable to agricultural production.

Auctions as a Compromise between Different Interest Groups

The village meetings arranged in the kolkhoz probably facilitated a clearer identification by kolkhoz members of where their interests lay. An interviewee from Kooraste estimated that the later chairman listened to people's opinions and did indeed try to take them into account in his proposals for action.

> I'm convinced that he found the best possible solution for the dissolution of the kolkhoz. Everything had [already] been decided at higher levels [i.e., the government]. With these meetings [the later chairman] tried to find out what the people wanted. Our present situation is a result of that: [we now have] the joint stock companies and the co-operatives. He shouldn't be blamed for anything. (A specialist with an intermediate education)

The underlying factors behind the "little revolution" did not simply involve a lack of confidence in the board, but also conflicting interests with regard to the reform plan. One should bear in mind that the interest of the specialist and machine drivers, which was to preserve as large a kolkhoz unit as possible, had been the most important driving force behind the "little revolution".

It is hard to tell exactly how stable this agglomeration of interests remained during the period of "widespread thieving". The board of management, in particular, as well as the circle of specialists close to the board, were able to obtain a large amount of machines, equipment, spare-parts, fuel, etc. One would assume that the interests of the members of the board and the core of the reform committee at that point separated from the interests of the specialists and the machine drivers.

> In my opinion the board members [gained the most]. That close circle of friends: specialists and managers. (A local amateur historian)

> These people were 'right next to the pump' [*pumba juures*], and the chief 'pumpman' among them all was the kolkhoz chairman. (Former municipal director)

It would be naive to think that the board of management simply aimed at executing the agenda dictated by its opposition background and by local public opinion. In any case, there was no unified public opinion, although most people on the whole supported the preservation of the kolkhoz as a single unit. Different people – specialists, tractor drivers, people living in old family farm homesteads and ordinary workers who had just recently moved into the municipality – most certainly attached different meanings to the term "preservation". Tractor drivers and specialists would have preferred maintaining the kolkhoz as a large-scale production unit for an indefinite period of time, while ordinary workers and especially the members of Kaitseliit and other nationalist organisations probably only wanted to delay the breaking up of the kolkhoz.

> The majority of the people were in favour of breaking up the kolkhoz in a different way: in several stages, which would correspond to the [unspecified] 'economic stages' of the kolkhoz. But that kind of a process would have taken a lot of time. (A kolkhoz electrician)

The board members were also well aware of how difficult the situation had become for any profitable agribusiness, and they had already started considering alternative options. During the reign of the later kolkhoz chairman the board or at least its core formed a group characterised by many locals as a "secret society".

> Our company was founded [about a month after the decision to auction kolkhoz assets was made], but we had already discussed and negotiated the matters among ourselves from the turn of the year . . . The six of us had made future plans for the [use of the] tractor depot, etc. (Later chairman of the kolkhoz)

The excerpt above illustrates how the core of the board had started preparations for the kolkhoz dissolution well before the issue was brought forward for public debate. What actually did and did not occur during this period of time will remain pure conjecture. Anyhow, this period preceding the kolkhoz auction was the most opportune moment for transferring kolkhoz property into private hands, especially those assets that could later be utilised in non-agricultural enterprises (e.g. tractors and cars) or assets that could be easily liquidated (e.g. spare-parts and fuel) to facilitate investments in a new business or as its working capital.

The later chairman's company was called MTJ (derived from *masina-traktorijaam*, i.e., Machine and Tractor Station) and the six owners displayed especially great interest in the forestry business; initially they had been more interested in agriculture, but they pulled out of that sector as they became doubtful of its profitability.

> We focused on timber trading from the start. Agriculture was just a sideline. It was supposed to provide the flour for our bakery. If everything had gone according to our plans at that time, we would have sown on our fields. [But] agriculture has been the cause of the failure of Kanepi co-operative [currently the largest enterprise in Kanepi]. If we had taken up agriculture, we would be in trouble too. (Later chairman of the kolkhoz)

As MTJ took up production and public operations after the auction, farming no longer played any part in their plans, and the company profile was reoriented.

> Initially our aim was to repair agricultural machinery, make agricultural field machinery, cut timber, process timber and set up a bakery. (Ibid.)

The formation of the new profile of the company was, however, also influenced by the outcome of the auction – the owners of MTJ did not manage to acquire all the production facilities they had desired. Anyhow, these plans devised by the then kolkhoz chairman and his allies illustrate the point that the top kolkhoz management recognised the economic decline of agriculture and were disengaging themselves from it. Probably this also paved the way for the dissolution of the kolkhoz.

Perhaps the possibilities for gain explain why the specialists were no longer as hostile as they had been initially towards the reform plan originally proposed by the former chairman. The opinions of the agronomist who had been a member of the reform committee might in fact reflect a more general the change of opinion among the specialists. (But note that this change did not reflect the thinking of those specialists who had the closest contacts with the board and who had already resorted to activities more lucrative than agriculture.)

> During the kolkhoz times we had three departments ['brigades'], where every-one lives, in Kaagvere, Kooraste, and so on. I thought [that] the kolkhoz assets should be divided among them, according to the areas. The cowsheds [are there and] the men are there, [so] let us share the land and the funds equally [between the villages and brigades]. (A member of the reform committee, representative of the kolkhoz, future employee of the Kanepi neo-collectivist co-operative)

In this model the machines would have belonged to independent local complexes, in which case their maintenance and functioning could have been secured. In the new smaller units there were only a few posts available for specialists and managers, and therefore only a small segment of the educated specialists could pin their hopes on them.

Perhaps the drivers were reassured by the fact that they were allowed to take the machines home as if they owned them, and "they also hoped to get these vehicles for themselves," said the later chairman.

However, the auction would prove the hopes of this faction to be an illusion (more about the fate of the cars, tractors, etc. later). All those who were either planning to make a career outside agriculture, or who were going to exchange the property purchased by vouchers at the auction into cash on the open market, were interested in exactly the same property. One of the interested parties was the MTJ company. Moreover, the small-scale agricultural producers, whether current or prospective producers, were not ready to renounce their claim on the machines and other technical implements in favour of either the new large complexes or the tractor drivers. It is quite understandable that in addition to the land that was being restituted, the restituees "also wanted to get back machines and other implements," as agronomist X said to the researchers.

In principle, the dissolution of the kolkhozes could have been carried out on terms set by the small farmers – in which case the kolkhoz assets could have been interpreted as profit yielded by the appropriated (collectivised) private property, restricting the sale of machines and implements to these small farmers (cf. Tamm, Chapter 8). A member of the reform committee who entertained plans to re-establish the restituted estate of his grandparents was typical in holding this view. His personal dislike of the new large-scale units was so overwhelming that he called them all kolkhozes, despite the fact that only one of them actually became legally a co-operative, while the others were set up as private farms.

> I represented the municipality in this reform committee. I was personally against the reform. In my opinion the committee members were [just] playing with the property of those people who once laid the foundation of the kolkhoz. The members of this commission wanted to get hold of the assets that [rightfully] belonged to these people. Now [that the reform has been accomplished] the farm is divided into three pieces – it only amounts to three little 'kolkhozes.' [When in fact] the kolkhoz should have been broken up into pieces and all of its assets auctioned. As it is, people lived for 50 years in a situation where someone always told them what to do. Now it is exactly the same in these three [remaining] 'kolkhozes'. The kolkhoz property should have been sold in lots as small as possible, and if someone then wanted to establish some sort of a small kolkhoz with other people, and continue that way, it would have been a different matter altogether. Today, the co-operatives are only held together by the property they were given. Now they [just] keep wasting those assets, until there's nothing left. And eventually everyone will have to go. (A member of the reform committee, representative of the municipality)

Along with decline in the general conditions for agriculture, the stealing and destruction stirred up more and more discontent among the people.

A cowshed in Vana-Karste was in operation for more than ten years, now it's [been] closed. Another cowshed in Kaagvere kept going for only a year. And within a very short period of time many cowsheds have been closed down. The main reason: the board left, took for themselves whatever was available, and what remains is in poor shape. (Former manager of the kolkhoz electricity works)

This brought about a conflict among people, those who were no longer working and who were on a pension, and a section of those [people] who were capable of working. They [the former groups] didn't get [or need] any machines, and [hence] they wanted to divide out all the assets at auction. (Kolkhoz agronomist)

Within the kolkhoz, people tried to find another option. Agronomist X in particular, who had been one of the key opposition figures when the former chairman had been drafting the first reform plan, was once again very active. He had no position in the inner circle of either of the kolkhoz boards. Nor is there any evidence of his participation in the actions of the former organised opposition. Instead, he seems to have been a keen observer of different interests, and a skilful inventor of alternative plans of action. He also seems to have enjoyed considerable support among the people, and eventually he ended up as the manager of the largest farm in Kanepi, the agricultural co-operative in the central village.

In my opinion [there was] one man who made a difference to the people by raising the advantages of an alternative model [alternative to the later chairman's model]. He's the manager of the Kanepi unit [neo-collectivist co-operative] here. He wanted to be completely fair and square with everything he did. He wanted people to get back everything they were entitled to. But it's impossible to draw that kind of a line, someone would [always] be left without restituted funds, or would have been forced to relinquish his share to some enterprise. He didn't want that [to happen]. As a result we didn't succeeded in dividing the kolkhoz [resources simply] in four parts. (Owner of a cowshed complex in another village)

The decision to choose auctions as the method by which privatisation was to be realised cannot, on the basis of the interviews, be linked to any particular person. Prior to the decollectivisation people were reluctant to speak to each other and very confused about the changes. However, the arrangements at the beginning of the meeting of 26 February 1993 implied a clear vote of non-confidence in the later chairman.

I was supposed to open the meeting and pick the persons who would preside over the meeting, the chairman, the keeper of the minutes, and so forth. And then people elected the former [kolkhoz] chairman [to chair the general assembly] by common consent. [Professor] Mati Tamm explained to people what it was all about, what would happen and that it was inevitable. We presented the reform plan, people understood that it was a scheme for carrying out a reform, but they didn't get the substance [of it], and didn't understand why the assets had to be divided by an auction. They were happy with the method by which the workshares were calculated [by workdays]. A new thing that was brought up was that the price of some small article could climb really high, if there were many people interested in it, and that's just what happened. Mati Tamm explained how a Savings and Loan Association worked. (Later chairman of the kolkhoz)

Although the auction solution obviously was something quite unfamiliar to most of the kolkhozniks, we can perhaps agree with the evaluation of agronomist X, that it was understood as a compromise between the private farmers and the kolkhoz departments. Nevertheless, the interviewees almost without exception emphasised that from the standpoint of a kolkhoz member everything happened far too quickly. This might be due to the fact that the issue was never adequately discussed. Perhaps the "little revolution" carried out in the name of preserving the kolkhoz had forestalled the discussion of feasible alternatives – such as the model offered by the Põlva co-operative for example – in public debate.

Still, it must be remembered that events were happening quickly on a national scale, too. It was all the harder for the kolkhoz to cope with the unforeseen nation-wide economic collapse, and the collapse in morals, which merely became more acute as time passed. "The auction became 'a must' after the rumour spread that too much was going in the pockets of the bosses," pointed out the former municipal director, explaining the basic causes behind the collapse in morale. "There was no discipline left whatsoever in the final days of the kolkhoz," commented a milker.

Our study has only superficially touched upon the subject of Kalev kolkhoz, the other kolkhoz in the same municipality, and on the basis of our data it is impossible to form any coherent picture of the course that events took there. However, it is clear that the dissolution of the kolkhoz could not be postponed there, either. The question of the methods of achieving this, auction or otherwise, became a central issue in Kalev as it did in Kanepi. In Kalev kolkhoz the dissolution process, however, resulted in the preservation of technologically more viable production units furnished with the necessary machinery and facilities.

When the final breaking up of Kanepi kolkhoz was at hand, the reform committee would have preferred not to proceed with the auction directly.

They wanted to leave the door open to the possibility of a consensus in dividing the assets, to prevent prices from rising excessively. The idea was that by putting together their vouchers, a group of buyers could still get the articles they wanted at book values. How to organise the negotiative and conciliatory proceeding which would have been a prerequisite for this option was not specified. In the final analysis, it may be that irrespective of all the confusion concerning the auction system, conflicting interests and the general suspicion of the kolkhoz board of management were so high that a straightforward auction was the only outcome people would accept.

> The participants at the big meeting insisted on . . . that everything be put up for auction. An auction means the highest bidder [gets the article]. (Later chairman of the kolkhoz)

The same meeting decided on the relative proportions of the assets that were to be auctioned and those that would be reserved for restitution. There were some problems, though. For example, those who had lost their property in the collectivisation had been awarded compensation amounting to 190,000 roubles during the former chairman's period, but the new currency, the Estonian kroon (EEK), had been introduced since then.

> The general meeting . . . resolved that 190,000 roubles would equal 190,000 kroons. We had no other choice. (Later chairman of the kolkhoz)

Some other remuneration was made as well. Considering the matter as a whole, this extra remuneration was of minor importance. Nevertheless, the phenomenon deserves to be described as a detail illustrating the general atmosphere in Estonian society at that moment:

> [The former chairman] gave one tractor [as compensation], too . . . The man [whose tractor had been forcefully collectivised in the late 1940s] was very interested [in getting a more modern tractor in compensation]. So he dug up some proof of ownership and produced a paper, to document that it [the tractor] hadn't been given up voluntarily, but that it had been taken at gunpoint . . . That man [the man whose tractor was collectivised] had a document dating from the period [of forced collectivisation], he laid the paper on the table at the party committee and [finally the former chairman] released a tractor. (Later chairman of the kolkhoz)

The Auction Strategy of the Kolkhoz Leadership and the Tactics of Other Interest Groups

In Chapter 8 Professor Mati Tamm argues that delays in the decollectivisation process may have resulted from the interests of the kolkhoz and the political elite, not only in the kolkhoz of Kanepi, but also in the whole of Estonia. Some farmers of course required more time to set up their farms, but the delays also served the purposes of persons capable of transferring the resources of the kolkhoz to themselves, i.e., the kolkhoz leadership.

To the great majority of kolkhoz employees the dissolution of the enterprise was simply terrifying: as far as they could see, there was nothing positive to be expected from it. Moreover, the whole process remained to a considerable extent unstructured in the minds of the people. In the light of the Kanepi material it appears that the two kolkhozes in the municipality were not broken up until compelled by absolute necessity, and many other kolkhozes in the country were not even able to keep pace with Kanepi. However, it is arguable that even though the pace of Kanepi may have appeared far too brisk from the viewpoint of ordinary kolkhoz members, any slow-down – for the reasons we have discussed in connection with our case in Kanepi – would simply have meant a further deepening of all the problems.

In preparation for the privatisation of the kolkhoz, its total assets had been valued at 4,000,000 million kroons (EEK). This figure was a book value, in which the wear and tear on all pieces of property as shown by the books (depreciation) was taken into account. However, book values were fundamentally affected by the Estonian monetary reform: the earlier values in roubles were converted into kroons (EEK) by equating 10 Russian roubles (RUB) with one Estonian kroon (EEK). Thus one could claim that any privatisation based on book values denoted the privatisation of kolkhoz property at substantially undervalued prices. The portion of the assets not earmarked for restitution to the pre-collectivisation owners and their heirs was divided among all present and former kolkhoz workers in the form of share vouchers, whose face value had been calculated according to the workdays they had accumulated over the years. The value of one workday was set at 60 cents (EEK 0.6).

Although the kolkhoz general meeting had agreed upon auction as the appropriate method for the last stage of privatisation, there remained the task of turning the decision into a concrete auction strategy; in part this was determined by the law, and in part by the kolkhoz leadership and the reform committee. These definitions of policy were by no means neutral from the perspective of the people entitled to either restitution or participation in the auction. Among other things, carrying out the auction called for answers to the following questions:

- how to group the property that was to be privatised into lots ("objects");
- how to determine minimum bids and the sequence of the auction;
- how and in which order the unrestituted and uncompensated pieces of nationalised property would be restituted or compensated for at the final stage of privatisation;
- what the auction timetable would be;
- who would be entitled to participate in the auction (Would it be only "entitled subjects"? Would it be individuals in person or also their authorised representatives? Only authorised voucher recipients or also people who had bought vouchers from others?);
- how voucher trading would be organised (Without any control or under the supervision of the municipality, for example?);
- how the auction purchases would be paid for (By vouchers or in cash? On credit or not?).

The decisions made provided for the interests of different social groups participating in the auction, but with varied success. Although many social groups certainly shared parallel interests, people's overall comprehension of the situation varied, and accordingly their auction tactics took different forms. In any case, the auction should not be viewed solely as a conflict between different private interests. People's ability to recognise their own interests varied greatly, and these interests were not by any means unambiguous: Estonia was not a stable country at the time, but a society undergoing tempestuous and upsetting changes, in which any preparations for the future were on shaky ground.

A great deal also depended on the ideology embraced by each individual and the social networks linking an individual to his or her fellow-citizens. The social network of a person who was both a specialist and a member of the board of management was quite different from the network of the ordinary specialist, not to mention the networks of tractor drivers or private farmers. Moreover, each department (e.g. the planning department, the tractor station, a cowshed or a brigade) exerted a lot of influence on its members and provided them with more or less individual trump cards. For example, specialists working in the planning department, such as accountants and economists, possessed a lot of strategic information, even if they were not members of the board of management. Pensioners, of course, principally remained outside the crucial networks. Another factor that played a great role was the residential environment, that is the villages, since the villages formed a kind of a community background for the people. Interests, moral outlook, and the level of knowledge could vary a lot from one village to another.

Be all that as it may, perhaps the most important strategic decision involved the grouping of auction lots and the sequence of the auction.

> We chose this kind of strategy – the cowsheds and other production buildings were the first to go, and only after that did we move on to the machinery. (Later chairman of the kolkhoz)

The decision to separate production buildings from agricultural machinery was of course in the interest of family farmers and those who were about to set up a farm. Thus, they would be able to improve the mechanisation of their own farms. Those who did not yet have a farm could prepare in advance for the farm they expected to be returned to them in restitution, while others bought tractors in the belief that they would later buy the fields around their current house.

The conflicting interests of private farmers (or the "conservatives", as some people still called them in old Soviet terms) and the upholders of the "combinate" (the "progressives") is particularly emphasised in the interviews. The decision to separate machinery from facilities may be regarded as a concession to family farmers both old and new, who were thus offered the possibility to convert their workshares into usable pieces of machinery. The decision was likewise advantageous to all those who planned on becoming agricultural contractors or partners in larger firms involved in contracting in the future (such as MTJ). The decision also facilitated the transfer of machines out of agricultural use. Lorries and excavators in particular but also farm tractors could be used for contract work, for example in a construction or timber business. In addition to this, the object or machine bought with workshares at a low price – often a give-away price – could be converted into cash at its actual value in dealings after the auction.

Some parts of the kolkhoz assets indeed laid the foundation for future businesses, but others produced mere transient wealth, which was quickly exhausted. The latter form of wealth was often called the "cream of the kolkhoz" in Kanepi, and a livelihood based on it was labelled "living off the cream of the kolkhoz".

In retrospect, the auction strategy was probably optimal for the six-person alliance formed within the board of management (and their company MTJ). The alliance had already come to the conclusion that agriculture as such was not a profitable branch for investments, and the search for alternative forms of economic activity, still based on resources available in the kolkhoz, had started a year in advance of the meeting on 26 February 1993. It was fortunate that the conflict between the family farmers and the supporters of large production complexes was settled – seemingly spontaneously – in a manner favouring the six-man alliance.

Regarding the fate of the large production complexes, it was perhaps unfortunate from the point of view of long-term agricultural development in the country that ordinary people, as well as agronomists, zoologists, members of the board of management, and on the whole those with the best agricultural education, were so convinced of the poor prospects of the agricultural business. At that moment the market for Estonian livestock in the local slaughterhouses was completely blocked, which is why pessimistic sentiments dominate interview excerpts.

> That's where the problem was, they all knew too well that it will profit you nothing if you buy it [a cowshed], because there is no place you can sell the meat. Nobody buys meat [right now], and what is one going to do with a cowshed like that? And land was another problem, it was other people's property and the cowsheds were located on other people's property. (Later chairman of the kolkhoz)

But for all these groups the auction system involved the risk that a high demand for machinery could lead to competitive bidding and inflated prices, and that people coming from outside the kolkhoz community proper could be participating in the auction. People included in this group were, for example, persons who had worked in the kolkhoz in the past but who had moved to the cities, or the children of pensioned kolkhoz employees, representing their parents at the auction. The decision on the auction strategy was not made at a general meeting; it was formulated by four people, including the chairman of the reform committee and the later chairman of the kolkhoz.

The auction sequence included one further aspect. Those subjects entitled to restitution, and their heirs, could also take part in the auction. Even after the auction the portion of the *unrestituted property* that could be returned in kind, e.g. cows and other livestock, was to be given to persons claiming it.

This sequence may appear strange, since it would of course have been sensible to restitute cows and livestock in general before the auction. But according to an interview with the later chairman of the kolkhoz, the sequence was not for the reform committee or the kolkhoz to decide; it was based on the law.

> When the auctions were over, two dates were set for paying compensation [properly speaking restitution in kind] for assets that had once been taken. It was a government decree; it had to happen. Two days were set for handing out cows and heifers back from the [kolkhoz] cowshed to all the people who wanted them. Some 124 animals were taken. (Later chairman of the kolkhoz)

Afterwards there were complaints from all the parties involved. The recipients claimed that only the most inferior and sickest cows had been given to them, while the givers maintained only the sickest cows were left at the kolkhoz cowsheds. However, it seems that this procedure did not have any particularly traumatic consequences. Since the kolkhoz at that stage had hardly any animals or pieces of property that would have corresponded to private property in the era of horse-drawn agriculture, the property restituted in kind was limited to cows.

The compensation for collectivised property, the other side of the same coin, was nevertheless under the authority of the kolkhoz general meeting. A part of the compensation had already been paid to people in cash during the rouble era, and according to the Estonian privatisation law, compensation should take precedence over other parts of the property that was to be privatised. The kolkhoz general meeting, however, came to a different conclusion: they decided to reverse the order of priority. The auction would be organised first, and only the owners of workshares would be eligible to participate. Only after that would compensation be paid for the collectivised property out of the kolkhoz assets that remained after the auction.

> A crucial error in the administration of these matters occurred, when the order was reversed. The people whose land had been annexed to the kolkhoz by force were left last. (Former chairman of the kolkhoz)

The importance of this decision lies in the fact that after the auction the authority responsible for the arrangements for the assets to be returned and compensated for would be the Savings and Loan Association, and thus the fate of those remaining assets became dependent on the repayment capacity of those people who had acquired kolkhoz assets with their workshares. The researchers were told by the later chairman of the kolkhoz that theoretically, the total value of property awaiting restitution amounted to EEK 800,000. Prospective recipients could have traded a part of the forthcoming compensation sum into so-called "yellow vouchers" (EVP privatisation vouchers given out to all Estonian citizens) that could be used for procuring property from outside the kolkhoz, such as an apartment. But apparently this exchange option was not known to everyone.

> I only have money received in compensation deposited in the Savings and Loan Association. Later we found out that one could have traded shares for 'yellow vouchers.' We had no prior knowledge of that option. I might have bought another house. But that's hindsight, I should have been wiser then. (A construction worker in the kolkhoz, heir to a collectivised farm)

Everyone with work or restitution shares from the kolkhoz had the right to take part in the auction itself. This had major repercussions on the auction, since the decision brought with it people from outside the kolkhoz, even from outside the municipality.

> The right to participate in the auction was also granted to people who were entitled to compensation in the form of land or funds . . . Pensioners who were too tired to attend the auction themselves gave their younger relatives the authorisation to represent them. (A member of the reform committee)

Also the *sequence of the auction* was of great importance. Because of the rapid destruction of kolkhoz resources, it was essential to carry the process through as quickly as possible. On the other had, the demand for information among ordinary people was great, and more time should have been reserved for discussions and public meetings. The interval between the last general meeting of the kolkhoz and the auction was only a couple of weeks.

The alliance that had been formed within the board of management started systematic preparations well in advance of the auction. The decision to set up a shared joint stock company (MTJ) and the systematic preparations for the auction were not public, although the most intent observers did notice that these men had teamed together.

> It was indeed clear that these men spent a lot of time together, but it was not the talk of the town. It might be true that they were co-operating, but we only found out about it later. (Agronomist X)

> You can't be sure of anything, but I believe that [the members of the board of management had] some plans. (Former brigade leader)

At the auction the six owners of the MTJ, a new joint stock company named after the kolkhoz machine and tractor station (*masinatraktorijaam*), realised their acquisition plan to the best of their abilities. The later chairman describes the background of the MTJ company in the following way.

> When we set up the joint stock company, there was myself, a department manager, and then there was the manager of the repair shop, and the manager of the truck depot. So it was [only natural] at that time to plan so that now we would be dividing it [the kolkhoz] up between ourselves and taking the best parts. (Later chairman of the kolkhoz)

The opposition that rose to power in the "little revolution" had accused the then kolkhoz leadership of dividing up the property of the collective. Now this charge was brought against the former opposition members themselves. Whatever the truth, the strategy of these kolkhoz board members created a comfortable basis for getting the MTJ off to a good start. At any rate, the alliance was satisfied with the prices they paid for the machinery.

> In the end we did get them [the machines needed]. All our machines, except the large forest tractor, were acquired from the kolkhoz. (Later chairman of the kolkhoz)

In this case *information* was, quite literally precious, i.e. worth money. The members of the board of management possessed the greatest amount of information about people (the number of vouchers people had and the personal characteristics of their holders) and the technical and commercial prospects for agricultural production.

Similarly they were, because of their standing, best able to understand the complicated kolkhoz privatisation process, whose stages they themselves had drafted and proposed to the reform committee. In this way, through the reform committee, they were in principle able to direct the auction procedure in whichever direction was most favourable to them. This does not mean that they would have been from the onset attempting to maximise their own interest by joining the board or the committee. In any case the disagreements within the reform committee suggest that at least some of the family farmers were left unsatisfied. Perhaps not every aspect of the dissolution procedure could be fixed to maximise the benefit of the board of management, but it was in their interest (and that of the reform committee in part) to familiarise themselves with the pros and cons of the chosen procedure particularly from their own point of view.

As far as the large agricultural complexes are concerned, it was not just a question of information. People who felt the desire to buy a large unit such as the Kooraste cowshed complex had to gather a sufficiently large number of people who would put their vouchers at their disposal (on loan), since no single person had enough vouchers. It is unprobable that anyone apart from the members of the board of management and the reform committee could have been fully aware of the future role of the Savings and Loan Association. At the auction the only method of payment was workshare vouchers. People had to make up a plan and simultaneously convince others of the wisdom of what they were proposing. The buyer of the enterprise would also have to solve a great number of problems, ranging from work ethics to machinery.

> We covered 40% with shares. We got our shares from our own employees and other people, [such as] pensioners . . . We bought shares at low prices from other people.

> The matter was talked over with the people. [We] invited them to a meeting, [and we] asked whether they would agree to invest their own shares and whether they would agree to work for us. We wanted to survey the overall opinion [and] we got a positive result.

> There were discussions of how much land and [what kind of] machines would be needed, and based on that, we bought items at the auction. We also discussed matters such as if we bought a tractor, for example, would the tractor driver be willing to work for us. So that the drivers would stay the same – so that a person who knew that particular piece of machinery would come and work for us.

> We did not have much time for planning, [only] approximately one week. (An owner of the cowshed complex)

Great haste also characterised the privatisation of the Kanepi cowshed complex, although the work for the establishment of a new complex had admittedly been started there well in advance of other villages, perhaps thanks to the foresight of agronomist X. In Kanepi, however, the process was more complicated, since the intention of the employees was to establish a neo-collectivist enterprise, an agricultural co-operative, instead of a joint stock company. In terms of size alone the Kanepi complex was significantly larger than the one in Kooraste.

Two months before the auction we had our hands so full . . . that we simply did not have time to watch and observe what other people were up to. The founding agreement of Kanepi co-operative [*osaühistys*] was signed before the auction. When we had decided that we would buy three cowsheds, we also had to buy half of the machine station in order to make the cowsheds economically viable. Besides that we also needed an oil and petrol distribution point. There was an interval of a couple of days. And [then we bought] hardware and machines. (Agronomist X)

From the standpoint of the ordinary machine operator or family farmer the situation was difficult. In many cases a driver wanted to buy the tractor most familiar to him, but whether he would later be able to put the machine to any profitable use was very unclear. A family farmer, on the other hand, required quite a different type of machine, but if the farmer did not have any previous experience in running a private farm and the size and type of equipment required, drawing up a sensible purchasing plan might not have been that easy. There were a lot of different needs to be met, and there were not enough of all the necessary machines at the auction: for example tractors were in short supply. Where would one start in the mechanisation of one's own farm?

On the other hand, those family farmers who had started cultivating their own farms during the rouble era had in many cases already acquired such basic machines as a tractor. Thus they were able to concentrate on other deficiencies in the mechanisation of their farms. Their preparation for the auction may therefore have been very rational from a technical viewpoint, since they knew from experience what kind of equipment was needed in their particular situation.

I had authorisation from my two grandfathers, and therefore I had the opportunity to take part in both [Kanepi and Kalev] kolkhoz auctions. They had a real auction in Kanepi kolkhoz, [whereas] in Kalev kolkhoz all the better machines had been given out before the auction. I bought three tractor-trailers, one hay rake, one harrow and an old car in Kalev. Furthermore, [I purchased] a potato harvester, it was a new piece of equipment from Germany, and I bought it because nobody else wanted it, since it was considered too complicated [to operate]. I bought it because it was dirt-cheap. If I do not find a use for it myself I will sell it off. It only cost me 2,000 kroons and I got it with vouchers. (An owner of a family farm, modern by Estonian standards, set up in 1988)

The Importance of Information in Preparation for the Auction

Since the Soviet Union had no auction tradition whatsoever, the auction event was unfamiliar to everybody, and of course strangest of all to the common workers, pensioners and marginalised people (alcoholics, single parents burdened by many other problems, etc.). Although people chose a direct auction at the general meeting held on 26 February 1993, the later chairman of the kolkhoz nevertheless takes the view that "they did not understand anything. At that moment I realised that they did not grasp what was about to happen, who was going to be the master of the house."

If the people of Kanepi had difficulties in anticipating and grasping major changes in ownership, it is not surprising that they also did not fully understand the significance of the vouchers.

> Many people believed that these shares could be [best] realised by exchanging them for cash [as soon as possible]. There were many that traded them for a bottle of liquor . . . it seemed as if people did not understand what was actually happening. People were used to being told and getting explained to them what to do, but that wasn't going to happen now, there were only rumours. (A successful businessman)

Just as the six-person alliance formed within the kolkhoz board of management kept the agreements they had made to themselves, the ordinary people also cut themselves off from each other.

> People became very cautious after the meeting. Prior to the auction everyone kept as little contact with other people as possible. People only talked when it was absolutely necessary. Nobody wanted others to know what he was going to buy with his shares. It was self-defence in a manner of speaking. (Kolkhoz electrician)

In their minds people also feared the forthcoming auction and its effects on the value of their vouchers, comparing it to the fateful consequences of the 1992 monetary reform.

> It was also a question of the fact that nobody's real money went far at the time roubles were converted into kroons. People lost their bank savings. In a sense [people] were a little bit afraid of losing their shares in the same way. (Ibid.)

Many individuals also viewed these circumstances in the light of Estonia's turbulent history, which has included violence, with unpredictable turns and internal conflicts between different population groups.

> I was born during the war, and also during that time we had such a tyranny. [Everyone] was afraid, and you could never know how things would work out, and the competition [between ordinary people] was brutal. People had already lost a great deal, and it was not wise to talk about one's own plans with others – if you did you could lose even more. (Ibid.)

"Self-defence" is a very descriptive term, but as an auction strategy it was probably the worst imaginable. People should rather have made mutual agreements and compromises, and at the very least they should have clarified the nature of the auction in face-to-face talks. Alas, with the limited level of knowledge they possessed many people were easily duped.

It appears that making preparations for the kolkhoz auction was most arduous for those who wanted to set up viable agricultural production complexes (and not invest in non-agricultural businesses). Amid the prevailing conditions of general uninformedness, feelings of apprehension, secrecy and private speculation these people attempted to preserve certain integral units intact, the viability of which was threatened by the removal and sale of crucial machines and equipment. The situation of the non-agricultural complexes was different, since their machinery was not necessarily as easily detachable from the whole (e.g. the sawmill). The situation probably seemed less stressful for people whose objective was to purchase a single piece of machinery (cf. the earlier description of a family farmer), since they were usually offered a wider variety of choices.

The former chairman of the kolkhoz, who had also chaired the meeting on February 26, made the observation that people were not aware of the nature of the auction, and he proposed that there should be another meeting. The later chairman commented on the meeting in this manner: "[The kolkhoz was] terminated right there, full stop. There we were."

In the end the proposed new meeting was never arranged. It is not easy to tell to what degree the urgency was a calculated policy of the kolkhoz leadership, but undoubtedly they possessed a monopoly on information. The character of this monopoly is best described by the fact that even the university-educated agronomist X, who acted as the dynamo for public debate in Kanepi, lacked absolutely essential strategic information.

I had no idea of the contents of the kolkhoz accounts . . . Furthermore, I had no idea of all the items that had been sold during the last two years of the kolkhoz [before the auction]. And if I wanted to check something, there was no way the paper I needed was given to me.

To all appearances agronomist X was a person who did not lack ability and willingness to dig out the facts, but apparently obstacles were put in his way. He was not given all the essential information even if he made a direct request for it. Thus, information was to the highest degree monopolistic in nature.

Outside participants (retired kolkhoz workers, heirs and representatives of rightful restituees) had little or no precise knowledge of present kolkhoz resources, and it was more difficult for them to partake in the alliances that had been created inside the kolkhoz. If they had money, they could purchase more shares from those kolkhoz members and employees who were willing to part with theirs, and invest in those (ex-kolkhoz) enterprises which in that particular economic situation had the best prospects. Outsiders found such opportunities especially in the timber business and, among the kolkhoz departments, in the wood processing plant.

There was also an alliance of four businessmen, three of whom had served in the Estonian agricultural hierarchy in high positions. Only one of them had been a member of the leadership of Kanepi kolkhoz. He had once been the confidant of the former kolkhoz chairman during the "little revolution," but now he and the others had all been displaced from their positions in the agricultural hierarchy. Thus, these businessmen were very competent, but unlike the alliance formed by six members of the kolkhoz board of management, they were forced to construct their acquisition strategy from a more abstract perspective. The local people claimed that this group purchased a great number of shares from alcoholics and other destitute shareholders.

One of the interviewees sums up the importance of information in a fitting way, and from the context it appears that he sees membership of the board of management as of vital importance.

There was a big difference according to one's position in the kolkhoz. Considering it in concrete terms, one could say that the share of a specialist was worth more than the share of a worker. The share of a worker was a blank piece of paper. They [the workers] only wished and hoped that they would be given their rightful share. But [other] people organised matters for their own good. Not all people had the same amount of information about the true value of things. There were plenty of matters that were based on the lack of information. I believe [that the ones who benefited most from privatisation were] the people in the board of management. A very close circle of friends: the specialists. (A local amateur historian)

The interviewees, both ordinary people and specialists agreed on one thing: that the dissolution of the kolkhoz took place much too quickly. But on the other hand this most critical stage of Estonia's economic transition, which was accompanied by hyperinflation and price scissors on agricultural produce, called for rapid measures – without any guarantees of improvement.

In Kanepi kolkhoz everything happened as if we were going off to the war. I have not seen war in real life, but it was as if the Day of Judgement was at hand, everything had to take place very fast. We had to stick new lists on the wall at night; it was a real madhouse. (Later chief accountant)

In our case the crucial part was played by the time factor, since the future was shrouded in mystery and everybody's sole interest was survival. (Later chairman of the kolkhoz)

Further Information on the Auction Procedure

Who then were the authorised participants in the auction and which methods of payment were used at the auction?

If you had worked in the kolkhoz for longer than five years you had the right to get these shares. But if a person had worked for a shorter period of time he wasn't entitled. His workshare was calculated, but he didn't have the right to buy with the shares [he could only buy an apartment]. (Later chairman of the kolkhoz)

So five years was the limit. And even if all former and present employees were entitled to workshares, only workers with five years of experience or more could participate in the auction.

Nevertheless, there was one group of people besides the ones who had worked the minimum of five years in the kolkhoz who were also allowed to participate in the auction, namely the offspring or authorised representatives of the "more-than-five-years" individuals. Furthermore, those who were entitled to compensation for collectivised property (or other persons authorised by them) were also entitled to participate, Thus in the end, a large number of people with no local interest in the items on sale took part in the auction.

However, vouchers were the only accepted method of payment and nobody could use cash to purchase lots at the auction.

The reform committee, upon a motion of the kolkhoz board of management, was also able to influence the auction event in a fundamental way by resolving three other interconnected matters: (1) the regulation of voucher trading outside the actual auction event, together with checks on whether bidders could actually provide cover for the bid they made at the auction. These powers included two further arrangements, which cannot be understood separately from these initial decisions on the regulation of voucher trading. These further arrangements were (2) the method for disposing of kolkhoz-owned housing and the fixing of house prices, and (3) the foundation of the Savings and Loan Association and the formulation of its directives. We shall consider items 1–3 separately.

1) *An unofficial stock market was born* on the basis of workshares *since these shares were now bought and sold for cash*. The trade actually began before the auction itself, since "the vouchers had been written out well before the auction. It had the value of the [person's work] shares marked on it," said a kolkhoz member.

The former director anticipated the dangers involved in this, and consequently he made the following proposal at the meeting of 26 February 1993.

> Now [let's consider] the voucher. If an individual gives his voucher away, this should take place through the agency of the municipality. [Which would] ascertain that there is no possibility of fraud by giving [the buyer] a document certifying that so and so many people have handed over their shares to him, with the countersignatures of the sellers [in the document]. It [the proposal] was ignored. The [later] chairman [of the kolkhoz] wanted to act immediately and organise the auction in a matter of a couple of days. (Wife of the former kolkhoz chairman in a joint interview with her husband)

The implementation of the proposal would have created a public forum for the stock exchange. Counselling could also have been incorporated into the verification procedure. This would have been necessary because of widespread uninformedness, and because the patrimonial system was second nature to these people.

> As the kolkhoz was broken up, plenty of people kept on hoping that somebody else would take care of them again. (A Kanepi bystander, not a kolkhoz member)

There was no uniform way of dealing with the vouchers. It was haphazard in many ways. Many people believed that these shares could be [best] realised by exchanging them for cash [as soon as possible].

The situation . . . was such that nobody really understood what to do with those vouchers. There was a man who threw his grandfather's and his fathers vouchers onto the street, [saying] 'take that rubbish and give me a bottle of vodka.' And that way he might as well have given away several tractors. (Later chairman of the kolkhoz)

Putting the voucher trade under the supervision of authorities would perhaps also have compelled the reform committee to attend to the moral practices of the voucher trade. The downright stealing of another person's shares by taking advantage of the person's old age, feeblemindedness, sickness, alcoholism, etc. would have become more difficult – at the very least by making it blatantly open. As it was, the board of management even possessed information on paper about the alcohol-related problems of kolkhoz members, and in principle they could have easily made use of this knowledge, even though there is no proof that they resorted to this type of tactics.

Stock trading in its crudest form nevertheless became one of the most important mechanisms of the so-called original accumulation, before the auction, during the auction and after it. "Drunkards sold their own shares for 30–40 cents each. Wise people bought shares from them immediately," said a buyer of a large production complex who most probably had been one of the buyers. The former municipal director had noticed that "old men started selling their vouchers at rock bottom prices."

Many people trusted the buyers too much and it might have been that the buyers believed that they would some day pay for their purchases. Whatever the truth might be, the end result was as a general rule the same.

And the vouchers I sold. The man who bought them promised that he'd pay for them within five years. So far I've seen none of that money. (A pensioner)

It was like taking advantage of the situation. Many people sold their vouchers for a couple of bottles of spirits. (A policeman)

The buyers above included all those who planned ahead for the future. Of course, some people had an advantage over the others.

Those who had disposable cash in their pockets, [since they] were able to buy valuable property. (Former municipal director)

This group included local businessmen and other people who had made money in various ways.

> The one who managed his own business, [another one] who [for example] owned a bar, and other enterprising people . . . There was one who had worked in Germany. Their parents were kolkhoz members, so they had the right to buy. (Former brigade leader)

You could also increase your own capital resources by brokering vouchers (i.e. by buying cheap and selling at a higher price). "That was also going on," confirmed one of the interviewees when queried about the matter. Anyhow, those who invested their vouchers or a small amount of cash judiciously were sometimes able to acquire a sizeable property.

> We bought vouchers from the people, and that was why we could get the building at an affordable price. (Businessman 1, member of the four-man alliance)

> I bought the kindergarten. The building cost next to nothing. Objects such as the kindergarten should in reality have had a high value, but they were sold at very low prices. At that particular moment we had money. We made our payments on the days of the auction with money [i.e., they bought vouchers with cash]. [Most] people did not have money at that time, but I had money since I had been in Germany [as an agricultural trainee], and I had the opportunity to pay in cash. (Businessman 2, another member of the four-man alliance)

But the great majority did not have the courage to purchase anything.

> Anyone could have bought things [at the auction]. [But] many [people] were afraid of buying; they were expecting [repercussions] and what not. And later they had to buy [vouchers direct from people or from brokers] at a much higher price.

If one could not prepare oneself for the auction by acquiring more vouchers, the prospects for future entrepreneurship were significantly worse. Here a fellow citizen describes what happened to the new owner of an agricultural complex.

> Everybody else [bought and hoarded up vouchers . . . probably [they] paid 50 cents or less [per share]. He [the new owner of the complex] was hardly able to cover the cost of the property he had acquired. He only had those shares of his own . . . Maybe he couldn't even afford to pay those 50 cents. [Eventually that

agricultural complex went bankrupt.] (An accountant of the above agricultural complex)

Such regulations as the former chairman proposed would also have affected the prices in the auction event itself. If the buyer had always had to present a proof of ownership of the vouchers in order to cover his bid, the total price (book value) in kroons (EEK) of all the assets for sale would have remained unchanged (or at least it would not have rocketed as wildly as it did) during the auction. If the prices of some auction lots had increased above the book value used as the starting point, the prices of other lots would have correspondingly decreased. But there was no regulation, people were able to make bids and buy – as the Kanepi people expressed it – "with air." That was why the value of the workshares (the value of one workday) they used in bidding at the auction rose from the original book value of 60 cents up to 2 kroons 30 cents, i.e., the value was almost *quadrupled*. In the end, it was the lack of regulation that made the auction event incomprehensible to the majority of the people.

> An auction implies making the highest bid and the price of a workday started to climb, and it happened that [in the end] nobody knew its price. (Later chairman of the kolkhoz)

> That's why the total value of the property sold at the kolkhoz auction rose to 3.5 million kroons. The vouchers only covered half of that sum. (A member of the reform committee)

If the regulations suggested by the former chairman had been enforced, it would not have only reduced the exploitation of uninformed people and made the auction situation better organised, but also created a necessity to negotiate over the formation of various kinds of consortiums based on written agreements. In actual fact, there were few written agreements when the businessmen hoarded up vouchers, promising the sellers money or a share of future profits. It is probable that the kolkhoz auction would have had to be postponed to introduce this controlled procedure, but it would have resulted in a much more equitable outcome.

As it was, the unregulated nature and irrationality of the process only benefited those who were best able to understand the underlying character of the process, and were able to systematically orient themselves to it. Undoubtedly, it was most advantageous to the kolkhoz board of management, as well as to a group of people who had previous business experience and cash assets to secure vouchers in the unofficial "stock market". Based on the interview material, one cannot say whether the irrational character of the auction event was premeditated or not, but of course this possibility cannot be totally excluded. And it was certainly in the interest of a few individuals to increase the irrational aspects of the event.

2) The former chairman also showed keen interest in *the privatisation of kolkhoz-owned housing*. The last meeting of the kolkhoz decided that the occupant of each house and flat would have a preferential claim to the residence to be acquired with vouchers. The houses and flats were set a low book value, but they were not auctioned off because of the right of redemption clause. Since the value of workshares almost quadrupled thanks to the auction, the book values of houses and flats declined in proportion. Thus, the people who lived in kolkhoz housing and were able to purchase it benefited from the situation at the expense of others, and those who had the most highly valued residences benefited the most. Detached houses were the most valuable, and they were often inhabited by members of the board of management and leading specialists. Besides, as the wife of the former chairman commented in the joint interview with her husband, an ordinary flat could be redeemed with the "yellow vouchers" (EVPs or *rahvakapitalisobligatsiooni*) which were handed out to all citizens, while those vouchers alone did not suffice for a detached house. According to her, this was one of the reasons why the nominal value of a workday (in vouchers) rose at the auction.

> However, [the rise in the value of a voucher] worked to the advantage of one specific group. The value of a day was not calculated on the basis of the value set at the kolkhoz; instead, the value of a day was determined at the auction itself and this made acquiring very valuable objects very easy. (Wife of the former kolkhoz chairman)

The action of the former chairman at the meeting of February 26, when matters pertaining to the auction were agreed upon, appears to have been based on his expert knowledge plus a highly developed sense of social responsibility. As the former chairman of the kolkhoz he could also have gained various kinds of personal benefits in the course of the process, especially at the auction stage – for example, his family lived in an old detached house he could have purchased. This does seem to prove that the former chairman, as a person elected to a position of trust, kept to his old line of patrimonial responsibility familiar from the Soviet era, even though his proposals were no longer accepted. It was most likely that this caring attitude motivated people to elect him chairman at that particular meeting.

A senior official in the Põlva County stated in an off-the-record conversation that the former chairmen of the kolkhozes and sovkhozes as a rule did not take part in the "public thieving"; he believed it was more characteristic of the new leadership of the transitional period. The former chairman of Kanepi kolkhoz had angered the younger generation with his authoritarian approach, but during the dissolution process they appear to have reconsidered their opinion of him.

> Now our opinion [for him] has changed for the better. (A young specialist with an intermediate education)

Among the older age groups attitudes such as the following appeared to be fairly common.

> I am sure that the former chairman would have acted in a different way. The new man holding the post of the chairman of the collective farm was not the same in his conclusions. (Former manager of the kolkhoz construction team, not a member of the board of management)

The "little revolution" had been carried out in the name of securing the future of the kolkhoz. People feared the break-up of the kolkhoz, and it was one of the factors that had enabled the opposition to gain power. However, the objective of the revolution was right from the outset in conflict with the political orientation of the opposition leadership, and after they had gained power they relied on the support of the kolkhoz council of representatives, not the general meeting.

It might be said that later, as the kolkhoz was being broken up, the conflict was resolved to the advantage of the right-wing political groupings at the local level and at the Estonian national level. Patrimonial care was abandoned, since the new kolkhoz leadership (together with those members of the old leadership who were not classed as supporters of the former chairman) was in the first place interested in looking after its own interests. This was ideologically in perfect harmony with the neoliberal doctrine, which legitimated the pursuit of individual interests as a social virtue. The kolkhoz members and workers saw this, and they sought support from the former chairman during the last months of the kolkhoz. But the influence of the former chairman remained very limited in these situations, despite his attempts. Besides, his illness had by then exhausted his powers.

The privatisation of housing, however, has one more sub-plot, which has especial theoretical interest from the viewpoint of the problematics of the structuring of capitalist social relations (the so-called original accumulation). This sub-plot is *the battle for the ownership of the housing* built in the neighbourhood of the Karste and Kooraste cowshed complexes. The battle arose from the conflict between two new laws. On the one hand the law placed the kolkhozes under the obligation to sell all the cowsheds and other possible major production units as technically undivided complexes. The housing of the local workforce was often kolkhoz property, which was why the kolkhoz had the authority to decide what to do with them. But on the other hand, another law ordained that the tenant had the right of first refusal to his/her residence.

According to a senior official in the County of Põlva, this conflict situation was typical of the problems encountered in the process of privatising agriculture. Since the agricultural reform was accomplished before the law on the privatisation of housing became effective, "the ones who could get a hold on something prior [to the actual privatisation of housing] . . . were the winners, you couldn't get anything back." However, the Kanepi kolkhoz tenants were not forced to move since the last general meeting of the kolkhoz on February 26 had decided that the current tenant of each flat or house had the right to purchase it. But the realisation of this decision was preceded by a fierce fight. Despite the decision (and unlike all other kolkhoz-owned housing) the detached houses built next to the cowsheds in Karste and Kooraste were sold in the same bundle as the cowsheds. That caused a conflict situation between the residents and the kolkhoz leadership.

> We had a disagreement [with the later chairman]. [The matter was discussed] four times at the office of the municipal council, and we nearly ended up fighting. Lawyers arrived from Põlva, and one of the lawyers tried to settle the disputes between us. (A pensioner living in a disputed detached house)

The venue for the proceedings was the municipal council, which according to the law on agricultural reform had to validate the privatisation of each individual batch of collective farm assets. The citizens of Kooraste and Karste lost the first round of the battle.

> But the board won . . . The entire fight was very depressing. Why do the bosses get [what they want], and we don't? There's no justice. (Ibid.)

The residents felt as if it was all a game, but luckily the game was not yet over. The tenants discovered a trump card as a result of an imaginative cloak-and-dagger operation.

> We were in fact so furious that we even stole. We had not been shown the minutes of the last meeting of the kolkhoz, but we took them in secret and copied [them]. The same thing in Kooraste. With the man from Kooraste we then went to Põlva . . . We wanted justice and equality. We protested against the fact that all the assets had been handed out to them [the new private owners of the cowsheds], and there was nothing left for us. A lawyer in Põlva proved that the official record of the meeting included a clause that everyone living in a detached house had the right to buy it. Nobody knew of our visit to Põlva, just the wife of the man from Kooraste. She helped us. And there was one further person that helped us to get the minutes of the meeting from the safe. We were so angry we weren't even afraid. Our only fear was that they [the board of management] could have made changes to the official record, not forge it, but to change it [by making a new decision]. [The later chairman] maintained that the content of the minutes was totally different until we brought forward [our copy of] the minutes. (Ibid.)

Now the men had their trump card, but it was still up their sleeve, which was why the later chairman of the kolkhoz at first kept on making the same claims as before.

> He just read [out loud the list of] all the collective assets [to be sold]. And [that was when] we brought our own paper forward, [the one] we had copied in secret. He became so angry that we almost started to fight. That happened at the meeting [of the municipal council]. Then he said, 'you still won't get anything.' There were three lawyers present [for reasons unrelated to this issue] and they confirmed that we were right. (Ibid.)

The tenants in the detached houses in Karste and Kooraste had thus been victorious in their legal battle. It appeared to be something that the chairman of the kolkhoz found hard to digest. But this series of events reveals a lot about the nature and the methods of the later kolkhoz chairman. He had already, prior to this, repeatedly uttered blatant lies about the contents of the official record of the meeting, at an occasion in which the new ownership of privatised property was officially validated. The later chairman was not the only one who was involved, since the chairman of the reform committee and also many other key personalities involved in the privatisation had to be present (as members of the municipal council), and there were lawyers too, one of which had been especially appointed to supervise the legality of asset transfers.

Although the case had been the subject of a lengthy dispute, nobody had compelled the chairman of the kolkhoz or the chairman of the reform committee to prove the authenticity of their claim by bringing forward the official record of the meeting. Without the espionage-type operation by the men from Karste and Kooraste described above, an obvious wrong would have remained uncorrected. Even after the truth was disclosed no public debate arose about the matter – let alone any question of imposing a punishment on the culprits. The members of the municipal council and lawyers closed their eyes to a clear case of wrongdoing.

The motivation of the later chairman was unclear, even though it is known that he was a personal friend of the individual who had bought one of the cowshed complexes (they had both been members of the group that opposed the former chairman). But the case in question was not just a matter of loyalty between two friends; it also included an interesting theoretical aspect from the viewpoint of the structuring of the society, connected with the availability of labour.

The villages of Karste and Kooraste are located a long way from Kanepi township centre, which is why the new owners of the cowshed complex had to depend on the local labour supply. All the larger agricultural enterprises in Kanepi are today concerned about the quality of their workforce. They claim that the working population these days is apathetic, lazy, unenterprising, alcoholic and sometimes prone to pilfering. (We will deal with these accusations in more detail later.) Besides, a large part of the workforce in the villages of Karste and Kooraste consisted of "migratory birds", who were particularly notorious. Once the occupants had been given the right to purchase their residences, the new (capitalist) enterprises became dependent on the local labour supply. If the buyers of cowshed complexes had taken possession of these residences the situation would have been reversed, as one of the new owners of cowshed complexes frankly commented.

> I've got no options. Who else could I employ? The others, the ones that I could hire, are the same or even worse [than my current employees] . . . If I was offered a choice [of employees], then people would work harder. [Today, detached houses] belong to the people who occupy them. Originally I was told that I was to become the owner of those houses. It would have been easier, since I could have stated my terms to them. But now they keep making me all kinds of demands. (Owner of a private cowshed complex in another village)

The precondition of functional capitalism is a sufficiently large "army of surplus labour" (Marx) of wageworkers. The decollectivisation of the kolkhozes indeed created a mass of underprivileged people in rural Estonia, but the privatisation of housing prevented the creation of a sufficiently large local labour reserve. Only a large surplus of labour would have imposed a situation of competition on the workers in a single village, and consequently would have forced individual workers to reconsider their work ethics, among other things.

3) The need to set up a *Savings and Loan Association* was a direct consequence of the decisions made. It was the legal successor of the privatised kolkhoz, but the founding of an independent organisation for this purpose was unnecessary, since the kolkhoz could have had some other form of legal successor. The Savings and Loan Association was established to solve a single problem: *the "air" included in the uncovered bids made at the auction* had to be determined as a debt to those people who had not used their vouchers at all, or to those who had not yet received any compensation for their collectivised property.

> The original price of a workshare was 60 cents per day, but the price kept on rising at the auction as the bids soared . . . In the end it was 2.30 [kroons]. There was the danger . . . well, we – the reform committee and I – had the situation under control so that we somehow managed to set up the Savings and Loan Association, since otherwise there would not be any arbitrating agency or any organisation that would make up the difference between the air and reality. (Later chairman of the kolkhoz)

The Auction

Further Problems Arise

Organising the main auction (11 to 23 March 1993) decreed by the general meeting necessitated a number of technical preparations. Some smaller illegal auctions had already been arranged in 1992, but this was something quite different. All those entitled to participation were registered, and only those on the registration list could take part in the auction. A starting bid, based on the book value of each lot, had to be placed on all items, and also an exhibition of the goods had to be organised prior to the auction. At that point

the individual machines that had been taken to the homes of kolkhoz employees became a problem.

> Many people had also kept a kolkhoz lorry as if it was their own, and they hoped
> they would get it for themselves. One of the terms set at the meeting [of
> February 26] was that all the machines had to be gathered at one location, or else
> you would not be allowed to attend the auction. All our [kolkhoz] machines had
> been countersigned, so nobody could hide anything in the forests, and all those
> items were gathered up. And we placed armed guards [from the] Kaitseliit
> [nationalist paramilitary organisation] on them. I was there myself guarding [the
> machines], too. (Later chairman of the kolkhoz)

According to the deputy head of the local Kaitseliit unit "there were
attempts at theft and the situation was becoming chaotic," proving that the
armed guards were indeed necessary.

Already the first stage on 11 March 1993 indicated people's profound
confusion. Some people believed they could only use their vouchers at the
auction (while kolkhoz tenants, for example, could have purchased their
homes with them), while others trusted that they would be able to change
their vouchers into cash after the auction. The source of this confusion was
the fundamental lack of information regarding the vouchers.

Yet it was not only a question of the obscurity surrounding the vouchers
and the overall nature of the auction. The basic flaw in the whole auction
system was the lack of any checks on the vouchers that were supposed to back
up people's bids. (The starting bids were set in kroons and the auction
participants also made the bids in kroons, although the only approved method
of payment was vouchers.) The ordinary bidders themselves knew little about
their vouchers, except their original nominal value (EEK 0.60 per workday).
Competitive bidding eventually obscured the kroon value of the vouchers.

> Rivalry at the auction was markedly increased by outsiders who were not
> kolkhoz employees. They might have been the relatives or former and current
> kolkhoz workers, who were also entitled to restitution. For example, old people
> who were not fit enough to attend the auction gave their younger relatives the
> authorisation to represent them. And they [the outsiders] messed up all [our]
> plans. Some . . . stranger came and bid for the machine I had planned to buy. (An
> agronomist)

Thus the rivalry between bidders inflated the prices of the lots offered
for sale. Because of this "the [nominal] value of a workday [in kroons] started

rising . . . and [in the end] nobody really knew its exact price," said the later chairman of the kolkhoz.

Agricultural and Non-agricultural Complexes

The auction (11 to 23 March 1993) was originally to be divided into two stages. At the first stage the intention was to sell off the production complexes (agricultural and non-agricultural complexes and other large buildings, such as the new administration building of the kolkhoz, the kindergarten, the shop, etc.), and only at the second stage sell all the movable machinery and equipment, plus any other collectively used assets that remained. The new owners of production complexes were obliged to employ their present workers as established employees. Dismissal would only have been possible by paying the employee a severance pay equal to eight months' wages.

An auctioneer was needed and once again people turned to the former chairman, who handled with due dignity this task that would lead to the closing down of the kolkhoz, which in itself was highly undesirable for him.

During the first phase the bidders were quite clearly divided into two groups. The ordinary members of the kolkhoz were largely incapable of forming alliances and probably perceived that they had been edged out from the sale of the large complexes on purpose, since the vouchers of an individual person did not suffice for the purchase of a cowshed, for example.

> An ordinary field worker did not even know how and what was being privatised. [He] was not familiar with the mechanisms of getting more vouchers. Legally, of course. [He didn't know] how to buy and how to act. (Municipal councillor)

On the other had, some alliances such as the kolkhoz board of management appeared to look after their own. Social processes that would involve ordinary employees as owners were only developing in respect of the three cowsheds in Kanepi kolkhoz centre.

It is true that a great number of other local people were also involved in the process of establishing new enterprises. Besides selling their vouchers, many people also gave them on loan to the new owners (but not as investments).

The assumption that everything had already been divided would account for the emergence of a carnival atmosphere among the people who felt they had been left out.

> People were walking about drinking, most of them were drunk, and the atmosphere bore a resemblance to the times when [private farms were collectivised and] the kolkhozes were formed. Nothing was sacred any more. (Later chairman of the kolkhoz)

At the core of the carnival atmosphere was a protest directed not only at the leadership of the kolkhoz, but possibly also at the political elite of Estonia. This element of protest was tinged with the bitter taste of a final farewell to the kolkhoz way of life with its established customs and workplaces, but there was no choice, just as there had been no choice at the time of forced collectivisation over 40 years previously. One era was coming to a swift and unnatural end, and the future was shrouded in great mystery and uncertainty.

Some of the most important players in the first stage of the auction were enterprises formed by various types of alliances, registered as several kinds of *"ühistys."*[3] However, these enterprising individuals and alliances invested primarily in the non-agricultural product industries of the kolkhoz (e.g. the sawmill, wood processing plant, repair shop, mills), plus machinery in general, along with the spare parts and stored supplies of the kolkhoz (the secret MTJ joint stock company formed by the core of the kolkhoz leadership was especially interested in these) and real estate. (Other alliances were interested in, for example, the new administration building of the kolkhoz, the kindergarten, the commercial buildings, song festival stage, and so on.)

The interest in the agricultural complexes remained low, with plans for the establishment of only one co-operative in Kanepi (one half of the Kanepi centre agricultural complex) and for a private farm in Kooraste. These units were sold on the first day, one at the starting bid and the other at a slightly higher price. There was more competition for the other production complexes. For example, the MTJ did not get the sawmill and wood processing plant (furniture workshop) it wanted. These premises were sold to a businessman from outside the municipality who made a higher bid. At the time when the kolkhoz came to an end, the timber business was considered highly profitable.

> There were certain [interesting] moments . . . in connection with [the auctioning of] the sawmill. It appears that they hitched its price up on purpose. (Later chief accountant)

---

3   An *ühistys* (i.e., company) is not a company form in the legal sense of the term, but simply a designation local people have applied to most types of new enterprise that employ outside labour.

By contrast, non-productive real estate, the kindergarten in particular, was sold off relatively cheaply (see Nikula, Chapter 4, and Ruutsoo, Chapter 5). Furthermore, most of the individuals who acquired the complexes at a low price were local people.

Since several dairy production complexes remained unsold, and the kolkhoz board as well as the other business alliances showed little interest in basic agricultural production, the reform committee had to take special urgent measures. The later chairman of the kolkhoz feared that "there was the danger that nobody would attend to cowshed chores any longer."

Again, there was a situation analogous to forced collectivisation. But now the kolkhoz was the object of liquidation. Back in the late 1940s "everything was given to the kolkhoz, and nobody knew who would care for the animals" (account of an amateur historian in Kanepi). From the perspective of the livestock the result would have been the same.

> And then, in a couple of days there was the new auction . . . And once again we offered them [the cowsheds for sale] almost by force. [We urged people to] think about it; why wouldn't you take those buildings and the cattle . . . We found an owner, and we ordered right there that the signer [of the purchase agreement] should go to the cowshed right away and start taking care of urgent matters, since the cattle were starving. The necessary machines were there; we handed out a few further pieces of equipment for the cowsheds [to the new cowshed owners] from the yard of the repair shop. Everything was entered into the books, all the things each person got. (Later chairman of the kolkhoz)

These first auction events were clearly indicative of the fact that a large proportion of the people – who after all, saw their future as being in the new complexes – had not been adequately prepared for the auction. The ones who would have had the best qualifications, the managers and the specialists, were searching for opportunities outside basic agriculture. Thus, many of those who finally did buy cowsheds did so on the spur of the moment.

For the sake of comparison, I could mention that according to the later chairman a large cowshed typically cost around EEK 100,000 (approximately DEM 12,500), livestock included. The low prices undoubtedly contributed to the impulsive nature of the purchases.

> [There was] an old man who entered the cowshed [under auction], he was a bit drunk, [and eventually he ended up] buying the cowshed for 73,000 [kroons]. When his daughters heard about it, they left home [and moved into a larger town]. Only his son-in-law, the husband of the younger daughter, [remained in the household] and he commented [on the impulse purchase by saying only],

'let's see what comes of it.' The craziest thing of all was that there were five cattle minders in that cowshed and from the moment he [the old man] signed the paper, they were on his payroll. (The later chairman of the kolkhoz)

I got excited at the auction, I ventured a bit and that's how I got the cowshed. On the one hand I felt a little bit guilty, since everybody else was buying something, and I wasn't buying anything and the cowshed might even remain unsold. That too was one reason for the purchase. (A man who bought a cowshed complex; presently a pensioner)

Table 3.1 shows the eleven most important new enterprises established in connection with the first stage of the auction. Six of them practised basic agricultural production, while five were involved in non-agricultural businesses.

Altogether eleven separate units came into existence that way; they were formed on the basis of the property received from the kolkhoz. The largest was Kanepi co-operative, with a total asset value of 3.4 millions [EEK at the time the enterprise was founded], the smallest was the Ojakivi company, with total assets of 617 kroons. (Later chairman of the kolkhoz)

In 1995, two years after the auction, all the non-agricultural enterprises except the planned hotel were still in operation. The kolkhoz office building that was to be turned into a hotel was eventually sold to Eesti Energia, the national electric utility company. The fact that none of these four "spur-of-the-moment" cowshed complexes is still in operation is convincing proof of the lack of advance planning. However, one of the purchasers managed to make a change from milk production to small-scale wood processing (a small sawmill and the production of wooden articles). The initial capital of the wood processing enterprise was derived from the sale of the cattle from the now defunct cowshed.

Machinery, Equipment and Other Movable Assets

The second stage of the auction consisted of selling off all the movable machinery, equipment and other movable property within 2–3 days. The buyers who had been active during the first stage had held a meeting before that, in order to divide up the objects for sale in advance, and thus avoid unnecessary competition in the bidding.

Table 3.1 The eleven largest enterprises formed from the decollectivisation of Kanepi kolkhoz (restituted farms not included)

Name of enterprise	Line of activity	Status in 1998
Kanepi co-operative	Agricultural production (dairy farming)	Dairy production in full activity. Pork production given up
Karste Piim (private entrepreneur)	Agricultural production	Went bankrupt. Some of the buildings have been sold to new owners, whose plans include a wood processing plant
Kanepi MTJ (limited liability company)	Agricultural production, forestry, retail trade, and bakery production	In operation. Current lines of business are forestry and retail trade
Liivasaare (private entrepreneur)	Agricultural production	In operation
Filippos (private entrepreneur)	Wood processing plant (sawmill and furniture manufacturing)	In operation
Laete (limited liability company)	Hotel planned in the kolkhoz administration building	Building sold to AS Eesti Energia
Ojakivi (private entrepreneur)	Flour-mill	In operation
Igor Põldsepp (private entrepreneur)	Sawmill	In operation
Ritsike (private entrepreneur)	Agricultural production (cowshed and storehouse)	Cattle sold. A sawmill has been set up in the storehouse by the son-in-law of the former owner
Gagarin (private entrepreneur)	Agricultural production	Went bankrupt
Heiki Põkk (private entrepreneur)	Agricultural production	No activity

> We certainly had an agreement and in theory the machines had already been divided up in advance. The ones who kept raising the prices were [other] people standing next to us. We [the local buyers mentioned above] had agreed not try to outbid each other. (Buyer of cowshed complex 1)

However, the agreement did not hold and the competition for machines turned into a merciless battle. There were many reasons for this. Firstly, certain types of machinery (e.g., tractors, lorries and combine harvesters) were absolutely necessary for the people who had bought large production complexes. Naturally, they could in principle have bought agricultural machinery outside the kolkhoz, but they could only use their vouchers in the kolkhoz; furthermore, buying with borrowed vouchers (with borrowed money in a manner of speaking), without guarantees, was only possible inside the kolkhoz.

> The book value of a combine harvester was a couple of thousands, but the price we paid for it was 45,000 kroons – ten times higher . . . I was one of the people who pumped up the price of many machines, [simply] because I needed them; the mower cutter for example. I fought fierce battles for the machinery at the auction. (Buyer of cowshed complex 2)

Secondly, those buyers who were interested in machinery faced competition from existing family farmers as well as those who were planning to set up a farm on the expectation that it would be restituted to them. Unlike many ordinary people, family farmers and the representatives of alliances "were not drunk, but they quarrelled and tried to outbid each other," said the later chairman of the kolkhoz.

The third group were the former machine operators, whose sights were not set on a family farm, but who instead were planning for a future as independent contractors. However, the general decline of agriculture later deprived them of employment opportunities. According to the former municipal director, "today, there are many people who have tractors that are useless. They are just sitting in the yard." "When agriculture doesn't provide even the tiniest income, there is no money to pay for [a contractor's] services," explained a senior agricultural official at county level.

The most interesting objects were lorries, tractors, excavators, and pieces of machinery that were fit for almost any use, and which could also be employed outside the field of agriculture. That was why many machine operators lost the specific machine they had driven and kept in the yard of their own home. The fourth group, the outsiders who had stirred up the competition, was especially interested in these multi-purpose machines. According to a family farmer "there were many who made a big profit at the auction. You could buy [machinery at the auction] with vouchers, and sell them [a few days later] for cash."

The consequences of this behaviour were described in this way.

Tractors and cars were the most sought-after items, and their prices soared. (Former chairman of the kolkhoz)

All the cars changed ownership. Many [kolkhoz members] had kept the kolkhoz car as if it was their own, and hoped to get it for themselves. (Later chairman of the kolkhoz)

For contract work [future entrepreneurs] only wanted to buy machinery that could be used in the forest. (Agronomist X)

There were also several types of purely agricultural machines, such as harvesters, and the demand for these items also vastly surpassed the supply at the auction.

The starting bid for a combine harvester was 1,435 kroons. I bought one for 20,000 kroons. The starting bid for a tractor was 792 kroons. I paid 48,000 kroons. (Buyer of cowshed complex 2)

The fifth group that put up the prices at the auction consisted of people who were not actually interested in purchasing anything, but who attempted to raise the value of their vouchers by making bids. These were often outsiders or people who merely owned an apartment.

Some people who knew that we needed machinery raised the prices to a very high level, but [in the end] they themselves did not buy anything. (Buyer of cowshed complex 1)

There were two men who kept boosting the prices; they were [just] bidding. (Buyer of cowshed complex 2)

Certainly there must have been some brains behind it. I really believe that the men coming from the city were responsible for it. (Later chief accountant)

Somebody was constantly making [higher] bids. It might as well have been a dummy hired for the purpose. (A kolkhoz electrician)

It was like a 'black auction,' since there were people [present], who did not want to buy, but who made bids and kept prices going up. That's what happened with the pork production complex. (Agronomist X, purchasing for Kanepi co-operative)

But this was not all. Prices were further inflated by a sixth group, people who lacked plans for the future altogether or whose plans remained very obscure.

It bore some resemblance to a circus, [it was] a shocking situation. There were only a few buyers who knew in advance what kind of machines they would need. People bought just to be on the safe side, [since] you never knew when a particular piece of machinery would be needed. (A local amateur historian)

There was a man who bought a peat roller, which can only be used in boglands. The next day he gave it to somebody for free. (Former chairman of the kolkhoz)

We wanted a tractor, but the price was too high [at the auction], and we thought that we wouldn't be able to buy one. A couple of days after the auction the same man [who had purchased a tractor at the auction at a high price] approached us and told us he was sorry he'd made such an excessive bid. [Then he said] 'you could buy the tractor for yourself, I don't need it.' [But] I didn't buy it. (Buyer of cowshed complex 1)

Some people made their bids in an advanced state of intoxication.

People had been drinking alcohol; [some] even took their bottles to the [auction] hall. And then [as a consequence of this] they made bids on a few lots solely to prevent another person from getting the item, and before the end they gave up. Prices rocketed to inconceivable heights, from 900 kroons to 92,000 kroons to give an example. One guy bought a fridge with 4,000 workshare kroons and now it's been dumped somewhere in the woods. Quite impossible things were bought at quite impossible prices. (Later chairman of the kolkhoz)

There was this alcoholic woman who bought an old wreck [unspecified] that is completely useless. (A kolkhoz construction worker)

There were mechanics there, and when the auctioneer asked [them] about the state of a specific piece of machinery, they told people about it. There was a trailer that only had an axle and a towbar, and it had been set at a very low starting bid. Someone had eyed it in advance and made a bid. Another fellow just heard that a 'trailer' was up for sale and he also started bidding, so the price rose. And in the end it became mere play-acting. (Later chairman of the kolkhoz)

Some people wasted their money due to lack of information. Perhaps they just thought that the vouchers would not have any value after the auction – so they believed they had better squander all their money there and then.

> When the auction was over everybody had a great time. Many [people] thought that you wouldn't be able to buy anything with the vouchers, and they wasted their shares by buying impossible things at impossible prices. [For example] the briefcase of the kolkhoz cashier was sold at an astonishing price. (Buyer of cowshed complex 1)

Ignorance and drunkenness were thus closely connected with the general lack of knowledge about the auction system. The irrationality of the auction was further heightened by the lack of enough public meetings before it. For most ordinary people the six days between the general meeting and the first auction was insufficient time for the preparation of personal plans.

By contrast, the representatives of each *ühistys* and the family farmers acted much more purposefully. It was a case of serious rivalry between neighbours and they were not always able to get the machines they required. Thus, in their eyes the comedy had turned into a tragedy. But in reality the auction was a tragedy for the majority of the kolkhoz people from the very beginning.

The only group that got immediate and unambiguous benefit from the sharp price increases at the auction were those who were about to redeem their flats or houses for themselves. The nominal value of a single workday soared, thanks to the effect of the auction, from 60 cents to 2.30 kroons. Since the price set for the house or flat remained unchanged, these individuals were able to purchase their flat or house for about a quarter of the workdays that would have been needed prior to the auction. Due to this increase in the value of a workday many people were able to buy a home of their own and an additional flat or even several flats for their children – who as occupants had the right of first refusal, but did not have enough vouchers to redeem their residence themselves.

Today the houses formerly owned by Kanepi kolkhoz are "mostly owned by the occupants," said the later chairman of the kolkhoz. However, "there was a lot of dealing after privatisation – for cash this time – or [people could alternatively] swap [their flat for another] flat or a car or something else." (ibid.)

By liquidating a residence that had been redeemed at a relatively low price one could acquire expensive durable goods, and perhaps in some cases it also facilitated a move out of the municipality. In this way, old kolkhoz flats passed into the hands of new owners coming from outside the kolkhoz, which aroused feelings of bitterness in some people.

> When the kolkhoz flats in the kolkhoz centre came up for sale, they were bought [redeemed] by total strangers – people from outside the kolkhoz – and at a much lower price than my mother paid with her vouchers. (Daughter of a kolkhoz member)

But even if housing was cheap, machinery became ever more expensive; nevertheless, the future of most residents depended on the use of machinery.

> The *ühistys* enterprises were not even able to buy decent machines at the auction. And the pieces of machinery that did they manage to buy were bought on credit. [Now,] the enterprises are deep in debt. (Ibid.)

Since prices rose unexpectedly, the funds accumulated by interested buyers for the auction fell short and their plans went awry. The solution was to resort to taking a loan from the Savings and Loan Association after the auction (see section titled Savings And Loan Associations as a Solution for Unrealised Vouchers for details).

Basically the auction was a tragic and dishonourable drama, and its basic character was actually intensified by the comic elements. Moreover, the second auction event was crowned by a disgraceful climax.

> Hell really broke loose at the moment they started dealing out the machines [that had just been sold at the auction]. People were swapping spare parts; and [many felt that] machines had been [wrongfully] taken away from some individuals. Men stood on guard there and [those who had worked as kolkhoz tractor drivers] knew the exact condition of each individual machine. And if a machine [tractor] that shouldn't have had new tyres had new tires, they were taken off [stolen]. In the end, however, they managed to divide everything, but some [pieces of machinery] are still there in the clearing . . . It was as if we were at war. An armed guard kept watch at all times and once he even had to fire a shot because there was thieving. (Later chairman of the kolkhoz)

The auction grounds were located close to the modern building that only served for a short period of time as the administration building of the kolkhoz. The fine building and the beautiful park-like surroundings resembled a battleground after the auction. A large number of machines and other pieces of scrap were abandoned simply to rust away. It was a huge mess, as if the machines had met their end in a fierce battle. Nobody showed any interest in this debris, although in the third stage of the auction even outsiders could have purchased unprivatised assets with cash.

The Auction and the Social Structure

The kolkhoz auction was a definitive loss for all the citizens of Kanepi: the community structure of the township was damaged because of the careless and chaotic breaking up of the kolkhoz. We have already referred above to the sale of the new kolkhoz administration building and the kindergarten. The municipal council of Kanepi would have had a clear need for these premises. For example, the municipal office has had to operate in very modest quarters, while the modern kolkhoz administration building remained unused and was slowly falling into decay.[4]

The damage was not limited to the change of ownership of socially vital resources from the kolkhoz to private ownership. Those kolkhoz buildings that have not changed hands and become the private property have been vandalised completely. Everything that might have any value has been stripped out. Many former cowsheds, warehouses, etc. now look as if they had been attacked by termites. Not only has everything of value been robbed; anything left has been destroyed as if in a fit of blind rage. In addition to removing almost every removable item, the windows have been broken, the doors have been ripped from their hinges and so on.

From the perspective of an outsider the fate of the kolkhoz district heating plant seems emblematic. It used to provide heating for the flats and houses of all the residents in the centre of Kanepi as well as kolkhoz members.

> During kolkhoz times the kolkhoz paid for the fuel [of the heating plant] and other such costs, but now it lies idle. It was built with care during the kolkhoz. People have broken the district heating system up [by taking building materials from the premises]. Everybody wants heating, but nobody is able to pay for it. (A local amateur historian)

When our researchers were gathering interview data (1995–1996) people were building little stoves in their flats out of the bricks, and chimneys were sticking out from the windows of private flats in some buildings. All this has come about because the heating plant and other major facilities were

---

4   The building has since been sold to AS Eesti Energia, the national electric utility company.

owned by the kolkhoz, and because of the narrow profit-oriented thinking of the board of management and the reform committee, which simply aimed at "disposing of all ballast, everything that was unnecessary" (later municipal director); plus the fact that the municipality did not have the financial resources to buy the district heating plant. Consequently, parts of the kolkhoz that were vitally important to the community ended up in private ownership with all the consequences described above.

Numerous individual objects changed ownership and the huge totality of the kolkhoz was divided into smaller units at the auction. The basis of the local social structure was transformed and the process itself caused a great deal of material and moral damage.

All the employees, except some office workers, had been given notice.

> I gave notice to the kolkhoz workers . . . by April 1st. Only . . . five accountants and a secretary were left. All that went on after that was compiling archives, drawing up and finalising documents, paying and collecting . . . debts. (Later chairman of the kolkhoz)

The Savings and Loan Association as the Legal Successor of the Kolkhoz

The legal closure of the kolkhoz and the disbanding of the reform committee took place simultaneously, at the end of May, with the Savings and Loan Association becoming the legal successor to the kolkhoz. The following description of the closing down of the kolkhoz indicates the situation.

> Then there was the switch over to the Savings and Loan Association. The reform committee was in operation until the 28th of May. That day we organised a little party and at nine o'clock in the evening I locked the office door, threw the key onto the lawn and left. At that point we no longer had anything, all the property had been divided, the office was empty, the desk of the chairman had already been sold, everything [was gone]. The doors were left wide open, electric wiring hung from the ceiling, anyone could take anything he wanted from there. (Later chairman of the kolkhoz)

The assessment of the immediate economic consequences of the dissolution of the kolkhoz is not, however, sufficient for a full understanding of subsequent developments. Both the vouchers and the items bought as the kolkhoz dissolved later created an aftermarket, the mechanism of which can be properly understood only in connection with an understanding of the operation of the Savings and Loan Association. The new economic units developed within this special environment.

A board of management was elected for the Savings and Loan Association, and the later chairman of the kolkhoz was elected as chairperson. In addition to the chairman, the board also employed a secretary. The mission of the association was to act as a channel of investment for those vouchers that had not been used to claim restitution or at the auction. It was against the value of these shares that an *ühistys* (company) or an individual could receive a loan to pay for the bids made at the auction.

At the time of the interviews (June and July 1995) the association controlled vouchers worth EEK 1,200,000 and remaining kolkhoz assets worth EEK 800,000. This covered the difference between the "air" created at the auction and reality – as the later chairman formulated the matter. In fact it covered more than that, in that each agricultural *ühistys* was (in the spring of 1993) provided with the seed corn, fertilisers, etc. necessary for sowing, so that production could be started up. The materials were provided from kolkhoz assets. This was deemed necessary, since the new agricultural enterprises did not have any working capital, nor could they take out a loan from the bank since they could not provide sufficient security.

The Savings and Loan Association was also responsible for making sure that the debtors did not waste their assets, i.e. sell their livestock and machinery in such a way that the property given as security for the loan did not dwindle away to nothing. (Incidentally, it has since been discovered that there is in fact no legal means of controlling the use that individuals make of these assets. Furthermore, it has been shown that the entire Savings and Loan Association system lacks a legal basis.)

The Savings and Loan Association covered its wage costs (the chairman and a secretary) and running expenses with the interest on the loans it provided. The debtors had to pay a very reasonable 1% interest per annum, but the total amount of the debt itself had to be repaid to the association by the year 2003. The paying off of the loan should have been started earlier than that, since the Savings and Loan Association was supposed to have paid back the first vouchers for which they were liable in three years, i.e. by 1996.

In addition to the interest and possible amortisation payments, the association received a dividend from the stocks of Põlva dairy (Põlva Piim) and Värska sanatorium that had been handed over to it. Beyond this it did not have any other assets except for three buildings: two cattle feed silos and one pigsty. These were left unsold at the auction, and they were no longer in active use. The chairman and the secretary were both employed part-time only, and they received most of their income from another occupation. The main source of income for the chairman of the association (the last kolkhoz chairman) has probably been the MTJ. In the mid-1990s it was one of the largest companies in the municipality, and the later chairman is one of its six owners.

It was (and still is) possible to buy housing after the kolkhoz had been broken up, but the current occupants of each flat or house had the right of first refusal, so in this respect the use of the vouchers remained limited. But the holders of vouchers did have other investment opportunities besides housing. They could become shareholders in Kanepi co-operative, and when the co-operative increased the number of its members this way, its debt to the Savings and Loan Association correspondingly diminished. By becoming members of the co-operative they improved the chances that the co-operative would be able to pay its debts, and that they would some day be able to convert their vouchers into kroons at face value; if the enterprise was a success, they could even receive a dividend.

Another alternative was to lend or sell their shares to an *ühistys* or private person, who was indebted (as a result of a purchase of a tractor, for example) to the Savings and Loan Association, with similar consequences. Many different kinds of terms regarding both the loan period and the method of repayment could be specified in the loan agreement. A typical agreement would perhaps include a clause stating that the *ühistys* was committed to doing contract work on a person's fields, so that half of the payment would be deducted from the kroon value of his vouchers and the other half paid to the *ühistys* in cash.

> [I rent my harvester] from the MTJ. I've got 14,500 kroons worth of vouchers invested in there. That's why I can use the services of the MTJ. I have to pay half of the price of the services rendered in cash and the other half in shares. Now I save half the price of the services, I have to pay less . . . The MTJ gained a benefit from people's shares after the auction. MTJ men bought machines and other things at the auction, but they were unable to pay back their loan to the Savings and Loan Association, since they had [been forced] to use other people's vouchers. (A new family farmer, who has only a few pieces of machinery himself)

So the *ühistys* enterprises are able to pay off their loans by providing services instead of paying in money, and the new farms with their inadequate mechanisation are able to cultivate their fields with the help of indebted contractors by resorting to their vouchers. Older people in particular appear to make use of this alternative throughout the county. According to a senior agricultural official at county level "it provides older people with a chance to keep on farming. I believe it's a widespread practice." All the companies owning agricultural machinery in Kanepi appeared to engage in this kind of activity.

There is even the possibility that one can purchase the majority of shares in an *ühistys* and become the owner oneself. One can make an offer to the owner of the *ühistys*, acquire the majority of shares and gain absolute power – this would also apply in respect of co-operatives, at least in Kanepi. After that, "the one who has the controlling interest dictates [his demands] to the others," as the chairman of the Savings and Loan Association put it. This way the ownership may also be concentrated in companies that were originally employee-owned, except in those cases where the legal form of the company was a traditional co-operative (as with Kanepi co-operative).

In some cases it happened that the owner of a particular piece of machinery was driven into financial difficulties, since he had bought partly on credit but then found out he was unable to earn an income with his machines. In such instances one might sometimes acquire the machine at a very affordable price, for example by buying the associated workshares from the owner, and by taking over his debt to the Savings and Loan Association. Could this be what happened in the following case?

> The lorry under the Fiskars [crane] cost 35,000 [kroons]. The balance he owed [to the Savings and Loan Association] was 18,000. And we didn't buy it for 18,000, but at a negotiated price, which was much less. And we didn't have to pay it all up front: we signed an agreement that we would pay it [in instalments] over a period of several years. And this is how those machines were paid for. The MTJ could fall back on the forests; they [always] provided [us] with an income. (One of the MTJ owners)

Although vouchers cannot be converted into money at their nominal value like bonds, for example, they are not entirely worthless. Their ultimate value of course depends essentially on the economic prospects of those enterprises whose assets are held as securities for the shares. The local black market for vouchers was created on the basis of speculations such as the following.

> At the auction, the price of a day was established at 2.30 kroons. A new market started up, in which these cards [vouchers] were traded, but they were no longer sold at the same price as in the beginning.

> Shares are sold on the black market for 30 cents a day; the lowest price by far has been 5 cents a day. (Chairman of the Savings and Loan Association)

Having bought vouchers on the black market and having validated his transaction with the municipal council an individual could now pay his debt with vouchers.

> Smart people buy shares with cash and a piece of property comes along. If one is quick on the uptake, one can make a fortune out of nothing. And I'm not at all interested in how he has acquired that card [voucher]. (Ibid.)

The balance to the Savings and Loan Association could also be paid in cash, but in that case the amount due would be calculated according to the nominal value of the share, not at the current black market price. That nominal value is 2.30 kroons per workday. Thus, one can pay back one's auction loan more quickly through the black market, if one happens to have funds to buy the vouchers. In the early days one could not take out a loan from a bank to repay the association, since the types of assets people possessed did not usually qualify as securities for a loan. In Kanepi an opportunity for acquiring capital was offered by the timber business right after the auction.

> There was still one further option. If you had something you could sell, maybe a cow, or if you got [income] from the sale of milk, you could [if you did not owe money to the tax authorities] ask for a paper from the Tax Office certifying that such and such a company didn't owe any money to the government, the taxes had all been paid. The Erastvere forestry area is located close by, and [the government] organised timber auctions [where the rights to fell trees in a certain area were sold]; [some companies and individuals] felled timber and got money from that. This is how the MTJ paid its debts. Others who have gained a great deal [of capital] this way are the farm [of cowshed complex 1] and Kanepi co-operative too. (Ibid.)

But vouchers will not be available on the black market forever. Some people have asked for the price reached at the auction for their vouchers, and in 1996 the repayment by the borrowers should have already started. We will come back to these problems later when we look at the future prospects for different types of farms. However, at this stage we can already establish that many *ühistys* enterprises soon met with insuperable difficulties, and they had to be closed down. That was why many owners of vouchers consider shares handed over to the Savings and Loan Association to be lost. Although the situation in reality is not as simple as that, it is obvious to these people that if the Savings and Loan Association were now to start collecting all the outstanding debts, the real property that forms the basis of the outstanding claims would be largely – perhaps entirely – destroyed. Thus, "if everyone . . . wants to get his share, there will be nothing left of them," as one of the MTJ owners said.

In principle the Savings and Loan Association also has to check that the debtors do not waste real property. In the case of agricultural co-operatives, even the sale of a single cow would have required the approval of the Savings and Loan Association. Despite this, some wastage has occurred, and the ("half-Russian") owner of one *ühistys* did flee to Russia shortly after he had purchased kolkhoz assets. Attempts at theft are quite systematic.

> When the assets of the *ühistys* came up for sale because of bankruptcy, the assets should have been handed over to the Savings and Loan Association. But assets like these keep getting 'lost' all the time. Even before the bankruptcy people somehow bought the tractors, cars, [and] agricultural machinery from this *ühistys*; even cows have been stolen in that manner. (A policeman)

Still, the greater part of the material property remains, or so the chairman of the association believes: "All the property is there, [or at least] 95% [of it]."

However, in the light of recent information the chairman's impression has proved too optimistic. One of the three cowshed *ühistys* enterprises that went out of business left all its debts unsettled. When the Savings and Loan Association took legal action against the owner it turned out that the association in fact had no legal right to demand the repayment of the debt.

We shall revert to agricultural enterprises later in this chapter, and other types of enterprise will be discussed by Jouko Nikula in Chapter 4. However, the following citation serves as a provisional summary of kolkhoz privatisation.

> And that's how the kolkhoz property was dissolved. There were plenty of people who got a lot of assets and many that got nothing. But all that was scattered around [in this way] was the result of people's work. It was divided among different people in an unequal way. (A pensioner and family farmer)

It might, however, be appropriate to emphasise that in fact very few people got rich as a result of this. The later chairman mentions two groups.

> I'm not really able to say, but [it appears] that businessman Q, he bought a lot . . .
> They bought the sawmill, [and quickly] disposed of the cattle [they had bought]

and [then] bought the buildings with the money. Then there is the MTJ Company, in which I'm a partner, too. At first they operated in forestry, sold timber, got money. [Today] their property is 4.5 million [kroons]; they started out with 300,000.

The other extreme may consist of the segment of the population that is incapable of any independent initiative, notably the elderly.

When the kolkhoz was broken up, many people [just] waited and expected that somebody [else] would [once] again take care of them. Especially the older people, who'd once given all their property [to the kolkhoz] . . . At the moment the only real worry for the elderly is whether they'll be able to buy a coffin for themselves or not. (A local amateur historian)

The Future Prospects of the Various Farm Types

Three different categories of production units immediately came into existence on the basis of Soviet-type agriculture in Estonia: (1) large-scale agro-industrial units (*ühistys* enterprises which could take various legal forms, from co-operatives to joint stock companies, and from direct individual ownership to family ownership); (2) plot farms (modest production buildings using largely unmechanised farm implements, a small herd of cattle, up to one hectare of land) and (3) garden plots. In addition to these, the period of perestroika had brought about (4) peasant farms proper (much larger in acreage, partly modern mechanisation, production buildings suitable for modern family farming) and (5) expanded plot farms (at first the maximum area was three hectares, but it was later increased; often based on old production buildings). Perestroika also made possible the selling of kolkhoz machinery to private farms at advantageous prices based on book values, in addition to which many new farmers received second-hand agricultural machinery from the West at a nominal price. Note also that (6) the restitution of landed property, together with (7) the right granted to country people to redeem about two hectares of land around their house (even the complete holding, if the person(s) entitled to its restitution had no interest in having it returned) have made possible the creation of numerous new small-scale farms. In fact, at the moment, (8) agricultural land is available for rent to anyone who wants it for nothing more than the payment of the land tax, at least in such remote areas as Kanepi.

The breaking up of the collective farms tore agriculture away from its associated product industries (it separated industry and in many ways also trade from agriculture). Furthermore, the process strengthened the government and made it more independent of enterprises at both national and local level.

The new agricultural enterprises evolved as a result of a more or less anarchic process, which split up and then reassembled the various elements of the Soviet agricultural system, and separated the developing agricultural enterprises in terms of division of labour from private entrepreneurs in other branches of the economy, as well as from the public sector. Of course, the new units have not been born ready-made from the standpoint of the new social order; they have had to undergo a profound process of change themselves. They are more or less temporary conceptions by nature, which are only gradually developing into the forms of enterprise characteristic of capitalism. With regard to the division of labour in Estonia, the overall trend of the process conforms to general ideas of modernisation within social theory (see e.g. Parsons, 1971).

Capitalism as such does not prescribe any specific type of enterprise, and in the course of history capitalist economies have included enterprises based on serfdom (Prussian and Russia), slavery (the Southern States of the USA and Caribbean colonies), wage-labour (England and Scotland) and even quite early in the modern history of Western Europe, family farming (France and Denmark). The spread of parliamentary democracy has made the occurrence of the more archaic manifestations less frequent and abolished such forms of capitalism from many countries.

A Systematic Picture of the Agricultural Enterprise Structure in the Light of Two Surveys

The overall picture of the enterprise structure of the Estonian agricultural sector is clearly observable in the results of the nation-wide agricultural survey[5] conducted contemporaneously with the Kanepi interviews. The survey data shows (unlike the publications of the Statistical Office of Estonia) cultivated hectareages and the extent of agricultural cultivation and

---

5   The survey was based on a random sample of 1,000 respondents living in the Estonian countryside. Small towns, of which Viljandi with at least 20,000 inhabitants is the largest, were also included. This survey was carried out by Nordic and Baltic researchers participating in the "The Privatization of Agriculture in the Baltic Countries" research project.

gardening by households for their own use. In the table below I have only selected those households where the surveyed interviewee belonged to the economically active population.

My inferences from Table 3.2 are based on the fact that in Estonia gardens and plot farms under 3 hectares are almost exclusively sources of additional income only, and that only in a few exceptional cases do they provide the main source of income for a household (Alanen 1998a, 56; see also Table 3.3). Since the branch of employment has been classified by the main source of income of the interviewee, we may reasonably assume that those plot and garden cultivators (on a cultivated area under 3 hectares) employed in agriculture are in fact wage-workers in larger enterprises.

Table 3.2 Classification of the economic branch of the interviewee by cultivated land area in 1995

Cultivated area (ha)	Employed in agriculture %	(N)	Not employed in agriculture %	(N)
Not at all	22	(21)	47	(198)
0.3 or less	21	(20)	23	(95)
0.31–3.0	27	(26)	18	(76)
3.1–8.9	8	(8)	5	(23)
9 or more	22	(21)	7	(31)
Total	100	(96)	100	(423)

First of all, the table indicates that the majority of interviewees engaged in any type of cultivation did so merely in order to gain additional income, since their main source of income was outside agriculture. Secondly, we discover that the majority of those employed in the agricultural sector, especially those who do not practise any cultivation, together with the bulk of the plot and family farmers (categories from "Not at all" up to "3 hectares") – in all 70% of the interviewees – are essentially agricultural wage-workers. Thirdly, the statistics bear evidence of the fact that even on larger farms cultivation is often practised solely to provide supplementary income for a wage-worker household, since the majority of farmers with over 3 hectares of land (only 29 cases in agricultural households compared with 54 cases in non-agricultural households) derived their main income from non-agricultural occupations. However, the relative over-representation of farms with over 9 hectares of cultivated area among those employed in the agricultural branch implies a fourth conclusion: that the real full-time family farmers are most likely to be found in this category.

We had conducted a previous survey in early 1994,[6] that is about eighteen months before the survey above and about six to eighteen months after the decollectivisation of the kolkhozes and sovkhozes. The table below (Table 3.3) bears further witness to the hypothesis that wage-work dominates Estonian agriculture.

Table 3.3 Classification of agricultural households by their primary source of income in 1994

Primary source of income	Percentage of agricultural households (%)
Wage income	75
Entrepreneurial income	18
Mainly plot farming	7
Total	100 (N=73)

According to table 3.3 a wage or a salary was the primary source of income for up to 75% of the households in the agricultural population, whilst only 18% were agricultural entrepreneurs proper. Despite the fact that plot farming is very widespread in Estonia and that many households endured grave economic hardships after the decollectivisation, only 7% gave it as their primary source of income. Note that plot farming, chiefly referring to farms with 1–3 hectares, was a legal term in the agricultural reform and on account of this was also applied as a category label in our 1994 survey; hence the results of this survey are fairly unambiguous.

It can be argued that plot farming (and cultivating one's own farm in general in Estonia) usually forms an integral part of the coping strategy of the wage-worker, regardless of whether the rural household in question derives its primary income from agriculture or from some other branch of the economy.

---

6   A random sample of 1,500 respondents living in Estonia. This survey was carried out by Nordic and Baltic researchers participating in the "Baltic-Nordic Research Project".

The two surveys demonstrate that there was no significant shift towards family farming over this period of time, since entrepreneurs proper made up such a small part of the population deriving their primary income from agriculture. The small number of family farms can be attributed to the failure of decollectivisation, the disinclination of the kolkhoz and sovkhoz employees to break up the large-scale farms, allied to their unwillingness to take up family farming, and the failure of government policies favouring restitution and family farms, all this in a background of difficult external circumstances.

The arguments presented above serve to demonstrate that the agricultural enterprise structure created in Estonia is to a great extent dominated by wage-work and large-scale production. Figures released by the Statistical Office of Estonia verify that in 1994 47% of overall agricultural production was generated by large-scale farms, 15% by family (peasant) farms, and 38% by plot cultivators (auxiliary farms) (Alanen, 1998b, 159). The production structure created in the immediate aftermath of decollectivisation has since remained relatively unchanged (Agriculture and Rural Development. Overview 1998, 64). Even the restitution of land and other privatisation processes, which have resulted in a highly fragmented land ownership, have not significantly deconcentrated production (ibid. 67).

The Kanepi case gives us further opportunities to examine the microlevel mechanism that produced the macrostructure delineated above.

Back to Kanepi – Difficult External Circumstances

A lack of experience in private entrepreneurship in the early stages can itself lead to practices that are unfavourable to long-term prospects. But improving one's knowledge of constructive practices has been made more difficult by the instability of the economic and political environment. Such macroeconomic measures as the abandonment of customs duties and price control had multiple effects at the level of individual enterprises. All in all, the economic and political environment of new businesses has undergone and is still (1995–1999) undergoing rapid and unforeseen changes.

> Development is totally unpredictable and nobody can influence those development processes on his own. When we got that farm in the first year, I promptly electrified everything. Now, a year has passed and the price of electricity has risen so much that I've had to switch from electricity to other [sources of energy]. And that's caused [us] great expense. I [also] got Danish automatic feeders for the whole farm. The price of electricity has since come down, but the price . . . that I've had to pay for that extremely expensive equipment, I can't

work out how I'm going to get it back. (Buyer of a pork production complex from the neighbouring kolkhoz)

In addition, the competition so essential to the dynamics of a capitalist economy is developing unevenly from a macroeconomic viewpoint. At the same time as most of the large-scale farms are being split into units so small that they cannot influence the market by themselves, the monopolies of the Soviet period remain in the food processing industry. The processing monopolies have managed to react to the decline in consumption and the low retail prices of food products by shifting the burden downwards, onto basic producers. (This has also been one of the major characteristics of the Russian economy, see Clarke, 1993.) At the time of our survey, the interviewees referred to the strong position of the dairies. In the county of our research the commanding position of Põlva dairy was experienced as a particularly pressing problem, since the majority of the newly formed private production units were specialising in dairy farming.

We have given up – [actually we have] not given up yet, but will soon finish – raising dairy cattle. The [milk] quality is low, [and] the cattle have somatic cells [in their milk]. According to the veterinarian the reason for this is that the cows are stressed [because they do not get enough cattle feed or when some person shouts at them] . . . [Because of this problem] we lose over 1,000 kroons each day . . . (An agronomist at Kanepi co-operative, July 1995)

The Võru dairy went bankrupt . . . In Põlva [dairy] all the technology has been imported from the West, [while] in Võru it came from Lithuania. The technology in Põlva is of high quality; they detect all the bacteria, etc. Last month we should have received 130,000 kroons from the dairy for our milk, but we only got 80,000 kroons. We lost 50,000 kroons. The reason was the [poor] quality of the milk. We pay [our employees] 40,000–45,000 kroons in wages. Money also goes on fuel, and spare parts for the machines, [but] there is no money for new technology. (An agronomist at Kanepi co-operative, July 1995)

Põlva dairy is listed in the catalogue of the fifty best businesses in Estonia. We feel that their success results from exploiting fifty enterprises that are in a worse state. How else could it buy milk in Pärnu and sell finished products in Holland? (An agronomist at Kanepi co-operative, July 1995)

The quality of the milk produced by the small farmers is not even monitored; instead they are automatically classed as providing the lowest quality class of milk.

And now they say that we should join forces with the housewife next door, together we would get 100 litres of milk [per day], and then they would perform a test [for us together], and if it is milk of the highest quality, they [would] pay [us] a higher price. That would be like a new kolkhoz. For the highest quality class they pay 1.90 kroons in the summer, 1.70 kroons for the first [class], 95 cents for the second [class], 60 cents for the third [class] . . . It's also an interesting point that the producers are paid different prices, but later in the dairy all the milk goes into one single tank, and [still] the final product is of 'high quality'. But [of course] the milk for export is properly checked . . . Money – the money that comes in always goes straight out. It's not possible to buy [any new technology]. Last year [1994] we had two cows, we got [paid] 6,000 kroons [for the year's milk], which is a month's wages for one person. (A farmer's wife)

These policies of the dairies wield a great deal of influence on the technological modernisation of agricultural enterprises and favour the centralisation of production. Naturally the pressure by the dairies also creates bitterness.

The people living in the country believe that . . . the dairy is one big mafia. (Policeman)

In 1995 the bitter feelings had not yet resulted in any organised actions or pressure by the farmers, but later in the 1990s there were organised expressions of opinion against the dairies.

The Modes of Reproduction of Agricultural Enterprises

It is possible to categorise the agricultural enterprises characteristic of modern capitalism by the types of labour on which their internal reproduction is based. The classification consists of the following types of enterprises (Alanen, 1991 and 1996): (1) marginalised enterprises, (2) semi-proletarian enterprises, (3) capital-intensive family farms, and (4) capitalistically organised large-scale enterprises based purely on wage-labour.

In the Baltic republics, and in other post-socialist countries as well, another enterprise type could develop as an alternative to or parallel with large-scale production based on wage-labour, namely (5) large-scale production units collectively owned by the employees as co-operatives, or other similar legal entities. The types of enterprises that will dominate in the future will determine the basic nature of the structure of production in agriculture.

At the time most of our data were gathered (1995), these enterprise types and the production structure determined by them were only just evolving, and the future production structure was still obscure. However, with hindsight (Alanen, 1999) we can establish that the structural basis of Estonian agriculture had already acquired its present character.

Following the agricultural reform in Kanepi (and especially the dissolution of Kanepi kolkhoz) the development tendencies in enterprise structure discussed below can be observed. I have omitted from my analysis (regardless of the acreage cultivated) the kind of hobby gardening and plot farming that is practised not for economic reasons, but rather for recreational reasons or as a manifestation of the Estonian custom – also typical of other Baltic republics – of preparing and preserving an abundance of garden produce for private use; housewives in particular tend to regard this as a duty.

Marginalised or Marginal Small-scale Producers

This group has little significance on either the market for agricultural produce or the labour market. Its marginal status determines the type of reproduction involved. In developed capitalist countries people classed in this group of producers include those who have fallen into the poverty trap because of a lack of professional skills, poor health, a lack of education, geographical location, deficiencies in the social security system and other such reasons, as well as so-called multi-problem families and individuals. In numerous developing countries this type of small-scale production is in fact (according to several empirical studies) numerically dominant (Alanen, 1991, Chapter 4.4.4).

In developing countries, marginalised farms form a part of the stagnating informal sector, which is made use of by the export-driven and technologically modern formal sector. Developing countries are also characterised by the generally undeveloped state or plain non-existence of any social security system, in which case the unemployed, the elderly and other people incapable of work are cared for by the members of their community, especially their closest relatives, rather than by the government.

Plot farmers cultivate a small piece of land using traditional methods involving a lot of manual labour. They consume the produce themselves or sell it at less than the national price level, mostly in local markets. Their production of cheap foodstuffs tends to lower the wage demands of the local labour force. At the same time they themselves constitute a large and flexible reserve of cheap, but unskilled labour. Since a large part of their livelihood is derived from their tiny plots, the farmers are able to take on outside work at a lower wage than other potential employees, and to return to their plot when they meet with unemployment. This informal sector brings down the general level of wages both in industry and in large-scale agriculture, which in turn reduces the domestic market, and deepens the circle of underdevelopment in the nation. Since plot farming in part acts as a substitute for a social security system, according to Claude Meillassoux (1981) the existence of plot farms renders "super-exploitation" possible. A small farm thus becomes a structural element in such a society, indeed the element by which the majority of theories on developing countries explain the subordinate status of a country in the world system (Amin, 1977, 21; Wallerstein et al., 1982, 438 and 440; in the Baltic context see Alanen, 1995 and 1998b).

In Kanepi the marginalised small-scale producers appear to be evolving from several quarters: out of former garden and plot farms, out of restituted farms and new family farms, or in some cases from persons and families already marginalised who have taken up this kind of production. The foundation of traditional plot farming had been its symbiosis with large-scale production. Now this symbiosis has been broken. According to the former chairman of the kolkhoz the breaking up of this symbiosis, which resulted from the 1993 auctions and the setting up of new enterprises, was a big surprise to a great many plot farmers, and it brought about a rapid abandonment of plot farming. The fracture has, however, been *softened* by the redemption of shares – the method by which the *ühistys* enterprises with activities in agricultural production or agricultural contracting have *raised their paid-up capital by redeeming the vouchers* of small-scale producers (including people other than traditional plot farmers); an *ühistys*, it will be recalled, is able to repay its debts to its shareholders by providing various services on the shareholders' fields with its machines. Although in practice all the people still living in rural areas have the opportunity to acquire land for cultivation, not everybody has the skills or the material necessities. The most important of these, i.e. the first major problem is the *lack of agricultural machinery and production buildings*.

> In my opinion the greatest problem is the machinery. There is no mechanisation. (A man who got his farm back in restitution)

> In the early years they gave loans to independent farmers. Now the time of loans is over and people are saying that [agriculture] isn't economically worthwhile.

[They received second-hand agricultural machines from Sweden and Finland, but that is over now]. (Agronomist X)

At the moment farming is possible only for those people who were able to acquire machinery during the kolkhoz, that's at the auction or prior to that, from [19] 88 onwards. There are only a few of these. (A member of the reform committee)

In today's conditions, setting up a farm in not even worth considering.

No, I haven't [even considered] taking up [agriculture]. [It would only be possible] if your parents have left you something, [since] you have to have implements, mechanisation . . . If you don't have the machines, where do you get the money to buy them and what could you do without them?

Brand-new small-scale producers may also be induced to start up because of the low level of income from the primary occupation of the family breadwinner, but only if they have the necessary basic prerequisites.

[The Kanepi] co-operative is at present the largest employer of men [in the Municipality of Kanepi], and they are lucky to get 600 kroons after taxes. Can you call that a man's wages? 600 kroons is [these days] supposed to be a good wage. In the forestry business they get 1,000 [kroons per month]. (An unemployed woman in the centre of Kanepi)

1,000 kroons [per month], that is a fantastic job. (21-year-old salesperson in the centre of Kanepi)

The potato field . . . I've only had it for two years. We get the potatoes from there, [so there is] no need to buy them. [We have got shares in the *ühistys* for] over 4,000 kroons. But the value [total amount] of [our] shares is decreasing, since we get services [from the *ühistys*] in the cultivation of our potato field. We pay a part of it in vouchers and another part in cash.

The citation above comes from a joint interview with a married couple. Both are working as milkers in Kanepi co-operative. In practice, the *ühistys* is their only employment opportunity in the municipality, but moving away is not easy either, because of problems related to housing.

I feel that the people in the cities do not know how difficult life is here [in the countryside]. It could be that I'd be able to find the same kind of work elsewhere, but I have my own privatised apartment here, and I won't be able to get a similar one elsewhere. (Wife)

Consequently, people are resorting to plot farming, because their *wages are low and they are unable to move to another place* where they could get a job that would provide a higher wage.

Other groups of people typically involved in plot farming are *elderly pensioners*, who are still fit enough to cultivate a small piece of land. Pensions are so small that they require *a supplementary income*, but the residence may also be so remotely situated that plot farming is a virtual necessity.

> The pension is 738 kroons [per month], [but] in September there should be a rise. My hard work [at the kolkhoz] was of no use whatsoever, because those who didn't work at all got exactly the same. [However,] the house is mine. After my mother's death the village soviet gave me entitlement according to which the buildings belong to me, but not the ground. [I've got a] plot [at my disposal] where I grow potatoes. Taking a larger piece of land is not worthwhile, since using a combine harvester [as a contracted service] would be too expensive. I have only 0.1 hectares of arable land. I gave the *ühistys* some of my [vouchers], because I hope they'll send me a tractor to work on my field. [I've got] one cow, one pig, chickens and rabbits. [I would not get along without my plot, because] in that case, there would be nothing to eat. I would have to go to the market each week to buy potatoes. But there are no potatoes for sale in Kanepi market. Outdoor cucumbers and tomatoes, it's so easy to grow them on your own plot. [The cow] is for my own use only. I don't [sell milk]. (Pensioner, living in an old detached peasant house)

It seems to be even more common that plot farming is practised by *a network of close relatives or an extended family*, which includes pensioners and unemployed persons in addition to family members employed in regular wage-work elsewhere. Small-scale farming has thus become an integral part of a coping strategy in which people band together to form a social network based on barter between its members. Indeed, it is less common for plot farming to be done by a single person or a nuclear family. An illustrative example of this social network is a family with three school-age children, a wife in early middle age (former kolkhoz accountant, today a municipal official) and her husband (former kolkhoz lorry driver, currently unemployed). They and their closest relatives obtain an income from plot farming in the following manner.

> My husband does some work on the field. His father has received [in restitution] some 40 hectares of arable land . . . They are not able to cultivate all this acreage, but he helps out [his parents] as much as he can . . . Personally, I don't have the possibility to keep livestock, [since] we live in a large block of flats, but my

mother and my mother-in-law are able to do that, and we're all a little bit like partners [in this enterprise]. I spend virtually all my summer holidays making hay. And then we also have a tiny kitchen plot where we grow potatoes . . . There's no need to buy milk and meat. And with my wages one couldn't. I'm paid a fixed wage [of EEK 1,000 per month], but my husband is unemployed. If he's able to sell some agricultural produce that's [his] sole income . . . Yes, you've got to find a place where you can sell. He's taken potatoes up to Tartu and even [as far as] Elva . . . You just have to find a location. Usually we don't go to the market place, our car is too old and it keeps playing up, we would have to rent a car to be able to go to a public market. But somehow we've always dealt with the matter . . . we've even bartered potatoes for something else we need . . . Others [other farmers] have, for example, offered us seed corn . . . [Our] son sold mushrooms [he had gathered], and bought a pair of shoes.

Yes, groceries are, nevertheless, the most important expense. We come up with our own milk, and potatoes, and sometimes even meat, but that's not enough. There are things that you have to buy from a shop, such as sugar, macaroni, and items like that. And I think food is very expensive. And take shoes [for example], they are also expensive. Our relatives help us too . . . [I also] do some needlework. I've knitted all the socks and mittens. My mother-in-law keeps sheep, and that's how we've got our yarn. (Ibid.)

The collective farm was liquidated in 1993 [and my husband] has been unemployed since then. For a while he was registered as an unemployed person, but he only received the benefit for six months. In the winter he got some [short-term] job in forestry, transporting timber. He takes whatever chance he finds to earn a little extra money, [since] we're not able to make a living on my wages . . . Farmers in our village, even the ones with big farms, say that they're not making any profit. It could be that the farmers who purchased their machines while they were still cheap, it could be that [cultivating] might be profitable for them. But to start now [is an impossibility]. (Ibid.)

So the husband is reckoned among *the labour reserve* for most of the year, and in principle he is willing to take any work available. The production of their allotment mostly goes to their own use, or, as a matter of fact, the consumption of a large network of family members; *only the small surplus is sold directly to non-related consumers*. Despite the farm being fairly large in principle, the family appears to be drifting towards partial marginalisation.

There is plenty of arable land available for prospective farmers, but right now furnishing a new homestead with modern machinery and production buildings is virtually impossible.

We have more than 40 hectares of land, and I can't even imagine how large a loan we'd have to take to be able to buy the machines we need. Nor do we have any production buildings, just a house [fit for residence in the summer only, on the farm in a remote village; the family also have a main residence in the centre of Kanepi]. (Ibid.)

We have a small tractor, and [my husband] ploughed the fields last year. [That way] it's a little easier. We only have to buy the fuel. If you have to rent a tractor and do the job with that, I can't imagine how we could have afforded that. (Ibid.)

We've also got a potato planter. But we haven't got any combined sowing and fertilising machine, sowing machine or [unspecified] planter. (Ibid.)

We've made a loss [because of the plot's non-profitability]. We don't have all the machines that we'd need, although we have managed to get some. Now they've had the haymaking season there [in the remote village where their farm is located], but we don't have any harvesting machine of our own, we had to rent one, and in exchange we had to make their hay. (Ibid.)

The difficulty of building up a farm from scratch today can be clearly illustrated by considering *the expenses and risks involved in the purchase of an agricultural tractor*. The price of a second-hand Soviet-era tractor in fairly good condition is about 50,000 kroons.

The price of a house in the country is about 50,000, this means that a person should mortgage his property in land and his house, and [then] buy that tractor. Then a couple of parts break down in the tractor and in 2–3 years the bank will send him packing from his house. (Wife of the former chairman of Kanepi kolkhoz in a joint interview with her husband)

That . . . a person would be able to purchase new technology from his own work on these Estonian wages, that is totally impossible in the present circumstances. (Former chairman of the kolkhoz in a joint interview with his wife)

A few can do it, but the majority can't. (Wife of the former kolkhoz chairman in a joint interview with her husband)

Those who are able to buy machines with money acquired by selling timber or from the forestry business are a small percentage. (Former chairman of the kolkhoz in a joint interview with his wife)

Of course, a tractor alone does not make a farm. A farm received in restitution requires other agricultural hardware as well; otherwise the tractor could stand idle too. And even if the neighbours would like to contract the tractor owner for various tasks, they simply cannot afford to do so.

There's a farmer who bought himself a tractor. Now this tractor stands in the yard of the farmer, and he won't use it for the benefit of other people [plot farmers]. (Director of Kanepi co-operative)

What about the income provided by a small-scale farm or a plot farm? Four cows is the maximum amount of livestock that will typically fit into an old cowshed in a plot farm. To what extent can one rely on that?

We have four cows, [but] we don't send all the milk [to the dairy], [since] our children also come and get their milk [from us]. Last month [summer of 1995] we received 1,900 kroons [from the dairy], and 300 kroons was deducted from that to cover the cost of transport, etc. I bought one or two things with the money and that's about it. Some was also spent on repairs to the tractor we bought. Another family and we pooled our vouchers to buy a tractor for our common use, but it is in bad repair. (Former kolkhoz agronomist, today a milker in the co-operative, cultivates a one-hectare plot together with two pensioners, earned income about EEK 2,000 per month)

The proceeds from the milk from four cows and other earnings (e.g. meat, calves) are *mainly used on consumption*, they do not suffice to equip a farm, although in this case the earned income is still well above average (about twice the average). Setting up a farm completely from scratch is, of course, a much more demanding endeavour.

Just to be able to construct a farm with a house to live in, a million won't be enough for that. Just acquiring the cows [at the time of the interview he had 21 cows, four heifers and calves] and these buildings [he owned a cowshed and some warehouses], a million [kroons] won't go far. (Owner of a modern family farm)

Hence, if a person did not get the agricultural machinery he needed by the time the kolkhoz was broken up at the latest, it was usually totally impossible to construct and mechanise a farm received in restitution after that date. And what about the *plot farms?* Most of the plot farms are under-mechanised, while others are overmechanised.

It's not normal for people that cultivate a holding of about two hectares to buy a tractor. If a person buys a tractor he [soon finds out that] using the tractor is so costly for someone who only wants to cultivate his own little patch that he simply gives up. (Former kolkhoz member, today a successful shopkeeper)

And even a plot farmer needs other machines besides the tractor. If there are no machines, one has to purchase the services from an outside agricultural contractor.

In reality, *the distinction between family farmers and plot farmers is being obscured*, since nobody is able to expand production, no matter how much cultivable land a person might have at his disposal. Most of those who have received land in restitution are in fact former plot farmers. They are able to continue (after some futile attempts at expansion) the way they did before, since they have the necessary buildings and some of the implements – and they want to continue small-scale farming from force of habit.

In addition to the shortage of modern machinery and buildings, the second *major problem is marketing*. The volume of production on ordinary plot farms is so small that direct sales are the only worthwhile form of marketing. Kanepi is located in an outlying district away from the largest population centres in Estonia, and the traditional markets for the local farmers have been in Russia.

> Our neighbour's got two oxen and a cow. They built a cellar for their own use. But I believe that at the moment no one can sell the products of plot farming. [People only farm] for their own consumption. (Former vice-chairman of the kolkhoz)

> The farmers face the same problem [with the location of the municipality as with all other business enterprises in Kanepi]; in the old days they used to go to Pechory and Pskov, and sell potatoes, vegetables etc. in the marketplace. [But] after the border was closed everything became very complicated. Back then it was easy for plot farmers to sell their produce in Russia, but now it's practically impossible. (Municipal councillor)

> People want to grow something in their fields but they've got problems in selling their produce. If this problem of selling the products of an Estonian peasant farmer could be solved, at the 'normal' price [evidently referring to the good price they got in kolkhoz times], they would enter the market. In my opinion it was a big mistake of the [Estonian] government to close the Russian border. (Former manager of the kolkhoz construction team, now a successful shopkeeper)

> Our [government] policy turned its back on Russia. The whole of our production used to go there. At the moment people have a surplus of everything, they aren't able to sell all their apples, potatoes . . . (An agronomist formerly employed at Kanepi co-operative)

Now this great purchaser, Russia, [has] disappeared. A person can no longer even get rid of the small amount he produces. (Former chairman of the kolkhoz)

It is in fact difficult to estimate how much Estonian politicians could contribute to the reopening of the border, if Russia is simply not interested in the matter. People do nevertheless expect some sort of initiative from their own government. We were even presented with a calculation of the concrete significance of the trade for one family during one of our interviews.

Throughout all these years that we've been married, we've also grown some cabbage, vegetables [and other products for sale]. (Wife)

But this year [we planted] potatoes for our own use only; if something is left over, that would be perhaps 2–4 sackfuls. We used to grow [potatoes] for sale, and we did get a lot done in the past, but the year before last we were unable to make any profit, instead we sustained a loss of 1,000 kroons or thereabouts. We aren't wealthy enough to pay anything extra for our own work, and therefore we've given up and left the field uncultivated. Yes, in the summertime we prepare all kinds of conserves and . . . we're well stocked for the winter; usually we're not even able to use them all up during the winter. We've got no market here. The prices are low here [in Estonia], and we cannot produce any extra for Russia, [since] there are borders and taxes and high transport costs. (Husband; a young couple with two children in a joint interview, both in regular wage-work)

An elderly plot farmer who has now been restituted his old holdings has also found *cultivating* them *unprofitable*; however, he has developed his own method of direct sales. This may only be feasible in the centre of Kanepi.

We can't keep too many cows, [since] we've got trouble with marketing. If I send it [the milk] to the dairy, they'll tell me that I'll only get 60 cents a litre. Now I sell the milk at home and I get two kroons per litre. I sell it directly to the people and there are plenty of customers. We also make cream at home and sell it as well. I've got one cow [and] it gives me 30 litres of milk [each day]. The customer comes along, and brings [his/her] own 3-litre jug for example, takes the [old jug with the] milk, leaves the new empty jug [for the next day]. It's their own business whether they come on time or leave the milk waiting. The payment is due once a month. So far we've had no problems with the payment. People are honest. (A man who received his farm back in restitution, but whose production is based on the cowshed and the warehouses of the plot farming period)

Because of the problems in marketing, people are reducing the number of their cattle to the level of their own consumption.

> At the moment it seems that people are cutting down on their cattle. The whole herd is not disposed of; [instead] they leave just a couple of cows for themselves. Fields are cultivated and cattle are raised solely for their own consumption. For example, milk production is no longer profitable. The dairies won't pay the highest price for the [small] farmers' milk, [in most cases they pay] only 60 cents per litre. (A member of the reform committee)

The rural population is thus increasingly switching over to *subsistence farming*. This type of old-fashioned agriculture is exercised in the first place by the unemployed, families with dependent children and old age pensioners, in other words, groups that have surplus labour and a large number of dependants.

> Young families are in trouble without plot farming. But on the other hand, I have to spend my two months' pension on cultivating the plot. I made calculations on the basis of one hectare. I paid 1,200 kroons [to contractors for soil, fertilisers and other such things]. In addition to that I had an old tractor which I used for ploughing the plot, to prepare it for cultivation. For large families the plot offers one possibility of obtaining a livelihood, but it's not a solution. I calculated what would happen if I bought a pig. [First of all, it would cost me] 400–500 kroons. The powdered milk costs 500 kroons. That's 1,000 in all. With that kind of money I could buy a lot of meat. It's just not worthwhile . . . With that money I get to buy 50 kilograms [of meat from a shop]. (Former vice-chairman of the kolkhoz)

Despite her similar experiences, a municipal official who has also conducted interviews for the Statistical Office of Estonia (as a part-time job) has observed that the total area of the farming plots is surprisingly large.

> Single parents don't bother to grow anything. Among the other groups, about 90% have a plot. But whether it's is profitable or not, I'm not sure. There are families for whom plot farming is an important source of income; at least that's what they've told me. I know about this because I work for the Statistical Office [of Estonia] every once in a while [conducting interviews]. (A social worker in Kanepi)

In the interview material we found cases such as the following.

> 'We've got a plot,' (wife). 'A potato field and a plot,' (husband). 'Now we also have two little pigs,' (wife). 'In principle growing anything for sale isn't profitable,' (husband). '[Economically] it's [however] very important [for us]. We wouldn't be able to buy them [the foodstuffs],' (wife). 'Just think what it would cost if we bought them [at a shop],' (husband). 'Without the plot we'd

starve,' (grandfather). 'My sister lives in a country town, in X. She doesn't have the chance of an allotment. This year we gave her cabbages and tomatoes from the greenhouse. Cabbages, vegetables, tomatoes for our own family. In theory we could've bought those cabbages, but since she had nothing, we helped her out,' (wife). (Two generations of a family living in adjacent houses: grandparents, grandmother a milker and disabled grandfather; the younger generation, consisting of an employed husband and his unemployed wife, with a four-year-old child)

Clearly a great number of people find that plot farming for their own consumption is of considerable economic importance. However, the social worker quoted above indicated that in her own case and certainly also for a great number of other people plot farming is little more than *a cultural convention.*

> For one thing, it's not profitable for me, but I have in a way got used to cultivating a small patch. It's part of the tradition in the countryside. But economically it isn't efficient. (A social worker in Kanepi)

Cultural traditions do not change at the same pace as financial conditions. Older people in particular keep on farming, some because of the additional income the crop provides, or because of the difficulty of obtaining groceries, or because of the poverty of elderly people and the long distance to the nearest shops. At the same time it strengthens family ties among relatives and is therefore highly important for social reasons alone.

Others continue simply out of the old tradition of plot farming, and a few others out of a burning desire to reconstruct the old family farm.

> Elderly people [practise agriculture on homesteads that have been given back to them]. Personally, I don't know any young farmers. Elderly people have to have something to do . . . (21-year-old woman in Kanepi)

The young do not generally show any interest in farming; they would rather move out of the municipality. According to our survey, *migration from Kanepi* to the cities is much more widespread than the information gathered by the Statistical Office of Estonia would lead one to believe. This does not only concern the young, but also many adult occupational groups.

> And I don't know any young farmers either. I really can't recall any. (15- year-old schoolgirl in Kanepi)

> I'm afraid that our children aren't interested in agriculture. [But] they could be some day in the future . . . (Woman from a family cultivating a restituted farm, with children aged 9–14)

> And for me the only chance of changing the course [of my life] is to move to Põlva. (21-year-old woman in Kanepi)

> At first he worked in the kolkhoz, then at his parents' farm, but the farm was not profitable, which is why he decided to go and work in Võru. (Currently unemployed milker, talking about her husband, now employed)

But agriculture continues to decline and rural people are often tending to give up the keeping of cattle.

> I live in a village, in fact, on a real farm. It's owned by my father and mother. The farm is quite big, I'm not exactly sure how many hectares, but it's a fairly large farm. We used to have dairy cattle, but there's no sense in keeping them. There's no profit in agriculture, [since] today you've got to pay extra for [the 'privilege'] of working in agriculture. Today there are just potatoes. It's more or less for our own use. And everything that's left over is sold. And people are baking bread themselves in the village. (17-year-old shop assistant)

Nevertheless, in the areas worst affected by unemployment such as Karste, the growing of vegetables is a necessity.

The amount of uncultivated acreage is rising because of the decline in the intensity of agriculture and the diminishing use of restituted land.

> It is highly regrettable that the farmers took the fields for themselves, but they're not making a livelihood out of it. [Today these fields] are overgrown with weeds. (Agronomist X)

As a result of this development, the *ühistys* enterprises which are engaged in large-scale production are today able to pick up all the fields of the highest quality, and rent them for the cost of the land tax only.

> These [350 hectares cultivated by Kanepi co-operative] are fields received back by farmers [in restitution]. The people who took the land, have now rented their lands to us. We don't pay them any [actual] rent, but we pay the land tax [to the municipality] on their behalf. If three years ago we had difficulty in getting land from the people, now there is so much arable land on offer that we cannot take it [all, not even for the remittance of the land tax only]. People don't need their fields for themselves, they haven't got the strength to cultivate them . . . We don't need [fields] any more [or as much as before, since we had to cut the

cultivated acreage by 30% because of unprofitability]. During the kolkhoz the size of a field was approximately 3.3 hectares, [while] our largest fields are 20–30 hectares. We don't have any fields of 50–100 hectares. People often offer us fields of 2–5 hectares, [but] we only pick the best of those. A lot depends on whether the field is level enough, if it's easy to cultivate. We only pick fields that require the minimum amount of labour. [A large percentage of the] land remains unused. We have fields here that haven't been cultivated by anyone for three years. That's the future. (Agronomist at Kanepi co-operative)

Due to the loss of the virtually unlimited All-Union market, the opening of the Estonian domestic market to unrestricted imports of agricultural produce and the decline in consumer demand, agricultural land is being lost to cultivation, just as Karl Marx (1966) pointed out in his theory on the differential rent. This is particularly conspicuous in Kanepi where holdings are mostly small in size and where the soil quality is below the Estonian average, but it also reflects the local failure in agricultural decollectivisation.

As an interim summary one could argue that both plot farmers and independent family farmers, especially those who have started agricultural production on fields only recently restituted, *basically* fit the pattern of undeveloped small-scale agriculture found in developing countries. Agriculture is only being practised on a small scale, mostly for the family's own use and the family income is supplemented by selling some of the produce at the local market. The system is based on *a low level of social security and low wages.* At the same time, unemployment and the local grocery market sustain the low wage level. This results in a low demand for services and poor opportunities for local service providers.

At the national level the rural population, despite its size, does not form a significant group of consumers because of its low demand for products and services. Thus, the problems of agriculture and the rural areas are ultimately also visible in the macro-economic development of the nation as a whole.

Nevertheless, *Estonia is not an underdeveloped country.* The Estonian social security system has marked deficiencies, but its coverage is, nevertheless, reasonably good. Moreover, the labour force is for the most part skilled thanks to the kolkhozes, and in addition to the best educated employees, young people in particular may find permanent employment in the cities, especially in the Tallinn area. Furthermore, the producers are only rarely able to market their produce locally, which is why their influence on the level of prices is marginal. In these respects the conditions for Meillassoux's super-exploitation are only partially fulfilled. Thus we may presume that the present plot farms together with the (mostly restituted) medium-sized private farms are largely a transitional phenomena. Production on these farms often yields little or no profit, and it is largely carried on by older people, who tenaciously continue cultivating their old family farm or a modest plot as a part of the internal barter system of a more extensive social network. For some people, especially families with a large number of children, such farming does still play an important role economically. One factor in common with all these groups is that they are all unable to move away from their present place of residence for a variety of reasons (e.g. lack of housing in the large cities).

In this respect it is not a question of modernisation, but the reverse side of the so-called original accumulation: the formation of an army of wage-workers dispossessed of the means of production as a part of the formation of capitalist relations. The future will show to what degree this transitional phase will also result in the problems characteristic of Western societies: families with overlapping problems, alcoholics and mentally disturbed individuals, or people who have fallen outside social safety nets, i.e. people of working age who have been completely displaced from the world of work. It seems reasonable to expect that many will fall into this category.

> The situation in the countryside today is that people who have got a farm and forestland sell timber and drink and celebrate. Nobody thinks what he'll do when the money runs out. (A small-businessman engaged in various kinds of dealing)

In this respect the process not only produces wage-workers, but individuals totally displaced in society, or in other words it produces *a lumpen proletariat,* unfit and unmotivated for work. The fate of the small-scale producers in Kanepi is not only indicative of the so-called original accumulation, but also of the catastrophic failure of land reform and its immense human toll. From a theoretical viewpoint, a total avoidance of human suffering might have been impossible; certainly it was by no means a part of the ideology underlying restitution. The following observation, however, best corresponds to the facts about the restitution policy and the success of its implementation – at least in the light of the Kanepi material.

> I would say that the private farmers don't have a future. In my opinion it was a great mistake to break the kolkhoz up that way and parcel out large fields into small pieces, and to give these pieces of land to the people. People are practically starving; they keep a cow and a chicken to survive. (Former manager of the kolkhoz construction team, now a successful shopkeeper)

But at the same time we may presume that agriculture – to the extent that it will continue to exist in Estonia in current conditions – is going to be restructured in a relatively short period of time. The present small enterprises are being replaced by larger ones. The present dwelling houses are going to be turned into detached houses and summer cottages, but if they are in bad repair and have little monetary or recreational value, they may simply be abandoned. This assumption may be further examined and possibly refined by analysing the other types of reproduction.

Semi-proletarian Enterprises

This small-farm segment is decisively dependent on wage-labour, which also determines the dynamics of reproduction within their families. Semi-proletarian groups are probably the largest groups of small producers in the developed capitalist countries, and apparently their proportion is on the increase. The persistent existence of the segment is explained by the income derived from wage-labour. This segment is typical of small-scale production in developed capitalist countries, since capitalist economies provide a labour market with the appropriate level of income and other characteristics (e.g. the regular availability of work) necessary for its existence (Alanen, 1991, 97–103).

In Estonia the occupational backgrounds of the people (especially the former non-agricultural occupations of the new farmers, or the former agricultural occupations based on a far-reaching division of labour) and the relatively high standard of education could provide suitable prerequisites for combinations of wage-work and agricultural entrepreneurship in the future.

Not a single person in the Kanepi interviews could be clearly classed within this category. However, one family who had received its lands back in restitution could well be developing into the semi-proletarian category. They would not like to give up the farm, since it is the family farm of the husband; indeed, the farm is being developed further, since the wife was thrown into unemployment when an agricultural *ühistys* went bankrupt.

The family did not purchase any machines, neither prior to the kolkhoz auction nor at the auction itself, which is why the mechanisation of their homestead has had to start almost from scratch. Their chance of developing into a semi-proletarian farm characteristic of developed capitalist countries is based on the husband's good vocational (electrician) training (four years at the Tallinn Technical University), and the fact that his total wages in a well established company are fairly high, as a worker and shareholder (EEK

26,500 per annum). This gives them "some opportunity to accumulate money and plan purchases ahead" (husband). Last year their income from the milk from two cows totalled EEK 6,000, and now they are increasing the number of cows to four. Tractor services are obtained by investing the family's vouchers lodged with the Savings and Loan Association on a tractor, which is to be bought together with the former tractor driver of a bankrupt *ühistys*. Their immediate plans include buying a hay tedder. The difficulty in their mechanisation efforts is characterised by the fact that the price of an old machine such as this is almost as high as the annual yield provided by two cows. They also foster thoughts of constructing a new cowshed.

Estonia certainly already has some of the semi-proletarian farms characteristic of developed capitalist countries, but they are more likely to be located in the vicinity of large population centres.

Capital Intensive Family Farms

These are enterprises that are thoroughly integrated within the agricultural product market. The term also refers to the high level of economic and technological capital bound up in this type of enterprises. Capitalist enterprises that seek profit mainly by employing labour from outside the family are not included within this category. However, that part of the petty bourgeoisie which gets some additional income from outside agriculture is included within this definition, if the reproduction of the family is primarily dependent on the agricultural product market. The development of capital intensive family farms as core agricultural producers in Western countries has been a lengthy process, and one which has required great economic input by governments as well as a complicated regulatory system. This kind of ideal of family farms was the vision promoted by the cultural and political elite in Estonia once the independence of the country had been reinstated in 1991.

The majority of such farms already started up during the rouble era,[7] whilst the subsequent agricultural reforms have produced hardly any new family farmers in Kanepi or elsewhere. But they may have reinforced the position of existing family farms. The following farm was brought up as possibly the best example of the farms set up as a result of restitution.

> Mr KK . . . Former tractor driver. The technology [partly] originates from the auction. He has been obtaining technology both now and at earlier stages,

---

7   In the rouble era almost 30 private farms were established in the area of Kanepi kolkhoz alone.

without any help from any federation [Taluliit organisation that acted as distributors of used Western agricultural machines]. As far as I know he has six cows. (Member of the kolkhoz reform committee)

But there is also at least one (and probably only one) technologically developed family farm set up during the favourable rouble era that comes up to Western standards and surpasses all subsequently restituted farms. The farmer was born on the same homestead where he and his family are today building a new house and production buildings. "That project cost me 900,000 kroons," said the family farmer. Right now some of the buildings are only half-completed, but the majority of them are finished. The farm specialises in breeding pedigree cattle alongside the usual dairy cattle; in their cowshed they have "pure-bred cattle" that came from Finland. These were described by the farmer as a "super elite." "To begin with we had 5, now [we have] 20." The family members cultivate both their own and rented fields, but they do have plenty of land of their own, since the current farm is made up of the restituted farms of three of their relatives. Out of his own acreage "31 hectares are in intensive use and 20 hectares are in reserve," said the farmer himself.

The construction of the farm started early on in the rouble period, but the family did not move in until 1991. The delay was caused by the farmer's work as regional vice director of the technical department of the Võru branch of the national agro-industrial concern ATK,[8] and subsequently (at around the time he and his family settled on the farm) chairman of the Taluliit organisation in the rayon of Põlva. These appointments enabled him to create an extensive network of social contacts, not only within Estonia, but also (through the ATK) in other republics in the former Soviet Union, and (through the Taluliit) in the West, especially the Nordic countries.

My nature as an individual is such that I've always been inclined to build relationships with other people. I've always had good friends and I've been able to give up the bad ones. And people have indeed been helpful to me. To give an example, my son is now in Denmark and my daughter is studying at the [private] Concordia University [in Tallinn]. (A family farmer)

The Finnish cattle have in fact been acquired from Saint Petersburg and the machines (all of them, except for five tractors) originate from the West, although most of them are second hand machines originally donated for free

---

8   Agro-toostuskomplex, i.e. agro-industrial concern. A Soviet-era organisation that is now defunct.

to Estonian farmers. "And we really do appreciate the help, and there's been quite enough of it, too," comments the farmer cheerfully with regard to the donations.

Most of the tractors originate from Russia. They were cleverly purchased from various kolkhozes at advantageous book values well in advance of the start of decollectivisation proper. Later, the farm mechanisation was to some degree supplemented by acquiring machines at the auctions held at Kanepi's two kolkhozes (with their grandparents' vouchers). However, it is not simply a question of the ability to acquire various kinds of machines and materials. "I've seen, how others [other farmers] are doing as well here as abroad. And we had better learn from the mistakes of others when we're making our own plans," stresses the farmer. "You can only turn in a profit by concentrating on one field." Thus, the family agreed upon their line of specialisation at an early stage. The preparatory work was amply facilitated by the mental capital, the technical college education of the farming couple, and the experience of everyday agricultural production acquired by the farmer in his previous capacities, both in kolkhozes and private farms. His wife, for her part, had gained her own perspective by studying in other Soviet republics, at the universities of Minsk (Byelorussia) and Riga (Latvia), which gave her the appropriate training for using computer programmes in the accounting of the kolkhoz.

The work of the farming couple is also characterised by long-term thinking and the ability to anticipate the future. "When I started out as a private farmer, I'd already planned what I'd need [initially] and even beyond that." The tractors were bought with a rouble loan (one extra tractor to provide spares for the others), but they also raised another loan for the construction work on their farm. "We could've bought 20 cars with that money," but of course, if they had done that, they would have lost a unique opportunity. Everything was remarkably cheap at the time, and the loan taken in roubles had later shrunk to nothing because of Estonia's hyperinflation. In the farmers own estimation the mechanisation of the farm is not yet quite complete. "The hay harvesting technology, for example, is not up to date – I would like to get a hay crusher, but there's no money," he says.

Besides the rouble loans, the couple has managed to raise capital through business activities outside agriculture. The husband was a member in the alliance of four agricultural executives mentioned before, which had prepared for the Kanepi auctions with great care.

We [four persons] had a shop and a small bar. It was for the purpose of selling my own production. I was the chairman of this *ühistys* for three years. I worked there for free, but I managed to sell some of my own production. In 1992 the annual turnover of the *ühistys* was 1.2 million [kroons]. (A family farmer)

Since then the farmer has given up this partnership and invested (with another businessman) the vouchers received from his grandparents and bought on the black market on various items including the newly built administration building of Kanepi kolkhoz (at well below its nominal value). In actual fact, the building remained unused for several years, but it has subsequently been sold to Eesti Energia, the national electric utility company. These investments indicate the *good relationships* he has managed to create with *the other former members of the agricultural elite*, who have served as his business partners in the post-socialist era.

The social capital of the farming couple is not yet exhausted. The construction of the farm has been to a large extent a project for the whole family, but also for friends, who have pitched in to help at times.

I've mobilised all my relatives to work here, friends, too. We help each other. Yes, everybody does lend a helping hand, although there's no money in it. For example, [my] father-in-law has made all these doors and windows. And if I hadn't had all these good people, it would have been impossible. The money received from milk, for example, doesn't go anywhere. (A family farmer)

According to the calculations of the farming couple the production of ten cows would render the farm profitable, that is without additional investments. Their present cowshed would accommodate a herd of up to twenty cows. But the family wanted a larger cowshed, and would have had it built if they had been granted a loan by the government of Estonia for that purpose.

If we'd been granted the loan, the cowshed would have been larger, for forty cows. That would have been a production farm and not a sort of subsistence farm. Once it had been completed it'd already have been profitable; also the interest on the loan would have been paid. (A family farmer)

Perhaps the sale of the administration building has now provided them with this opportunity. And certainly there are also other alternatives, as shown by the example of another farm (see section titled Capitalist Large Scale-enterprises) that was supposed to be a family farm. In any case the family trusts in its own abilities. "If we can't make it then who will [succeed]," asks the farmer, and the interviewers were convinced of this from what they saw.

This farm is clearly progressive, of the type that is bound to play a part in the future structure of Estonian agriculture.

At the end of the interview the farmer praises life on the homestead in a way that would put many novelists to shame.

> I've always been working for society, and now I've discovered how beautiful the succession of summer and autumn is, and how important family relations are and how important mutual support is and also your support for others. Relations with my children have changed, and between the parents, as well as between relatives, now that we've started keeping this homestead. That's why I'd never change this life. I feel sorry for the people who live all their life in the city and who don't see any real life. And even if there ever came a time when the best thing for us would be to leave for Siberia for example, I'd never leave here. (A family farmer)

Nevertheless, Estonian agriculture will hardly be based on family farms in the future. Four such model farms were in fact established in the early 1990s in one of the rare government investments in agriculture. Several of our interviewees told us how at least two of them, perhaps all of them, ceased production.

> I've been there; one was a dairy farm and the other reared cattle. Now they've both given up. I was thinking that when a person gets everything easy, everything will go easy. (Ibid.)

> There are four [model] farms near Tartu. Two of them have been closed down. The machines and [the rest of the new] technology were sold off, and they [the farmers] got the money for themselves. I'm not aware of what happened to the others. (Agronomist X)

The family farmer profiled in the pages above is the only clear success out of the 30 or so private farms set up during the last years of the rouble era. Other farms established during that time do not appear to have fared any better than the farms established under less favourable economic conditions after Estonia had been declared independent.

Dynamic family farms such as this may after a relatively short transitional period evolve into capitalistically organised agricultural enterprises. At any rate, there are plenty of opportunities for this kind of development. In the following section dealing with capitalist large-scale enterprises there will be a concrete example which illustrates this.

Capitalist Large-scale Enterprises

This group includes the enterprises whose model of reproduction is characterised by wage-labour and the pursuit of profit.

In principle capitalist large-scale enterprises can develop in post-socialist countries in the same classical way as they come about when a feudal system breaks down and capitalist markets develop. Within this larger process, they may on the one hand evolve as a result of the centralisation of small-scale production, i.e. internal class-differentiation in agriculture; on the other hand, they may evolve through the gradual capitalisation of originally non-capitalist types of enterprise. In the following analysis we will start off from the capitalisation of small-scale production in Estonia, and only then will we discuss the transformation dynamics of former large-scale farms, and the smaller complexes formed as these were broken down, both privately owned and neo-collectivist.

The background of our illustrative case bears a close resemblance to the technologically developed family farm described above. We have a couple in which both the husband (Mr A) and his wife have had a good education and also a career in the Communist Party. The husband first received the intermediate education of a zoologist, but after that he studied for four years at an Estonian college, and then continued with legal studies at the Leningrad Communist Party School. Subsequently, A served as the vice-chairman of a kolkhoz in a municipality neighbouring Kanepi, but resigned in 1989, when the local kolkhoz chairman was replaced on political grounds at his kolkhoz, too (in the same manner as in Kanepi). Thereafter he served as the managing director of a freezing plant, a part of which he owned (an enterprise which later made money mainly by importing alcohol). The firm had a considerable turnover, and when he parted with the shares of the company he had considerable initial capital in his possession.

With the help of this initial capital A started setting up a family farm in Kanepi in the summer of 1991. Today he and his family live in a modern detached house (in an area that used to belong to Kalev kolkhoz), which is surrounded by a modern cowshed, storage buildings, a grain dryer and machines of good quality. It is not situated on their own land, but fairly close to it they have 20.3 hectares of their own land, most of which is owned by A's wife. The rest of the acreage that they cultivate has been rented from the municipal council or from private farmers. The cattle consist of pure pedigree cattle only, with 21 cows, four heifers and some calves. In terms of quality "they're the best cattle in the county, the fruit of my own and my wife's efforts," says the farmer with pride. In addition to his own capital, A got "at the last possible moment" a loan with which he bought a new combine harvester costing 80,000 roubles. "I feared that during the kroon era its value would be 8,000 kroons, but a couple of years later the value of that harvester was 750,000 kroons. It was a beautiful investment."

It is evident that the farmer (like the owner of the technologically developed family farm) has good sources of information: the family have connections with important people in the area of agricultural production, both the old Estonian agricultural elite as well as the new business circles. For example, the farmer himself was a member of the previously mentioned alliance formed by four former agricultural officials. They have also received pedigree cattle from an *ühistys* that replaced the Estonia kolkhoz, with which they had "old contacts." This farming couple have indeed managed to construct a technologically advanced family farm. Their contacts are not limited to the former Soviet Union only; they also have contacts with the West. Indeed, the farm has visitors from the Nordic countries, too.

> We have taken a loan and we're paying it back. We've got no problem with that. [Recently] we asked for an assessment of all our fixed assets [landed property not included], [that is] an assessment of the real estate. [According to that assessment] it is worth 1.7 million kroons. Twenty cows were a large property in the Soviet era, a huge fortune. Now these twenty cows provide a living for our family, but we're not thinking of acquiring a new car, for example, [or] hiring a farm hand or a milker, [because] there's not enough work for everybody. (A family farmer)

Farmer A also talked about the need to provide work in the area. It is unclear whether the farmer was referring to the people in the surrounding countryside or his relatives (two of whom later became his employees) when he was talking about the lack of work, but in addition to providing employment he was also motivated by the desire for gain. So farmer A and his wife quickly seized the opportunity when *the private cowshed ühistys* formed on the basis of Kalev kolkhoz came up for sale. "We bought a dairy farm to provide work for everyone. At the moment [summer of 1995] it has 66 cows and 20 heifers," said the family farmer.

The story of the *ühistys* they bought is descriptive of the problems that have been faced by most enterprises of this type in the municipality of Kanepi: a struggle with debts, and attempts at adapting to the new economic system which have resulted in problems of leadership and management. In particular, problems in work discipline have been acute, related to the irrationalities privatisation brought to the economy of the cowsheds, the problems caused by outdated machinery, exhaustion, etc.

This is how the previous owner herself described the difficulties.

And then the [time of] break up came, and Mr B, the vice-chairman [of the kolkhoz] paid us a visit. He strongly recommended that I should take the cowshed. [Subsequently, when I became the owner] there was panic and confusion, some people were disappointed. There were people willing [to work at the cowshed] from further away, but we took people who lived nearer, because of the [shorter] way to work. There were some unpleasant incidents; [for example] one of the employees had a heart attack. (An agronomist who bought a cowshed complex, today working as a milker in the cowshed she sold)

To begin with, I feared I'd not be able to make it, but I did get along for three years. We paid the auction price with vouchers. 43,000 for the cowshed, 1,500 for the car, 2,000 for the tractor . . . Along with fertilisers and other movable assets that totalled EEK 100,000, a part of which we owed. For my own part, I'd been given vouchers worth 10,000. Part of the money we paid with the shares [of those people] that worked here and later we had to pay them back. We also made the repayments with the little money we got from milk; there was nothing else, and sometimes we sold animals. We paid the wages and other expenses of the workers mostly with the income provided by the milk. (Ibid.)

There was also a shortage of labour. At the time we took over the cowshed, we had altogether ten employees: there were three tractor drivers, a feeder, a night watchman, a dairyman and the milkers. In the summer, during the haymaking season, we had some extra labour. But then trouble arose with our employees. It manifested itself in this way: they claimed we paid them too little in wages, but at the start you couldn't pay [more], since you had to pay your debts. That was how our milkers received 1,300 kroons a month. At times there was also trouble with people who were drinking too much. The guards [who were required to prevent thieving from the cowsheds] were the worst cases. They kept on drinking. On a few occasions I was left all alone, as the women [milkers] left [the workplace] to gather berries. And I had to care for the calves, too. I had to milk all those 70 cows. On top of that I had to take care of all the other things, get cattle feed, etc. There was one worker [who only] came back after the berry season was over. Also, the machines received from the kolkhoz were in bad repair, and they started acting up, and spares were very expensive. There wasn't a single pasture available near the cowshed, [because] the farmers had been restituted their lands next door. The first year we had a good harvest, but then the weeds started to grow. Our fields were all far away, 7–8 kilometres away. (Ibid.)

And at home my sister died as well. There are two pensioners at my home [five kilometres away from the cowshed] and it became very difficult as I had to spend all my days in the cowshed, and you couldn't be at home. Everything was so depressing; I often thought why did it have to go this way? Wouldn't it have been easier to take care of things some other way, by forming a co-operative or something? But we were simply not offered any other choice. It is difficult being alone and a woman, and my health deteriorated markedly during that period. (Ibid.)

I was already thinking of selling the machines one day, paying off the debt and giving it all up. I wanted to do that back in the spring, but then I decided to hang on until the summer. At that point I was wondering where I'd find a man who'd take it [the cowshed] over and told A about the matter. Of course, he thought I was kidding to start with, but then he said he'd think about it for a week; he thought it over and took [the cowshed]. I found one fine individual, that's Mr A; he took it. He agreed to take it, [although] some of it was still unpaid for, but he took over the debt. I've still got 52,000 to pay. Now the work is easier, I stayed on working for him. [Beside] myself, only two milkers, a night watchman and a dairyman stayed. The discipline is tight under Mr A. He is strict, if you don't work you'll get sacked. (Ibid.)

Undoubtedly the cowshed was an advantageous purchase for Mr A: it was completely free of any risk, since its value could be realised immediately. A part of the price had already been paid and inflation had in any case raised the true value of the property above the nominal value of the vouchers. But the intention of Mr A was not to turn his investment into cash at once, but to further develop the business to yield a higher profit. Mr A must have pondered over the purchase once or twice, since the fields at the cowshed's disposal were located far away, and there were no adequate storage buildings in the immediate vicinity of the cowshed. Still, he had gathered enough experience in private farming to realise the potential for making a profit in certain types of agricultural production. He was not alone. In the summer of 1995 there were also other signs of new dynamic development, and this did not go unnoticed by the Savings and Loan Association.

A couple of months ago [in the autumn of 1995], it started to become apparent that [agricultural] assets had gained more value. It could be that this'll provide us with a chance to pay back [to the people who had handed over their shares to the co-operative]. People's interest in machines and farming has been re-awakened. The property will end up in the hands of the most industrious men. They've learned to understand life, that something must be done, and what can be done they are capable of working out for themselves. And as soon as someone gets more land or initiates something, that's a sign of intelligent thinking. (Chairman of the Savings and Loan Association)

It is not apparent from our material (the interview was interrupted at this point by the visit of a neighbour) how Mr A had financed his investments. Perhaps he simply assumed full responsibility for the debt attached to those shares that the former owner had not yet managed to pay up.

The influence of the new owner on the business has been remarkable.

The situation of that cowshed [at the time of purchase was that] the milk yield was 610 kilograms of second class milk. Some 15 cows were seriously ill. In four days the [milk] quality rose [to first class], and production was upped to 850 kilograms in ten days. If the former owner of that cowshed earned about 25,000 kroons per month, then we are at the moment making 66,000 kroons, and there are ten cows less than before.

Essential to this transformation was the reorganisation of the whole work process, in which the owner was assisted again by his own relatives (one as a foreman, the other as a milker), the replacement of the poorest employees with better ones, and better overall work discipline. But in the background there was also deeper knowledge, with experience in corporate management, animal husbandry and hygiene. And most important of all, the owner has proven his personal ability to reform the enterprise using practices suitable to transitional Estonia. He possesses the kind of business acumen that is capable of making the most of the exceptional opportunities offered by the present transitional period for moving from small-scale farming to becoming a large-scale farm owner. The following excerpts from interviews portray his personal characteristics.

First, Mr A himself cites an artificial inseminator who had been explaining A's methods to a group of people who were astonished at his success.

You know what A said [to the milkers]? 'You have to take your own milk from the same tank from which the milk delivered to the combinate [i.e. dairy] is taken.' [And then Mr A goes on explaining:] Those people had been keeping another two cows at home, [while they were tending] 70 cows at their workplace. There was no alternative [but my strict rule], if a person does not trust the work she's done. The first condition placed on the people who were employed by us as milkers was that they shouldn't have cows at home. The other condition was that when they want milk, they have permission to take milk for their own daily use [since they can no longer keep cows at home].

He also overcame the problem of somatic cells in his new cowshed. According to him, there are "110 different reasons" why they would appear in the milk. The major principle of husbandry in his cowsheds, however, is, that "a cow should be treated like your fellow man."

> When I was working as a zoologist in Väimelä, I tried to get the milkers to give up a certain habit. It wasn't very humane [towards the milkers], but nor it was right for the cows. I took the object the milkers used for hitting the cows, and hit a milker instead. 'Why?' asked the milker. 'The cow wouldn't even be able to ask that question,' was my response. In my own cowshed I had the following rule: you weren't allowed to yell at the cows, not to mention hitting them; even the screams of children were banned, running inside the cowshed, any extra disturbances just won't do. And the cows should always be fed on time. (Mr A)

This narrative with its highly personal touch goes on to explain the correct organisation of feeding, the positioning of the cows, motivating the tractor drivers, the prevention of drinking on the job, etc. The new master really appears to have discovered a solution to these problems, and this has enabled him to raise the quality and productivity of the work on his farm to an altogether new level. The workers, too, have benefited. Their monthly wages are twice as high as those in the neighbouring co-operative. Their take-home pay is 2,000 kroons (excluding overtime compensation). Compared to the neighbouring co-operative their working hours are more reasonable and also the work in general is better organised, with the needs of the employees taken more into consideration.

The dynamic entrepreneurial grip of Mr A and his family has been maintained and strengthened. At the time we interviewed him, he was expecting 25 heifers for his new cowsheds from his old acquaintances at the former Estonia kolkhoz. In addition, the herd in the recently purchased cowshed is scheduled to be replaced by a high-quality herd even though the existing herd is not bad. Credit was needed for these arrangements, but the loans granted to farmers are not "ordinary bank loans:" the terms are more disadvantageous, since the banks "don't trust the agricultural business," as Mr A put it.

A few months later we learned that Mr A had bought two more cowsheds. Likewise, the area under his cultivation has been steadily increasing. In 1995 he cultivated 370 hectares, in 1998 842 hectares, and today (1999) he cultivates a total of 1,100 hectares. Most of this land is rented, but he has acquired 260 hectares of his present lands by outright purchase. Although there is plenty of farming land available for rent, Mr A claims that he has not been able to add to his cultivated area as fast as he would have liked.

If he is successful in his endeavours, the capitalist agribusiness that is being established in Kanepi could be considered fairly large even by Western standards. It would also prove the viability of large-scale agribusiness in today's Estonia, even in its remotest corners.

What about the various *ühistys* enterprises founded on the basis of Kanepi kolkhoz? What has been their fate? Some of the cowshed complexes ceased operation very quickly, as we have stated earlier. In some cases they formed a part of a firm with branches in more than one line of activity, and the cattle may have been sold off to strengthen the capital base of the more profitable industrial activities. In one instance the former cowsheds are now (at least in part) used for industrial production. Six of the eleven new enterprises formed were conceived as agricultural enterprises from the outset. Four of them promptly went out of business (two of these being unable to pay off their liabilities). One of the remaining complexes (in the village of Kooraste) was owned by a private person, while the largest, that is, the Kanepi *ühistys* (in the centre of Kanepi municipality) was owned by the co-operative. Although the private and co-operative enterprises have a lot in common, the problematics of a neo-collectivist enterprise do nevertheless differ from the problematics of a private enterprise. We shall return to the special characteristics of a neo-collectivist *ühistys* later.

The fixed costs of all types of *ühistys*, both private and co-operative, consist of social security payments, health insurance payments, income tax, value added tax, land tax (on the fields they cultivate) and salaries. In addition to this they all owe money to the Savings and Loan Association and individual stockholders. The repayment period to the Savings and Loan Association was set at ten years, so "the shares and the debts should be paid by the year 2007," said the chairman of the Savings and Loan Association.

Meanwhile, those shareholders who had handed over their vouchers for the use of a private *ühistys* have been able to make a great variety of different agreements with the owners. The most common arrangement, however, has been that the *ühistys* could purchase vouchers (both from members of the co-operative and from people who had simply placed their shares for the use of a private *ühistys*) by performing contracting services with its agricultural machines on people's fields.

> We bought a cowshed and 170 cows, young animals, cowshed machinery and equipment, tractors and other agricultural machines. [Everything] was bought on the promise that in ten years we'd have to pay everything back. It might be that in ten years we'll be able to pay these people their shares back, [on the other hand] it might be that we can't. If we get [enough] income, then we'll be able to do it. We've got 40% of our shares covered. We got the [rest of the] vouchers from workers, other people, pensioners. [To pay] for the shares, we help the

pensioners in cultivating their land, to give an example. You could [also] buy vouchers at low prices from other people. Some of these people haven't yet received anything from us for their shares. It could be that many of them don't even want to get anything. [They] just gave away their shares to us. (A cowshed owner)

Because of the chaotic nature of the auction the prices were established at a relatively high level (vouchers only covered about 40% of the total price of the cowshed in the example above), much higher than had been assumed in the plans of the buyers of the Kooraste and Kanepi cowshed complexes (plans which had been carefully prepared, considering the short time available).

We didn't know how and when we should pay back. Only after all the machinery had been [transported] home, only then it did start to became clear how I should repay [the price of the machines bought]. I don't recall what the exact requirements were right there at the auction. (Buyer of a cowshed complex)

The owner of another private farm bought his cowshed almost on the spur of the moment, without any deeper thought. Since he had not acquired (bought or received as investments without immediate compensation) the necessary capital (vouchers), and had not given thought to the organising of the work, nor indeed given much thought to his future activities at all, he soon came to a dead end. Here are some characterisations of that cul-de-sac.

The farmer took up drinking, in the mornings you could chat with him, but by the evening he was drunk. He's lost hope. (Chairman of the Savings and Loan Association)

He [the owner] didn't show any interest in anything. I can say that if I hadn't taken care of the paperwork, he would've had the tax authorities or somebody on his back long ago. He wasn't really interested or maybe] he didn't really understand things either. At times I had to force him to [get up and] find some papers. (A worker in the cowshed)

They even stole my welding leads! . . . People are no longer interested in working. They just want to live. During the day they sleep, at night they steal. (The owner of the cowshed)

It wasn't in good shape [when he started] either, there were big problems with the feed, either he didn't bother or he didn't know how to organise it, the storage of the hay, for example. (A worker in the enterprise)

Production was very low. When I made those reports [related to production], according to them the production per cow was 0.5 litres. It is so little that I was told by the statistical centre that I had the wrong figures. The daily production of the 70 cows totalled 35 litres. (An accountant)

[The *ühistys*] went bankrupt, because the firm had the wrong person as its director. (A villager)

Today the enterprise described above is *de facto* bankrupt, and the Savings and Loan Association is attempting to sell off the remaining assets. There are not many prospects for the sale of the building, and there is no new entrepreneur who would take it over. A catastrophe for a single individual has at the same time been a catastrophe for an entire village, especially for those people who had moved there to work in the cowsheds. Only a handful of people still leave for regular work every morning from the blocks of flats built in the village for kolkhoz workers. "Life in this village is a catastrophe," says one of the few men who have regular employment. The municipal officials agree and the researchers were likewise convinced of the fact when they conducted interviews in the area.

The other agricultural *ühistys* set up outside Kanepi Township has also had its problems. The owner and his wife work long hours, but they make an incredibly meagre income. Most of the problems have an economic foundation, although problems related to employee motivation and quality of work also play a part.

At the moment we employ twelve people. At first we had more people, [but] six people have left. There were people who were very old, and there were younger ones, but they weren't interested in working. I didn't sack anyone; they all left of their own accord, right at the beginning. Among the [remaining] workers there are only 3–4 persons I can trust, besides my wife and myself. I would like to [get rid off] three people [right now], if only it was possible. (An owner)

The greatest problem is still the macroeconomic environment in Estonia.

I've got 80 cows right now, plus young cattle, 200 [head] in all. [After the auction] we took some of the cattle [the sick and the weak cows] to the slaughterhouse. The alternative [to dairy farming would be] growing crops or raising beef cattle. We haven't made our minds up yet. The question is what would be the most worthwhile investment? At this moment there's so much uncertainty that we are afraid of making any plans for the future. (A family farmer)

The income of the agricultural *ühistys* enterprises was derived, because of their production structure, mainly from milk, and to a lesser extent from meat and the sale of cultivated crops. The greatest immediate problem is the lack of working capital. In conjunction with the auction the kolkhoz provided each *ühistys* with the initial seed corn, fuel, pesticides and fertilisers (on credit, which consequently increased their debt to the Savings and Loan Association), but already by the autumn there was a crying need for cash. They could not get a loan on the open market, since they had no securities. (However, later a more successful private enterprise was able to raise a relatively large loan from a special fund after getting backing from a wealthy individual.) Furthermore, they were all equipped with mostly Russian machines, already outdated, with a high fuel consumption and prone to breakdowns, but they absolutely could not afford new, let alone Western machines. A lot depended on the *ühistys* employees' ability to repair the old machines by cannibalising spare parts from other similar pieces of equipment.

Since the privatisation of the kolkhoz the running costs of the *ühistys* enterprises have gone up as a result of rising taxes and fuel prices. For this reason alone the wages paid out by them have been very low – "they usually get 450 kroons [per month]," said the chairman of the Savings and Loan Association – although claims were made in some of the interviews that most enterprises as a rule paid a part of their wages in cash to circumvent social security payments and taxes. Still, it is clear that the possibilities for paying unreported wages are much more limited in an agricultural *ühistys* than in other types of business – if such opportunities exist at all.

It is indicative of the difficult circumstances of agricultural *ühistys* enterprises that none of them has even been able to pay to the Savings and Loan Association the 1% annual interest on their loan. Initially, the two enterprises were able to pay back a part of their debt by commercial felling. But felling has now become unprofitable because of changes in the market situation and government decisions concerning the price of standing timber; thus each *ühistys* has been left to rely on its basic products.

This trend, however, is in line with the possibilities we have already discussed. Quite clearly it is in favour of large-scale production. But before we move on to an analysis of the structural basis of these opportunities, let us take a brief look at the neo-collectivist type of reproduction.

Collectively Owned i.e. Neo-collectivist Large-scale Farms

This form of enterprise should in theory have been able to develop on the basis of the existing, relatively developed production equipment, plus the specialised professionals and educated employees of the kolkhozes. It may be assumed that its mode of reproduction differs in principle from large-scale production based solely on wage-labour, since the production strategies of the enterprise would have to take the employees into account as owners.

In Estonia – as in many other former socialist countries – there has evolved a tendency towards the formation of neo-collectivist enterprises. Government policies did not contribute to this development; indeed, these enterprises were set up despite government opposition, and overall resistance and distrust at national level. At the kolkhoz level, however, people's attitudes had clearly moved in this direction.

> It might have been better to leave kolkhozes the way they were, and not break them up at all. [Instead,] the structure of the kolkhozes should have been changed [too much money was being wasted, etc.]. The kolkhozes should've been adapted to modern-day people and production. The breaking up took place under duress, on orders. It wasn't what the people wanted. (Private owner of an agricultural co-operative)

> People have realised that kolkhozes weren't so bad after all . . . Perhaps it'd be best if you could set up an enterprise that would be somewhere between a kolkhoz and a homestead. It could be a farm with 500 to 1,000 hectares. (Chairman of a neo-collectivist agricultural enterprise)

Nevertheless, this type of enterprise could not simply continue its operations the way it had done in the Soviet mode of production. The transition from a "command economy" to a market economy also requires reorganisation within neo-collectivist enterprises.

The legally constituted form of neo-collectivist enterprises is not the same in every case. Only Kanepi co-operative out of the many *ühistys* enterprises providing data for this study is a co-operative in the sense in which co-operatives are understood in the Nordic countries. In the Nordic countries each member of a co-operative has only one vote. But in many of the Estonian *ühistys* organisations we studied (such as the Põlva limited liability company) the right to vote depends on the number of shares in the firm. As a matter of fact, these neo-collectivist firms bear more resemblance to a joint stock company. This type of company is characterised only by the fact that it is not owned by a single individual or a limited group of people, and that the former kolkhoz employees are typically (but not exclusively) owners. (Only those kolkhoz members and employees plus former members and employees who had received vouchers in connection with the dissolution of a kolkhoz or a sovkhoz were entitled to ownership.) The number of owners is however decreasing since it is possible to purchase agricultural contracting services from co-operatives in the same way as such services are offered against shares in a privately owned *ühistys*. The interest of the voucher owners in making use of these services slowly dwindles, and ownership becomes concentrated among those who retain their shares.

Vouchers may also be traded concentrating share ownership within the enterprise; or alternatively, if it is in accordance with the statutes, an outsider might also take over the enterprise. In most neocollectivist enterprises in Kanepi the shares may be sold to members only. In Põlva the number of shareholders has rapidly diminished from the original 300 to under half of that figure, and now ten of the largest owners hold over 50% of the total capital stock. It is quite possible that the controlling interest in a co-operative may in practice be transferred into the hands of a small group, and thus it may in fact become a capitalistically organised enterprise. Out of the 180 people currently employed at the Põlva co-operative only 50 are still owners. (The information is based on an interview with the director of the company.)

The price of Kanepi co-operative was established at a little over two million kroons at the auction. The co-operative managed to pay the start-up debts (seed corn, fuel, fertilisers, etc.) by commercial felling. "We've only [got] debts to people for their shares," says agronomist X, the chairman of Kanepi co-operative, who was probably the leading ideologist behind the construction of the whole enterprise. He gives the following overall description of the co-operative.

> We have 200 shareholders, each of them has given [invested the minimum of] 1,000 kroons, some [up to] 20,000 kroons. But we've got [only] 50 employees. First thing: the level of [our] assets has remained [the same], the assets have been preserved. On top of that we've bought some machinery. When the auction was organised, they wouldn't sell us young cattle at that time, only to others. Now we've again got young cattle. The number of our cows is a little higher than before, and now we are able to raise young cattle ourselves. That's why we converted one of the pigsties into a cowshed for the young cattle. We didn't want to buy any of the cowsheds for young cattle at the auction, because these cowsheds were located too far away. In all, there are 200 cows, 57 young cattle,

90 calves. 400–500 pigs. [In the old days] we used to have 5,000. Economically it's been profitable and it is enough for our own consumption only. We've rented 320 hectares of cultivated land, [and] with the meadow lands that is altogether 740 hectares, which also includes the pasture. (Agronomist X)

Half of all the prices of assets have been paid in shares, the other half hasn't been paid yet, but if we sold the cattle, we would then be able to pay the other half. And then the machinery and the buildings would be left to the shareholders, [and] that would then be the property of 200 people . . . Kanepi co-operative holds responsibility for its loans to the owners of the shares. If their investment fails, all their assets will then be passed on to the Kanepi Savings and Loan Association. (Ibid.)

In the summer the co-operative was in grave difficulties, because its milk did not fulfil the requirements set for the highest grade of milk by the Põlva dairy. Milk production had suddenly become unprofitable, and there was a debate about whether they should put an end to it. They considered switching over to grain cultivation only (which likewise was barely profitable). In the view of many outsiders the co-operative was in fact facing bankruptcy. However, the situation took a turn for the better in the early autumn, when Põlva dairy lost its *de facto* monopoly. Changes were brought about by the emergence of competition: Swedes bought and relaunched its competitor, the Võru dairy, which had gone bankrupt earlier.

Our principal source of income is milk. When we sold milk to Põlva dairy, the price we got was 1.60–1.70 kroons per litre at the lowest. From August onwards we'll take our milk to Võru dairy and then we'll get 2.70 kroons per litre for this milk, [since] it's of the highest quality. There's fierce competition between the dairies, and this explains the differences in prices. (Agronomist X)

Nevertheless, the fate of the enterprise had not yet been settled and was still in the balance.

The basic problem is the relation between the prices [of production input and output]. The prices of our products are low, but spare parts and fuel are expensive. Taxes are going up all the time. The land tax, the prices of electricity and fuel are going up. We won't increase the number of cattle. The fields were ploughed in the autumn, but it seems like we'll have to reconsider in the spring whether it is wise to sow and how much to get a good crop, what the quality would be like, so that it would be economically profitable. Some of the fields that have already been ploughed may be left to lie fallow. (Agronomist X)

The reorganisation of the co-operative has been a painful process. Undoubtedly the most difficult part has been the orientation to work.

> [The number of employees is] 46, the number has remained the same, ten have left, but ten new ones have arrived. We've had to let a couple of people go [because of poor work ethics], [but] people have understood that they do not have a chance to move somewhere else. (Agronomist X)

In principle, the situation of the co-operative and the other (private) enterprises is the same. Nevertheless, there have been signs of a change for the better in the co-operative (as well as in the other types of enterprises).

> Oh yes, the [work] ethics are better now, but there are some people that still haven't been able to change their approach. A third have taken a new attitude towards work, while two thirds have kept to their old ways. [Particularly] the milkers have noticed that with care you can produce the highest quality. (Agronomist X)

The understanding of the leadership and the people with the "new attitude" appears to be much the same.

> We've got shares, this means [we are] owners, all of us. We're all equal. There's no boss as such. Some of us still only work strictly fixed hours. Not according to the amount of work to be done, but [only] until the working hours come to an end. But each job has to be finished. You can't leave just like that, just because your hours are up. (A milker)

The wages in the co-operative are extremely poor, both for the management and the employees. Indeed, the salaries of the managers are not any higher than those of the employees. This is due to the fact that the enterprise is currently struggling for its survival. It is difficult to say how motivating a factor being part of a co-operative has been for the individual employees, but interview excerpts such as the following should be encouraging to the constructors of neo-collectivist enterprises.

In the interviews, moreover, the workers' attitudes toward the present leadership seem to be decidedly positive. "He [the chairman of Kanepi co-operative] is one of us. But we don't meet too often. We get along well with him. He's very helpful, helps us in our work if help is needed," said the milker.

Based on our data it is, however, impossible to determine how representative these kinds of opinions are. The managing director of the firm, agronomist X, has according to our information done everything he can to turn the co-operative into a successful business enterprise. He was described as a "thoroughly unselfish person" by one of his specialist colleagues in the co-operative. Agronomist X had been working for the co-operative earning the minimum wage since it was founded, regardless of working hours – and until last summer – without any leave whatsoever. He was ready to admit that if he had known what the job would be like, he would not have taken it on – since it has been so hard. Some members of the surrounding community, for example about half of the municipal council members, have taken a negative attitude towards his co-operative enterprise largely for political reasons. It has been nicknamed the "little kolkhoz". This attitude appears to be shared especially by the members of the later board of management of the kolkhoz, as well as by the specialists who used to work in the kolkhoz. "The specialists and the [later] members of the [kolkhoz] board of management don't have a positive attitude toward him," said a milker.

Although there has been improvement in the work ethics of people over time, this aspect has still been the greatest disappointment to agronomist X. He said he "wouldn't have believed [when he was founding Kanepi co-operative], that changing the ways of a man [an employee] takes such a long time."

On the whole, the basic problems of the Põlva limited liability company do not differ from those in Kanepi. However, Põlva *ühistys* was founded significantly earlier, as early as 1992, and, furthermore, it is much larger, since 80–90% of the agricultural workers of the kolkhoz that preceded it wanted to preserve the collective farm as an entirety. Economically it is clearly better stabilised, and it has managed to begin replacing old machinery with more modern equipment. They have even bought agricultural machines from the West, a detail proudly stressed by the chairman of the co-operative. It is also making a profit (EEK 1,000,000 in 1994) and it is capable of paying dividends to its members (25% of the profit), although the wages paid to its employees are at a markedly higher level (1,800–3,000 kroons per month per milker) than in Kanepi co-operative (1,000 kroons at most).

The Põlva *ühistys* is considering expanding its production by buying cowsheds in Kanepi, but the primary goal, however, is to raise its productivity. New equipment is being purchased in co-operation with three other large limited liability companies, and some employees are being sent abroad for training. (This information is based on an interview with the director of Põlva enterprise.) Nevertheless, the director of Põlva neo-collectivist company believed they had still to establish their position firmly. According to him it will eventually be determined in a kind of race between the old "Russian technology" and the co-operative's ability to replace machines that are falling apart with new "Western technology".

Later interviews conducted in 1999 suggest that the Põlva *ühistys* was considered possibly the best agricultural enterprise in the whole of Estonia and even the Kanepi co-operative appeared to have weathered its first crisis. Both enterprises, particularly the Põlva *ühistys*, had invested heavily in new technology. A continuing investigation would look at how the Russian economic crisis in late 1998 affected Estonia and created new problems. However, the analysis of its impact lies outside the scope of this book.

A Summary of the Directions of Development

Private or neo-collectivist – the constituted position still seemed unimportant in 1995 – there are many factors that appear to be favouring large-scale production in agriculture within the former socialist countries. The infrastructure has been inherited from a large-scale farm system, so have most of the production buildings and an essential part of the existing machinery. Likewise, the old vocational education of the farm workers, the experience gained by specialists (foremen, milkers, tractor drivers, etc.) in dividing up tasks, as well as their way of life as wage-workers instead of independent farmers – all these would appear to favour large-scale production.

Correspondingly the same factors are working against the family farm system, even apart from the fact that its basis has been markedly weakened by the anarchic nature of the decollectivisation process. Furthermore, there are still other factors related to the transitional period that seem to be favouring large-scale production (at least judging by the Kanepi survey data).

The *first* of these is the fairly high rate of inflation, which appears to be erasing a part of the inflated prices of the auction. There are two mechanisms for this: (1) The real value of fixed assets rises in relation to the book value (nominal value) of shares. The results are the same, whether the *ühistys* owes money to stockholders through the Savings and Loan Association, or directly. The rate of inflation was 89.8% in 1993, the year the kolkhoz was dissolved; in 1994 it was 41.7%, in 1995 28.9%, in 1996 14.8% and in 1997 12.5% (see Table 1.3). Each year the nominal value of the share buys less and less real property; on the other hand, during this period the debtors are only obliged to pay a meagre 1% interest (which has not even been collected) to the Savings and Loan Association. Those shareholders that have given their vouchers directly to the *ühistys* have not received any interest on their investment.

Inflation has eaten away much of that debt. The value of property has gone up. [A debt of] 100,000 [kroons] is no longer a problem, so I gain [i.e. the Savings and Loan Association gains, if the firm in question becomes insolvent] whatever the outcome . . . [This is the case] despite the fact that some fellow [who has borrowed money] drinks a couple of hundred thousand down his throat. (Chairman of the Savings and Loan Association)

(2) As the local currency depreciates the *ühistys* enterprises are charging a higher price for their services to private farmers (plot farmers and others), which are usually remitted half in vouchers owned by the farmers. This is how an *ühistys* can manage to free itself of its debts to its private shareholders at a quickening pace.

In my opinion they've been able to reduce their debt by doing some work [for their shareholders] on a contract basis. A lot of this has been going on. But how is the share actually eaten away? All the time the price of the services keeps going up, [while the price of] the share doesn't rise. One day the shares [will] dwindle to nothing. It's eaten away, [and the shareholder] is left without a share . . . and [the *ühistys*] is left with the property. The only one who loses is the person who has to part with his own share. (Chairman of the Savings and Loan Association)

Nevertheless, the farmers keep on struggling, fighting year after year – albeit on extremely low wages. If a farmer manages to take care of the running costs, and somehow keeps the old machines in operation, the debts will eventually dwindle to nothing. At the same time, the assets of the business will serve as security when applying for a new loan, and a new, dynamic phase, with investments in new machinery, buildings, etc., may be possible.

You just have to bear it. Yes. And we trust in the future. And they [the farmers] trust, too. Their wages are so low, but they've still got a chance, they've got land and an opportunity to do something. A big animal dies slowly. (Chairman of the Savings and Loan Association)

But there is also *another* reason, which speeds up the concentration in large enterprises. The assets of an *ühistys* which goes bankrupt (because of the drinking of the owner for example), and which is indebted to the Savings and Loan Association, can now be bought with vouchers. The effective value of these vouchers has not simply decreased. Rather it is possible to buy these same vouchers on the unofficial stock market at a price significantly lower than the nominal value. This has been caused both by the uninformedness of the voucher holders and by their inability to trade them for productive assets (because of old age and other such factors). An *ühistys* may, of course, also be sold to an interested party when it is facing insolvency or in cases where it has got into difficulties for other reasons, such as the failing health of the owner (as in the case of Mr A above). The new owners will in all likelihood resemble Mr A: they detect a business opportunity in agriculture and are capable of organising a profitable enterprise.

But there is also a *third* cause, which functions the same way as the case mentioned above, but is applicable to an *ühistys* such as the Pölva enterprise. Somebody might buy the majority of shares in it.

> He brings out the statutes . . . and states that since he's the biggest shareholder, he's got the right to call together a meeting of the *ühistys* and put matters in order. The one, who has the controlling interest, he dictates to the others. This is one of the existing theoretical possibilities. (Chairman of the Savings and Loan Association)

Consequently, debts are gradually being nullified, the assets of inferior large-scale businesses are being transferred to better ones, and production is being both intensified and centralised. In the light of the Kanepi data this would appear to take place specifically through the modification of old kolkhoz structures, and no longer by way of setting up new family farms. The significance of family farms, at least in this part of the country, would appear to remain peripheral. This view coincides with the estimates of county level experts.

> But in Estonia [the principle] appears to be the larger [the agricultural enterprise] the better. (A senior agricultural official at county level)

> People are going to understand that anyone who wants to succeed has got to take up large-scale farming. A small proportion may remain as some sort of hobby farmers in cases where one of the family members, for example, is a government employee. There are farms of 5–10 hectares. They don't provide a person with a basic income. (A senior official at county level in charge of small-business matters)

However, it must be stressed that this dynamism leading to large-scale production is still fragile, although it might well be – at least in municipalities like Kanepi – the only clearly positive tendency from the viewpoint of advancing agricultural production. The overall picture is heavily negative, and a vicious circle of pauperisation predominates in agriculture. In this respect the following generalisations are justified.

The one who fares the worst at the moment is the farmer. (Chairman of the Savings and Loan Association)

Here [in Kanepi] the costs of agriculture are too high. It simply isn't profitable. (Director of a wood-processing enterprise)

Agriculture is simply not profitable in its present shape. I cannot even imagine how it would turn in a profit. (A small businessman engaged in various kinds of dealing)

If there are no changes in agricultural policy, the land will be left idle, and the fields won't be cultivated anymore. (Agronomist X)

Many cowsheds, pigsties, warehouses and other production buildings have been left unused and have fallen into disrepair.

Kanepi, of course, is still a fairly large municipality, but at the moment the situation is that as we drive here [in the more remote villages], [we can see] the former cowsheds and kolkhozes, they've been overcome by desolation. I get the feeling a war has swept over [this place]. (A small businessman engaged in various kinds of dealing)

A great quantity of buildings, machinery and even mental capital has been destroyed. The infrastructure necessary for all agricultural activity has been eroded.

During the kolkhoz times there were soil improvement systems that had been constructed with government money; drainage channels have to be cleaned out and maintained all the time. The kolkhoz handed these jobs over to the municipality through the reform committee, and the municipality doesn't have any soil improvement specialists . . . That was the first thing that they'll have to pay dearly for, since those [underdrainage systems] are going to get blocked and clogged up. It's a great shame, but most likely it's going to happen. (Former chairman of the kolkhoz)

The whole landscape is changing; first the fields grow weeds, then they start sprouting coppices. The imprint of human hand disappears from the landscape, as do the aesthetics produced by continuous care. Only then will it be noticed that the national landscape has its own gardener, the farmer – once he is gone.

> It isn't the worst thing that [agricultural produce] is being imported. There's also the standard of people's homes, their ability to do something, take good care of their own houses and their surroundings. A beautiful field is beautiful; a beautiful hayfield is beautiful. (Wife of the former kolkhoz chairman in a joint interview with her husband)

Although the interviewees' sentiments were gloomy in 1995, Kanepi was in fact already entering a more stable period, just as the chairman of the Savings and Loan Association had optimistically predicted. This new phase (from 1995 to early 1998) did not prevent the marginalisation and gradual destruction of plot farms and technologically backward family farms, but the economic stability contributed to the strengthening of the best family farms and particularly the best (and largest) agricultural enterprises. The data from our Kanepi project are in keeping with the preliminary observations made by the present author (cf. Alanen, 1999). Figure 3.2 presents the overall picture of the development from the symbiotic production structure of kolkhozes and sovkhozes to a few capitalistically organised large-scale enterprises, complemented by a group of advanced family farms.

Understanding the Failures

But *what went wrong with the reform* and how should government policy be changed to remedy the situation? The failure of the reform has usually been attributed to a *failure in integrating the dissolution of the kolkhozes and sovkhozes with the restitution of land and other assets;* and this in turn has been explained either by too much haste or by a lack of advance planning.

> I've never defended large economic [units], kolkhoz discipline, etc. I [just] opposed the breaking up and the sudden changes. I think people were a little deceived, and nobody knew how and what would happen to people's assets. Professor Tamm made an attempt at explaining matters to the people, but . . . I spoke with Tamm a year ago and he said that they'd offered choices to the people. I asked him, what would a senior citizen know about such alternatives? I don't know anything about them, neither do you. Then he said that even they weren't certain [about a great number of issues], [so] we were all fools. But that's the way things went. The one who bought machinery, he didn't have land to cultivate, and he didn't have the money to repair and maintain the machines. (Former chairman of the kolkhoz)

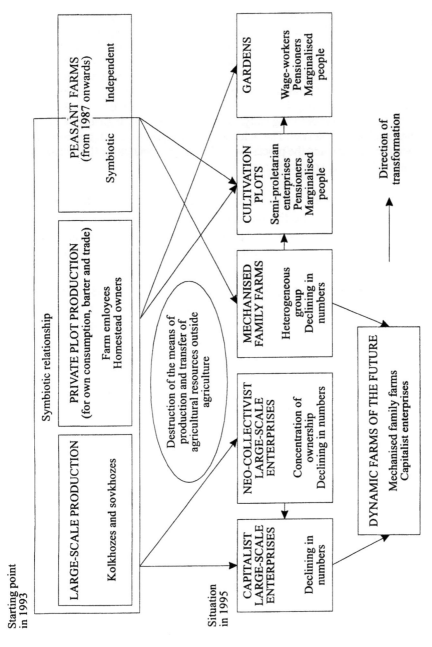

Starting point
in 1993

Symbiotic relationship

LARGE-SCALE PRODUCTION

Kolkhozes and sovkhozes

PRIVATE PLOT PRODUCTION
(for own consumption, barter and trade)

Farm emloyees
Homestead owners

PEASANT FARMS
(from 1987 onwards)

Symbiotic   Independent

Destruction of the means of
production and transfer of
agricultural resources outside
agriculture

Situation
in 1995

CAPITALIST
LARGE-SCALE
ENTERPRISES

Declining in
numbers

NEO-COLLECTIVIST
LARGE-SCALE
ENTERPRISES

Concentration of
ownership
Declining in numbers

MECHANISED
FAMILY FARMS

Heterogeneous
group
Declining in numbers

CULTIVATION
PLOTS

Semi-proletarian
enterprises
Pensioners
Marginalised
people

GARDENS

Wage-workers
Pensioners
Marginalised
people

DYNAMIC FARMS OF THE FUTURE

Mechanised family farms
Capitalist enterprises

Direction of
transformation

Figure 3.2 The emergence of a new enterprise structure: the transformation process in Estonia

> In my opinion, the breaking up of the kolkhozes should have taken place in stages. It shouldn't have been done at one go. [Breaking up the kolkhoz very rapidly] is possible in theory, but the people's thinking and psyche wouldn't keep up [with the pace], and it's now clear that they didn't. If the land reform could have been brought about calmly, we could have slowly started forming homesteads. Things shouldn't happen violently, but voluntarily. Although they say that it was voluntary, it was still a forced liquidation, and as it took place by force, it didn't proceed logically. It would have gone logically if the land question had been solved. The fields would have got owners, farms could have been formed then and the process would have gone smoothly. (Later chairman of a neighbouring kolkhoz)

Perhaps it would be wrong to assume that all the critics disapprove of the restitution that became the basic postulate of the reform, although no doubt some do. The perspective of these critics might be better understood from a technocratic viewpoint: restitution is a given fact, but there might have been more productive ways of putting it into effect.

In his article (Chapter 8) Mati Tamm reckons that it was the speed of Estonian agricultural reform that explains its relative success. No doubt Estonian agriculture has not fared worst compared to the all other post-socialist countries (although more accurate comparisons still remain to be made). Perhaps the relative success of the Põlva *ühistys* is explained by the fact that there – and in a number of other kolkhozes – the reform was carried through relatively quickly compared to the kolkhozes in Kanepi; also the fact that they managed to avoid the intermediate period that destroyed assets, and maintained the entire farm as a more or less unbroken economic unit.

Integrating the restitution of the family farm system of the former period of independence with the breaking up of the kolkhozes would certainly have required much more time. But still the results could not have been very good: the transformation of the resources of the large-scale farm system for the use of small farms would have been an impossible task – with the exception of a tiny proportion of the machines and appliances. Success would probably have required the redirection into agriculture of an enormous amount of resources from other sectors of the economy. But of course, there were no assets that could have been transferred to agriculture – not even if there had been the political will. A more methodical process would also have required a larger body of government officials, which the state of Estonia simply did not have when the reform was started. The inadequacy of the civil service and the associated control system were most likely the main reasons why the reform finally became "just wholesale stealing and robbing" – as the later chief accountant poignantly expressed the matter.

Another large group of critics continue to defend the preservation of kolkhozes, either as large entities or divided into "little kolkhozes". This brings us again to some kind of a Põlva model. Indeed, the clear majority of the kolkhoz workers and members placed their hope in this direction. Still there were a great number of Estonians who wanted to establish a small private farm or who wished to continue cultivating an existing small farm. And many wanted – at least on paper – their old family farm returned. But parting from the kolkhoz was quite another matter. Perhaps some kind of a compromise could have been reached between all these conflicting desires, instead of carrying out a land reform based on the main principle of restitution. For in any case, the family farm principle is willy-nilly turning into a victory for private large-scale agriculture, in so far as anything dynamic is being reconstructed at all right now. The alternative could have been the following, for example.

The breaking up of the kolkhozes – I believe I can say that – it was criminal, since there was no plan whatsoever. And now those, who want to engage in that kind of [agricultural] work, they have to make a fresh start, because all the resources have been destroyed. And that's why all the people with common sense are now moving from the country to the cities, and that's why the contrast between the country and the city is greater than ever. If you just look around, there's plenty of new stuff in the city, but people only use old things in the country. The social system has been disrupted too. In the old days the kolkhoz used to take care of that, but now it's the municipalities. Unfortunately, the municipalities aren't yet capable of doing everything. And although it's been said that everything's been stabilised, that isn't really the case, everything is still going downhill. (Owner of a technologically advanced family farm)

It's a question of psychology. In the old days we had successful kolkhozes, and many of them have remained [usually as co-operatives or limited liability companies]. There could be some of these, but there could also be private entrepreneurs. What's important is that the buildings would have been kept up and they would be bustling with workers. Everyone could have learned from each other. I feel that the most important factor [in the dissolution process] was an individual's fear that somebody else might get more profit. That's why there was no proper planning. At the same time as they were given the right to make up their own mind at local level, people were unable to find the right way forward. If there were knowledgeable people present, everything went fine. (Ibid.)

In my opinion, the only necessary thing was to find an owner for each and every item. After that, [economic] self-regulation would already have taken over. It would have taken time, but it would have worked.

> It wouldn't have been necessary to grant rights to one side only [private farms or co-operatives], both could have worked together. (Ibid.)

The other pivotal question is: *how should Estonian agricultural policy be revised to repair the damage?* This is clearly an issue of general politics that cannot be resolved at local level.

> Agriculture has got to develop. We [in the municipal administration] cannot do anything, it all depends on government policy, which is debated in the parliament. All those protective tariffs and government subsidies, whether they should be applied or not. And the loan system, so that a farmer could get money for the purchase of machines, everything depends on that [the government policy]. (Municipal councillor)

One thing that the farmers agree on is that further land reform should be carried through, since entrepreneurship requires a secure legal foundation for agreements to be made.

> I really can't say what this place will be like in five years. There are so many open questions in the countryside. Private ownership hasn't yet been established in the country . . . There's a temporary user, but no master. That is the general attitude. You cannot plan anything ahead. (Later chairman of the kolkhoz)

Mr A, a large-scale agricultural producer who bought three large cowsheds pointed out that one need not own the land one cultivates. Still, there has to be some assurance that one can carry on a business in the long run, for example with a lease.

Another issue on which the farmers appear to agree is that there is a need for a workable loan system, and that the produce must have a secure market. Land reform does have an influence on the granting of loans in so far as landed property serves as security for a loan. As a rule farmers are unable to provide this kind of security. However, in such a remote area as Kanepi this would not be enough, because of the low value of arable land. Perhaps in the future, if agriculture recovers from its present desperate situation, the ownership of land may gain importance in this respect. However, all across the developed capitalist countries separate credit systems have been created specifically for farmers. These take into account not only the issue above, but also the other special characteristics of agriculture (e.g. the slow circulation of capital). Agriculture requires a national credit institution specialised in its problems, and the government (or international credit institutions) should aim to appropriate a sufficiently large capital stock to set up such an institution.

What about the market? Many people in Kanepi see a market in Russia, since the region used to have close trade relations over the Russian border. But trade links to Russia were cut off for political reasons, and Estonia alone may not after all have sufficient impetus to solve this deadlocked situation.

In any case, it may be that Estonians have a mistaken impression of today's Russia as a market for agricultural products. Russia no longer suffers from a shortage of food products, since foreign agricultural produce is imported in large quantities to Russia as well as to Estonia. The thing Russians are lacking may simply be money. Because of this, opening the borders might not actually solve the problems of the Estonian agricultural market, or it would do so only marginally. The problem that farmers in Estonia (as in most other countries) are facing is the lack of a stable market for their produce, a market that would make possible the long-term planing which agriculture requires by its very nature.

> The main problem is that the prices have no guarantees. If Estonia, too, had a guarantee system, as other countries do, then it'd be safer to take a loan – if they [the farmers] knew what its expenses would be in 1–2 years time. (Agronomist X)

Even if Estonian farmers could agree on this, when we start considering the variety of measures available, we face ideological conflicts which are deeply rooted in the ultra-liberal business atmosphere of the country. The thousand-dollar question is how it would be possible to establish a stable agricultural market – some type of a system of guaranteed prices, that is – without any trade barriers on agricultural products. On border issues, i.e. on taxes and import duties, farmers indeed appeared (1995) to be divided into two factions, defenders and opponents. Since there are no trade barriers on the border, a system of guaranteed prices cannot be created, and there will hardly be any need for a credit institution. And failing such an institution, who would be willing put the sort of money into the buildings, mechanisation and land that agriculture requires, with its long natural cycle and consequent need for the long-term investment.

As of today (1999), farmers largely appear to have united behind the demand for increased trade barriers.

Robber Capitalism, Anomie and Resistance

Patrimonial leadership and other social relations intrinsic to Soviet-style agricultural enterprises and rural village communities have already been irreversibly replaced by social structures based on wage-labour and the private ownership of the means of production.

Although the new society is undoubtedly capitalistic, its final form is still incomplete. The final form will be determined both by the local people themselves (from below upwards) and by society as a whole (from the top downwards). It will be affected by the general conditions for economic development, political decisions, legislation, and the new, national regulatory bodies that are still under development. Judging from the Kanepi data, we can estimate that rural Estonia is currently undergoing a phase which can be effectively described by the terms "robber capitalism", "anomie", and "resistance".

Robber Capitalism

By the term "robber capitalism" we are in this chapter referring to only one of its aspects, i.e. the characteristics acquired by entrepreneurship and wage-labour in today's Estonia. These characteristics will be more precisely under-stood in a broader context. In using the term "robber capitalism" we are not referring to the so-called original accumulation; nor are we referring to the "public thieving" which was mostly prevalent at the time of the actual privatisation of the kolkhozes and sovkhozes and which for the most part is already over. Thus, by "robber capitalism" we mean the stage of development that has followed privatisation.

The term "robber capitalism" is often used in articles published in social science journals dealing with post-socialism, and occasionally newspaper articles. Usually it serves only illustrative purposes, but in the following treatment it is linked with Durkheimian thinking, as presented in his works *The Division of Labour* (English translation 1964, Chapter 7) and *Suicide* (English translation 1951), although the term as such is not actually used in these books.

According to *the Division of Labour*, social circumstances analogous to robber capitalism are characterised by the incompleteness of the moral foundation of society. Although the foundation of new social relations may have already been laid qualitatively, time is also required for the development of a new kind of "traditional authority" on the basis of "experience". Only that will create a moral order as a prerequisite for everyday social exchange between individuals. Thus, we are primarily dealing with a moral principle, although legislation in line with this principle is also being developed.

The moral order is not grounded on explicit interpersonal interests, but on a system, and – in Durkheimian functionalist terms – "the supra-individual sphere of transcendent values", which is ultimately rooted in every society. By contrast, in robber capitalism people are only connected by immediate interests; moreover, the association is only "temporary", since ever-changing circumstances divide and pull individual interests in different directions. Thus, robber capitalism effectively consists of everyone at war with everyone. Adhering to the terminology used in *Suicide*, it is one of the representations of an *anomic* (normless) social condition. However, the reverse side of selfishness is a notable and widespread social helplessness (people's inability to defend themselves) which make it easy to deprive them of their property.

The following interview excerpts illustrate this social situation further from the viewpoint of robber capitalism.

[All] I can say is that the kolkhozes spoilt Estonian farmers. People don't have any practice in getting a grip on their own affairs. In my opinion, the biggest problem is that we were all wager-workers, but now that everyone should look after himself, people are incapable of doing it. In my opinion it's the people themselves that are the problem, and not the [lack of] money as such. (A successful businessman)

People themselves don't know how a farmer-proprietor should act. There are many young farmers here, well, they aren't really farmers, they've been restituted their former [family] estate . . . I don't now how many thousands they got for the timber, but two hundred kroons was all he [the young farmer, who sold timber] had in the end. And he's drunk every day. (Later chairman of the kolkhoz)

We don't have the kind of continuity they have in Germany, where they hand over the farm from one generation to another and it's a matter of pride to keep on [farming]. (A small businessman engaged in various kinds of dealing)

When the kolkhoz was broken up people just stayed waiting there for somebody to look after them. (A local amateur historian)

Work ethics have deteriorated compared to the Soviet era, when people worked hard and were paid, too. (Later chairman of a neighbouring kolkhoz)

Old workers have the same old habits, the young ones don't. Young people are more flexible. They are more eager to learn. (23-year-old worker in a small firm)

The board members of the [leading private enterprise] are respected people. Their grabbing is now called 'entrepreneurship'. (A local amateur historian)

The books are [formally] in order, and whatever is paid under the table, it's certain that it'll never be discovered [by the tax authorities], there are no documents whatsoever [about those payments]. (Person familiar with the methods of tax evasion in local businesses)

[The only matter that interests entrepreneurs in the economic policy of the Kanepi municipal council] is to get hold of the felling areas, or get hold of something [of value], get a share of the pie, get to the source. This is the situation everywhere, not just with us. (An activist in the Isamaa Party)

The most serious problem [in the municipality of Kanepi] right now is corruption . . . The most corrupt body at the moment is the forest management, especially concerning the sale of areas for felling. In that place nobody knows who's bribing whom. (Former municipal director)

The above excerpts refer to the following characteristics of robber capitalism:

1) *A minority* acts without scruples for its own benefit. Corruption is rampant and even positions of trust are viewed from the standpoint of personal benefit. Social organisations (e.g. in elections, see Ruutsoo, Chapter 5) are primarily based on temporary individual interests (e.g. in relation to local administrative bodies), and organisations dissolve as these interests are reformed.

During the interviews, the leading businessmen gave us the impression that entrepreneurship is for them a big adventure or game. Tax evasion and the grey economy are currently considered a perfectly normal part of the game. The data indicate that the most important players are those who were either members of the core kolkhoz leadership at the time of the privatisation, or else they are young adults who have had no previous standing in the power hierarchy, but whose business strategies have proved to be most inventive and flexible.

2) *For the majority of people* the transformation of them into the economic subjects of capitalism (as entrepreneurs and wager-workers) has been extremely painful. Patrimonial relationships of the Soviet type thrust the

majority of the population into passivity: today they are still waiting for a "carer" or a "white ship". This applies to middle-aged people in particular. Most of them received some sort of productive capital in restitution and/or at the auctions, but they lack the ability to regard it as an investment (i.e. there is a lack of a "master mentality"). Instead they tend to make short-term plans, solely from the viewpoint of consumption. In extreme cases, which are not exceptional, the assets are simply squandered by drinking, buying a car, etc.

Labelling all this as "robber capitalism" may be too black and white, since – as we have already seen – there is evidence in the data of the development of a new type of entrepreneur and wager-worker, and people do express moral criticism directed against robber capitalism. But Durkheim underlines the "organic" nature of highly developed capitalism, and Kanepi has a long way to go before it reaches a comparable structure of solidarity. All in all, these concepts of classical sociology (organic solidarity, and anomie as a disturbed state of solidarity) portray remarkably well the post-socialist crisis, although they were originally formulated to describe the birth processes of an industrial and partly capitalist society.

So, robber capitalism prevails in Estonian countryside. Estonian legislation has, nevertheless, been constantly developed, and has apparently succeeded in setting a limit to the grey economy. It has, for example, made the illegal felling of timber much more difficult. The development of a moral order involves, however, a much more complicated process than just the enactment of normative legislation. As long as legislation runs ahead of its moral basis (a situation explained, perhaps, by the fiscal constraints of the public economy and the rapid adoption of foreign models), people's attitude towards the law will remain external. This tends to work against the success of legislation, and in any case, businessmen regard legislation as a mere hindrance to their activities.

Apparently, legislation still lacks, at least in part, the respect which in a capitalist society consisting of individuals pursuing their own interests may only originate from a moral foundation – a foundation that transcends the immediate interests of individual actors. Hence, it is only understandable that trust, social capital, and the fundamental role of informal institutions in regulating and making the functioning of formal institutions more efficient have come up as central themes in today's debate on post-socialism.

Anomie

As a background to anomie we find on the one hand the dissolution of the old system and a disillusionment with the promises of Estonia's Singing Revolution, which had enthused people immensely, but on the other hand, perhaps even first and foremost, made them realise their real inability to act in a structurally new situation. In Durkheim's works this inability is linked to the underdevelopment of moral codes, but in Kanepi the analysis is confused by the fact that effective social activity lacks many material prerequisites as a result of unemployment, low pensions and low wages, an underdeveloped social security system, and so on. The moral aspect is within the focus of this analysis, but the following excerpts point towards the necessary material prerequisites for such activity.

> The municipality guarantees minimum subsistence. Out of the 3,150 inhabitants in the municipality 900 [are] pensioners, and 300 are unemployed. (Later municipal director)

> As you chat with the elderly people [you definitely get the impression that] they've fallen to a level where we're talking about survival; whether they will get something to eat every day, whether they'll get bread, whether they'll get heat. (Leading person in a pensioners' organisation)

> There's a milker [who] works for me, she's got electric heating in her flat, and it costs 850–900 kroons each month. Now that she gets 2,000 kroons in wages from me each month, half of it she must spend on the heating. (Owner of a cowshed complex)

> Who would hire a woman of my age these days? I can't even dream of it. If you have good connections, maybe. 36 [years of age], that's too much, nobody wants to employ a person this old. (An unemployed woman in Kanepi)

> There are some 300 recipients of welfare benefits. Out of this number a quarter are single males who've never really worked. We have a quarter of the people with an agricultural education, they've got their own home and they're elderly. Single parents, families with many children and mothers on maternity leave make up 25%. The registered unemployed, who get [are qualified for] a start-up grant for the setting up of a farm or a business, there are 20% of them. Employed people, whose wages are much too low, though – make up 5%. (A social worker in Kanepi)

It is descriptive of the level of welfare benefit that pensioners are not included in the number of welfare recipients, although pensions are considered to be fairly low. However, the wages of many workers are even lower than this. In addition to the customary groups (unmarried males who have never worked) and groups that are facing impoverishment in the West as well (single parenting mothers, etc.) the high percentage of "elderly" individuals with an agricultural vocational education is noteworthy. This reveals the true nature of the agricultural reform. It not only resulted in a sharp decline in the volume of agricultural production, but also in the displacement of a large number of agricultural specialists.

The following excerpts describe genuine anomie.

> The people have become terribly indifferent and apathetic, and the only thing that's left is drinking, and they do drink an awful lot. I can see it just from [the fact], that we [the MTJ] have got our own off-licence down at the corner, and its turnover used to be much smaller than it is now . . . Today everything is so uncertain. You waste [the money], you eat, and you drink everything right away. Why wait for tomorrow? (One of the six owners of the MTJ)

> The thing that's going on in the countryside is horrible. As soon as they get some benefit money, it's spent on liquor. People are deeply depressed, since they don't get paid. [They are] the middle-aged generation that's living for the moment, drowning it all in a stupour. The attitude of the city people is most likely summed up in the comment by Siim Kallas, chairman of the Reform Party: "No development is possible in the countryside, because you don't sober up until noon." Nobody bothers to think of the true cause: that people don't get their wages. To give an example, [when] a husband arrives home, the wife starts complaining, the husband gets in a bad mood, goes off to a bar, gets drunk and so it goes, their life's a dead end. I've been watching as an onlooker. (A small businessman engaged in various kinds of dealing)

> The world of the people has collapsed. They have lost touch . . . [From a] psychological [viewpoint], during the kolkhoz people collaborated with each other, there were possibilities for interaction, it was possible to meet people at the workplace. Now people are lonely, associations are no longer formed. During Soviet times all the needs of the people were satisfied, and in the evening they escaped to the seclusion [of their homes]. Today, they can't get away from the isolation, you can't get away from the structure . . . The situation is worst in the new villages, kolkhoz villages, [those] half-villages with blocks of flats . . . Like in Russia, they're living from day to day. When they get money, they drink it away. (Later chairman of the kolkhoz)

And you don't meet any people anymore. I haven't met some people I used to see often for a long time. (23-year-old unemployed woman from Karste)

There's a great deal of drinking [much more than during the kolkhoz times]. Crime, serious crime where people are killed, has gone up. [People] are killed because of the assets restituted to them, everyone wants to have the assets for themselves, and that's why they're killing their next of kin. And the weapons, [the police] cannot check the firearm certificates of Kaitseliit [paramilitary organisation] members, etc. There are lot of unregistered weapons. The men of the Kaitseliit have misused the rights granted to them. The whole year the Kaitseliit used to collaborate very actively with the police, keeping up public order. But now they [themselves] have no discipline at all: everyone who's got a weapon at home does whatever he pleases with it, [even] threatens other people, etc. (Former chairman of the municipal council)

There are thefts. The largest objects being stolen are tractors. [They are stolen by] the young unemployed. Their main occupation [however] is robbing the forests of timber. Another group is the alcoholics. A third [group of people] are those who arrived here after the restitution of assets. (A policeman)

We are pessimists and completely disillusioned with life in general. (21-year-old kiosk saleswoman, talking about herself, her fellow workers and her mother)

There is drinking, and violence between family members and also between neighbours often turns serious. There is thieving, once in a while by people with a gun in their hand, and many kinds of petty crime.

In addition to increased drinking and crime, also social isolation and the lack of prospects are also emphasised in the excerpts. These phenomena were particularly apparent in the opening and closing moments of the interviews. Many of the interviewees were at first very reluctant to talk and suspicious towards the interviewer. Many of them had recently been in contact with nobody but their closest relatives. But frequently they opened up and welcomed the interview in a therapeutic way. After a long interview session the interviewee often responded to the interviewers' thanks by saying how important it had been to be able to discuss problems with an outsider. Discussing these matters with one's neighbours or acquaintances is too difficult, since they too are burdened with similar kinds of problems. Repeatedly we got the impression that in the interview situation even family members imparted to each other matters they had not managed to discuss with each other. Despite this, in most cases the only social network that really worked, the one that really connected people to each other, consisted almost exclusively of close relatives.

Resistance

People felt that the breaking up of the kolkhoz was a socially irrational and unfair act, almost regardless of the other opinions they might have had of the kolkhoz system. The people of Kanepi described the dissolution process with negatively charged expressions – just as the Bulgarian rural population did in a study carried out on a local community (Creed, 1995).

In both countries the expressions used originated from the days of forced collectivisation, some fifty years ago. Thus, the breaking up of Kanepi kolkhoz is consistently called its "liquidation", and its last chairman has been nicknamed the "liquidator". The use of the term indicates that ordinary people considered privatisation analogous to the liquidation of "enemies of the state" in the kulaks.

During the actual process of dissolving the kolkhoz, Kanepi people found at every step negative analogies from the times when the kolkhozes were created. Overwhelming governmental pressures were applied in both cases. Overwhelming punitive taxes had once forced farmers to join together within the kolkhoz; now they were used to accelerate the economic ruin of the kolkhozes. While the kolkhozes were being formed, the last days of the private peasant farms were found oppressive and without prospects: no one could imagine what might lie ahead. The same phenomenon has reappeared, now that the kolkhozes are being dissolved. And individuals have reacted in a similar way. Today, just as back then, even men who have not been known for their liking of alcohol have started drinking. And both at the time when the kolkhozes were formed and when they came to an end, people left the livestock uncared for to such an extent that they almost died of thirst and hunger. The list could go on. On both occasions people's old way of life had been violently interrupted and their comprehension of the new direction their life would take was nothing more than a faint idea, and one which embodied more fears of worse to come than hopes for the better.

In kolkhoz times, most of the people in Kanepi kolkhoz could wield very little influence over the way things happened, and the only role reserved for them was that of a conformist. There were very few conflicts of interest that would have required conciliation through trade unions, political parties, etc. There is nothing remarkable in that, since such institutions would have required the fully-fledged existence of something which was merely embryonic: a developed civil society with all that belongs to it, including unionisation, professional ethics, and so on. In situations such as this, the most intense collective reactions, such as violent rebellions, are typically romantic in nature: people strive for the restoration of the past. However, there was no activity of this kind in the kolkhoz of Kanepi.

Nevertheless, many phenomena related to Kanepi kolkhoz and the situation that ensued may be interpreted as indirect manifestations of *resistance and protest*. For example, in connection with the auction, we have already noted its carnivalistic aspect, which is in a way a combination of distancing and protest. We have also heard of cases in which the unemployed reacted to the offer of a job by retorting that "a little hunger is better than hard work." This too can be interpreted as a protest: against the new ownership, low wages, a new kind of regulation of work, etc.

The woman who had bought a cowshed complex told us that her employees experienced their transformation to the role of wage-workers under her as a shock, which led to a number of unfortunate incidents. At one point some of her employees simply refused to obey her orders, went berry picking and left her all alone with a large herd of cattle. That cowshed owner and also the manager of a new manufacturing firm felt themselves completely powerless.

> [The manager] isn't able to pay them wages [comparable to wages] at the national level, he only pays them local-level wages . . . The manager has told them that if they'd work [properly] they'd get good wages. But right now, they don't really want that. There's a certain limit up to which they'll work. [Then] they just close the doors and go out on a drinking spree. They drink for several days in a row [just as in kolkhoz times]. There's nothing [the manager] can do about it. (Later chairman of the kolkhoz)

On the whole, collective reactions such as these are rare. It is much more common to ridicule people behind their backs: for example, the owners of cowshed complexes are called names, more specifically the owners are labelled "kulaks" using the Soviet-era pejorative.

Although the overall impression we got during the interviews is that the work ethics of employees in local enterprises are progressing in the direction of more discipline, this tendency is not found everywhere. The owner of a cowshed complex which was widely known to be insolvent, and which was totally unable to pay its wages or honour its other commitments to its employees, considered that the situation was, on the contrary, getting worse day by day.

He also believed he knew the identity of the person who had stolen his few remaining assets (e.g. his welding leads), but he did not dare to speak the name of the person aloud, because he was afraid of his house being burnt down. The threat to the property of this alcoholic owner was not imaginary, since one case of arson had already occurred in Kanepi. The cowshed of an another entrepreneur was burnt down after he had declared his intention of putting it up for sale. Threats of violence were indeed common, although the actual use of personal terror such as this was not so frequent. (Indeed, there was serious violence, but people mostly directed it against their next of kin or next door neighbour.)

These acts of violence lack manifest social content. We did hear of one possible exception, however. The chairman of the reform committee in a neighbouring kolkhoz was murdered and the same threat was made to his successor as well as to the former chairman of that kolkhoz. The threat and the act were undoubtedly connected to the reform, but our data are not specific or detailed enough to interpret them as a protest against the new social relations.

During the past five years three savage murders and several manslaughters have been committed in Kanepi, a rural municipality of about 3,000 inhabitants.

Resistance is certainly not an exhaustive interpretation of the phenomena described above. The carnival atmosphere of the auction might have arisen simply because of the unique nature of the event, and the fact that many matters related to the auction were not understood. Drinking, thieving and gossiping behind people's backs can also be traced back to people's behaviour in kolkhoz times. But in many cases the criticism was clearly directed at the new social relations (with one term of abuse being "new kulaks"), and in some cases existing phenomena intensified in the new situation (for example thieving in the instance mentioned above).

Whatever the case may be, we are definitely dealing with resistance to some degree. And although there might be continuity from Kolkhoz times, it may well have gained new intentional content in the new circumstances that have arisen under the guise of a superficial similarity.

The theory of *the moral economy of peasantry* was formulated by James C. Scott (1986) for somewhat different circumstances (primarily for the study of the peasant communities of the Middle Ages and in developing countries), but it still provides us with a useful means of interpreting phenomena related to the dissolution of the kolkhoz and its aftermath as a reaction against the *negative characteristics* of capitalist relations.

Resistance is a reaction against proletarisation and marginalisation, and the loss of previous respect – which had been shown towards ordinary kolkhoz workers, but especially to such vocational specialists as a milker or a tractor driver in the patrimonial and other Gemeinschaft-like societal structures of the kolkhozes (cf. old villages).

Scott links the roots of resistance with the ideological meaning system of peasant culture, which has its roots in the "historically deep" vein of "peasant culture", constructed on the basis of the "tight social network" of village communities. In Estonia we would have to add to this elements related to the kolkhoz times (cf. the labelling of the owners of large-scale farms negatively as "kulaks"). According to the former municipal director, the Soviet concept system still dominated the minds of many local people. Although ethnic Estonians as a rule felt deep hatred towards the Soviet occupiers, many had over decades adopted the Soviet metaphors of "workers and revolutionary seamen and the Great October Revolution". This type of tradition, in Scott's theory, "legitimates" the "forms of everyday peasant resistance".

Scott's listing of resistance forms (1986, 29) appears surprisingly similar to that which one observes in the Kanepi situation. The forms of resistance include for instance deception, superficial adaptation or indifference, shirking, pilfering, slander, gossip, lack of respect for the elites, strike, arson, sabotage, murder, and so on.

Furthermore, Scott emphasises the everyday character of resistance. The relations within the peasantry (including relations between classes) and relations between the peasantry and the external elite are to some degree questioned every day, and therefore reproduced as they are or transformed gradually into other forms in the social processes of interaction in everyday life. This resistance is typically both in form and intentional content highly personal. At first sight it is also without any collective elements (e.g. thieving from the rich for the use of the thief's own family, or hiding assets from the tax authorities, etc.), but this does not exclude the collective cultural conditions and consequences of these actions, nor their culturally determined nature overall.

According to Scott, the intention of an individual also originates from conditions of collective resistance. Peasants are scattered in small communities. They lack the institutional instruments for organised activity, since political liberties themselves are seldom sufficient, and elites are generally capable of controlling collective organisations (Scott, 1986, 28). Of course, the latter part of Scott's exposition does not apply to Kanepi as such. Estonians are endowed with the formal rights of assembly, but few such organisations exist because of the underdeveloped civil society.

Nevertheless, in Kanepi too it is possible to interpret the form as well as the content of individual resistance as a manifestation of *de facto* collective resistance, since the dissolution of the kolkhozes does not automatically signify the disappearance of the "climate of opinion" which provides an individual's intention with a collective justification.

Although the day-to-day resistance of ordinary citizens of Kanepi does not call capitalist society itself into question, it still has an effect on the formation of classes by "the constant process of testing and renegotiation of production relations between classes" (Scott, 1986, 18). In such a community as Kanepi single acts of resistance construct normative (economical, political, etc.) structures which determine relations between classes, just as the life processes of individual anthozoan polyps create coral reefs that obstruct the passage of ships (Scott, 1986, 8). Thus, resistance by kolkhoz members does have an effect on the formation of the special characteristics of new social relations – relations whose foundation was laid in the so-called original accumulation, and whose reformation is at present dominated by robber capitalism.

References

Agriculture and Rural Development. Overview 1998 (1998), The Ministry of Agriculture, Tallinn.

Alanen, I. (1991), *Miten teoretisoida maatalouden pientuotantoa* [How to Theorise on Agricultural Petty Production], Jyväskylä Studies in Education and Social Research. 81/ 1991, University of Jyväskylä, Jyväskylä.

Alanen, I. (1995), 'The Family Farm Ideology, the Baltic Countries, and Theories of Development', *Eastern European Countryside*, vol. 1, no. 5, pp. 5–21.

Alanen, I. (1996), 'The Privatization of Agriculture and the Family Farm Ideology in the Baltic Countries', in R. Blom et al. (eds), *Between Plan and Market. Social Change in the Baltic States and Russia,* Walter de Gruyter, Berlin, pp. 141–168.

Alanen, I. (1998a), 'Petty production in Baltic agriculture: Estonian and Lithuanian models', in M. Kivinen (ed), *The Kalamari Union – Middle Class in East and West,* Ashgate, Aldershot, pp. 39-70.

Alanen, I. (1998b), 'Baltic Agriculture After the Decollectivization', in L. Granberg, and I. Kovách (eds), *European Countryside in Transition,* Institute for Political Science of the Hungarian Academy of Sciences Publications, Budapest, pp. 144–167.

Alanen, I. (1999), 'Agricultural Policy and the Struggle over the Destiny of Collective Farms in Estonia', *Sociologica Ruralis*, vol. 30, no 3, pp. 431–458.

Amin, S. (1977), *Imperialism and Unequal Development. Essays by Samir Amin,* Harvester Press, Brighton.

Clarke, S. (1993), 'The Contradictions of the State Socialism', in S. Clarke, P. Fairbrother, M. Burawoy and P. Krotov, *What about the Workers? Workers and the Transition to Capitalism in Russia,* Verso, London.

Creed, G. W. (1995), 'An Old Song in a New Voice: Decollectivization in Bulgaria', in D. A. Kideckel (ed.) *East European Communities: The Struggle for Balance in Turbulent Times*, Westview, Boulder.

Durkheim, E. (1951), *Suicide*, The Free Press, New York.

Durkheim, E. (1964), *The Division of Labor in Society*, The Free Press, New York.

Hirschhausen, C. von and Hui, W. (1995), 'Industrial Restructuring in the Baltic Countries: Large-scale Privatisation, New Enterprise Networks and Growing Diversity of Corporate Governance', *Communist Economies and Economic Transformation*, vol. 7, no. 4, pp. 421–443.

Laird, R. D. (1997), 'Kolkhozy, the Russian Achilles Heel: Failed Agrarian Reform', *Europe-Asia Studies*, vol. 49, no. 3, pp. 469–478.

Liepins, V. (1993), 'Baltic Attitudes to Economic Recovery: A Survey of Public Opinion in the Baltic Countries', *Journal of Baltic Studies*, vol. XXIV, no 2.

Lieven, A. (1993), *The Baltic Revolution*, Yale University Press, New Haven.

Loko, V. (1993), 'Current Situation and Perspective of Estonian Agricultural Policy', in *Agricultural Development Problems and Possibilities in Baltic Countries in the Future*, Finnish-Baltic Joint Seminar in Saku, MTTL – Maatalouden taloudellinen tutkimuslaitos (Agricultural Economics Research Institute, Finland), julkaisuja (Research Publications), Helsinki, no. 72, pp. 7–9.

Marx, K. (1954), *Capital, Volume I*, Foreign Languages Publishing House, Moscow.

Marx, K. (1966), *Capital, Volume III*, Progress Publishers, Moscow.

Maslovski, M. (1996), 'Max Weber's Concept of Patrimonialism and the Soviet System', *The Sociological Review*, vol. 44, no. 2 (May 1996), pp. 294–308.

Meillassoux, C. (1981), *Maidens, Meal and Money. Capitalism and the Domestic Community*, Cambridge University Press, Cambridge.

Pajo, M., Tamm, M. and Teinberg, R. (1994), *The Restructuring of Estonian Agriculture*, Estonian Ministry of Agriculture, Midwest Agribusiness Trade Research and Information Center, and Center for Agricultural and Rural Development at Iowa State University, Ames.

Palm, T. (1992), 'The Suurupi Program: Estonian Economic Policy for the Transition', *Journal of Baltic Studies*, vol. 23, no. 3, pp. 283–298.

Parsons, T. (1971), *The System of Modern Societies*, Prentice Hall, Englewood Cliffs.

Raig, I. (1989), 'Viron sekundaaritalous', *Kansantaloudellinen aikakauskirja*, vol. 25, no. 1, pp. 61–66.

Scott, J. C. (1986), 'Everyday Forms of Peasant Resistance', *Journal of Peasant Studies*, vol. 13, no. 1, pp. 5–35.

Selden, M. (1994), 'Pathways from Collectivization. Socialist and Post-Socialist Agrarian Alternatives in Russia and China', *Review (Fernand Braudel Center)*, vol. 17, no. 4, pp. 423–449.

Vasary, I. (1990), 'Competing Paradigms: Peasant Farming and Collectivization in a Balaton Community', *The Journal of Communist Studies*, vol. 6, no. 2, pp. 163–182.

Wallerstein, I, Martin W. and Dickinson, T. (1982), 'Household Structures and Production Processes: Preliminary Theses and Findings', *Review*, vol. V, no. 3.

Weber, M. (1978), *Economy and Society, Volume 1*, University of California Press, Berkeley.

World Development Report 1996: From Plan to Market (1996), The World Bank, Oxford University Press, Oxford.

The centre of Kanepi township is small but prides itself with long traditions of culture and trade. Today the population of the Municipality of Kanepi amounts to about 3,000 inhabitants. (Photo: Kanepi kolkhoz archives. 1960s)

On entering the vicinity of Kanepi kolkhoz a visitor encountered signs like this by the roadside. Note the slogan: "Austa tööd, hinda aeg!" ("Respect work by valueing time!"). (Photo: Kanepi kolkhoz archives. Early 1980s)

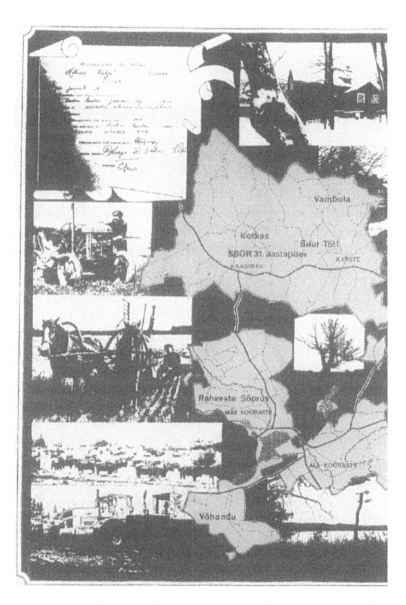

The map of Kanepi kolkhoz includes Kanepi township, where the administrative building of Kanepi kolkhoz and many other kolkhoz facilities (large cowsheds and piggeries, the machine and tractor station and the central

warehouses) were all located. Large-scale cattle sheds and blocks of flats were also built in two other villages within the municipality — Karste and Kooraste. (Photo: Kanepi kolkhoz archives. 1988)

Harvest-time in the early 1960s when the mechanisation of Soviet agriculture was well under way but horses were still used alongside combine harvesters. By the time of decollectivisation all the horses had been retired from agricultural use. However, when the kolkhoz was broken up many aged farmers demanded the return of the horses that had once been forcibly taken from them. (Photo: Kanepi kolkhoz archives. 1963)

Maize sowing by hand in Kanepi kolkhoz. On returning from his tour of the USA in September 1959, Soviet leader Nikita Khruschev pushed for maize cultivation in the USSR, even in areas which were unsuitable for it. The maize varieties used never ripened in the Estonian climate, but the maize was sown, because that was the order from the leadership. (Photo: Kanepi kolkhoz archives. Early 1960s)

Kanepi kolkhoz was specialised in dairy farming and pork production. (Photo: Kanepi kolkhoz archives. Early 1980s)

A large pigsty in Kanepi kolkhoz centre. (Photo: Kanepi kolkhoz archives. Early 1980s)

The kolkhoz was extensively mechanised. Shown here is the line-up of heavy agricultural tractors in front of the kolkhoz machine sheds. The prime objective of the Estonian privatisation policy was the re-establishment of family farms, but huge tractors such as these were quite unsuitable for use on the small farms of most private cultivators. One reason for the robust construction of these tractors might have been their secondary military application. Some people believe that the largest tractors were in the first place designed to tow missile launchers. (Photo: Kanepi kolkhoz archives. Early 1980s)

The kolkhoz also included industrial departments. The ownership of this sawmill and the associated wood processing plant was the subject of a fierce battle at the time of privatisation. (Photo: Kanepi kolkhoz archives. Early 1980s)

The new administration building of the kolkhoz. After the kolkhoz auction these offices remained vacant for several years and the plan to convert the building into a hotel was never realised. Recently the building has been sold to AS Eesti Energia. (Photo: Kanepi kolkhoz archives. 1984)

A political meeting (Poliitpäev) in Kanepi kolkhoz. On the right, representatives of the kolkhoz board of management and visitors from the Communist Party rayon executive committee. On the left, kolkhoz workers who have been ordered to attend the meeting to hear the latest party line. (Photo: Kanepi kolkhoz archives. Early 1980s)

The detached house of a specialist in Kanepi township. Note the potato fields surrounding the house, leaving no room for ornamental garden plants. All private plots and gardens, even the back yards of blocks of flats, were intensively cultivated. Vegetables and all other types of economic plants were also frequently cultivated in plots and gardens. (Photo: Kanepi kolkhoz archives. Early 1980s)

A terraced house constructed for unskilled workers moving into Kanepi from other parts of Estonia and the USSR to alleviate the constant shortage of labour. Some of these people were so called "migratory birds", who were often less respectful of their surroundings than the local population. (Photo: Kanepi kolkhoz archives. Early 1980s)

A streetscape in the centre of Kanepi settlement today has not changed much from what it would have been decades ago. (Photo: J. Nikula. 1995)

Combine harvesters in a Kanepi field after decollectivisation. Kanepi kolkhoz was replaced by a number of large-scale enterprises in which production is mainly based on the machinery and production infrastructure inherited from kolkhoz times. The picture also shows that the open fields in Põlva County are often bounded by large spruce forests. (Photo: Kruusla. 1997)

The post-decollectivisation atmosphere in Kanepi is crystallised in this photograph. At the time of our research the most profitable branch of the retail trade in the municipality was embodied in two outlets specialised in selling alcohol. One of them (pictured) was simply called "Vodka". The overall number of shops in Kanepi is declining, but today the number of specialised alcohol shops has gone up to three and alcohol is also readily available at grocery stores. (Photo: J. Nikula. 1995)

Some private farms were set up under the Farm Law (1989) prior to the decollectivisation of agriculture proper. Special perks were offered to the farmers and the overall economic conditions were also more favourable at that time. The best of these farms have managed to build modern detached houses and cowsheds. In this particular case the family farm was just an intermediate step and the enterprising farmer has progressively expanded his production by acquiring more land and several ex-kolkhoz cowshed complexes. (Photo: Kruusla. 1997)

The detached house of a prosperous farmer with his new car in the foreground. (Photo: Kruusla. 1997)

Most of the machinery used by the private farmers dates back to the Soviet era, as with this ageing Belarus tractor. (Photo: Kruusla. 1997)

The most successful farmers have also managed to modernise some of their equipment. This Zetor tractor comes from Czechoslovakia and the Class baler was imported from Germany. However, only a small minority of the new farmers are as prosperous as the owner of this combination. (Photo: Kruusla. 1997)

4 Surly Cream

JOUKO NIKULA

Introduction

The first phenomena of emergent capitalism in every post-socialist country were small traders who sold various goods in the streets. They did not appear unexpectedly; they had already existed for a long time. The distorted, or should we say, the other kind of modernity in Soviet style societies mainly emphasised the development of heavy industry, whilst the production of consumer goods and adjoining services was hindered. The result was a kind of lumpen consumerism coupled with restricted luxury. This resulted in the growth of a second economy – including bribery, the exchange of black currency and other types of informal exchange. The main cause behind the rise of a second economy was the possibility of getting hold of scarce goods. This represented a resource that served as a means of exchange, and replaced the bogus money that had no real value in a situation of constant shortages. Therefore, gaps in the provision of services and consumer goods created fertile ground for the proliferation of entrepreneurship in the socialist countries, whether official or unofficial. Under socialism, private entrepreneurship served merely as a source of extra income and not as a basis for class formation. Before the disintegration of the two collective farms, there were no private enterprises in Kanepi. All services, such as shops, hairdressers, and repair services were part of the kolkhoz, or collective combine, whose employees were ordinary wage earners of the state.[1] In 1987, as a part of perestroika, some liberalising measures were taken to make the Soviet economy more efficient. A part of that effort was a decree that made it possible to establish co-operative enterprises. This provided Soviet citizens with an opportunity to start building the foundation for private businesses. It also rendered it possible for the existing forms of informal economy to begin their transformation into legitimate enterprises. In Estonia, these opportunities were heightened by the adoption of the IME programme,[2] which aimed

---

1   Of course, a grey zone also existed then, where people provided services based on reciprocal exchange or personal barter.
2   Isemajandav Eesti, Estonian Self-Management.

at making Estonia economically independent within the Soviet Union. Later this programme turned into a programme for independent Estonia, which would be based on the principles of a market economy, private ownership and a multiparty system.

In Kanepi, the extensive formation of private enterprises did not start until 1993, following the decision to dissolve the kolkhoz. Prior to that there had begun a process of "initial accumulation" of capital and people, especially persons who wished to exploit the gaps in the existing inadequate services.

In the following pages I will describe and analyse the ways of establishing private firms and especially the preconditions that determined success and failure in exploiting the opportunities that the dissolution of the Kanepi kolkhoz created. It appears that the ability to use these possibilities was dependent not only on organisational capital, but also on such things as education, skills and personal qualities, such as management capabilities.

The dissolution of the collective farm was an incident in which huge properties were redistributed, as preceding chapters have shown. The property consisted mainly of forest areas and machinery, both agricultural and non-agricultural. This property represented the 'cream' on which people's prospects for the future were built, and their prospects for success were not equal. These were determined by the initial financial and social resources of the persons involved.

Sometimes success and failure have followed from the inherent forms of organisation that characterised Soviet style enterprise – e.g., the fact that managers and workers were in many ways dependent on each other, a typical feature of Soviet economy where waste and shortage existed side by side (Clarke et al., 1993; Burawoy and Lukacs, 1992). In this situation, the most important thing for managers and workers alike was the survival and reproduction of the labour collective, not economic results or profit as such.

The Era of the Rouble was the Golden Era – the Importance of Organisational Capital and Social Networks

Diversified Company I

The significance of social networks in the success of a private firm is evident in the development of the most prosperous enterprises in Kanepi. For example, the co-owner of the largest private firm was the former chairman of the kolkhoz, and his present business partners had held managerial positions in the kolkhoz. In late 1992, these three men got together, planned the organisation of their future firm, and decided upon its areas of operation. The next step was a meeting held in March 1993, where the threesome agreed on the procedures relating to the auction of the kolkhoz. They made decisions concerning their bidding policy, objects to be bought, and other such matters.

The registration of the company did not take place until the end of 1993. So, as the former chairman of the collective farm threw his office keys on to the lawn and walked away after the last general meeting of the kolkhoz, he and his partners had already formed a clear plan on how to survive the stormy weathers of collective farm dissolution; they would become businessmen.

Actually, their firm is a conglomerate of different firms under one name. The origins of the enterprise lay in the kolkhoz machine shop, and initially the founders operated in the fields of agriculture, forestry, and the maintenance of these machines.[3] In addition, the town bakery was an original part of the firm. Since then, agriculture and forestry have become more marginal and they have been replaced by a grocery shop and some cafeterias.

The firm's initial capital consisted of forests, trucks and agricultural machines bought at bargain prices with privatisation vouchers. The company director himself estimates the value of the machinery at around USD 30,000, although that may be too low, since it includes several heavy trucks and plenty of agricultural machinery, such as a combine harvester and many tractors. The time factor played a crucial role in the establishment of the firm and the accumulation of initial capital. The director himself said that, "The future was completely in the dark and everyone wanted to survive . . . The break-up of the kolkhoz resembled the shipwreck of the [passenger ferry] Estonia. Everyone tried to stay afloat, grabbing at whatever they could, because that time was terrible. Many earlier agreements were broken, of course. There were quarrels over machines that had already been distributed to people, excessive prices were offered, fistfights were common and drunkenness prevailed."

The quotation above aptly describes the general strategy in obtaining capital, not only in this particular firm, but also around the country. The strategy of helping oneself to machinery through 'honest robbery' was not only a common scheme, but also common knowledge among the citizens. As another villager stated, "Well, one location [where stolen farm machinery was stored] was probably his [the kolkhoz chairman's] father's farmhouse.

---

3   The founders of the firm strove to acquire the sawmill and the wood-processing plant that the collective farm owned, but they lost the bid to a businessman from Tallinn.

I've visited the place with my daughter and the tractors are there, and they even carry the markings of the collective farm . . . [Then] there was the case of a collective farm tractor: the bulletin board of the local shop had an announcement offering a tractor for sale, [and the phone number given turned out to belong to one of the kolkhoz leaders] . . . part [of the price] was to be paid in cash and part in vouchers," (former kolkhoz worker).

The former kolkhoz chairman describes the situation himself, as follows, "[After the last meeting of the collective farm] people started going crazy. Some had already put kolkhoz assets to one side. I was also accused of that but at that time I had not taken anything, but later on others took more and I did not remain a bystander either."

'Honest robbery' was a possibility for the people who, for example, were able to manipulate the bookkeeping of the collective farm – especially at the point when records were being transferred on to computers. Some of the information would be lost in the process, and together with that information, parts of the kolkhoz property would also go missing. Since that property no longer existed in the records, it was nobody's property (see Alanen, Chapter 3).

Besides 'honest robbery,' which refers to the illegal privatisation of collective property for personal benefit, machinery was also acquired by buying it at very low prices. Starting bids at the kolkhoz auction were based on book values that were significantly lower than the actual values of the items up for auction. In addition, the value of a quota day (the amount of quota days was written in the vouchers) was unstable as they climbed in value from the original 60 cents to over two kroons in the course of the auction.

Overvalued vouchers made buying machinery a real bargain. When the value of the machinery acquired by the diversified company was recalculated after the auction, it proved to be much higher than the purchase price. That provided good securities for more loans to expand the activities of the firm.

According to the director, the most dynamic parts of the firm today and most likely in the future, are the bakery[4] and the grocery shops, which are expanding their operations within the village and in a nearby city. A key factor in the success of the present firm has been the low wage level of female employees – their wages are two or three times lower than wages in similar occupations in the cities – at least officially.[5]

---

4   The bakery went bankrupt in the autumn of 1996.
5   One interviewee noted that "there is this practice of brown envelopes. It is ridiculous to claim that he pays only 300 kroons to his employees and that somebody would be so naive as to believe him."

Other activities continued by the firm, but which are becoming unprofitable, are commercial felling and repair shop services for agricultural machinery. In particular, the capital invested in agricultural machines (the machine shop) is rapidly losing its value. The overall economic conditions for agriculture have become gloomier – production is on the decline and farmers cannot afford to pay for the services provided by the machine shop. The more affluent farmers have their own tractors and machines, so the machinery and equipment at the machine shop mostly lies idle and rusts in the company yard. The original plan was to offer repair services at the machine shop, "We calculated that if farmers needed help in repairing broken machines, we would have the necessary equipment and skills, but nobody started farming here [in Kanepi]. If there is no activity, machines will not break. Our services were just not needed."

The company had a very poor reputation among the villagers in the beginning. People regarded the managers as a bunch of thieves and not without reason. Some demonstrated their antipathy by refusing to sell timber to the firm. Today, the company has been accepted as a necessary evil because it provides employment for a large number of villagers.

The director of the company, who had previously held the office of kolkhoz chairman, explained that he was driven to entrepreneurship by the "necessity of doing something" when the collective farm ended. According to him, his principal motivation was the benefit of the community and not his personal self-interest.

Diversified Company II

The present co-owner and departmental manager of another large company has held managerial positions since 1981, when he became a manager almost by chance. He soon found that the prevailing egalitarian attitude aroused hostility and envy amongst his co-workers: "It was very difficult to talk to other people [his subordinates], due to the fact that I had had no previous experience in managerial jobs. Many of them had worked [side by side] with me, but they automatically changed their attitude towards me. [Also] their behaviour changed and sometimes they even acted against me. Those were very trying times for me."

According to the manager, the duties of a kolkhoz manager in the early 1980s were more indefinite; there were several persons with unclear responsibilities. In addition, the prices for services and the measurement of productivity were more arbitrary then. Only after privatisation were these matters taken seriously. Today, the prices charged by the manager's company are firmly based on actual costs.[6]

The idea of a privately owned business was conceived by the employees at the electricity works of the collective farm. Consequently, the manager together with three of his colleagues bought that department. Since these four men were not wealthy, they turned to a larger regional company for financial support: "We went to see them [the owners of the regional company] with our vouchers and we exchanged those vouchers for shares in the company. When the collective farm was broken up, I bought all the necessary materials at the auction under my name and then we collected all our vouchers and bought them."

Today, the electricity works are a part of the regional conglomerate mentioned above, which operates in many different sectors. They produce and sell electricity, sell electrical components, do electrical installations, trade in timber, breed cattle, grow plants and run a machine shop. There used to be a couple of cowsheds as well but both of them have been shut down. The manager's opinion about the causes leading to the closures is clear, "The board [of the cowshed] took [stole] every usable thing, and whatever remained was no longer in working order."

Despite its problems, the company is prospering these days. The manager viewed the lack of skilled workers and the workers' attitudes towards work as the two biggest problems. "We have had problems with the local workmen. The kolkhoz had about ten workmen [that would have been suited to our jobs], but when we contacted them, they refused [work] due to problems with alcohol. Some even claimed that a little hunger is better than hard work. The local population has a strange attitude towards work – it is the collective-farm mentality: even if you worked hard, your pay remained small and if you simply idled away, you sometimes got paid much better. We had the roof repaired last year. The worker, who was skilled and could have done the job, offered at least a hundred excuses for not doing it but we had an agreement and he finally conceded."

Furthermore, the manager explained that it is very difficult to find industrious and skilled workers locally in Kanepi, or anywhere else. The hard-working generation that aimed at quality is already dead, and the present generation of employees has been spoilt by socialistic morality. For this reason, he regarded the outlook for the community as a whole as bleak: "Compared to 1950, there are twice as many people, but the state [of our

---

6   Many villagers argue that the prices of the firm are monopolistic because there are no competitors.

small town] is terrible. I do not believe that things will get any better in the future. Not even during kolkhoz times was there as much negligence as there is today."

Shopkeeper I

There are two relatively prosperous tradesmen in Kanepi. The stories of their lives are quite different and the underlying factors behind their successes are also dissimilar but in both cases, high levels of education and good social relationships have played an important role. The first of these men used to hold a managerial position in the kolkhoz. Before that, he had received higher education in Tallinn and worked in different parts of the former Soviet Union. During the dissolution process, he lost his job in the kolkhoz and he was forced to reorient his life – to transform himself from a state worker into a private entrepreneur. He was opposed to the last chairman of the collective farm. Other villagers say he was one of three men that were supposed to have become the managers of new agricultural co-operatives, if the former chairman had managed to carry out the reorganisation of the collective farm into three or four smaller ones. "It seemed that the collective farm was already being divided between three men: the former chairman, the manager of the forestry department and the manager of the construction department," (former owner of a dairy farm).

If there was such a plan, it failed. The chairman of the collective farm was ousted from his post and, with the adoption of a new reform plan, the people around him were temporarily defeated. During his holiday, the manager, who had supported the former chairman, received a note saying: "in connection with the breaking up of the collective farm you are relieved from your duties as of today."

Later, in the auction he and his partners bid on the sawmill, since they all knew that the prospects for the lumber business were bright. Like the last chairman of the collective farm and his colleagues, he lost the bid to a businessman from Tallinn.

The initial capital of the joint stock company founded by him, two partners working in another firm in a neighbouring town, and a relative from Tallinn, was the value of his car: "At that time there were no exact requirements on how big or small the initial capital of a joint stock company should be." Most likely, the investments of the company have been financed by the other shareholders, with capital derived from the sale of property restituted to them.

The first shop opened in 1992 – on the very same day as the kroon (crown, EEK) was introduced as Estonian national currency. Another shop followed a year later. In addition to these two shops, the tradesman bought half of the kolkhoz kindergarten-premises with privatisation vouchers, and he is planning to refurbish the building and open a third shop, as well as a cafeteria, there. He and the other local shopkeeper (shopkeeper II) have established a special joint stock company to hold the ownership of the kindergarten and refurbish it into a kind of a 'shopping centre.' His vision for the future is to merge his outlets with those of the other local merchant into one large joint stock company: "I think it is obvious that one day these two joint stock companies will be merged, although I have not yet discussed [the matter] with the others [other shareholders in his own company]."

The greatest problems in running his business are the shortage of qualified labour and difficulties in getting loans. There are other concerns, too. His business policy differs from the strategy of the larger retail company. The shops of the latter are relatively shabby and somewhat disorganised, but he puts every effort into keeping his shops clean and orderly. In addition, while the other shops make money by selling alcohol in small plastic cups, such as in a bar, his shops only sell alcohol in bottles. This policy has been adopted because he is not fond of the five or six customers "who stand at the door waiting for a 'friend' to buy them another 100 grams of vodka." However, alcohol sales in his shops also make up the bulk of the income – approximately 80–90%.

Shopkeeper II

The other shopkeeper in Kanepi has attended the Estonian Agricultural University (Eesti Põllumajandusülikool) in Tartu and the Tallinn University of Educational Sciences (Tallina Pedagoogikaülikool). He worked as a mechanic in the kolkhoz for several years and later spent some time in West Germany learning more about agriculture. He accumulated some foreign currency whilst abroad and his intention was to start farming in Estonia. He had already bought three tractors and other agricultural equipment at a very low price from Russia before Estonian independence. However, as he said, "I could see what was happening to the collective farms." Judging by his experiences in Germany, he concluded that practising agriculture would not be profitable in Estonia and therefore, he decided to set up his own business in the retail trade. He and his wife, and another family started by buying two shops from the local Consumer Co-operative. His friend's wife used to work at the economics department of the collective farm, so she could provide the joint-stock company with valuable economic information. Nowadays she works part-time as a bookkeeper in a local bank.

He spent some of the capital accumulated in Germany on privatisation vouchers (EVPs or erastamisväärtpaperid) bought from other villagers. As another interviewee said, "The drunkards sold all their shares for 30–40 cents to the most aggressive privatisers, even before the auction . . . The buyers were mostly young businessmen, the children of collective farm [employees]. Some of them had been working in Germany, some had pubs, but all of them were enterprising."

The entrepreneur himself says that, "The street value of the quota day was still 60 cents or less. We had cash then. We paid for these days [i.e. vouchers containing kolkhoz quota days] with cash. [Other] people did not have cash at that time, but thanks to my stay in Germany I had cash and had a possibility to buy with cash."

He invested the shares in purchasing the other half of the kolkhoz kindergarten, which has not yet been put to any productive use, but still acts as collateral for loans. He bought it because "It cost next to nothing. This was a result of the [sudden] reform [of the kolkhoz]. Things that should have had value were sold very cheaply." The favourable loan terms offered by the Savings and Loan Association were another reason for this investment. If you bought something with a loan taken from the association, you had a ten-year period of repayment and the interest rate was only 1%. Since the rate of inflation in Estonia has been something like 25–40% per annum, the debt has been eroded relatively quickly.

The firm has grown fast – today they have three shops and a fourth one under construction. These days their problems revolve around financing expansion, as well as the day to day running of the firm. According to the entrepreneur, it is not profitable to run a business using commercial loans anymore, since the price of money is much too high, and loans are generally on a very short-term basis (2–3 years) only. In his opinion, setting up a business is "Next to impossible now. You may be able to maintain your family [for some time], but it [the money] will soon run out. Everything is so expensive that you are forced to give up. The right time [to start a business] was during the period of the rouble. That was the golden era." He was also afraid of the big department stores and multiple store organisations, which are gaining ground even in the countryside – his own evaluation was that "We've still got some ten years or so."

For both of the businessmen above, the role of social networks and relationships has been of vital importance – both in the form of capital from friends and relatives, as well as in the form of advice regarding the day-to-day running of the firm. These two men had obviously realised the importance of 'strategic alliances' which are invaluable for a business facing tough competition and increasing costs.

In the Grey Zone – Informal Economy as the Basis for Entrepreneurship

Great societal upheavals create ample grounds for several types of semi-legal entrepreneurship that may serve as a basis for 'respectable' entrepreneurship. Timber trading, which has served as an important source of wealth for many firms, is a good example of this kind of activity. The ways in which forests are used for creating and accumulating capital include legal, semi-legal and illegal forms. The loopholes offered by inadequate legislation and the deficiencies of control mechanisms are exploited by firms that are ostensibly operating according to the regulations – they buy, cut and sell timber. However, as one interviewee said, "If that business was done according to the law, nobody would ever get rich." There are many ways of evading the law – you can do business with your acquaintances and claim that you are buying firewood at the price of one kroon (EEK) per cubic metre, when, in fact, the company is buying wood for paper. As the interviewee said: "Those cubic metres were [officially] traded at a bargain price, and all this was done because it gave [the businessman] a possibility to show such high expenditures, that he could prove it [trading wood] was completely unprofitable for the entrepreneur." Another company did black timber business by buying wood from itself – the firm buys timber from its owner using go-betweens. "They buy from themselves and take advantage of the purchase tax. They are clever people, they make money out of money." The most common form of timber robbery is, however, the use of one felling license on several different wood lots – the firms even rob state-owned forests: "They take five logs from here, five from there and so on – let us say 10 cubic metres, and only the best trees. Trees for felling are selected at daylight and cut during the night. Everything takes place quickly and in the dark" (a businessman).

Sales of black timber are accomplished by using specialised brokers who know the sellers, and find the buyers and take a 10–15% commission from the total price. Both entrepreneurs in commercial felling, as well as tax officials, agree that the opportunities for benefiting from 'black timber' are rapidly diminishing. However it is still the most profitable form of business, especially now that smuggling semi-precious metals and brokering used cars have become very difficult or unprofitable – at least for small firms.

Another example of entrepreneurship in the 'grey zone,' is a firm owned by a young man in Kanepi. He started his business under socialism by smuggling semi-precious metals and petrol from Russia. He said, "The border [between Estonia and Russia] was still open, [and] we transported petrol illegally, or whatever you might call it, because there were no laws [dealing with the import and export of petrol between the two countries] at all." The smuggling of semi-precious metals continued until the summer of 1992, when all the roubles accumulated through smuggling were exchanged into US dollars, to prevent the loss of these fortunes by inflation. Though smuggling semi-precious metals was illegal in principle, "It was no secret, [and] our quantities were rather small, while Mrs Silves [the most famous of the semi-precious metal traders] and others, operated by the same principles but on a much larger scale. The scrap metal was obtained by purchasing it directly from people in marketplaces and elsewhere [in Russia]. Here [in Estonia] it was sold to brokers, who advertised all over the country. The most active people collected the metals here and exported them to Europe."

Later, he started smuggling used cars from Finland to Estonia and from Estonia on to Russia. "There was no plan [in the early days]. I bought Zhigulis [here in Estonia], repaired them and sold them at the [local] marketplace. Russians simply came here to buy them. In the beginning of the car trade there was no organisation." He and his friends made trips together to neighbouring countries and all of them closed deals for their own personal benefit.

Opportunities to make money out of used cars have diminished now that this line of business has been taken up by large companies, which have organised systems for the acquisition and transport of used cars. "Nowadays, only a handful of individuals are in the business, but it is not profitable [for them] anymore because the only people who can make a profit [today] are those who operate with big [car transportation] trucks."

All the social contacts that he created with businessmen and so-called Mafia structures locally, as well as in Russia and Poland have been essential to his success. In his own experience "They [Polish Mafia] are regarded as terrible rogues but, in fact, they are very peaceful. They approach you and tell you nicely that you should pay them if you are going to the border. If you pay, they wish you a pleasant trip and they phone on ahead to others and tell them not to touch these people as they have already paid. The local police are also involved – they are another Mafia. They [Polish policemen] take your driver's license away and say that you must pay a fine. When you ask them why, they mumble something in Polish so that you do not understand anything [that the policemen are saying], but if you pay you can go." Later, he switched over from the car trade to brokerage of antiques and timber. As with other examples mentioned earlier, these businesses do not require any formal organisation or office – they can be taken care of by one man, a car, a mobile telephone and photocopied leaflets. "People who want to sell, contact us. We go there, evaluate the pieces and offer a price. We do not take anything by force and if the person wants to sell [the pieces] at our price, we make a deal and phone [antiques] dealers in Finland or here in Estonia."

This businessman is an outstanding example of a person who, without any special education, operates successfully in circumstances where norms and legislation are underdeveloped. His only resources lay in his ingenious capability of taking advantage of the situation and building relationships with other similar businessmen. As in 'official' business, it is vital to know and follow the norms and rules in the grey zone. In the case of the black market, however, the informal, unwritten rules are the key to survival and prosperity. Another precondition for survival and success in Estonia, for official and unofficial businesses, is the ability to evade state control, such as taxation. As the young man said: "Naturally we do not pay anything to the tax authorities, otherwise it would not be profitable at all." "Businessmen make deals between each other and they trade by barter to show small profits" (a businessman). "I have been in contact with the tax officials and I think that they are so stupid they [tax officials] will never be able to track them down [the businessmen]" (a villager). "Farmers pay taxes, not businessmen" (manager of an agricultural co-operative).

This story also demonstrates that, due to the development of state control and legislation, the possibilities of operating in the grey zone are becoming more restricted. New legislation forces an entrepreneur to move swiftly from one business sector to another, "It has been a process of continuous change. Those who, in the beginning, started out selling cars got rich, moved into dealing with huge amounts of semi-precious metals and then, when they could no longer do that, they moved on to the lumber industry etc. They keep on having to establish new companies."

Depending on the skills and resources of an entrepreneur in the grey zone, the result is complete marginalisation or a move to the formal economy as an ordinary businessman. The latter option was the goal for this man. His plan was to accumulate enough capital to be able to move to another city and set up a respectable firm, as a "business consultant or something like that, where you don't have to do any physical work."

Just Making a Living – Business Enterprises as a Means to Avoid Marginalisation

The dissolution of the collective farm also created a large number of people who had a chance of starting private farming, or a private business, but who were unable to get loans or modernise their source of livelihood simply because their possessions were too modest to provide security for a loan. In the case of farming, the rise in production costs has long since overtaken the prices paid for produce and, since many farmers do not have the resources to buy any new equipment, they are constantly forced to reduce production. In the end, they often become subsistence producers living mainly on social benefits and the produce they cultivate on their plots.

On the non-agricultural side, the situation is not quite as bleak but some firms there, too, are on the brink of collapse, as the following story of a hairdresser shows. Under socialism, she had been a hairdresser in a service oriented collective combine, which employed about ten hairdressers around the countryside. She was forced to quit when the combine was closed down. In the auction, she was able to buy some hairdressers' appliances from the village service-centre and she became a private entrepreneur. She believed that setting up her own business was her only option, "Maybe I could have worked in a canteen but since there wasn't one, I had no choice." The first months were difficult. She operated her business in an old wooden house where plumbing and drainage were inadequate. The council officials let her a room in a kindergarten, but when it was later sold to a local businessman, she had no possibility of carrying on her business in that locality.

The initial capital for the business comprised of her and her husband's wages and savings that were adequate for financing the purchase of old equipment. Now she has been running her business for three years and very little has changed since she started. The equipment is still the same. She has no new customers and it is difficult to even keep the old ones, due to the constant decline of living standards in the village. The firm is barely surviving. "Women in the countryside have reason to celebrate only once or twice a year. They might come [to the hairdressers] once in the spring and then [they come] again before Christmas. They might not have the money for more frequent visits." Keeping her customers requires flexibility and the ability to be content with a lower income. "Every once in a while, an old man comes in and asks, 'What would it [a haircut] cost? Can I [the man] afford it?' and I say, 'OK, come in, I'll give you a discount.'"

Her network of colleagues and friends helps her to keep in touch with the latest developments in hairdressing and in obtaining the necessary materials. She cannot afford to take any special courses, "Hairdressers from Põlva have gone on training courses in Sweden but I do not make enough money to be able to go. During the winter I have to have an outside job to manage." The future of the firm appears uncertain for her, "I don't know; it would be good if there was enough work and I could continue. I would like to carry on, but I really don't know. There's other work for me and you must work – I can't imagine what else I could do, not that I don't want to do anything else but I can't think of what else there is." Her future is very 'iffy.' "If the cost of living does not go up too much, and if people can afford to go to the hairdresser, and if I stay in good health – because I can already feel signs of strain in my feet, hands and neck . . ."

A car repair shop represents a different kind of firm that is barely surviving. The owner does not work in the firm himself but has a job in the municipal council. He used to be the manager of the collective farm's car-repair unit and when dissolution came, he and his friend bought all the repair shop tools. Establishing the firm required a lot of money and was, in part, financed through barter. "We took timber as payment [for car repairs] because we saw that something was going to happen [in the timber business]." Some of the private loans he took were paid off through barter, "We got [borrowed] money from people we knew and they all have cars. Later, they brought their cars for repairs to us and we paid off our loans that way."

The firm's operations have remained relatively small in scale. They just handle basic car maintenance, as well as some quick repairs that car owners used to do themselves in the old days. Even though the basic problems of the socialist period are over, and there are enough spare parts and tools now, the problem today is the lack of money – neither customers nor entrepreneurs have any. Like everybody else, the owner of the car repair shop told us it is no use taking a loan because the terms are too strict.

Changing business legislation also creates problems for the firm. In the near future, all companies will have to register in order to make taxation more effective. But the entrepreneur believes that, "It is no use registering this small firm as the documentation is much too expensive and you would need an accountant to do the book-keeping and all that means more expenses. Therefore, it is not wise to set up a [registered] firm and the only official document is my partner's mechanic's license." Today, the firm simply shelters the owner's partner from unemployment. New investments are not being made, the firm still uses old spare parts, inherited from the car repair unit of the collective farm, to fix mainly Russian manufactured cars – all other cars are sent to the nearest town. "We used to have expansion plans to carry out more difficult and complicated repairs but that is only a future plan; for now we go on with our work as before because this state of affairs suits us much better."

The Spirit of Capitalism Arrived, the Community Spirit Went Out of the Door – the Losers

When the collective farm was disbanded and collective property was privatised by auction, many former employees truly believed in the promises of the ultra-liberal government and that the days of growing prosperity had finally arrived. However, for many the outlook for the future turned bleak and they did not become wealthy entrepreneurs but destitute wage earners or even unemployed. The following two entrepreneurs, who were facing that future, share a very similar history.

Wage Earner Turned Business Person and Back

The first one used to work as a brigadier in the collective farm's cowshed where there were a hundred cows and four work groups. Later the workforce dwindled into four milkers who did all the work. At the time of the dissolution of the collective farm, she was persuaded into becoming the owner of this cowshed. She agreed because, "I was worried about my work-mates and also about the animals." The price of the building and machinery was paid partly with privatisation vouchers that she and the other workers had and the rest was covered by a loan taken from the Savings and Loan Association. The establishment of the firm was not expensive initially because the buildings and machines were bought at book value prices. However, since the new entrepreneur had to pay back the privatisation shares to her workers and buy cattle feed, seed grain, fuel, etc., the firm rapidly ran into debt. She, also had plans for expansion but she gave them up because she could not make the struggle alone. The problems started to surface shortly after privatisation, "The first year we had a good crop but after that some of the fields remained unsown and were overgrown with grass. Also some of the machines broke down and all the farm work was delayed." Nevertheless, the main problem and most important cause for her failure as a private entrepreneur had to do with the work ethics of her employees. As the workers learned that their former brigadier had become an independent entrepreneur and the owner of their workplace, "There was panic and confusion, some of them were disappointed . . . there were some unpleasant incidents. It was all so depressing and very often I wondered why it had to be like this, why the collective farm had to disintegrate." She was not able to get a grip on her workers during the three years that she owned the cowshed. The workers always maintained their "autonomic approach" to working hours and work ethics. "There was, for example, one worker who left her workplace when the berry picking season began and only came back after it was over. I had to do all the work by myself while she was away – milk those seventy cows, feed them and take care of everything else, too." One reason for deserting the workplace during the berry season was the pay, "They [the workers] claimed I paid too little but in the beginning I could not pay more because I had to repay the debts [of the company]. The milkers received some 1,300 kroons per month."[7]

There were also problems with alcohol; some workers used to drink daily without taking any notice of the entrepreneur's warnings. The owner of the cowshed did not react to these disciplinary problems, as a capitalist entrepreneur would have done. She did not warn the workers and finally fire them but she tried to manage the problems by doing the work herself. There was no shortage of labour because when she was setting up her business, there were willing applicants from other villages, too. However, "I only took those who lived close by and I was used to my own workers [from kolkhoz times]." These attitudes represent features typical of the Soviet-style organisation of work: the work collective was a kind of mini-community with close relationships between the workers and their immediate supervisors. Workers held a relatively wide autonomy because a supervisor, or even a manager, had no means of coercing workers due to the full-employment policy, and because the kolkhoz was as dependent on its workers as the workers were on their superiors in acquiring better jobs, wages, benefits and social services. In a socialist enterprise the most crucial task for a manager was the reproduction of his or her work collective, likewise, that was the main goal for the new owner of the private cowshed – it was not only the success of the firm that counted but also the well-being of her workers.

---

7   The wages of milkers were clearly above the average wages in the village, for example a salesperson received only something like 500–700 kroons and workers in sawmill got 1,000 kroons – at least officially.

The consequence of the problems with her workers was complete isolation and burnout, "Being secluded as a woman was very difficult and I began to lose my health." Even though most of the problems were socio-psychological in nature, there were also problems with the cowshed – the animals were old and produced very little, and the tractors were completely outdated and in bad repair. Finally, she was forced to give up the business and sell it at a loss to a new owner who agreed to take over her debts to the Savings and Loan Association. Only after the change in ownership did the spirit of capitalism enter the firm. The new owner fired some of the old workers, raised the wages of the remaining ones and started production in a decisive manner. The organisation of work was radically changed as the new owner set clear rules based on responsibility and result, "I have said that what I do in front, nobody will do behind. The workers know this and take care of their duties." According to the new owner his predecessor had lacked the necessary managerial skills: "There was one thing missing [in her firm] and that is: there was nobody who gave the order that now we [the employees] have to do this and it requires this much of that [work effort or resources]. Before there were dairy technicians and the chairman of the collective farm, but now there had been nobody."

The managerial skills of the new owner are based on vocational education and extensive practical experience as a vice-director at the collective farm and as the manager of another large private firm. During his service in the private enterprise, he was able to accumulate capital and take out loans to make the necessary initial investments in agricultural production. These early investments acted as security for subsequent loans, which in turn have enabled him to improve productivity and expand his firm.

Cowshed Entrepreneur by Chance

The second entrepreneur had worked for decades as a department manager on the collective farm but for the few years before its dissolution he served as an ordinary worker, following some disagreements with the then chairman of the collective farm. When the plan of the dissolution was published, he felt relieved, "At first, I was very enthusiastic, I thought that my life would get better. I had been there for so long and I knew all the people . . . The feeling of liberation was overwhelming. Everybody thought that family farms would be restored and that everything would get better. On the whole, people were happy about the changes."

The caring, even patriarchal, attitude of managers who have got used to working and living for the work collective is used by him as justification for his eventual decision to buy a cowshed: "I sat there [at the auction] and saw how very little [of the kolkhoz property] sold easily and so I got involved myself. At first, I was not sure if I would participate but then I thought that my people [fellow kolkhoz workers] would be left with nothing. That is when I consciously started buying the machines and everything I needed." A few days before the auction, he had talked with the former chairman of the collective farm who had coaxed him to buy the cowshed. "I [the chairman] told him he should take it [the cowshed] and even if it went bankrupt, it would not be the end of the world. And as it has turned out, it [bankruptcy] has not [been the end of the entrepreneur's life]. Life begins anew. People buy machines again, we negotiate again and who knows where it all ends." The former chairman, like all the other people who had knowledge about the situation of agricultural business in Estonia at that time, knew that buying a cowshed would not be a profitable investment: "They [professional people] knew very well that buying that kind of property would not yield anything because there was too much beef [on the market], so nobody bought any [beef]. The cowshed was useless and the fields were somebody else's property." However, the former employee of the collective farm bought the cowshed, mostly by raising a loan from the Savings and Loan Association, with the idea that a successful business would easily bring in enough money to pay back the loan in ten years. His own financial contribution was very small, "He bought property worth nearly one million kroons, but his own vouchers only covered 11,000 kroons. The reason why he did not buy shares from other people was that he probably did not have enough money to even pay the minimum of fifty cents for each share. In the beginning, he and his wife were doing quite well, but later it all went downhill."

The deterioration of the general economic situation in Estonia also played a role in ruining his plans, "Yes if, . . . if several things had gone differently from what they did. I had 100 cows and each yielded about 3,000 litres of milk a year and if the price of milk would have been three kroons a litre, I could have made a million in profit . . . All these oil price increases and decreases in the price of milk have driven me to the point where I evidently will not be able to fill the obligations in that loan agreement . . . If I had known that inflation would be so high and life would become so crazy, I would not have undertaken all this."

Other villagers view the reasons differently, "I guess the reason why he bought the place was his girlfriend, she was a very aggressive woman." The firm operated for only one year, after which he was forced to close down the cowshed. An immediate reason for the closure was the rapid decline in production. "Production was minimal. When I compiled those statistical reports, it turned out that each cow produced only half a litre of milk per day! In the statistical office [of Estonia] they suspected that I had given false figures because seventy cows produced only 35 litres of milk per day," (a former employee).

As owner and manager, he felt he did not experience such severe problems with his employees in terms of work, as the entrepreneur described above: "I got along very well with my people and I always tried to be fair to them. I knew each of them personally from the past so I was aware of what to expect and what not." However, the dissolution of the collective farm had a negative influence on the morale of his employees as well. The degeneration of morale was evident in the growth of larceny, "After the break-up of the collective farm, people started stealing everything. The electrical wiring of machines was even cut off and taken and the cattle feeder, too. All kinds of things were stolen. If you turned your back, everything would be stolen, including the milking machine." He had trouble sleeping because of the thieving: "I could not sleep well at night, and when I woke up in the morning and got to my farm I kept wondering what had been stolen this time . . . it was very difficult and it was getting worse all the time. I haven't have a day off since [I became the owner of the cowshed] . . . I wished I had never [started this]." Even in this situation, he swears loyalty to his people on some level, "Usually I could guess who had taken a particular item, but I cannot point my finger at any man or woman. Many [of them] have large families and no providers and many have served some time in jail. I cannot accuse them [of theft]."

However, when the business went bankrupt, the manager had nothing to worry about since, "He [the owner] is not indebted to anybody – not to the tax office, not to the state, nothing at all. The firm has no debts to the state, only to the Savings and Loan Association," (a former employee of the firm). The workers who used to serve in his firm comment on his failure more frankly: " . . . the business went bankrupt, because the manager was simply the wrong person for the job, he was misled," (a former agronomist). His former employees claim that his own work morale collapsed completely. In the end, he could not care less about the success or even the survival of his firm, "He was not interested in anything at all – he did not care neither did he understand anything."

Both of the stories above testify to the difficulties that relatively uneducated people, who can only rely on their years of work experience, face when they become entrepreneurs. Both of them appear to have assumed that everything would go on as it had done before, but in different circumstances. The biggest worry for them, in reality or perhaps in afterthought, was the survival of the work collective – "their people and their animals," and they could not foresee what lay ahead – that the spirit of capitalism would require totally different kinds of management skills and a different type of work organisation. The continuity of socialist behavioural models on the workers' side was evident in their attitudes to the use of working hours, work habits and ownership. It is probably appropriate to quote Richard Ruzicka's (1996, 220–222) description of the consequences of the socialist period in this respect: "The long-term feeling of entrepreneurial hopelessness led to desire and belief in a quick, just and socially supported development of the private (particularly the small private) sector. On the other hand, it produced a mass attitude of resignation and a longing for safety. It resulted in a personal strategy of consumption which misused the so-called 'common productive wealth' (e.g. working time, tools of work and others)." He continues with a list of likely risks for an entrepreneur. These include things such as "nobody understands your entrepreneurial (especially financial) situation. The egalitarianism that existed for decades contributed to the cultivation of envy and hostility. People working for you are still accustomed to the lack of the responsible working style of the former ownership system (e.g., not to use their working hours for you, to use your things for their purposes only, not to respect your time, etc.) The distinction between former 'common property' and the new private property does not exist for many people."

Wood Processing Through Thick and Thin

A third narrative, which also illustrates the above-mentioned problems of new private enterprises in the transformation, is that of a small industrial firm in Kanepi. The wood processing plant was privatised at the kolkhoz auction. The selling price was relatively high and was partly paid with privatisation vouchers and the bulk with a loan from the Savings and Loan Association.

The company was very reckless in the beginning. It bought timber from around the municipality and farther away. The firm got heavily into debt and it failed to pay its taxes. Consequently, the firm lost its creditworthiness, failed to raise new loans, and finally, after running out of working capital, it was driven into insolvency. Following bankruptcy, the state had to bear the tax losses because the debts were left to the old firm, whilst a new firm was set up very soon – with old management and personnel. One interviewee not involved in the activities of this company said, "The old firm was left there with all the debts and it was replaced with a brand new firm. Nowadays they do not trade in timber anymore [because] it is too expensive. The manager shouldered the responsibility for the debts to the Savings and Loan Association, but not the debts for the timber. Those debts remained with the old firm and nobody knows anything about them anymore." A representative of the re-established firm explained that "We don't want to take out a loan because it is too 'modern' for us, we have no use for it." According to him, the problems of the firm can today be attributed to outdated machinery and the shortage of labour, which is caused by low wage levels. "Our company cannot pay wages [that are competitive] on the national level, [our wages are competitive] only on the local level. If it would pay something like two or four thousand [kroons per month], maybe then [they would have enough good workers], but he [the director] cannot do it." Also the workers take up the same problem, "The management pays too little to the workers, the money runs out before the next pay-day. Workers get 500–600 kroons [per month]. This is the norm. In our village only one man gets up and goes to work in the morning. Also Aivar and one other. Altogether, only three men. The older men do not work," (the wife of an employee).

The machinery at the wood processing plant dates back to Soviet times and is obsolete. "We should replace the machinery, it is too old and requires refurbishment," (a foreman). "They wanted to have new machines and start manufacturing so called Eurostands [a special piece of furniture]. That plan did not work. And now, since we have the work-benches, we make doors and windows," (a worker).

The markets of the firm have remained mostly local, although the firm can produce good quality products. The problems of the firm continue because it is unable to get loans to expand its production or to renovate the machinery. This has resulted in the deterioration of work ethics, constant interruptions in production, machinery breaking down and so on. It is common knowledge amongst the employees, that although the present manager is a skilful and conscientious person, he cannot help the situation because he is unable to find new workers who are willing to work for such low wages. As one interviewee said, "The firm is operating, but there is an internal problem – all the workers are old, people who already worked there under socialism. They had and still have a [problematic] habit – once they start drinking, they drink for days in a row. Nothing helps, not the wage, nor threats, nothing at all."

Those problems were smaller in the early days of the company, but as soon as economic problems started to mount, people took to the "old habits." Now, the situation is similar to the times of the collective farm, "If you wanted to get something done, you had to bring a bottle [of alcohol] and the same thing goes on even now. Although the owners are different, the ways of the workers have remained the same. Sometimes the doors of the factory are locked and the workers are drinking in the bar [next door]." Most of these problems are with the older workers: "Our boss wants to get rid of the old staff and only hire young people, just because the older generation still has the that-will-do attitude of socialist times," (a worker). His wife continues, "That is something the young people do not understand. During Soviet rule . . . if you had a boss, he came [to you] and said, "Go and do this or that," and you had to manage yourself [perform the task the way most suitable to you]. But now when you are going to do some work, the boss says, "Do it [exactly] this way!" Both of them agree that the young are more flexible and more eager to learn new things, whilst the old have got used to following rules and regulations. "They are used to obeying instructions, the quality of work suffers and for older people it is more difficult to cope with the stress and bitterness" (a worker).

On the one hand, the problems of the firm can be attributed to rapidly changing economic circumstances such as rising prices and diminishing prospects of getting a loan. On the other hand, you can also argue that the work organisation inherited from the Soviet period is another major cause. The shortage of labour maintains and sustains the position and structural power resources of the old workers, against which the manager is powerless. However, the workers are also dependent on the firm because they are tied to their jobs. Their wages do not allow them to move to a big city and many of them have families, which also ties them to the village. The management is not wholeheartedly interested in the development of the firm – for some of them it only provides a means of accumulating money by evading financial obligations and dodging legislation.

As one representative of the firm noted, "The company has three kinds of problems: materials, machines and managers." It is therefore apparent that it is not the spirit of capitalism that guides the firm, but a distorted community spirit – the conservative tendency to try and ride out troubled times with the same machines, workers and products that already exist.

One can also interpret the workers' reactions as a sign of relinquishment in the face of growing uncertainties and unfulfilled promises. Their discouragement results in a retreat to 'asocial' forms of behaviour. These signal an informal protest against the present state of affairs, where they are forced to remain as underpaid workers with outdated machines and without any real prospect for improving their situation. As András Csite (1997, 12–15) writes, "alcoholism can be seen as a price of change; the increase in the use of alcohol is a special form of resistance – a means to get rid of the hegemonic project, refusal to stay with it. The feeling of being cheated – hopelessness, is the worst thing that can happen to a secularised person, who has lost his faith in God." Csite notes that one may try to break away from pessimism by starting to protest, by doing the same as the political leaders and managers do, lie and steal.

Conclusion

The stories of entrepreneurs in Kanepi show the extent to which the sphere of opportunities opened by the transition was exploited and the roles various factors played in the success and failure of individual businesses. A leading position in the old power structure, organisational capital, is without doubt a very important factor in successful entrepreneurship because it provides financial resources and knowledge. Organisational capital provides businessmen-to-be with sources of information that enable them to take advantage of such things as time. As the old saying goes, the early bird gets the worm. Those who could 'read' the signs of the times in the late 1980s and early 1990s could obtain financial and production capital in very generous terms. In this respect, the era of the rouble really was the golden era.

As many surveys and studies have shown, top managers are not necessarily the people who will become private entrepreneurs. More likely are the lower managers with their specialised knowledge. Of course, organisational capital as such is not a decisive factor, but personal contacts and capabilities are crucial. On the strength of these stories, it can be argued that to be successful, you have to be resolute, even to the extent of being rude. The chances of an ordinary worker, without the necessary social networks and skills, of setting up a profitable business are much more limited, or at least it requires much more effort.

These stories have demonstrated the importance of social networks in establishing and running a business. While many firms are one man ventures on the exterior, there often is an extensive network of people, who participate in and contribute to the institution and operation of the firm.

Thirdly, the stories demonstrated the role that informal economy plays in the evolution of entrepreneurship in a transitional society. In general, due to deficiencies in legislation the boundary between a formal and informal economy, and between legal and illegal business is vague during transitions. As one council official said, "There is no such law that could not be evaded by businessmen." A Kanepi businessman formulated the same principle as, "Clever businessmen are always one step ahead of legislators." In order to be successful in business you must know legislation and how to evade it without committing an explicit crime. Anyway, one can fool all state officials some of the time and some officials all of the time, but you can't fool all of them all of the time if you wish to become a prosperous businessperson. This means that the era of wild and free capitalism is ending even in such small localities as Kanepi. The strengthening of social systems and the institutions of control and regulation, the tightening competition of enterprise structures, and the growing ties between the Estonian economy and global economic structures all restrict the sphere of activities for small firms. It is becoming more and more difficult for a private person to set up a firm in a manner similar to that of a few years ago, when the quick and the witty exploited opportunities by amassing their initial capital from former collective property. The future is no longer bright for busy swindlers, but rather for those who are capable of making strategic alliances with large national or international corporations. What is left over from the past is the importance of networks; these are no longer created and utilised within the Communist Party hierarchy as before, but between businessmen, as well as between the business community and policy makers.

Still Waiting for the Good Times – the Future Prospects of Kanepi

The prevailing atmosphere in the little town of Kanepi is one of withdrawal – people just waiting-and-seeing while trying to manage. Southern-Estonia is not riding on the crest of the wave of economic development that prevails in the northern part of the country and especially around the capital. As a local entrepreneur told us, "I really cannot say what the future holds for Kanepi in the next five years – perhaps there will not be one stone on top of another. There are so many open questions in the countryside these days. There is no entrepreneurial initiative there and the state is holding back the development for some reason. I don't know."

Passivity and uncertainty are sustained by the unfinished and unclear results of land reform, the constant decline of the prospects in agriculture, and a vacillating regional and agricultural policy that which could be characterised as a policy of "cope as well as you can." There are some well-off firms and farms in Kanepi, but in general, the prospects for agricultural enterprise are not promising, unlike the foundation for future development in the town and around the municipality. The majority of the respondents we interviewed in the centre of Kanepi, as well as county officials, believe that success in agriculture belongs to the large farms. As one official said, "People are bound to notice that those who want success must establish a large farm. A smaller part of the population will remain subsistence farmers . . . there are farms with 5–10 hectares, but they will not provide a livelihood." One of the entrepreneurs in the town held a similar opinion, "I can say that small farms have no future. I think it was a great mistake to break up the collective farm and divide the big fields up into small plots and give those plots to the people. People are practically starving – they keep a cow and a chicken to survive."

Another problem, in the future development of agriculture and the town of Kanepi, is the loss of the Russian agricultural market. Quoting an official from Põlva, "We would live normally and have a decent standard of living if we could cross the Pskov–Pechory border easily as we used to do before Estonian independence . . . Russia is enormous. Our local agriculture would be normal, the agriculture of the whole region used to live off the markets of Pskov–Pechory and also Leningrad."

Kanepi as a community belongs to the least developed municipalities in Estonia. It has a lower percentage of working-age population and a higher percentage of elderly people than the national average. The income level of the population is very low and even if the official level of unemployment is not very high, it does not denote that there is not a remarkable level of underemployment or hidden unemployment. All this indicates that the future of private enterprise is not very lucrative, at least in the short term. There are only one or two non-agricultural enterprises with a viable basis for future development. For the majority of enterprises, such as shops, hairdressers, car repair shops etc. the future largely depends on the customers. Their wallets will determine the prosperity of the businesses. When vital demographic statistics indicate decline, the wallets remain thin because a large percentage of the people are old and the rest earn very low wages. The future of the community also depends upon its ability to offer jobs and services for the younger generation. In that respect the future looks even more gloomy as practically all the young people are planning to move from Kanepi, "There is absolutely nothing for the young. Everyone you talk to or listen to is trying to leave. There are no prospects for young people here in Kanepi." The exodus of the younger generation also affects local enterprises since they will not be able to hire new labour to replace old workers, or workers who are considered unsuitable for the firm. As one entrepreneur complained, "Personally for me, the greatest problem is my staff. I often wonder what will happen [to the business] the day I feel that I am no longer able to work." And an employee in another company said that, "We have a couple of men [in the workplace] whom they [the employers] want to get rid of, but they cannot be fired as there is nobody to replace them with."

An opinion, shared by both local council and county officials alike is that the future of the area lies in tourism. The views of the residents vacillate between cautious optimism and deep pessimism. Optimists agree with officials on future prospects and often their opinions are based on their own, relatively safe situation, while pessimists are mainly disappointed private farmers and wage earners, whose employment and livelihood are in jeopardy.

Both ordinary residents and officials share hostility towards the "Tallinn bosses." For them, Tallinn represents a completely different world and another reality, where there is no place for rural towns like Kanepi. As one entrepreneur said: "This state is a state for 1,000–2,500 people, the rest of the nation is missing. What could the new government bring? Nothing at all . . . All the shares have been given to the IMF [International Monetary Fund] which has decided that this nation of one million people must import all agricultural produce, and there is nothing we can do."

In the end, other problems are reduced down to the shortage of money, the difficulties of obtaining loans when securities are insufficient and when the means of local authorities to assist enterprises are very limited. As a council official noted, "The biggest particular obstacle is that people lack the capital to initiate anything. I myself have tried [to set up a firm] but in practice it is impossible to get a loan."

References

Burawoy, M. and Lukacs, J. (1992), *The Radiant Past – Ideology and Reality in Hungary's Road to Capitalism*, Chicago University Press, Chicago.

Clarke, S., Fairbrother, P., Burawoy, M. and Krotov, P. (1993), *What About the Workers? Workers and the Transition to Capitalism in Russia*, Verso, London.

Csite, A. (1997), 'En reaktionär betraktelse över tillståndet i mitt fosterland Ungern [A reactionary evaluation of the situation in my home country Hungary]', *Nya Argus*, 1997, no. 1, pp. 12–15.

Ruzicka, R. (1996), 'Small Entrepreneurs in the Society of Employees', in H. Brezinski and M. Fritsch (eds), *The Economic Impact of New Firms in Post-Socialist Countries: Bottom-Up Transformation in Eastern Europe*, Edward Elgar, Cheltenham.

5 From Village Soviet to Municipality

REIN RUUTSOO

Introduction – the Capacity for the Transformation of Social Capital

The restoration of the Municipality of Kanepi in 1991 was a political decision. Its revitalisation however is an integral process, calling for extensive economic, social and political transformations in the life of the local community. The village soviet was a local administrative unit responsible for functions such as the Voluntary People's Patrol (Rahvamalev) and community life – houses of culture, schools, kindergartens, etc. (financed via the state budget). Through organising clubs, sports events, entertainment and leisure activities, etc. the administrative structure, controlled by the Party, colonised traditional society. The economic responsibilities of the village soviet and the collective farm to uphold and support the public sphere in the local community were spontaneously intertwined and depended on the local situation (the wealth of the collective farm, personal relations, etc.) (for the basic structure of the Administrative System in the Estonian SSR, see Figure 5.1).

It seems the political decision to restore the municipality, which became invested with tangible power because of the regained independence of Estonia, was underpinned by several factors that made for a quick turnaround. Because of this, the reforms launched in the 1990s did not bring about the social collapse of community life, although the village soviet and the municipality were dramatically different as the so-called ideal types of organising social life. The administrative power of the village soviet began to crumble as early as the 1960s, with the changing nature of the collective farms (Erlich, 1985, 46). Inasmuch as realities permitted the actual needs of the people were the reference point in the daily lives of schools, cultural centres, libraries, etc. Parallel to and in defiance of the ideological prescriptions, it was the restoration of general human standards, the assignment of priorities to the actual

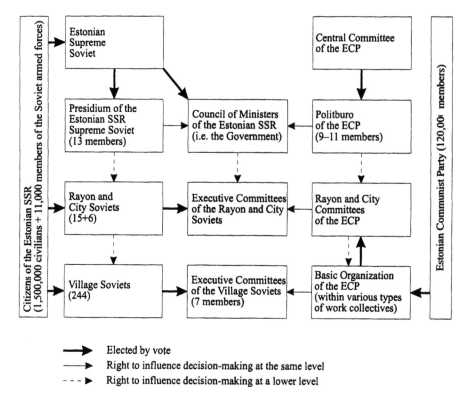

Elected by vote
Right to influence decision-making at the same level
Right to influence decision-making at a lower level

Figure 5.1 Administrative system in the Estonian SSR

cultural and social needs of people, that fostered natural co-operation between people, bolstering the local identity.

However, the social autonomy accommodating and adjusting the official prescriptions did not provide exhaustive support for new integral patterns of activities. It was not assisted by public democratic procedures or an alternative world outlook – these were not tolerated, and their formation was blocked. Consequently, the democratic changes triggered by realignment ('perestroika') and the achievement of formal municipal rights in Estonia could not rely on the extensive and multifaceted publicly available for *social capital* (organisational capital, reciprocity). Social relations became impoverished, the administration taking the place of management (authoritarianism, patronage), economic autonomy won by becoming pathologic (various illegal back door deals and 'blat', the attitude of 'I just don't give a damn about anything,' escapism, etc.). The latter is important to help understand the scope of the prevailing life-strategies that were inspired by reformers.

To date, there has been a basic focus on the problems of administration and economy when observing and elucidating the formation of municipalities (Ginter, 1992). It has to be admitted that the transition-related conflicts and paucity of resources are overpowering in this area. The sudden change of property relations and the downslide of the rural economy, receiving no significant resources from local industry, reduced the municipalities to a bureaucracy occupied mainly with distribution and largely dependent on the state budget. However, the development of self-government can fill the new municipal structures with democratic content.

The central condition for transforming the village soviet of Kanepi into a self-governing municipality is the development of its own local habitat. For overall success, the collection and mediation of social energy and access to social capital has to become possible in all main areas of life. The above is indispensable if they are to support democratic socialisation. Whether the formation of the preconditions for renewed social capital is underway can be discovered by studying the manifest changes in the organisation of cultural life, in school reforms, and in public safety and relations. The developments in these areas are analysed below.

Reforming the Village Soviet from 1989–1991

The democratisation process of local municipalities began on 8 August 1989 with a Resolution by the Supreme Soviet of the Estonian SSR. It was entitled 'Conduct of the Administrative Reform in the Estonian SSR'. It was supported by the 'Law on Foundations of Local Municipalities of the Estonian SSR' adopted on November 10 the same year. This reconstructing was part of the general plan for realignment, specifically underlined by a paragraph declaring that 'local municipalities must heed to the public opinion and act openly.'

Elections to local governments were held in December 1989 under the old laws. According to the Law on Administrative Reform, the new assemblies were to function as 'constituent assemblies,' until the municipal bodies were formed. A significant novelty was that several candidates were allowed to participate in the elections. However, the re-elected long-standing chairman of the village soviet said, "there were no great differences compared with the earlier membership. Those elected were all well-known people in the community, there were a couple of newcomers, like the general practitioner [the doctor] and a teacher. Among those elected were three women." In view of the number of tasks to be performed in the municipality, the number of officers increased from six to nine. The offices of land surveyor, population registrar and social worker implied the germination of new municipal functions.

After the development plan for the municipality was approved in Tallinn, Kanepi was granted the rights of a municipality on June 1, 1991. It became the third municipality in the County of Põlva. The Statute for the Municipality of Kanepi was adopted to legalise the activities of the municipality. The chairman of the village soviet was granted the title of Municipal Director (*viz.* Mayor) (Kuus, 1991c). The plan for the development of the municipality was verbose and diffuse, lacking in awareness. In summing up the current situation and municipal resources, its authors maintained that the future of the municipality would primarily depend on the reform of property. The main obstacles were perceived as the lack of laws on local self-government and the State constitution. Economically, there was the serious problem that almost any small production in rural areas would be liquidated and concentrated in towns and cities. The negative social and economic impact of this had been anticipated much earlier (Rüütel, 1985, 136).

The opportunities for the economic and cultural development of the municipality were considered satisfactory or even good. The tone of the document was overly optimistic. Unemployment was not anticipated. "The analysis suggests that in the near future unemployment will not likely be a problem, although finding a suitable job might be." Against the background of the general deterioration of state farms, hope was pinned on establishing private farmsteads. These were expected to increase to 200 in 1992! However, there was allowance for the farmsteads forming the basis of the municipal economy only after the passage of quite a few years (Arengukava, 1991).

A central issue facing the municipality was how to acquire the assets that were at the joint disposal of the village soviet and the collective farm. The vision of the former chairman of the village soviet revealed the collision of public interests and the burgeoning private interests:

> Contention centred on social objects, such as school and cultural premises. The municipality wanted to get hold of them. The Kalev collective farm addressed the issue with understanding. It transferred the open-air stage for singing and a 12-flat block of flats to the municipality. Kalev also gave the municipality some buses, trucks, and graders. The Kanepi collective farm yielded nothing. It tried to foist off the district heating plant heating 80 houses on the penniless municipality. The municipality refused to accept it. However, it did succeed in buying the kindergarten that was built with money from Moscow. The local bigwigs grabbed the main kindergarten office. The kindergarten building, which was obtained cheaply, currently houses the sports hall, the library, the bank and the

municipal guesthouse. This was an important acquisition for the municipality, without which it could not have got the things going.

That the municipality succeeded in getting the school heating system in good condition while Russian rouble was still effective was important for its economy.

Significantly contributing to the economic hardship of the municipality was the fact that the "leaders of the collective farm were unable to foresee what functions the municipality would be like." The former chairman reflected that a lot of materiel was auctioned, the municipality finding itself without equipment and machinery. The vagueness of ownership by the collective farm and the village soviet made the substantiation of requests for the transfer of facilities to the municipality complicated. The important factor compounding the adverse effect of the lack of clear-cut rules was the feeling of affinity, the solidarity of the leaders of the economy with the rural residents, and the heightened responsibility Kalev felt; i.e. 'regionalism, giving priority to the local interests' of the leadership of Kalev and the residents. The same had been evident earlier, when cultural questions were at issue.

The arrangements for mutual relations between the municipality under formation and the enterprises, institutions, etc. within its territory were no easy matter. Until then, the collective farms had substantially supported culture, maintained the road network, assisted the schools, etc. The new enterprises, having had those assets taken over, no longer had any responsibilities to the municipality. On the other hand, they often used the resources of the municipality at their own discretion. The small enterprises quarried sand and clay, and felled trees for their own use. For example, a municipal councillor complained that the Võru furniture factory carried on like it had in the old days; in 1990 felling 15,000 m^3 of timber and giving the municipality 300 cubic meters of plank in compensation (Kuus, 1991c). Besides the gaps in legislation, there was also the problem of rapidly rocketing prices.

The economic situation of the municipality was also affected by the restitution of church property. The process was initiated in Kanepi earlier than elsewhere. The church regained thirteen pieces of real estate, including land and buildings. The municipality supported the idea of legal succession. The restitution of property began during the time of the village soviet. As stated by the former chairman of the village soviet, the collective farm used church property and stood against the restitution. However, the village soviet advocated restitution. Unlike the village soviet, the people started to respect the municipality and to look up to the municipal director. "The municipal director no longer made the decisions demanded by some big shot – he fulfilled the resolutions. He was backed by the applicable law, and it worked," said the former chairman of the collective farm when describing the difference between the village soviet and the municipality.

Besides the clarification of the opaque property relations and economic reform, the municipality also became an actor in a more general process of transition, i.e. in the wider policy. Its independence, abidance to democracy and viability was repeatedly challenged (pressure by the occupying Soviet troops and the aspirations of the rightist Estonian Congress). Notwithstanding the changes in political supremacy (from the Estonian Communist Party to the Estonian Popular Front to the Estonian Congress), the municipal government never departed from its adopted line of policy nor deviated from the law.

The former chairman of the Kanepi village soviet prided himself on the support that the village council gave to the policy of reforms in Estonia at the time when it ran counter to the directives from Moscow. "We assumed the risk and responsibility, while supporting the reforms already originated when Indrek Toome's Cabinet was in power," reflected the chairman of the village soviet. In 1989 they sent a letter of support to the Government, to which the Government responded with a letter of thanks. It is highly significant that after four decades of repression and apparent "rule of the people" such a strongly ethnically motivated relation of trust was created with the reformist part of *nomenklatura*. As a result, the village leadership achieved a legitimate status in the eyes of the people. Local power was vested with democratic features before the official municipal reforms began.

According to the reminiscences of the chairman of the village soviet, after the Estonian SSR declared sovereignty (November 16, 1988), a full-scale enlarged session of the village soviet was held. As reported by the chairman, the enlarged session of the village soviet, called promptly after the Declaration, was attended by no less than one hundred people (regular attendance being 30–40 people). "Our unanimous decision (including members of the Estonian Communist Party) was that sovereignty was the single correct path. We also notified Tallinn about the said resolution."

In the spring 1989, the Estonian Congress launched the registration of the citizens of the Republic of Estonia; the village soviet supported the action, using their own staff. "The originator of the elections was the Popular Front in co-operation with the village soviet. The lists of the residents on the collective farm were distributed, so that everybody could register with the village soviet. The officer who used to handle domicile registration tackled the elections," said the chairman of the village soviet. The very fact that the chairman of the village soviet, who enjoyed the reputation of a circumspect and loyal citizen, spoke at the 'Days of Kanepi' in Erastvere prompted the people to register for the elections of the Estonian Congress. This had a potently encouraging effect, as intimated by one of the delegates to the Congress. The upsurge of nationalism conquered the ingrained dread and deeply rooted fear of the people.

The co-operative relations that were generated in Kanepi between the (formally) Soviet institutions and the Estonian Congress must be emphasised. The local authority clearly contravened the directives of the Estonian Communist Party, which urged the village soviets to treat the Estonian Congress as an illegal 'extremist movement' (Väljas, 1989, 14). Unlike the towns where the 'machinery of power' was prevalently Russianised and *nomenklatural*, the nationalist solidarity in the rural areas overpowered the dread of and loyalty to the Soviets.

From the perspective of rural development and the future of Estonia, the fact that the state administration in the backyard of Estonia took the side of the people can not be overestimated. Unlike the larger towns, the traditional intelligentsia in small settlements was too scarce to rebuff effectively the members of *nomenklatura*. The nationalist stance of local soviets secured an important place for rural areas in the Estonian revolution. Furthermore, it once more demonstrated to Moscow the cross-national support to the idea of independence for Estonia. The nationalist tune of the village soviets and the counties became evident on February 2, 1990. It was then that a 2000-strong meeting of representatives of all the municipalities in Tallinn declared, as the common will of the representatives of power, the restoration of the Republic of Estonia. In protest and to attract attention, the heads of the administrations in predominantly Russian populated Northeast Estonia and partly those of the soviets in the boroughs of Tallinn ostentatiously quitted the meeting.

Nor did Kanepi allow itself to be sidetracked and left on the fringes and in the backwash of the increasingly fierce struggle for a place as a leading agent of the revolution. In the spring of 1990, after the Estonian Congress was called together, the leadership of the national Estonian Committee[1] (working

---

1   The Estonian Committee was the executive organ of the Estonian Congress. It should
     not be confused with the Estonian Citizens' Committees (there were about 200 of them
     around the country) that were set up to register people prior to the elections of the
     Estonian Congress.

under the auspices of the Estonian Congress and controlled by the Estonian Party for National Independence) decided to take power. They relied specifically on the activists in the rural areas. For this purpose, a person shuttled the villages and counties, successfully agitating the people and recruiting supporters. The chairman of the village soviet, recalling the visit by Vardo Rumessen to the County of Põlva said: "After the session of Estonian Congress, Vardo Rumessen (an ideologist of the Estonian Congress) put in an appearance. He was very aggressive and delivered a speech. His goal was to secure support for the Estonian Congress from the local municipalities." The chairman of the village soviet remembers that municipality did not give Mr Rumessen that support:

> There were some people who did not like the role assumed by the Estonian Congress, and to be frank, some of the leadership staff in the County of Põlva were against the resolutions adopted by the Estonian Congress. In Räpina, the Estonian Congress met with support. However, elsewhere the leaders of village soviets did not deem the Estonian Congress worthy of attention and even displayed their undisguised contempt for it.

It looked as if the practical activities of the Congress, or rather the lack of a viable policy, were the factor eroding its support.

However, the chairman of the village soviet also had an alternative explanation to that phenomenon. "The individuals holding office in village soviets and opposing the Estonian Congress did not use to have any background relating to the Republic of Estonia. One had been the Komsomol organiser, another a member of the Party Committee. For example, the chairman of the neighbouring village soviet used to be the Party organiser." The elite in the rural districts did have a varied background and predominantly so-called Soviet identity. However, such an attitude can be explained by the fact that the Estonian Congress had been reduced to a party machine working under the aegis of the Estonian National Independence Party. It proclaimed the Soviet-period administration as the "illegal structure of an occupying power." It was only to be expected that the people involved in that administration were to feel endangered and baffled, thrown into puzzled confusion. The aggressive tactics in the struggle for power by the Estonian Congress augmented by its incapacity to pursue a practical policy, severely handicapped its efforts and ultimately turned against it.

The position of the village soviet in the period of transition was certainly controversial, affected as it was by different political forces and official Soviet authorities (Kuus, 1991a). As intimated by the chairman of the village soviet, the "village soviet played its subtle game, indulging in subterfuge. At that time, you had to practice double-dealing and be hypocritical. On the one hand, you had to do what was prescribed by the upper echelons of power; on the other hand, the Estonian Congress, very honest at the outset, also found some support in Kanepi." Hence, the chairman of the village soviet of Kanepi maintained steady contact with the Estonian Congress.

An important phase in the political development of Kanepi was the referendum on independence on 3 March 1991. The referendum was blatantly ignored in Northeast Estonia, while also the Estonian Congress appealed to the population to engage in a concerted refusal to participate in it. As remembered by the chairman of the village soviet "a special session of the village soviet was held in February 1990, to define our attitude to the popular vote. The enlarged session held in the house of culture supported the referendum on independence." The Estonian Congress was the loser. In Kanepi the referendum attracted 90–95% of the electors, which was typical turnout in the countryside and significantly higher than in the cities (Raitviir, 1996, 177).

However, Kanepi felt insecure over what was to be done if the confrontation with Moscow should become increasingly aggravated. The chairman sensed a growing helplessness and even fear in the people:

> The village soviet drafted a plan of action for an emergency situation. Several members of the soviet thought that it made no sense to take precautionary measures, that it was childish and that we did not have a chance against Russian tanks, and that indulgence in offensive talk would get the loudmouths in trouble. When final resolutions, the contents of which I do not remember, were adopted, several people left the room without voicing their opinion.

This statement is indicative of the deep-set fear of the people of Kanepi in revealing their standpoint. The past Communist terror generated the fear of relocation and exile to Russia.

In June 1990, the Soviet Army had a chance to display its power in Estonia by surrounding the small township of Tori, where former freedom fighters and German Army veterans were to gather. The Soviet Army destroyed a number of monuments commemorating the valour and dedication of the war veterans. The Army also trained the special 'black berets' elite military force to deal with conflicts in the non-Russian republics of the USSR, and to assist the International Front (Intermovement) inspired by the Russian ex-military and directed by Moscow.

The visit to the home of chairman of the village soviet by an officer of the Soviet Army in March 1991 during the referendum on independence was indicative of growing tension in the small township of Kanepi. As a rule, the local administration in Estonia did not have any direct contact with the Army. The latter did whatever it thought fit whenever it felt necessary. Here are the recollections of the chairman:

> The ground was still covered with snow when someone knocked at the door. There was a Russian officer standing behind the door. We offered him some coffee. He said what he thought of the situation. The officer alleged that there had been street riots in Võru, and the Army was to prevent conflict and bloodshed. He explained his visit by stating that there were rumours and evidence of anti-state activities in Kanepi and the whole of Estonia, – a result of which was the reported damage to a monument to Soviet soldiers in Kanepi. A moment later it turned out that he had photographed that same monument and found everything in perfect order.

The chairman of the village soviet was convinced that the officer was on a mission to find out the prevalent mood:

> I am sure that he knew very well what we were up to, and that the Soviet authorities had been tipped off about us having gone too far. He was evasive, however he hinted that some people in Kanepi are engaged in anti-Soviet activities. The officer also presented his view of the Ribbentrop-Molotov Pact, which he claimed to be enemy propaganda; he also elaborated on the voluntary entry of Estonia into the Soviet Union.

The chairman of the village soviet offered his vision, much to the alarm of the officer. "He wondered how a Soviet official dared speak like that. I said that I used to be member of the CPSU, however there was no Party left now; with the empire collapsing, the Party had admitted defeat and called it quits. He was very surprised . . . " When leaving, the officer had reportedly said to the chairman: "It is highly likely that a Soviet Army unit will be stationed in Kanepi."

In the chairman's opinion, the conversation was extraordinary and he surmised that the officer's aim in probing the prevalent mood was in anticipation of possible action. The military never did anything without permission and a definite mission. Contrary to the officer's ominous prediction, they never met again. Whatever the hidden motives and goals of that visit, it implied that policy was not only made in towns. The prevalent mood in the countryside and the rural districts was important for the authorities, and keeping the small settlements under control was deemed expedient. Hence, the support of dispersed village soviets to larger towns was highly necessary.

To a certain extent, the visit certainly achieved its goal of being a 'deterrent'. There was a collision of two irreconcilable world outlooks in the home of the chairman of the village soviet of Kanepi; it was just the matter of when and how the showdown would occur. The chairman promptly put his colleagues in the picture. Later, during the averted coup in Moscow on August 21, 1991, the warnings given by the military did sometimes turn out to be useful. You knew that you had to prepare to repulse potential action. "We set up our own committee, whose members were assigned tasks for securing general order, for hiding the documents of the municipality, for maintaining communications, etc. I was to hide the documents, because nobody knew when they would be needed," commented the now first municipal director of Kanepi on the first reactions to the coup attempt:

> We collected the documents of the municipal government and the council, the register of residents, etc. They added up to a bag full of materials. I had the cache under the house in the cellar, known only to my deputy and the secretary. Thereafter we set up a special committee, including Leo Vijard, the representative of the Kaitseliit [Estonian Defence League] and myself. We discussed the ways to defend people in case the army should take over in Kanepi. Vijard dispatched a group of Defence League volunteers to secure the Valgjärve broadcasting station. We set up patrols.

The level of danger to Kanepi is hard to estimate. However, according to the military personnel in Põlva, the Army had been issued rather unambiguous guidelines as to how to carry on in the county (Kuus, 1991b).

The last instance of calling for the firm resolve of the municipal government was during the collapse of the Moscow coup. "Even before Estonia was proclaimed a sovereign state, the municipal council decided that there was no other option left but the declaration of Estonian independence. A day later the Supreme Soviet adopted the same resolution." However, not everybody in Kanepi held the same opinion, and they referred to the 'the wisdom of the old'. The chairman of the village soviet, speaking about the then prevalent mood, recollected that:

> There were voiced isolated cautions to hold on a minute, lest everything fall apart. Such wise guys were found even among intellectuals. The second faction of doubters, vacillating between two choices, rhetorically asked whether we really were intent on wiping out our own people. Wouldn't it be better to hold developments at bay, biding time and refusing to take a political stand?

There are ample reasons to believe that those who considered the creation of soviet-style local governments in 1989 as just a legal trick, an attempt to pull the wool over the people's eyes, actually providing no wider guarantees, were essentially correct (Reino, 1998). The ECP believed that concessions at the local level would draw people's attention away from national politics. However, our research suggests that, from the standpoint of democratisation of the government and socialisation of the people, the years of transition (1988–1991) were more significant than the rules of formal democracy provided for.[2] The people living in far-flung places, distant from the large centres of Estonia, although sometimes experiencing the feeling of helplessness, had a hand in the national politics through local government. The views of the leadership of Kanepi were relatively close to the nationalist-radical direction. They were able to maintain poise between widely divergent impulses, not to support adventurism and risky improvisation in politics. The body of Soviet administrative control became a political subject in just a couple of years, effectively bolstering the aspiration to Estonian independence and political involvement at the grass roots level.

Development of the Municipality of Kanepi During Independence

The Constitution of 1992 proclaimed the municipalities as the main local (municipal) governmental units. However, until the elections in October 1993, the counties (former rayons) were also considered self-governmental (Mäeltsamees, 1994, 77). The Law on the Organisation of Local Self-Government in June 2, 1993 specified the economic rights of the municipalities. It detailed and extended the right to collect taxes, the right to establish imposts on residents, the right to apply compulsory duties and obligations, etc. Now, the focus was on how to set up and run the municipality as a legal structure. However, the institutionalisation of the municipality was difficult. The smallest historic community in the municipality was the village. Restoration of the office of the village elder, a position of considerable import in the interim years between the W.W.I and W.W.II had not been successful. Many of the villages had virtually dwindled to nothing, and the office of the village elder would mean working on an unpaid voluntary basis. Thus, the important basic structure for self-government had become extinct.

---

2   The vast majority of nationalist activities were *de facto* illegal according to the laws of the Soviet Republic of Estonia. For example, the elections of the Estonian Congress would have been considered anti-revolutionary a few years earlier, but in 1990 the ECP was too weak and too afraid to respond to effectively suppress nationalist movements.

In the opinion of a member of the council, the possibility for the municipality to make itself heard was too small, although the situation had improved lately:

> The municipality used to be represented on the county council [in 1991 or 1992]. However, that institution lacked a specific task. Now it has been replaced by the Union of Municipalities. The Union of Chairmen of the Municipal Councils of Põlva County also acts for the interests of the municipalities. Now one more body has appeared – the National Union of Chairmen of Municipal Councils.

The latter union promotes co-operation with the state on a contractual basis. At the Congress of Rural Dwellers organised in 1994 with support from the Association of Unions of Self-Governments, the municipalities of Põlva County promoted the acceleration of land reform, the introduction of a loan system and regional policy (Põlva Maakonna, 1994, 308–309). Hence, crucial issues came under discussion.

Lately, the underdevelopment of so-called direct democracy, and the officialdom-centredness of local governments has been perceived as a major shortcoming with Estonian local governments. That is true. In the opinion of the long-term head of the village soviet, the problem amounts mostly to the capacity of the human assets inherited from the past to actually participate in the community life.

> I am convinced that currently there are many people who are used to getting orders from the meetings of the collective farms like Kanepi in Estonian municipalities. The chairman of the village soviet would always set as an example of how the problems were to be settled at the board meeting of the collective farm . . . I admonished them that if we did not succeed in overcoming that way of thinking, we would hardly be able to build self-government. The entrenched customs are currently the largest problem; you get the impression that the municipal council is a common herd, just like the meetings of the leadership of the collective farms used to be, where people that had no idea of what was going on were driven just to vote by a show of hands. That pattern is so deeply established that it will take years to get rid of.

The current leaders of Kanepi see elections and open competition for filling official positions in institutions of the municipality as the important factor in the struggle against corruption and embezzlement. Corruption creates a crisis in confidence. The former chairman of the municipal council enumerated the problems of the municipality: "corruption, permanent unemployment, tax fraud, uneconomic use of municipal funds . . . families having many children, single parents. I would rather that the municipal government observed, in the first place, the resolutions and prescriptions of the council. Rules and regulations should take precedence," said the deeply discontented former head of the municipality. He saw the gravest problem as an ethical crisis, in the scarcity of honest people suitable to fill the positions. "One can not say that the former society lacked any corruption whatsoever, however, in the past years privatisation actually transformed into sort of 'privateering' (the illegal use of former public property), and immensely fostered corruption."

The restoration of independence has not brought about any large-scale changes in Estonian regional policy. As witnessed in Kanepi, support programmes are haphazard, contingent and patchy – i.e. repair in a hasty and shabby fashion. The overall economic situation of municipalities is rather unstable because, as formulated by a member of the council, vital state support is the 'standing object of haggling.' In Põlva County, the Municipality of Kanepi has the smallest relative budget. In 1995, expenditure was as little as EEK 1,743 (about USD 130) per person (Põlva, 1996, 79). As reported by a member of the council, there are many loose ends in the formation of the municipal budget, small as it was. "The budget for 9 months in 1996 was nearly EEK 4 million. Half of that sum comes from local taxes, the second half is contributed by the state." The existing structures are preserved with this money – road maintenance, school repairs, and municipal salaries. The school management is also on the payroll of the municipality. The councillor we interviewed told that:

> The municipality is also paying for in-service training. Paid out of the budget of the municipality are the salaries of nine municipal officers, the librarian, cultural workers, kindergarten teachers, etc – altogether the salaries of nearly 100 people. Nearly one-third of the municipal budget is spent on the secondary and primary schools. The neighbouring municipalities reimburse part of the school expenses. They pay for their children that are taught at the secondary school of Kanepi. The other major outlays are for environmental care and for the snow-ploughs that are used to clear snow off the roads.

The Municipality of Kanepi has not become a booming economic environment. Due to a financial squeeze, the work in the administrative apparatus of the municipality is an important source of subsistence to the residents of Kanepi. As a member of the council said, "we have still managed without artificial creation of municipal jobs, as seen in other places." The municipal budget is prepared, as reported by the same councillor, by four people – the chairman of the council, and three chairmen of committees, based on consensus. Although some wrangling is said to happen, a member of the council acknowledged that "there are no alternatives but to act as dictated by common sense." The same person said that, until now, the municipality has somehow managed not to run into debt (in this, Kanepi is quite an exception). Nevertheless, Kanepi has applied for financial aid and a loan for the renovating the Erastvere Care Home and the school heating systems from the World Bank and the European Union (Põlva, 1996, 58–59). However, the community lacks funds to pursue an active investment policy. A member of the council told us that:

> The sole resource is timber industry, however the situation is bleak there, too. Should the cultivation of crops fail, the county may be hit by disaster. There are no other alternative resources. It could be highly possible that the municipality would face bankruptcy. The people are disillusioned and they blame the municipal leadership for their passivity and lack of initiative. However, what can we do about it, with no funds available?

The municipality is now legally owns its assets. However, in actual practice it is hard to hold poaching, illegal woodcutting and unauthorised quarrying in check. On the other hand, both employers and employees conceal their incomes. As a member of the municipal council intimated, "at least half the wages are paid in envelopes " (unreported to the tax authorities, hence without tax deductions). He reckoned that the municipality is cheated out of at least EEK 100,000 income each month due to tax evasion, i.e. over EEK 1 million annually. When we consider that the municipal budget receives only EEK 2 million annually (Põlva 1996, 81), the municipality suffers huge losses. Although everybody knows about the fraud, there is yet no administrative or moral mechanism available to monitor tax payments. The residual mentality, derived for the Soviet era and amounting to a 'universal truth', that cheating is not a crime persists.

As maintained by a member of the council, "besides embezzlement, a major problem is flogging the assets of the municipality by receiving a commission, or purchasing useless goods, often at premium prices, for the municipality" (exemplified by what happened at the centre of the collective farm). A striking instance of corruption is the case of when "the new chairman of the council and the accountant, allegedly reducing the level of unemployment, had 185 cubic meters of wood logged and let it disappear into the thin air. The chairman of the council took home 5 cubic meters of planking."

As estimated by the councillor, nearly 20% of working age population in the municipality are unemployed. The number of unemployed equals the number of those earning wages – 300 people. The unemployment rate is twice as high as the average in the county, and is explained by the lower level of education for the population and the agriculture-centredness of the municipality (Põlva, 1996, 74). The councillor stated that the municipality is heavily weighted by the demoralisation of the unemployed – when offered a job they refuse to accept it. He suggested that such mentality might have been inherited from the organisation of work on the collective farm, which made it possible to conceal and tacitly accept unemployment, thus condoning the 'mentality of a dependent'.

The municipal leadership largely works because of moral obligation, 'in the performance of one's duty'. "There is no enthusiasm, the main driving force is the sense of duty, the inner urge to do something about it," said a veteran leading official of Kanepi, a man who had witnessed different eras – starting with the terror of Stalin and lasting until the Brezhnev era, rationalising his continuing active involvement in community affairs. "Whatever the acts of central authority, regardless of whether the money will be allocated and forthcoming, we have decided that what is to be done will be done, either by voluntary work, or by soliciting donations, etc. Our entire lives amount to patching the gaps, the voluntary work being of primary importance for the municipality to survive." The identity of the older generation of residents of Kanepi seems to be the spiritual resource keeping the municipality going.

The Kanepi study indicates a new, relatively stable social stratification, and the formation of an appropriate expert-centred mode of government. The majority of people suffer from deep depression; their position is defensive, they have no opportunity to improve their position by coercing the municipality and pressurising it into action, or by doing something radical by themselves. The bulk of the budget is expended on supporting those who are utterly destitute. The reform has somewhat widened the composition of the leading elite in the locality – besides the technocrats with the background of the collective farm, it also includes teachers and general practitioners. Women have won some representation in the council. However, the quality of the elite has deteriorated in the past decade – when competent people make their mark in the transformation process they are often transferred to larger centres or enter public service (the government administration, the border guard, etc.). Consequently, the circle of people shaping the outlook of the municipality will increasingly narrow, unless the new generation sets its roots in Kanepi.

The capital necessary to develop all areas, starting with economic capital and finishing with the moral capital of trust, is conspicuously lacking. The stagnation of Kanepi corroborates the more general summary conclusion that Estonia needs administrative reform for territorial development based on the actual situation and not on the conjecture of restitution.

The other resources and trends for the development of the municipality are elucidated in more detail later in this chapter, and in the chapter on civil society.

School and the Development of the Municipality

Historically, schools in Estonia have been the major 'engines' and driving forces behind local development, attracting the intelligentsia to the rural areas, mediating ideas, etc. There are two operating schools in the Municipality of Kanepi – the secondary school of Kanepi (350 students, 26 teaching staff) and the primary school of Põlgaste (100 students, 10 teaching staff). The construction of the latter was completed in the 1970s and the secondary school was enlarged. The secondary school is seen as a resource, giving the Municipality of Kanepi an edge on development. The plan for development of the municipality was finalised in 1991. However, in several respects it is rather controversial in how it handles the relations between the school and the municipality. "The school in Kanepi has been a closed establishment. At school, you are apprehensive of changes, viewing the future with unease. The teachers are isolated from the community life." The school in Põlgaste has left a better impression on the municipality. "The teachers interact with the people of the collective farm, maintaining relations of trust and support. They avoid encapsulation" (Arengukava, 1991).

The description of the schools in Kanepi, on the basis of the interviews, is essentially different from that revealed in the history of Kanepi, where the school was a major factor in the social and cultural life for over a century, until 1940 (Põldmäe, 1978, 198). What has affected the relations between the school and the local community over the past fifty years?

Village Soviet, School and Collective Farm

As with schools in general, the school of Kanepi promoted the democracy, initiative and patriotism of the native locality in the years of the bourgeois Republic of Estonia. The youngsters, who formed a cohesive body in the municipality, had an instrumental part in the War for Independence. The very scanty knowledge of the residents of Kanepi of that glorious period of history is the outright result of the Soviet system. In the annexed Estonia, the schools were part of the state system. In particular, the schools in the rural areas were designed as centres for the dissemination of Russian-Soviet ideology. The schools were developed to counterbalance to the 'backwardness in the perception of the world' in the rural dwellers and the bourgeois culture.

Hence, the controversial nature of relations between the school and the local community. The new rule contributed to the development of the school; however, the school was 'a thorn in the flesh' to the local community. The spiritual and mental attitude of the school was moulded by the supervisors of the CPSU/Estonian Communist Party, Komsomol and the Pioneer organisations (the 'Pioneers' was the Communist Party children's organisation). The attempts of students to consolidate nationally outside the state structure of mental colonisation were liable to wind up as culprits in a detention camp. The establishment of an independent organisation landed a group of students in Vorkuta, the transpolar coal mines. One survivor of the camp later became the chairman of the village soviet of Kanepi.

The Socialisation of Young People in Kanepi

The subjugation of the lives of the young people to the interests of the state, the 'nationalisation of the youth' created a state of powerlessness, incapacity to act, and paralysed the identity of the youngsters in the local community. Komsomol was an organisation that monitored political loyalty. One of its tasks was to bring the 'bloodsucker kulaks' (wealthy independent farmers) or nationalists to light, i.e. the destruction of the structures of the *ancient regime*. Non-membership in Komsomol made it impossible for a person to continue his or her education and start a career. As the retired director of the secondary school in Kanepi said: "After graduating from school I wanted to become a teacher. I was advised that without first joining the Komsomol I would have no hope to get the teacher's job. Later I was expelled from Komsomol on political grounds. That would have been the end of my career. However, the local Party organiser simply did not take my documents to Võru, so I could carry on teaching." That was how the man, later considered to be one of the most conscientious Party functionaries in Kanepi, described his trials and tribulations. After the expulsion and displacement of the 'kulaks' as well as the forced collectivisation of peasants through intimidation, Komsomol (and the school) focused, as from 1957, on the struggle with the influence of religion and the church (Toome, 1986, 125, 249). Thus, the school was again put in opposition with local cultural traditions and the generations set on a collision course.

The history of the Estonian Komsomol, at least partly truthful and factual, has not yet been written. However, it remained an alien body, imposed by force, used against tacit opposition in Kanepi as well as in other Estonian villages. The reminiscences of the authorities in Kanepi prove that Mikk Titma's research group missed the truth and it was totally off the mark when, transported with delight, it claimed that Komsomol was the 'forge of cadres', the bulwark of the development of rural youth and the bastion of self-realisation (Titma, 1980, 252). There was no mention made of the students' self-government in that study.

The former headmaster of the school reminisced that "as late as in the 70s the Komsomol organiser [a teacher] was dismissed, because there were too few members." The 1980s witnessed increasing disorganisation. The current headmaster said, "In the school of Kanepi, only 40% of students were members of Komsomol. It was actually a paper organisation. Only those who wished to continue education or obtain better jobs could be lured to inscribe their names in the membership register." The headmaster said, "in the years of realignment there was no longer any pressure to get more people to join Komsomol." The realignment put an end to blatant pressure.

In 1989, the inactive Komsomol surfaced unexpectedly when a joint letter by the teachers and students at the secondary school in Kanepi requested a halt to the activity of the Estonian Communist Party led Intermovement, which opposed Estonian independence (Kanepi Keskkooli, 1989). The defunct Komsomol local organisation was now manipulated and used by the nationalist-minded teachers against the Communist Party.

The emerging authentic self-awareness of Estonian youth made no attempt to use official structures for political purposes (implying the negative image of those structures); it obtained fresh life and energy outside the official organisations. For example, fame throughout Estonia was won by the Võru 'Youth Column No. 1', which tackled the restoration of the monuments to the War for Independence. This unofficial group of young people also participated in the reinauguration of the monument to those fallen in the War for Independence in Kanepi. The KGB officers were apprehensive in case the youngsters of Kanepi became involved. "When the Youth Column started activities in Võru, there were fears lest it arrive at Kanepi; we were warned to forestall riots," reminisces the then chairman of the village soviet. The way the leader of the movement, Mr Saar, was forced to leave Estonia illustrates the repressive character of the Soviet system. It repressed even a minor unsanctioned initiative as late as 1987. The fate of the young people in Kanepi would have been as dire if the truly nationalist spirit amongst them had not been effectively subdued in good time, particularly in the domains where it had been fostered.

The role and place *en principe* of the Pioneer organisation and its extensions – the Fledgling Hawks (Noorkotkad) and Pre-Pioneers (oktya-bryata – Soviet children of seven years or upward preparing to join the Pioneers) was the same as Komsomol. However, being more oriented to children, they enjoyed some popularity, which was only natural. "Children love building a camp-fire, hiking, scouting, etc," explained the former Pioneer leader. The opinion of the retired headmaster was that the Pioneer organisation had essentially become non-political by the 1980s. "Pioneers organised their own camps. That way, children could meet other children from their Latvian counterpart schools. It was absolutely non-political." There were natural reasons for the Pioneer organisation losing its 'militant' aspect – its outdated rituals and its form prompted jeers. In the words of a Pioneer leader: "and the teachers had to do something so that the outer form would not put the substance [of the Pioneer organisation] in peril." The Pioneer organisation ended its old ideological activities in 1988, and it became the Estonian Children Organisation (abbr. ELO in Estonian). In the autumn 1989, Komsomol stopped its activities in the rayon of Põlva. As the local Komsomol leader had said, it had no future as a political organisation (Aas, 1989).

The now officially tolerated research of the native locality was fully Sovietised, as emphasised the preface to an omnibus volume dedicated to history of the rayon of Põlva (Tarmisto, 1978, 7):

> The research of a native locality has a substantial place in the moral and aesthetic education of the Soviet people, in particular the young generation. Therefore, the research of native locality must deeper reflect the activities related to struggle on the fronts of revolution and war, the friendship of the Soviet peoples and the joint efforts in building the Communism.

It goes without saying that there was not a single line about the Republic of Estonia and the majority of the truly great men of Kanepi in the book.

As late as in the second half of the 1980s, the research into the native locality at the school in Kanepi was conducted exactly as prescribed in the programme 'The Soviet Union is my Native Land'. This was compiled in Moscow (Pugas, 1988). On the initiative of the leaders of collective farming, the school in Kanepi set up a one-room museum of local history in 1975. However, the Sovietised counterfeit of history did not have any major significance in the activities of the school or for the world outlook of the students.

The total failure of the students of the school in Kanepi to get involved in so much as even the 'singing revolution' was explained away by the headmaster: "Kanepi is no town like Võru, in the countryside the students are not active on their own initiative. They need to be guided." There is something in this statement. However, it is also evident that the teachers had given up trying to form keen minds in the students, to make them into patriots of Kanepi – and not without a valid reason. Even after the end of Stalinist terror, initiative was a risky business. The reminiscences of a teacher about the outcome of mild protest when he was at university were so traumatic that he refused to state his political views and convictions:

> When we were at university in Tartu, we carried a slogan carved out as a fox in one procession. It said: 'Hands off the fox!' The tail of the fox was the outline of the map of Estonia. The militia stopped us, interrogated us and accused us of anti-Soviet activities. We were set free only after the dean spoke to the chief of militia. Several people had trouble after that incident, and it has kept me far from politics ever since.

That teacher was right. The school came under special ideological monitoring. The teacher of Estonian at the school in Kanepi remembers the atmosphere at that time was quite stifled. The 'Letter of the Forty',[3] also disseminated in Kanepi, was quite an event and created "considerable elation, after years of grey monotony, and triggered speculation about the situation in Kanepi." The involvement of teachers in the political self-recovery of Kanepi remained very limited; they attended the meetings of the Estonian Popular Front, the Estonian National Heritage Society and the Citizens' Committees, but only as onlookers. The position of onlooker was, however, in blatant contrast with the traditional leading role of teachers in the social movements of Estonia. Hence, the school in annexed Estonia found itself one of the most homogenised, forcibly assimilated institutions of Kanepi with a declining intellectual capital.

There was no substantial interest and connection between the collective farm and school, or school and the village soviet. Economically, the collective

---

3   A letter signed by 40 established Estonian intellectuals was sent to Moscow and the republic authorities in 1980. The intellectuals spoke against the use of force against protesters, the russification of Estonian schools and other similar issues.

farm supported the school. As reported by a local amateur historian in Kanepi, the headmaster was an 'honorary member' of the collective farm. Without the support of the collective farm, the school would not have got its ancillary building. The collective farm also contributed money to support compulsory school attendance. On the other hand, the interest displayed by the collective farm was rather unsophisticated. The impression of the chairman of the village soviet was:

> The collective farm is interested in schoolchildren as field labourers. The schoolchildren were regarded as the future members of the collective farm. The intention was to turn the chairman of the village soviet into an overseer, and I was between the sledgehammer and the anvil when trying to protect the schoolchildren. The teachers were obligated to promote the collective farm amidst the students.

The relations between the collective farm and the school, and reporting to the village soviet, remained pragmatic and technocratic. What else could there be? Both were planned economic institutions directed from above. Besides, the political roots to alienation were reflected though the 'downstream' or 'vertical' organisation of power. This was a characteristic to the Soviet administration, with the flow of commands streaming from headquarters to actual doers.

The 'Soviet power', pushing political monitoring and control to the forefront, was successful in isolating the school and the local community in Kanepi. The normal 'excitation potential' of the school had gone unused, the official structures being impotent. The valuable initiative and common interest stemming from the identity of the native locality was never reborn in Kanepi. The scarcity of the social capital that is mandatory for organisation and co-operation seems to be a central problem for the future.

Post-independence Schools and Perspectives of the Municipalities

The restored Republic of Estonia views every initiative with a benevolent eye. The relations between schools and the municipality are largely formed by the boards of trustees for the schools, with the leadership of the municipality playing a significant role. Establishing the orientation of the school and the resolution of staff-related problems falls within the competency of the municipality. The relations of the school and municipality, however, have been over-ideologised. The termination of the Estonian Children's Organisation was only partly necessitated by the lack of funds. The state, and hence the municipality, decided to finance primarily patriotic structures. The former Pioneer organiser explained:

> In Kanepi, Leo Vijard is Chief of Defence League. He proposed creating the Noorkotkad [Fledgling Hawks] and Kodutütred [Home Daughters] [patriotic organisations affiliated to the Defence League] organisations at the school. Thence the idea. I tended to shun that idea first, but he made the children and me familiar with the programme and now there are 16 Home Daughters at the school. He himself is head of the Fledgling Hawks organisation.

The Fledgling Hawks group, acting under the supervision and support of the Defence League is the only organisation receiving funds from both the municipality and the county. They have their own room in the school, and the training they receive focuses on patriotic education and readiness to support the defence force in case of military action. For this, there is a shooting range and summer camps are organised. The interviewees lacked any information about the development of research into the native locality, the environmental protection movement in Kanepi, and any other such undertakings. These appeared to be lacking.

Hobbies and creative activity have been given second priority. Playing sports has not caught on. "There has actually never been a sports organisation in Kanepi, it has always existed on paper only. The interest in sports has diminished. We have two gymnastics teachers. They try to get something done, but the students are not very interested. It is also possible that the teachers are not very good. Nevertheless, we play ball games," the present headmaster tried to reassure the interviewer.

The parents in Kanepi are utterly discontented with the situation. "My daughter will never agree to continue studies in Kanepi. I can't understand why there are no hobby groups at school. They do not even play sports. In the summer, you can't find anything for the children to do. My son kicked a ball alone, there was nobody to teach him," complained the parent of a student at the secondary school. "I do not see any future for my children here." The opinion of one teacher about his colleagues was pulverising: "The teachers of our school are no patriots to this place. They and children do not display any interest to Kanepi and its history." Although the now municipality elects the headmaster, it is not easy to pick a right person, in view of the general moral breakdown. The person elected as headmaster in 1996 had forged his documents; he embezzled the school's money and had to be dismissed (Laas, 1996).

The objective reason for the disruption in Kanepi is understandably the discouragement with the increasing provincialisation of the run-down hinterland. "The problem is that teachers are considerably advanced in years, nobody wants to come to work in the countryside anymore. The teachers in rural schools no longer enjoy the privileges that they used to have. Services also used to be cheaper. Rents [today in Kanepi] are as high as in town, however goods there are cheaper," the master of curriculum said, illuminating the disinterest of teachers.

However, the overall low activity of the youth in the rural areas was already apparent in the 1980s, before the singing revolution. "The young people started to leave and the new tidal wave [the Singing Revolution] could not stem that process," reiterated one teacher. The weakening of the position of the school gave rise to a wider concern. "If we fail to attract the young people, it may well happen that the Green Movement, the Popular Front and the protection of national heritage will remain a queer hobby of the older generation," warned Andres Reimer, the then activist for the Defence League, as early as in 1988 (Reimer, 1988a).

At the end of the 1990s, the process triggered twenty years ago has been deepening. One shortcoming is causing another – weak teachers cause the bright and more talented students to leave the school in droves. As one parent in Kanepi said, "everybody with money sends their children to the town school, to make sure they get excellent education," and hence the prospects for future career.

The collective farm with its abortive attempt at modernisation is by no means the sole cause for degradation in Kanepi. However, having destroyed the natural historical regenerative mechanisms of the locality, the breakdown of the collective farm has left a vacuum that is not easy to fill.

Municipality, Revival of Cultural Life and Identity

One of the main sources of identity and the spiritual resources being reborn in the Municipality of Kanepi are the traditional cultural events, involving all or at least the best part of the population. The Choir Days held in 1925 were attended by 23 mixed-voiced choirs with 600 singers, 10 children's choirs with 300 singers, 5 orchestras with 92 singers, and also a score of dancing troupes – a total of 1,100 performers. In the 1934 Choir Days, even Mannstein's musical comedy 'Home of Happiness' was staged (Hirvlaane, 1988). Although one was allowed to speak of the so-called bourgeois period of

Estonia with recognition and respect only as realignment made headway, the autonomous cultural memory of the people was not totally effaced. On the contrary, it survived and continued to live in new forms, notwithstanding censorship and terror. What was even more important was that the cultural activity of the Estonian rural population (reading, excursions to the theatre) was several times higher than in Russia, Moldova, etc. This was that due to a tradition of attachment to long-term culture. Culture among those born and reared in the Republic of Estonia was in some aspects ten times higher that of their peers in Russia (Vihalemm, 1985, 102).

An important device to legitimise Soviet power and ideological control was the promotion of the so-called people's culture. The Leninist-Stalinist Cultural Revolution supplied it with sovietising and Russianising content. Cultural societies and their properties were wound up and liquidated, libraries were ransacked, the cultural life of the church (with the exception of music) was outlawed, and all initiative was subjugated to the supervision of the Estonian Communist Party and the NKVD (KGB). All the apparent national elements were raked out as 'nationalist' and 'bourgeois'. Cultural life concentrated in nationalised clubhouses, the renamed houses of culture. Mandatory indoctrination lectures were held there; readers were forced to familiarise themselves with propaganda literature; the singers were made to eulogise the Lenin-Stalinist Party; agitation films were show, etc.

The concept of the Soviet 'people's culture', essentially blocked the development of modern urban culture, but it became a source for restoration of national culture in the countryside. In the villages, out of reach of the wary eye of the Estonian Communist Party, people were ready to compromise, to tolerate the rebirth of the bygone 'bourgeois' culture, by the side of a 'flourishing' socialist cultural life. 'The shift of the boundaries of national culture', the redefinition of nationalism, etc. became possible only when the physical and spiritual terror ended, after Stalin's death.

As from the 1960s, the question of which of the two great narratives – the 'Russian-Soviet' or 'national' – would prevail in forming people's spirituality became the focal source of hidden political struggle. The two-layer or even three-layer focusing assumed an increasingly systematic form. However, the question of the emancipation from national cultural focusing amounted to social autonomy, the restoration of the mental prerequisites for civil society, until the formation of narrative autonomies, which finally materialised into institutional autonomies. For Kanepi, the last 'phases' of that process are observable.

The development of the cultural prerequisites for the rebirth of the municipality is primarily reflected in the transformation of three institutions – the house of culture, the schools and church. We shall focus on the first two. (The church will be handled in Chapter 6 dealing with civil society)

Disruptions in Cultural Life and Continuities in the Spiritual Life of Kanepi

The means and resources for the cultural life of an Estonian village in the Soviet era depended mainly on the relationship between two sources of finance – the village soviets and, in particular, the collective (state) farms. Those means and resources depended, to a considerable extent, on individuals in key positions, the appreciation of culture, the preserved identity of the native locality, and the overall relationships. The possibilities for the collective farms to 'sponsor' culture were both open and hidden, because 'black cash' (undeclared income) was part and parcel of Soviet management. Both collective farms in Kanepi were relatively well financed. One more source of funds came from the Kalev sweet factory in Tallinn, which was nothing exceptional (it was also dubbed 'patronage' – a relationship between two organisations in which one 'adopts' the other, or an arrangement by which an organisation takes a special interest in a priority construction project). Because the factory had a Pioneer campsite in Kanepi, it also supported the school. "They sent their workmen to help with the school repairs," said the former headmaster, explaining the background to the co-operation.

In Kanepi, the 1960s and 1970s are remembered as 'fat years', characterised by the growth of wealth and public weal, with the club life of the collective farm community in full swing. There is little left. "Compared with the Soviet era, people's involvement in cultural events has dramatically dropped. Then, the club evenings attracted hundreds of people. The evenings for the middle-aged and young were so popular that the house of culture was bursting at the doors. Those coming late found it hard to get a place," said the former culture organiser, describing the time when the collective farm was at its prime.

A number of people in Kanepi recollect that they used to live as a 'close-knit family,' everybody having money to hand out. Kanepi was visited by well-known musicians, writers, actors, etc. "We used to have money to pay to the performers. True, funds were sometimes procured from the coffers of the collective farm, circumventing the law, however we did find them," said the director of the house of culture when clarifying the background to financing cultural life. As far as he remembered, the leadership of the Kalev collective farm was less tight-fisted, less reluctant to part with money. "The former chairman of the [Kalev] collective farm was always ready to help if we were severely short of money, the former accountant was willing to overlook the rules of accountancy, should culture and hobbies need support." The former headmaster of the secondary school in Kanepi was nostalgic: "Kanepi was visited by the theatres of Tallinn, Tartu, Pärnu and Viljandi. Almost every week the bus from the collective farm took people to the theatre in town. Now the bus tickets are much too expensive. Then, the bus from the collective farm was provided free of charge."

The Estonian tradition of large national Song Festivals found many supporters among the population in Kanepi. The Kanepi choirs participated in all the song festivals held during the Soviet era. A brass band, choirs, and folk dance troupes (23 amateur groups) were all active in Kanepi in the 1970s. These groups were the most telling evidence of a keen interest in culture, even when we allow for a slight exaggeration, as was the Soviet custom. The achievements of the amateur talent activities of Kanepi were even recognised by an honorary letter sent to the village soviet by Moscow.

When comparing the collective farms of Kanepi and Kalev, the chairman of the latter seems to have been more culture-addicted. This left an impression on the local life, supporting the idea that an individual could play a significant role in the Soviet system. It was on initiative of the former chairman and the money from the collective farm that the poet Juhan Weizenberg was reburied in Kanepi in 1977. "When Kanepi commemorated its 300th anniversary in 1975, all participants at festivities were offered free bread and milk by the Kalev collective farm, with the Kanepi collective farm catering only for the performers," recollects a local amateur historian in Kanepi. It can be safely asserted that rural culture also had its 'great 60s' – not only in Kanepi but also throughout the rayon of Põlva, where there were numerous song and dance festivals.

The chairman of the Kanepi collective farm, who was not local, was primarily an administrator, a technocrat, who "was uneasy about the use of alcohol at amateur cultural activities," according to the former headmaster. Development of culture and the attitude to culture was primarily a problem of preserving local identity and family traditions. The local pastor in Kanepi confirmed this:

> I noticed that the 'mentality of the collective farm' had penetrated into the culture of Kanepi, everything had been reduced to 'the chase for credits'. The

chairman of the collective farm gave performance in work the highest priority. The oldest brass orchestra in Võru County, named Kungla is active in Raiste, where I live. It had started as early as in 1887 on the initiative of the school-teacher, Jaan Holster. The skills were passed from father to son, and everybody at Raiste considered it natural to do so. The chairman of our state farm, Heino Kuusik, supported the orchestra because he insisted not only on work but on the promotion of culture, too. It seems that culture was not considered to be of value in Kanepi, and the cultural tradition withered away, together with the ultimate victory of the collective farm system.

This is a very perspicacious observation. The system of collective farms that purposefully destroyed farming and made political control easier (even in spiritual life), was certain to distort the regenerative mechanism of culture, reducing village traditions to an object of 'socialist emulation'. The amateur cultural activities became considerably alienated. Alcohol abuse became all-pervasive on the collective farms. Cultural activities did not become an alternative to drinking – quite the contrary, amateur cultural activities went hand in hand with alcohol. The result was that the head of the Kanepi collective farm became stubborn and unwilling to support cultural activities.

The head of the house of culture thinks the reasons for culture having a secondary priority lay deeper. The head of the Kalev collective farm not only supported his people, but also subsidised the workers of the Kanepi collective farm in cultural matters with 'black cash'. "Heading that collective farm was Mr H, who was thoughtful about culture. In a way, he even competed with the collective farm Kanepi. He favoured the brass orchestra and had a choir stand built in Põlgaste. Under his leadership the cultural life of the Kalev collective farm overtook that of Kanepi," said the new pastor, exposing his vision. The head of the house of culture supported his statement:

> The decline started in the last decades of the Soviet power, when nobody cared about culture any more. The chairman of the Kanepi collective farm was no expert in culture. He lacked the cultural background one obtains at home, having been a ward in a children's home. He didn't give a damn about who became the head of the house of culture.

The position for the head of the house of culture in Kanepi lasted until almost the end of Party rule. It was held by a man who had drinking problems and not only did he fail to organise anything but he also sold a substantial part of the property belonging to the house.

At the beginning of the 1980s, culture also started to languish in Põlgaste. The Kanepi brass orchestra had long been dissolved and the one in

Põlgaste wound up its activity. The pastor described the decline: "When the orchestra was needed in 1988 for the reopening of the monument to those fallen in the War for Independence, it had to be commissioned from Põlva. The men's choir came from farther off."

The fate of cultural life in Kanepi reveals the essential feature of the Soviet system – patrimonialism could and did circumvent the restrictive prescriptions of the militarised state. However, due to the non-democratic system people were not able to overcome the negative results of authoritarian patrimony. The main enemies of the communist system were 'regionalism' or 'nationalism', and these were the characteristic traits of Estonian Soviet cadres. They were the most difficult to uproot and did not allow the administrative system to conclusively exhaust and deplete Estonia. With the state emaciated by militarism and going bankrupt, the 'regionalism' of the collective farms seemed to be the central origin of resources. However, it is clear that the 'organisational' resource of Bolshevik cultural life, intended to bolster the supremacy of Moscow, had utterly worn out; whilst the 'grassroots' resource of cultural life, which relied on farm families and village identity, remained subdued.

With economic resources shrinking, the idle Estonian Communist Party paradoxically boosted ideological pressure on culture on the eve of its dissolution. The daily newspaper in the rayon of Põlva always published the guidelines of the Estonian Communist Party. According to the guidelines, the only standard for the estimation of cultural work was to make people familiar with the resolutions of the Party, military-patriotic education, familiarisation with the Soviet foreign policy, etc. The guidelines were composed in a rather Stalinist vernacular and according to them, cultural life was to be subordinated to tighter control by the Party organiser (Vill, 1988). The document was ridiculously pathetic. Amongst those angrily speaking out against it was the long time promoter and organiser of cultural work in Kanepi, Ülo Leib (Reimer, 1988b). As it was, in spring of 1988 the *nomenklatura* of the Estonian Communist Party and the people lived in different worlds.

'Days of Kanepi' – the Restoration of Historic and Cultural Identity

The 'Days of Kanepi' is the name assigned to the song and dance festival in Kanepi. It drew on ancient traditions of song festivals. However, its social content was largely a political event, mobilising the entire population and transforming, within a short time, the balance of power in the municipality. The 'Days of Kanepi' was first organised in the summer of 1988 to represent the so-called heritage movement. This involved the whole of Estonia and its roots were naturally in the past. However, the Estonian Heritage Society later obtained substantial organisational and economic support from the Nordic countries.

The 'Days of Kanepi' was largely in the form of a nationalist anti-Communist protest, which it initially assumed during the so-called singing revolution of Estonia that began in the summer 1988. By politicising culture and suppressing the essential elements of national culture, the communists had reduced national culture to counterculture. The restoration of authentic cultural life was an important political act and simultaneously not at all formal a political undertaking.

The first attempt at 'cultural restoration' was in 1975, at the 300th anniversary of the foundation of the parish of Kanepi (in the time under Swedish rule). The song and dance festival held then was a clear continuation of the tradition of the bourgeois Republic of Estonia. However, the local newspaper did not contain the slightest hint of this. The censors were at work. Nor did the Estonian Encyclopaedia published during the Soviet era, make any mention of the Kanepi during the period of the bourgeois Republic of Estonia. In the Estonian Encyclopaedia the collective farms were regarded the benchmarks of Soviet identity, and the article on the district of Kanepi mainly dealt with the Great October kolkhoz.

The 'Days of Kanepi', were aimed at restoring local identity. They were held three times, in 1988, 1989 and 1990. The first was still culture-centred, a characteristic of the singing revolution. It was dedicated to the commemoration of the 120th anniversary of foundation of the Kanepi Song and Music Society. There were, however only about a hundred performers (cf. in 1925 there were almost 1,000 performers). In 1988 the procession of over 1,000 participants included almost one third of the residents of the old municipality of Kanepi. The old world of symbols was legalised and newly integrated into the culture through showing the national flag and the flags of the banned societies, and that of the Kanepi parish.

A seminar dedicated to the history of Kanepi played an important role in the restoration of identity. However, the Estonian Communist Party retained control over the microphone since the chairman of the village soviet was the master of ceremonies. There were also performers and guests from Tallinn and elsewhere. The event was largely financed by the Kanepi and Kalev collective farms. Hence, national rebirth was largely based on the economic foundation of socialist structures.

The 'Days of Kanepi' in 1989 were clearly part of political mobilisation. The questions of restoration of independence were on the agenda. An important place was taken by the election propaganda machine of the Estonian Congress, and the registration of people living in the old municipality, formed in 1939, was started.

The last 'Days of Kanepi' were held in 1990 and indicated the depletion of organisational resources. They were based simply on the restoration of identity. The events were oriented to the future, rather than to the past. An important event was a conference dedicated to the future of Kanepi, with the Member of Academy Raimond Hagelberg, a well-known expert in agricultural economy born in Kanepi, delivering a paper. Preparations for the all-Estonian Song Festival in Tallinn gave further impetus to the Days. Since the Kanepi boys' choir had won second place at the previous festival, Kanepi was picked as one of the twenty rural districts where the festival torch was lit and carried to Tallinn. The 'Days of Kanepi' show the depth to the cultural roots of the 'singing revolution' in Estonia. The developments that originated in 1988 largely repeated the 'singing revolution'. They started one hundred and twenty years ago and culminated in the creation of an independent state.

Modernisation of Cultural Life in the Restored Municipality of Kanepi

Due to collapse of the economic order of state socialism underlying the system of collective farms, the level of financing for cultural activities steeply declined in 1990–1992. The Soviet collectivist and ideological cultural pattern found itself in a deep crisis. Together with it, the revitalised patriotic culture also faced a deep crisis. The open-air stage for singing, designed for large-scale events in the nationalist euphoria in 1990, no longer had a purpose.

The cultural pattern of the Republic of Estonia to be developed was close to nationalist-conservative concepts. However, given the economic depression, making new laws and finding funding, etc. for cultural activities was complicated. The formation of new cultural needs and patterns was a lengthy process. However, cultural life was given a crushing and traumatic blow, both economically and in particular spiritually, by the rapid pauperisation of the population of Kanepi, casting them into a deep shock. The immediate goal for the reformation of cultural life was, primarily, to stop the downslide. "The only active choir in Kanepi was a mixed voiced church choir. It had started its activity in the [first] Republic of Estonia. The singers were no longer very young. Life in the house of culture had been extinguished," said the new pastor describing the situation as it was at the beginning of the 1990s.

In 1996, only one person organised the work of the house of culture in Kanepi (a second employee worked under contract). During the Soviet era, there were four people with an additional two people at the Põlgaste house of culture.

To his consternation, the new head of the house of culture of Kanepi discovered that the bulk of equipment and supplies for the centre (in particular musical instruments such as accordions, harmonicas, drums, etc.) were gone. The chairs had also been sold. The perpetrator turned out to be the alcoholic that had headed the house of culture in the 1980s. Only the upright piano had been overlooked. Even some of the windowpanes had been stolen. A fire in 1985 had interrupted the work of the house of culture and had contributed to its decline. The best electronic equipment procured under the Soviets (TV sets, radios, tape and cassette recorders) had found their way into the bosses' homes instead of the house of culture.

The primary concern for the head of the house of culture was to obtain the latest technical equipment. Otherwise, there was very little hope of attracting any young people. It took several years of effort to obtain some devices and equipment. Today, the main problem is the lack of money. Kanepi spends EEK 132 per resident on culture and holds an average place among the municipalities of the county. However, the sum is lower than the average in the county, which is EEK 186. (Põlva, 1996). The repairs to the house of culture in Kanepi have never progressed beyond patching up the old structures. As reported by the pastor, the house of culture in Põlgaste has never recovered from the intervening decline, no one has "succeeded in inspiring it with new vigour, and instilling new spirit into it."

The libraries in Kanepi accommodated themselves relatively well to the novel situation and are in good condition. There are active branch libraries in Põlgaste and Erastvere. However, the principles for operating the libraries are radically new. The propaganda literature that was forcibly sent under the Soviets to stock the library was withdrawn and left the shelves empty. "Orders used to be issued from the centre. Now we replenish the stock of the library at our own discretion," said the director of the library, characterising the current situation. No longer is there any 'work with the reader', which imposed propaganda literature on the readers. Only the children are guided and advised, to help them develop and preserve their skills in working with books, because "the books are costly and their bindings not very good."

As for the librarian, the municipality has realised the importance of the library. "At first it looked like the municipality did not care about us and did not therefore allocate enough funds. Books are expensive, but that cannot be helped. Nevertheless when we explained and substantiated our needs we obtained the absolute minimum of funds." The use of the library has increased. "In 1988, there were 400–500 loans per month, now it is 800–900," said the Kanepi librarian. "The majority of readers are old-age pensioners and the unemployed. The rate of readership increases proportionately with the unemployment rate. Men in particular are ravenous readers. The people lack money to buy books, newspapers and magazines, hence they read the latter in libraries." The librarian has found that the purpose in reading newspapers has also changed: "people now glean practical knowledge from them and study advertisements."

According to the head of the house of culture in Kanepi, the house is particularly important to children, especially to those that do not go to kindergarten. They are taught elementary knowledge in music, gymnastics, drawing and literature. Besides the children's groups, there is an active theatrical troupe of old-age pensioners in Põlgaste. Visits of the theatres in Kanepi have become rare, but there are few performances by the amateur troupes from Põlva and Otepää. Films are no longer shown in Kanepi, no one has any money. However, Vanemuine, the town theatre of Tartu, visited Kanepi once in 1996.

Besides hobbies and entertainment, the house of culture in Kanepi is being transformed into a training centre to more effectively meet the changing requirements of the people. The leaders of the municipality are also increasingly aware that training will help meet the challenge of deprivation, and the so-called brain drain, etc. The municipality will have a future only if it is able to retrain the best working men and active people in the locality. People are ready to stay in Kanepi on condition there are options for training, courses in computer literacy, sports facilities, etc. Training would help them adjust to the rapidly modernising environment and market economy. Upon the demand of residents of Kanepi, the municipality, with its expanding international contacts, has increased its support for courses in foreign languages.

Lately, there has been an increase in amateur cultural activities. Choral singing, folk dancing, and the musical activities of the young, etc. have drawn on the past knowledge of the long cultural traditions in Kanepi. Those past achievements were remembered by almost everybody we talked with in Kanepi. The support of the past primarily promotes identity and self-esteem.

The statutes and programmes of organisations once outlawed by the communists have provided the inspiration for starting anew. The head of house of culture explained that the development of the foundations has increased the chances of requesting subsidies for cultural initiatives. Choirs, theatre groups, clubs, etc. have been set up and developed into societies, because it is easier to request subsidies once they are registered. An important stimulus is the opportunity to have the chance to perform at the next all-Estonian Song Festival in Tallinn under the historic flags of the societies in Kanepi. People try to get new folk costumes for the choir. They have started to hold municipal song festivals every three years. There is a plan to send about 200 performers to the all-Estonian Song Festival in 2000 (Palli, 1998).

Besides the amateur groups, new vigour has been instilled in women's and girl's gymnastic groups and the women's choir. The head of the house of culture has also attempted to restart the folk dance group. However, cultural life has been thoroughly feminised – they succeeded in restarting a mixed voiced choir but the folk dance group was unable to recruit any men. Old age pensioners largely support the languid club life. The population lacks sufficient income to become involved in clubs. The head of the house of culture in Kanepi said that the local residents did not have enough money to for their families to attend a club gathering where a modest dinner was served at least once a month. The club-pass, which costs EEK 10–15, seems to be an insurmountable obstacle. Those economically well off have neither time nor interest in the village club. The former collective farm community is becoming deeply stratified.

Youth dances have been arranged on the open air singing stage but it is costly to invite musicians. However, the cultural organiser stated that the worst time of withdrawal from cultural life by the youth and the people in general seems to be over. Today, there is evidence of a revival. There also seems to be some interest in improving the spiritual environment of the municipality among the entrepreneurs in Kanepi: "I would set up a decent bar here, not just a place to gossip, but a place where even educated people would come to entertain their ideas and visions. Twice a month there could be musical evenings to meet celebrities." This vision suggests the influence of the traditions from the Soviet era.[4]

By 1996, Kanepi had recovered culturally. The municipality had restored the infrastructure for basic cultural services. However, the community

---

4   During the Soviet era there were two public spheres: the official (heavily censored) public sphere and the more free verbal sphere. Uncorrupted celebrities were often invited to perform and also to discuss delicate matters in rural districts.

as a whole has atomised and stratified. Economic hardship does not provide the majority of residents with civilised leisure time and the structures for social interaction remain fragile.

Public Safety in Kanepi – the People's Patrol, the Defence League, and the Home Defence

In the Estonia under transition, significant roles were played by grass-root voluntary organisations, both in maintaining public order and in the political struggle. In the towns, public order – the system that controlled activities – relied on the machinery generated by Moscow. In the rural areas, however, quasi-governmental, semi-professional institutions were of major importance in the social-political transformation at the level of local government.

Rahvamalev – the Voluntary People's Patrol The so-called Voluntary People's Patrol (Rahvamalev, the People's Militia) was an extension of the Soviet regime. (It was organised in the USSR from 1958–1961 to assist the regular militia in maintaining public order and combat hooliganism, etc.). The leaders of the People's Patrol were staunch communists to guarantee 'Party control' over the organisation. The People's Patrol in Kanepi had nearly fifty volunteers in its membership but only about twenty were active. The former chairman of the village soviet stated, 'with his hand upon his heart' that the People's Patrol fulfilled an important mission in maintaining public order, in combating drunkenness, hooliganism, traffic violations and other petty crimes.

However, in a state controlled by the KGB the People's Patrol was just a sophisticated instrument to upstage the sovereignty of the people. In Kanepi, the political reliability of the People's Patrol was tested in the spring and winter of 1988, when the authorities planned to disrupt the commemoration of the anniversary of the bourgeois Republic of Estonia. The people were going to burn candles at the remnants of the monument to the War for Independence, which was destroyed by the Communists. Plain-clothed militia and soldiers were used in the cities but in Kanepi, they had to use different tactics. At a meeting of the Party cell, the chairman of the village soviet was instructed to send in the volunteers of the People's Patrol, wearing red armbands, to 'enforce order.' The 'powers that be' planned to antagonise parts of the community to provoke the hostility. "Immediately after the meeting I told the Party organiser that I would not do it," the former chairman remembered. Open co-operation with the red authorities would have been shameful, "we would have been regarded as henchmen of the power," he reasoned.

We can only wonder at the nerve of the Estonian Communist Party in issuing such orders. When the fear disappeared, the disavowal of the *nomenklatura* for the People's Patrol and its renunciation of its criminal powers was a logical development (Semm, 1989). The People's Patrol passed into oblivion following the disintegration of the Estonian SSR. It is most significant that there was no succession or transition from the People's Patrol (Rahvamalev) to the new power structures such as the Defence League (Kaitseliit). One of the founders of the Defence League in Kanepi admitted that he "was the only person in the Defence League having co-operated with the traffic militia. All other members were new, without exception."

Kaitseliit – the Defence League The restoration of the Defence League was part of the restitution project, relying on the institutional resources of bourgeois Estonia. In the interim period between the W.W.I and W.W.II, the Defence League was the backbone in organisation of the village community. The recreation of the Defence League suggested the survival of the idea of independence; it manifested a combative spirit and an eagerness to fight. As a nationalist paramilitary power structure, the Defence League could only be created outside official institutions. For its ideological content, the union relied on the National Heritage Society. In Kanepi, the same people started both organisations. The Estonian Congress Convention in the spring 1990 gave a strong impetus to the development of the Defence League. The proponents for restitution considered the Defence League as their 'National Guard.' The conspicuous prominence of the union in Tallinn also stimulated local activists.

According to a farmer-member of the Defence League, the men of Kanepi were "among the first in Põlva County." However, there is evidence showing that some other places in the county also started early. An enthusiast of the movement in the County of Põlva, Andres Reimer, became officer at the Headquarters of the Defence League in Tallinn. "The idea to hold a meeting to set up the Defence League originated from Leo Vijard, who also started the local subsection of National Heritage Society, and the people around him. Leo Vijard was elected the leader of the Defence League, too," reflected the then deputy chairman.

An activist of the Defence League, a veterinary doctor, stated: "the movement found support first and foremost in Kanepi among the older men that had been members before the 1940 occupation." The first meeting to found the Defence League in Kanepi was held in the repair shop at the collective farm. The equipment and supplies issued by the Soviet Army to the collective farm and stored for mobilisation were now assigned to the Defence League. As one activist said: "part of the equipment, high boots and uniforms were bought with money from the collective farm." Officially, the Kanepi Detachment of the Defence League was restored on 19 June 1990, when the members gathered in the Fire-fighters House. The Detachment was headed by Toomas Lauk, who had been trained as an officer in the Soviet Army (Vijard, 1990).

By April 1990, the press had just enough freedom for the daily Koit to release an appeal to set up the Defence League of Põlva. Toomas Lauk, as the representative of Kanepi, attended the meeting to form the organising committee. He, as a founding member of the Defence League in Kanepi, considered the meeting at Põlva businesslike. "All gatherings were attended by Ralf Palo, the Chief of the Militia in Põlva. Palo said he had majored in law. He did not interfere, but did offer his advice from time to time. Those who were there were excited. They shouted and were noisy, some riffraff seemed to have mingled in the crowd."

It was amazing that the KGB did not interfere. The veterinary surgeon, an activist in the Defence League reflected:

> That made me wonder. Mr Tereste, the Chief of the Põlva Department of the KGB was personally known to me. Põlva is a small place; there are no secrets here. When meeting in the street, we sometimes discussed the situation in Estonia. It was evident that he knew what I was involved in. However, he never asked anything. His attitude to the KGB seemed critical. I was afraid lest he ask some probing questions, because I was not sure what I should answer. But, it never happened. I decided to keep in touch with him, because if there was trouble I could be tipped off or just get a hint of the prevailing mood.

Of course, the KGB knew more or less all about the Defence League. An enthusiast of the Estonian Committee in South Estonia and an activist of the Defence League Ville Sonn, who had also led the Defence League members in Kanepi in staking out the old Estonian-Russian border (which in itself created an international uproar) later confessed that he had worked for the KGB (Sonn, 1995).

Under the statutes for the Põlva Detachment of the Defence League, the members of the Estonian Communist Party could not join it (Eesti Kaitseliidu, 1990). However, as far as ethnic background was concerned, they kept to a republican pattern. Ethnic Russians were admitted as long as they were Estonian citizens and supported the movement.

Therefore, one of the first promoters of the Defence League in Kanepi was an ethnic Russian, whose Estonian was heavily accented. In his own words, he had never experienced "persecution or distrust on the ethnic grounds." The role of the Defence League was formed and transformed, as the opportunities and needs arose. The Defence League faced the same difficulties as the other undertakings in Kanepi. One of the leaders of the detachment admitted: "The overall level of activity is low. People displaying initiative and enterprise are scarce; as a rule they are better educated." The majority of the 'first wave' activists in the Kanepi Defence League had secondary or higher education.

As described above, the Deputy Head of the Detachment in Kanepi was an ethnic Russian that had been trained for the Soviet top army unit, the 'black berets'. He had been displaced with his parents from the County of Pechory (Petseri) to Siberia as a boy. He explained the goals of his activity: "I set myself the task of organising the people of Kanepi to bring public order back to normality. It was tending to fall apart. First of all we set up night patrols." However, there was also preparation for a conflict with Moscow: "We knew that if the worst came to the worst we would be among the first apprehended by the authorities. We built makeshift shelters in the forest to survive the worst period. We were given a wilderness survival course in Põlva. We were taught how to live in the woods. My group prepared a dugout in good time." The dugout was not needed. However, when the participants in the putsch in Moscow issued the order to take Estonia "under military control, we posted men from Kanepi to guard the Valgjärve [TV and FM] transmitters. Patrols from the Defence League also carried out surveillance on passing military units."

The Defence League stayed an unarmed until independence, although several interviewees maintained that weapons were obtained as early as the 'Russian period'. First, they only had shotguns, sports guns, and some pistols. All of them were deviously obtained. In 1991, following independence, carbines from W.W.II were delivered from Finland. As the then head of the Defence League recollected: "they were brought to Estonia taken to pieces and then reassembled."

After gaining independence, the Defence League was assigned to maintain public order with the help of the police. "During the disintegration of the collective farms, pending their auction, their saleable property was amassed in the centre. There were attempts to steal it and anarchy was imminent. Later we guarded the former storage buildings of Russian Army, and also participated in border guard details," said a member of the Defence League.

The Defence League also kept criminals out of Kanepi. If the police carried out major operations, the Defence League was also involved. Unlike the police, they were armed. "There was a time when the situation was dramatically out of control. Cars defied the traffic police orders to stop, muggers assaulted people – the intention to rob proliferated. We were brought in as a deterrent. We were issued helmets to look more frightening. The police was not taken seriously at that time," said the first chief of the Defence League in Kanepi, explaining its role.

However, the image of the Defence League was soon tarnished. "For just one year the Defence League was very active, co-operating with the police. Now, however there is disarray. Whoever has a gun at home does as he pleases, threatening to shoot his neighbour . . ." complained a constable in Kanepi. A former activist in the Defence League agreed with the criticism. However, he added that it all depended on the people themselves: "At Roiu, for example, the Defence League was very active in co-operating with the police." He also cast light on the motivation prompting him to leave the organisation:

> I believe that a member of the Defence League must have a decent family and social position; this would enhance the image of the Defence League. First, I succeeded in imposing my will but then the situation worsened. I opposed admitting pugnacious, quarrelsome fellows, or boozers into the Defence League. But there was no keeping them away; they were flocking *en masse* to the Defence League. When they had the upper hand, I quit. It seems that the authorities in Põlva were more interested in large membership than in its quality.

Kodukaitse – the Home Defence Besides the Defence League, another public safety organisation was created – the Home Defence. It was called into life by another political power – the Government of the Estonian Popular Front. The reason was that the militia was not reliable enough for an impending showdown with Russia, said the later chairman of Kanepi kolkhoz in providing his motive for supporting the local detachment of the Home Defence:

> The Home Defence was the brainchild of [Edgar] Savisaar [Prime Minister 1990–1992]. In 1991, when the village soviet transformed into a municipality, it seemed that the police could not cope on its own, and we needed the Home

Defence. The situation was serious, because every man carried a gun. However, the scope of the Home Defence was limited. It was to provide relief for the police, particularly at night.

Some men who hated the lack of discipline and the style prevailing in the Defence League also joined the Home Defence. The activist veterinary surgeon stated: "The Home Defence failed to become popular at Kanepi, nor was it very active. However, a group of men consolidated it. The group was not large because we insisted on quality." Besides policing the traffic "we settled accounts with some characters who were generally know as Mafia, because they get money by extortion. Some men of that type from Kohtla-Järve settled at Kanepi, too. We told them quietly and without fuss that we have our eye on them and that it made sense for them to leave. They did leave."

During Mart Laar's government (1992–1994), opposition to the Home Defence grew on purely political grounds. Besides their different political backgrounds, the two bodies also had different memberships. As the veterinary surgeon, who later quit the Defence League and went over to the Home Defence, said: "the Home Defence was first and foremost made up of men who were not interested in having a gun at home, but were keen on keeping the streets safe."

The perceptions (e.g., calling the latter an artificial formation) and rivalry in the parallel creation of the Defence League and the Home Defence reflect the wider struggle for power engaged in by the Estonian Committee and the Supreme Soviet (Savitsch, 1990). Because the proponents of the Estonian Committee failed to provoke a conflict-prone opposition at the levels of the village soviet or municipal government (with the village soviet organising the elections of the Congress), Kanepi was not torn by dramatic clashes between different power structures.

One of the first decrees of the Russian general that was appointed as Governor of Estonia by the participants in the communist coup attempt in Moscow in August 1991, was the termination of the Defence League and the confiscation of guns. However, this order was never enforced and the putsch was the hour of triumph for the Defence League. Unfortunately, the Defence League in the now independent Estonia caused a great deal of trouble and annoyance to the local governments. "There are people in the Defence League whose image is extremely tainted. One of them killed his father in Kanepi, another set a house ablaze," commented the headmaster. A founder of the Defence League recollected that the organisation was also used to settle personal disagreements: "One member was sent to prison for two cases of manslaughter; he had killed two Russian businessmen."

The dramatic inability of the Defence League, which had been born out of restitution, to accommodate itself to the new situation is indicative of the depth of the pit of degradation to which society had been cast during Soviet annexation. Before the hordes of Russians marched in (June 17, 1941), the Defence League mainly united the peasants that had fought in the War for Independence, making them the noble masters of land – owners of farm-steads. The Defence League was part of the village-centred hierarchy. The human assets in the 1990s were dramatically different. Generally, the coun-tryside had become a place to host those who had failed to cope in town. In addition, the most active and motivated members in the Defence League quickly moved on to the border guard, the defence forces, etc. The cults of power, violence and coercion that reigned supreme in the Soviet Army had also left their degrading imprints on young people.

Notwithstanding their shortcomings, both the Defence League and the Home Defence played an important role in the fight against the anomalies of a society in transition, particularly in the rural areas, the Estonian hinterland. The danger lurking in the mode of thinking underlying those structures, of the ambitions of the different power groups causing a conflict between the power structures, evaporated as soon as independence was achieved.

Both the weakness of military tradition and, in a wider aspect, the decline of the village community accounts for the fact that the stabilisation of the Republic of Estonia did not bring about a substantial improvement in the work of the Defence League. The rapid change of status from landless kolkhoz workers to independent farmers (carrying a gun!), not supported by a socialisation process, revealed the fragility of social tissues of the society. In the mid-1990s, the relations of the municipality with the paramilitary organi-sations normalised. The Defence League became an integral part of the Estonian Defence Forces, with the Home Defence transformed into a volun-tary police force.

Future of Local Government in Kanepi

The loose and arbitrary superposition of the allegedly collective, in reality the 'administrative property' (collective farm) and the Party-political territorial units that stemmed from the Soviet system, resulted in the degradation of rural areas. The responsibility of the village soviet for the community more often than not lacked economic cover. The traditions of Kanepi and its local interests as mechanisms to support the self-regulation of the cycle of life were excluded from the local administration. The 'local interests' had some hope of finding support, insofar as the 'Soviet cadres' harboured non-Soviet survival, such as interest in the history of the native locality, regionalism, nationalism, or cultural perception in reducing the virulence of Soviet technocracy. Hence, the traits of individuals in vital positions within the Soviet administration played an important role (Raagmaa, 1996, 43). Kanepi as a whole was happy to have passable administrators. In addition, the intensive Sovietisation over two generations was too short a period to wipe out the 'social memory' of the locality.

At the end of the 1980s, community life of Kanepi was largely under the direction of the collective farms, with the goal set to the cultivation of a single agricultural product to the exclusion of other land uses (monocultural plantation), or for the production at the meat packing factory. Farmers became farmhands. As this proletarisation progressed a type of landless farmhand emerged His leisure was increasingly occupied by drinking alcohol and indulging in unsophisticated entertainment.

For the collective farm, the district under the village soviet of Kanepi was the main resource for labour – the collective farm operating as the middleman providing odd jobs and entertainment. The Soviet-style centralised cultural modernisation, effected through the school and the house of culture, both promoted and homogenised the intellectual life in Kanepi. The main prerequisite for local self-government – the control of a citizen over his life conditions and his actual interaction, as an integral being, with his environment, was on the verge of extinction.

The quasi-reform of local governments under the guidance of the Estonian Communist Party in 1989 (with the leading role of the Estonian Communist Party preserved) was thanks to the initiative of the people unexpectedly filled with real content under the banners of political revolution and restitution. The dissolution of collective farms deprived the village soviet, renamed municipality council, of its main partner and economic support. The more or less balanced pair 'collective farm – village soviet' was replaced by the opposite 'municipal council – collective farm', which was followed with the coexistence of 'private interests – municipal council'. There is still a long way to go towards genuine co-operation. The elementary legal environment necessary for the rebirth of the municipality started to assume an outline in 1993. The tax policy, regional development projects and other vital factors are still being worked out.

The outbursts of local identity, which were based on traditional culture and linked the residents of Kanepi with one another at the end of the 1980s, crumbled in the rapid economic decline. The development of Kanepi is now stalled by insufficient economic, intellectual and moral capital. Hence corruption, massive tax fraud and disillusionment. The institutionalisation of the municipality as a unit of local government is not possible without a cultural-historical identity complemented with a modern civil identity. Positive socialisation calls for a developing environment.

The analysis of the development of the Municipality of Kanepi shows that the units of local government born in the upsurge of restitution are too small as carriers of intellectual and economic resources for the development that is necessary. Uniting the municipalities would increase the competition of the elite, consolidate the means, and create the absolutely necessary concentration of capital (provided the money sought from international funds is channelled into development programmes and not repairs, as is currently done). The reform of local governments is on the threshold of major improvements. Effective self-government is one the main conditions both for consolidating civil society and the economic development of the Estonian countryside.

References

Aas, P. (1989), 'Oodata või tegutseda? Tegutseda!' *Koit*, no. 106 (5969), 9 September 1989.

Arengukava (1991), *Kanepi valla sotsiaalmajandusliku arengu kava*, unpublished manuscript.

'Eesti Kaitseliidu Põlva Maleva põhikiri' (1990), *Koit*, 29 May 1990.

Erlich, R. (1985), 'Maa-asulastiku muutumine', in I. Raig (ed), *Maaelu sotsiaalseid probleeme Eestis*, Valgus, Tallinn, pp. 35–49.

Ginter, J. (1992), 'Omavalitsuse areng Eestis 1990–1991', *Õigus*, no. 5/1992, pp. 5–9.

Hirvlaane, M. (1988), 'Kodukant Kanepi', *Koit*, no. 90 (5800), 1 August 1988.

'Kanepi Keskkooli töötajate ja õpilaste koosoleku otsus' (1989), *Koit*, no. 38–39 (5901–5902), 1 April 1989.

Kuus, E. (1991a), 'Kas meil on vaja Eesti Vabariigi isikutunnistusi?' *Koit*, no. 5 (6221), 20 May 1991.

Kuus, E. (1991b), 'Lõhutakse võõrvõimu struktuure', *Koit*, no. 100 (6269), 31 August 1991.

Kuus, E. (1991c), 'Vastab vallavanema kandidaat Ülo Leib', *Koit*, no. 8 (6177), 19 January 1991.

Laas, M. (1996), 'Pettusega koolijuhiks', *Postimees*, 3 June 1996.

Mäeltsamees, S. (1994), 'Kohalikud omavalitsused Eestis', in *Kohalikud omavalitsused Kesk- ja Ida-Euroopas ning SRÜ-s 1994*. Avatud Ühiskonna Instituudi filiaal, Budapest, pp. 73–84.

Palli, I. (1998), 'Kanepi tuleb lauluga Tallinna', *Luup*, no. 14, pp. 8–9.

Pugast, L. (1988), 'Me kogume rahva enda jaoks', *Koit*, 31 March 1988.

Põldmäe, R. (1978), 'Kanepi kanged laulumehed', in T. Vello (ed), *Põlva rajoonis*, Eesti NSV TA, Tallinn, pp. 166–169.

Põlva maakond. Aastaraamat 1996 (1996), Infotrükk, Põlva.

'Põlva maakonna valdade seisukohad maaelu probleemide lahendamiseks' (1994), in *Maarahva kongress 3–4. Märts 1994*, Infotrükk, Tallinn, pp. 308–309.

Raagmaa, G. (1996), 'Regionaalplaneerimise uued suunad – alt üles toimiv strateegiline planeerimine ja avalik osalemine', in *Regionaalne areng ja vabaharidus*, Avatud Hariduse Liit, Tallinn, 7–49.

Raitviir, T. (1996), *Eesti üleminekuperioodi valimiste võrdlev uurimine*, Teaduste Akadeemia Kirjastus, Tallinn.

Reimer, A. (1988a), '.... Ei tule iial tagasi', *Koit*, no. 137 (5847), 24 November 1988.

Reimer, A. (1988b), 'Ärkamise eel Kanepi kultuurimajas', *Koit*, no. 76 (5786), 30 June 1988.

Reino, Ü. (1998), 'Eesti omavalitsustest 20ndate aastate esimesel poolel', in *Eesti Vabariik 80. Kaks algust. Eesti vabariik – 1920. ja 1990. aastad*, Umara, Tallinn., pp. 120–125.

Rüütel, A. (1985), 'Lõpetuseks', in I. Raig (ed), *Maaelu sotsiaalseid probleeme Eestis*, Valgus, Tallinn, pp. 134–137.

Savitsch, A. (1990), 'Kas Kodukaitse on Kaitseliidu alternatiiv', *Lõunakaar*, no. 7, 15 June 1990.

Semm, E. (1989), 'Muudatustest rahvamaleva töös', *Koit*, no. 19 (5882), 14 February 1989.

Sonn, V. (1995), *Võõras: jutustus KGB abilisest*, Marek Soonpuu, Elva.

Tarmisto, V. (1978), 'Saateks', in V. Tarmisto (ed), *Põlva rajoonis*, Eesti NSV TA, Tallinn, pp. 5–8.

Titma, M. (ed) (1980), *Kommunistlik noorsooühing noorte elus*, Eesti Raamat, Tallinn.

Toome, I. (ed) (1986), *Ülevaade Eestimaa Leninliku Kommunistliku Noorsooühingu ajaloost*, Eesti Raamat, Tallinn.

Väljas, V. (1989), 'Ettekanne', in *EKP KK XIV Pleenumi materjalid*, Eesti Raamat, Tallinn, pp. 3–16.

Vihalemm, P. (1985), 'Kontaktid kultuurieluga', in I. Raig (ed), *Maaelu sotsiaalseid probleeme Eestis*, Valgus, Tallinn, pp. 101–107.

Vijard, L. (1990), 'Kaitseliidu Kanepi Malevkond taastatud', *Koit*, no. 87 (6103), 26 June 1990.

Vill, R. (1988), 'See magus valus sõna KULTUUR', *Koit*, no. 33 (5743), 19 March 1988.

6 The Rebirth of Civil Society in Kanepi

REIN RUUTSOO

The Historic Resources and the 'Structure of Opportunities' in Realignment ('*perestroika*')

As a project of power, the Soviet system ruled out civic initiative independent of the State Party (Gill, 1994). The prevalent and all-encompassing Party State was the main vehicle for economic modernisation. In order to subjugate individuals under the dictatorship of the CPSU (the Communist Party of the Soviet Union), various additional control mechanisms were created, which lacked any material relevance to the aspirations or will of the people. The structures created by the administration (trade unions, Komsomol, the so-called friendship and peace movements) helped control and influence the initiative of the people through artful, unfair and insidious means and expand control over the whole of community life – even over the family (Rigby, 1990, 83–112).

In the post-Stalin administrative state, the significance of political terror decreased. However, this did not involve greater democracy for the society. Though the CPSU/ECP (Estonian Communist Party) did not give up their commanding position, the pervasive totality of control slackened. Some elements of 'directing' were added to the administration, meaning an increase in the internal autonomy of the administrative bodies. The indulgence in beliefs and practices differing from official politics and based on a lack of discipline or the demoralisation of the power machinery rather than on liberality functioned as 'repressive tolerance' rather than as a factor that enhanced the self-regulatory capacity of the society. Self-regulation in the domain of power and ideology, underpinning the foundations of the building the Communism, seemed ruled out *en principe* (Lane, 1996, 81).

Unluckily, the effect on the development of the social communication network and the added 'economic autonomy' (first and foremost the dwindling of the hierarchic character of control, the lessening of the ubiquity of

349

politics, and the partial dismantling of the 'Homo Sovieticus', etc.) as observed in the 1960s and 1970s is still inadequately researched. However, it is evident that many studies of the Soviet society, emphasising the new species of 'Homo Sovieticus', have overestimated the destructive effect on the individual in the Soviet system (Allik and Raelo, 1996, 332).

In Estonia, the inborn capacity for initiative and the expanding autonomy within the USSR could not assume the dimensions that would have justified the use of such concepts as the 'parallel society' and the 'second society', by which the success achieved in the West and Central European states in the creation of an alternative cultural life, independent trade unions, etc. could be characterised (Beyme, 1996, 35–42). Hence, both the 'second society' and alternative awareness had to assume hidden forms, within the official institutions.

The extension of social 'autonomy' meant concealed compromises to the doctrine of *dirigisme* in the name of efficiency in economy, culture, education, etc. In agriculture, permitting 'auxiliary farms' (i.e., plot farms) was a bashful retreat where one gained an increased volume of agricultural produce, without making additional investments (people were now permitted to toil away on leased plots of land in the evenings and during holidays). The invigorating effect of people's initiative in cultural life and the activities of trade union and similar organisation, where civic initiative drew upon ideas, were much more dangerous. Here, the pragmatic considerations for softening centralised control remained insignificant – the bureaucratic reports were easier to fake. The unpopularity of Soviet films, empty lecture halls, the yellowed volumes by Brezhnev on the bookshelves, etc., were all ascribed to 'weak ideological work', resulting in more pressure from the Party. Consequently, outside the sphere of the economy, the negative feedback amplified the counter-productive activity of the authorities; i.e., one found oneself in a wicked loop.

That was, however a falling spiral. The de-Sovietisation of the public sphere occurred as a cyclic process, when every reprimand from the 'centre' was accompanied by the concealed liberalisation of 'local' cultural policy – a slackening of control over leisure time, etc. This can be explained by the fact that the administrators really achieved, with less pain, some improvement in 'indicators' of the involvement of people, through this means.

Research into the concealed mechanisms and sources of added civic initiative is one of the goals of this chapter. It is clear that nationalistically motivated organised resistance to the Sovietisation of community life was impossible because of the forceful infiltration by the KGB (Waller, 1994).

Consequently, the resistance to the Soviet administration was largely hidden and spontaneous. It was based on democratic traditions and customs, and on the historic differences between the cultures of Russia (Greek orthodox) and Estonia (Lutheran). The principle of the 'facade'/Potemkin Village was habitual in Russia and characteristic to Soviet society. In fact, Russian bureaucrats welcomed the deceitful ('two-faced') behaviour of the population, which made their duty of reporting great achievements to Moscow easier. This resulted in the creation of a schizophrenic reality to all the parties involved.

Looking at the civil society will provide important additional information and a deeper understanding of the degree to which the collective farmers were social subjects during the transition (the potential 'masters of their own destiny'). What were the resources of the rural dwellers, their historical, value-related, and ideological 'capital', etc. and the communication networks for promoting co-operation and forming their future?

The 'Singing Revolution' in Kanepi in 1987–1990: Political Mobilisation and Mass Movements

The Singing Revolution in 1987–1990 will remain as the time of large-scale mass movements in the annals of history of Estonia. It involved the whole of Estonia and almost its entire population. The three largest among the numerous movements – the Estonian Heritage Society (Eesti Muinsuskaitse Selts), which was founded as early as in 1987, the Estonian Popular Front (consolidated in the autumn 1988) and the movement of Estonian Citizens' Committees launched in 1989 – were important boosters of civic initiative in Kanepi. Besides the important information about the development of the municipality, the recent history about the restoration of civic initiative in Kanepi is the first concrete study into the popular movements in small rural settlements.

Popular Movements in Kanepi – The Popular Front, Coupled with the Restoration of People's Faith in Themselves

The creation of the support groups for the Estonian Heritage Society and the Popular Front in Kanepi occurred more or less simultaneously. There was a slight delay in creating a support group for the Popular Front, which was explained by one of the initiators:

Pastor Raimond Peiker thought that creation of the support group would be successful if the meeting could be associated with a visit and a speech by some public figure. Peiker made an agreement with Jaan Kaplinski [a well-known dissident, poet and essayist] and Kaplinski delivered an impressive speech. Olev Pärna, the vice-chairman of the village soviet, was elected chairman of the support group.

An activist for the Popular Front, the present headmaster of the secondary school of Kanepi, remembered that activities started in June 1988. The "driving force of the Popular Front, as well as the Estonian Heritage Society was Mr D. He was our deputy to the first congress of the Popular Front. The self-assurance of the people had significantly increased." A deputy to the Congress in Tallinn on October 1–2, 1988 reported that it was "an impressive function" (although power was still in the hands of the ECP).

It seems the political agenda of the Popular Front became more prominent in larger towns. In the County of Põlva, the Popular Front assumed an outstanding place among other movements because its members belonged to the Council of People's Deputies of Põlva. In a small settlement like Kanepi, the Popular Front was largely construed as a common label for many types of resistance against the alien power (Vananurm, 1989b).

The ritual character in the use of political labels such as 'support for *perestroika*' by the Popular Front is seen in the composition of the board of the local Popular Front support group. The chairman of the local Popular Front was the vice-chairman of the village soviet (moderately critical of the Soviet system), his deputy was a radical nationalist, and also the anti-Communist pastor had a central role in the activities of the Popular Front. However, like its leader, the Popular Front had a moderate image: "In the societal scale he belonged neither to the right nor to the left, always staying in the middle."

According to a survey in the autumn 1989, the Popular Front had the trust of the majority of residents in Põlva County. Its candidates to the village soviets had the support of 52% of the electorate. The other movements had much less support. The ECP would have received 10% of the vote, the Greens 10%, the Rural Union 9%, the Party of National Independence of Estonia 3%, the trade unions 1.5% and the others a total of 5% of the vote (Vananurm, 1989a). The support group for the Popular Front created in Kanepi maintained close links with the Põlva umbrella organisation, and also benefited from its support at elections. According to a survey in January 1990, the Popular Front in Kanepi was supported by 83%, the Estonian Heritage Society by 75% and the Estonian Congress by 64% of residents of Kanepi.

Support for the ECP was as low as 6.4%. In relation to the marginalisation of the ECP, the then chief of the KGB in Põlva County, Mr Tereste, recommended that the leaders of the civic initiative associations be incorporated into the Soviet structures, possibly to neutralise them (Grigorjev, 1988).

An important idea on the political agenda of the Estonian Popular Front – the IME (Isemajandav Eesti, i.e., Economically Independent Estonia) project – did not have a significant profile at the municipal level. The plan of economic strategy for national independence had no direct bearing on the future of the people. In Kanepi, it was even regarded as just another 'campaign'.

However, on the initiative of the Popular Front it was recommended that the language law was to be passed expediently, and that the right to secede from the Soviet Union was to be pressed at all cost. A memorandum on this was to be sent to the Supreme Soviet of the ESSR in the name of the village soviet. A special session of the Local Council of People's Deputies of Kanepi (i.e., the village soviet) was organised for this purpose. Besides the deputies, it was attended by representatives from the support groups on two collective farms (Kanepi and Kalev) for the Popular Front and by the Estonian Heritage Society of Kanepi. A consensus that the all-Union draft laws, the law on constitutional amendments and the election law were unacceptable for Estonia was reached. The special session demanded the ESSR Supreme Soviet use its full powers (until secession from the USSR) to guarantee the sovereignty of the Republic. The draft language law was given a unanimous support (Pärna, 1988).

Olev Pärna, the leader of the Popular Front in Kanepi spoke up for openness, elections, the restoration of monuments to independence, and the movement of the Estonian Citizen's Committees at the council for the Popular Front of Põlva County (Vananurm, 1989b). In Kanepi, the Popular Front remained, in the public awareness, primarily the standard bearer of anti-Soviet nationalist protest. Its proof is in the fusion of the 'big policy' of two otherwise competitive political directions. "The Popular Front and the Estonian Congress were for us just the same. There was no antagonism", assured a man who used to be an activist in both movements. At the same time, he also expressed his opinion on the Estonian Heritage Society: "The Estonian Heritage Society had a more specific task, the Popular Front being more general – it embraced everything, like thin air. We had the same people in both the Popular Front and the Estonian Heritage Society. Once a person was active, he was involved everywhere." The heightened political radicalisation of the Popular Front in Kanepi was the background to the fusion in the whole of Põlva County and, in general, in the rural settlements. The Popular Front of Põlva County demanded the dissolution of the Supreme Soviet as an extension of the ECP as early as the autumn 1989.

The Estonian Popular Front left a deep imprint on the political awareness of the residents in Kanepi by organising the so-called Baltic chain from Tallinn to Vilnius on August 23, 1989. Three busloads of people from Kanepi, besides those that came in their own cars, stood in the chain. When the collective farm system was being dismantled, the Popular Front was a bystander – it lacked a respective programme of activities. The movement was injected new impetus in May 1990, when the Home Defence (Kodukaitse) was established.

The Struggle for Historic Memory – the Estonian Heritage Society in Kanepi

The Estonian Heritage Society won wider recognition in 1987 when it started putting the graveyards in order. First, the spirit of mutiny was manifested in that piece of Estonian culture that the Communists tried to remove – the restitution of the rightful place of religious culture and the Baltic Germans. In Kanepi Philip von Roth, the pastor at the beginning of the 19th century, was again acclaimed as a prominent local figure.

That the activities of the Society extended into politics in Kanepi was only to be expected. Like a drop of water, they reflected the foul tricks that the ECP and the KGB used to foreclose the restoration of authentic history. The channelling of protest against the state-controlled falsification of history, as was done in the research institutions manipulated by the ECP, into national heritage related activities resulted from an inability to keep civic initiative under check during perestroika. The antagonism between the Estonian Heritage Society and the ECP became more aggravated the closer the research area came to modern history. The 'white patches' of history, as euphemistically dubbed in the ECP vernacular were actually the wounds inflicted during Estonian history by the same party, were waiting to be studied. The crimes of the Communist Party were used by the national movement to 'delegitimise' the authority of the ECP and to stigmatise the entire system.

As with the Popular Front, impact from the outside was essential for the Estonian Heritage Society in Kanepi. A former public official of the village soviet of Kanepi said:

I remember that Mart Laar spoke in the secondary school of Kanepi, in 1986 or 1987 [most likely 1987] to introduce the activity of the Estonian Heritage Society. He also deliberated about the future of Estonia. It was a very interesting speech. They were planning to come with a larger group to put the graveyard in order, but the idea was to stir up the local population.

Kanepi was selected as the place to 'awaken' the people because it had had a glorious past and was rich in heritage. Hence, the half-forgotten history was still a resource. Mart Laar was the same young man who, in 1992, became the first incumbent Prime Minister of the newly independent Estonia.

The efforts of the ECP and the KGB to depoliticise the Estonian Heritage Society were also experienced in Kanepi. The residents of Kanepi had close links with the Heritage Society support group in Võru, having been subjected to repression by the authorities for their efforts to put the graves of those fallen in the War for Independence in order. The group was named 'Column No. 1 of the Youth of Võru'. The Communist harassment of the people putting the graves of the war heroes in order with bloodhounds, water cannons, batons, vandalism and arrest was counterproductive (Saar, 1998). The leader of the movement in Võru, Ain Saar (who was forced to emigrate by the authorities) managed to find time to visit Kanepi, too. Later, the Column participated, under its own colours, at the re-inauguration of the monument to those fallen in the War for Independence in the centre of Kanepi.

As in Võru, in Põlva the Society was also in peril of being closed down, because allegations were made that it was involved in politics (Konn, 1989). The open participation of the Põlva secondary school headmaster in the KGB-led campaign aimed at discouraging school students from joining the Society reflected the general attitude to 'work with schoolchildren'. This left also its imprint on the school in Kanepi and accounts for the 'passivity' of the students. Ostentatiously, the reason for the victimisation was that one of the activists in the movement was Lagle Parek, who had worked on the Kanepi collective farm for some time. (Later he became the chairman of the Party of National Independence of Estonia and the Estonian Minister for the Interior). A human rights activist and prisoner of conscience was not eligible, the KGB thought, to direct the campaign to set up a monument to Stalin's victims (Lehestik, 1988)! A former gulag prisoner and current resident of Kanepi was resolute: "They tried at all cost to prevent any public appearances by people who used to have a prominent place in anti-Soviet activities. Instead they gave preference to the people loyal to the system." In short, this evaluation holds the essence of the 'perestroika' initiated by Moscow. It boils down to sheer repressive tolerance.

Kanepi was also the target of KGB attempts to isolate the Estonian Heritage Society through veiled threats. A man who had served time in a gulag stated: "Through the grapevine, I learned that Mart Laar from the Estonian Heritage Society wanted to interview me in order to record my gulag experience. I was warned by the Rayon Committee to hold my tongue. In a few days, there was Mart Laar in my office with his tape recorder."

To prevent the publication of the reminiscences collected by Mart Laar, the State Attorney's Office of the ESSR charged him with libel against the 'organs' of authority. However, the KGB could do only so much. Any open discussion would have turned into a court session over the justification of the Communist system.

The Estonian Heritage Society of Kanepi was set up on June 6, 1988. About sixty people gathered at the house of culture, and 28 joined the Society. Not all dared put their signatures on the founding document. Mr D was elected as chairman of the Society. His deputies were Toomas Lauk and Merike Kaste, a history teacher at the secondary school (Vijard, 1988). The main business of the Society, besides documenting the crimes perpetrated by the ECP, and the restoration of national monuments, was to be disseminating of anti-occupation propaganda. The first chairman in Kanepi placed the main thrust of the Society in the latter. "It was not just the protection of our heritage, but it was also a political movement. The Society was the shield, the target was repudiating the authorities and goading the people into that line of thinking."

Some Reflections on the Estonian Citizens' Committees and the Estonian Congress in Kanepi

The movement of Estonian Citizens' Committees was spearheaded the restoration of a nation-state and therefore the public adherence to it was no longer a case of just manoeuvring under the cloak of perestroika – it was an open challenge to the power of the ECP. There was a realistic possibility that the movement would be crushed with overwhelming power. The ECP proclaimed the Citizens' Committees movement illegal, however it was politically impotent to fight it – there were few dedicated Communists among the Estonians and the rank and file members no longer feared the Party apparatus. As early as the spring 1989, the Põlva daily newspaper initiated discussion on the movement for independence. The Rural Union, which mainly consisted of the chairmen from the collective farms (nicknamed the 'red barons'), was the only organisation in Põlva County besides the ECP that openly considered the Estonian Congress as splitting the nation (Põlva, 1989). That summer, the daily Koit released a letter of support to Estonian Congress by other influential movements – including the Estonian Popular Front and the Estonian Heritage Society. The ECP remained in complete isolation.

There were no problems in co-operation between the Popular Front and Citizens' Committees; neither was there open opposition from official power structures to the movement in Kanepi (Rahvarinne, 1989). The chairman of the village soviet confirmed that the "promoter of elections for the Estonian Congress [called in February 1990] in Kanepi was the Popular Front and the village soviet." The deputy from Kanepi emphasised:

> The idea of the Estonian Congress reached Kanepi by that same Olev Pärn [who laid the foundation of the Popular Front]. He was an excellent organiser. Vahur Tohver, a teacher, was actively involved in the movement [he was also a deputy to the Congress of the Popular Front], so was the forest warden Rait Hirv and one more teacher whose name eludes me. They organised the registration and held the election.

One radical activist ventured that the support of the local soviet apparatus to the Congress was decisive in Kanepi: "People would not have had themselves registered at the election for the Congress, were it not for the chairman of the village soviet, who encouraged them." In addition to several functions organised by the Congress, names could also be registered at the so-called passport office of the village soviet of Kanepi.

Compared with the larger towns populated with Russian colonists, where the ECP structures were still viable, the official institutions in the countryside crumbled quickly. It seems that the feeling of national solidarity in the Estonian countryside overwhelmed the loyalty to soviets (notwithstanding the sore memory of deportations) by the autumn 1989. In Kanepi, the Estonian Congress had an effective structure, which relied on the Estonian Heritage Society, the Popular Front and Citizens' Committees. The elections to the Congress were far more important than just elections – they were an impressive showdown in the name of independence. The chairman of the municipal council was proud:

> All functions in Kanepi related to the Congress were well organised and of a high level. Also the visitors were classy [i.e., Kanepi was visited by well-known politicians]. The elections were held in the house of culture in Kanepi. The municipal council supported them. At that time [i.e., February 1990], it would

have been sheer madness to oppose the Congress, because that would have amounted to opposing the will of people.

By the time the elections were held, the Põlva daily newspaper Koit had shrugged off supervision by the ECP. As reported by the paper, the committee registering the candidates for the Estonian Congress was headed by Aulis Lokk, who was actively seconded by Uno Verrev (secretary), Marika Oksar, Are Kuld, Ilmar Turba, Enn-Leo Kompus, Maire Õunapuu, Väino Kaste, Helle Türna and Mäidu Kukk. The committee was accommodated at the office building of the Kanepi collective farm (Võrumaa EKK, 1990).

A newspaper article stated that Leo Vijard, Alar Inno, Ilmar Vananurm, Andres Maran and Relvo Värton were running for the Estonian Congress in Kanepi (Keda valida, 1990). As far as the chairman of the municipal council remembers, two deputies to the Estonian Congress were elected in Kanepi. "Here Leo Vijard was elected; actually Kanepi had two representatives, so there was also the pastor Jüri Pallo. Although Jüri Pallo's home was in Parksepa, since he belonged to the Popular Front and was generally active [in Kanepi], there were two deputies elected here." The leader of the Estonian Heritage Society however remembers that the second deputy to the Estonian Congress from Kanepi was Ilmar Vananurm. This discrepancy in recollections largely reflects the certain procedural confusion of the Estonian Congress as an institution of popular initiative.

The activists in Kanepi also tried to directly to affect the Estonian Congress and the work of the Estonian Committee[1] in Tallinn. On the proposal by the union of former gulag prisoners from Kanepi and Põlva, the Estonian Committee requested that the Supreme Council of the Republic of Estonia secure the compensation and all rights of the former political prisoners by law. The chairman of the municipal council, having wasted seven years in the mines of Vorkuta, pushed forward the request in the Estonian Committee in Tallinn:

> The Estonian TV news reported the proposition by the union of the ex-gulag prisoners in Põlva County in the Supreme Soviet and the Government, and also that the Estonian Committee supported it. The picture on TV of me delivering the speech was fuzzy and my face was not recognisable. That was a wise move. At that time, the KGB was still efficient and it was uncommon for the chairman

---

1   The Estonian Committee was the executive organ of the Estonian Congress. It should not be confused with the Estonian Citizens' Committees (there were about 200 of them around the country) that were set up to register people prior to the elections of the Estonian Congress.

of a municipal council to stand up in the Estonian Committee in such a demanding and vindictive manner. At that time such a move was unheard of.

The general fate of the Estonian Congress could also be observed in Kanepi – enthusiasm was followed by doubts and disappointments. Support in the Estonian countryside was recruited from the fundamentalist-restitutive and pointedly anti-Russian factions. The Estonian Congress relied on the countryside to try to overtake power from the Supreme Council. However, Kanepi was not among the municipalities that recognised the Estonian Congress as the sole legal power in Estonia. The chairman of the municipal council reflected on the attitudes of the leaders in Põlva. He summed these up as: "Devil take the Congress. The leadership of the county was made up of people that were against the resolutions of the Estonian Congress."

To find reasons for such an attitude is difficult. The Congress generated a widely spread feeling of disappointment and despondency because it failed to achieve anything of substance. A deputy to the Estonian Congress said: "The people were closely following the activities of the Congress, however its resolutions did not affect the activities of the Supreme Council. The impact was more of a psychological character." That same deputy also described what happened when Rumessen (an ideologist of the Congress) visited Põlva:

> [He was] giving speeches; some interested people gathered in the centre of the county. They were expecting direct help to cope with their daily problems. Rumessen's talk turned out to be far-fetched and much too general. Ploughmen expected some solution or relief. They were still waiting for the 'white ship' [magic wand] that would come and help. In the first place, they hoped for deliverance from the Russian Army and the Russians.

As to the opinion of a central organiser of the elections to the Congress, the "role of Congress to get life in Kanepi going was next to nil."

Hence, the causes for the erosion of the influence of the Congress – inflated hopes and its practical incompetence. The position of the people of Kanepi and, more extensively, the position of Estonia itself turned out complicated. On the one hand, one did not dare grant the Congress full power and on the other hand, one expected more conclusive and resolute activity. However, the plan of activities for the Congress was nothing but unsophisticated restitutionalism – the automatic restoration of property relations as they were before 1940. However, the more realistic vision for the future of the rural people included neither full restitution nor the collective farms. A just and rapid solution could not be achieved through property reform. The ironic reference to the 'white ship' clearly implied the utopian nature of the vision for the future of the village population. The role of the Estonian Congress in further development was the uncompromising execution of the restitutionist property reform.

The restoration of civic initiative in Kanepi gives rise to four fundamental conclusions. First, the massive participation of people in all three main movements corroborates the surmise that the 'singing revolution' was backed by the entire population and not just the city elite with their ideas. Second, the hegemony of the 'singing revolution' belonged to the intelligentsia of the humanities, represented by white-collar employees and officials in the rural areas. Third, the mechanism alerting the masses was the mobilisation of national identity, which later proved hard to translate into a language of 'interests'. Fourth, the community of Kanepi had no adequate social leverage and intellectual capacity for the clear-cut differentiation of movements and their programmes. All movements kept within the dominating national and anti-Communist narrative.

The Mobilisation of National and Local Identity in 1988–1991

The years of 1988–1991 will remain as an era of hope and good deeds in the history of Kanepi, as well as in the whole of Estonia. The collectivist economy and organisation of life were still valid but the added freedoms encouraged enterprise. The two pivotal 'personal resources' needed for civic initiative, leisure and money, were much more available than a couple years later. Those resources, as well as the novel employment of Soviet collectivism, supported the tidal surge of social energy.

The restoration of community awareness in Kanepi, the democratisation of relations, the authentication of collective memory, etc. reveal, on the micro level, how and to what extent societal prerequisites and social capital evolved into natural common activities and supported the restoration of the national-symbolic world of values. It is just as instructive to observe the methods used by the ECP to block national-anti-Communist mobilisation by using both the organisational and the symbolic world.

Local Identity Building and the 'Days of Kanepi' – 1988, 1989 and 1990

The public functions that attracted thousands of people over three successive years (1988, 1989, and 1990) are known as the 'Days of Kanepi'. Because these functions mimicked the festivities of 1926 and 1934 following the first independence rather than the more recent local 'song festivals' that brought the 'comrades of the frontline', 'fraternal peoples', etc. together, which were sanctioned under the Soviets (Kermas, 1978), the political content of those days was unequivocal. The cultural-symbolic restitution of independence was the first step. The 'organisational capital' deposited during the song festivals of the Soviet era and the 'civilisation competence' inherited from the so-called 'Estonian period' (the first republic) amalgamated.

The 'Days of Kanepi' is an excellent example of political mobilisation through the valuation of culture and the history of the native locality. Having censored much of the national character of culture, the Communists had in reality already created the expectation of a 'counterculture'. The 'Days of Kanepi' organically fused into the overall pattern of the mobilisation of the nation-wide 'singing revolution'.

The Days in 1988, even though the colours of previous banned national-ist organisations were already displayed, was still rather 'composed'. A resolution enacted by the Presidium of the Supreme Soviet on January 12, 1988 (Täiesti, 1993), following a confidential ordinance from the Central Committee of the ECP, made it criminal to use the symbols of the Republic of Estonia. That hastily composed resolution was published with exceptional speed in the daily newspaper, the Koit (Vaht, 1988). To oppose the resolution, a chimney stack at the local heating plant in Krootuse was painted with stripes in three colours one night in the spring 1988 – blue, black, and white – the colours of the banned Estonian flag.

The 'free microphone' was the highlight of the Days. It was attended by one thousand people and representatives of the church. Besides the tradi-tional dancing and singing festival, people spoke truths (more or less) about the past in Kanepi at a conference on history. The restoration of the monu-ment to the War for Independence played a significant role in the restoration of historical awareness.

The biggest successes for the Days of Kanepi were the events organised in 1989. They were openly political – the gathering was used to recruit support for the Estonian Congress; the songs, once considered 'anti-Soviet' (including the Estonian national anthem) were collected and printed in a booklet.

It was evident that the Days in 1990 lacked their earlier politically mobilising role. People were just getting ready for yet another all-Estonian song festival in Tallinn. To be exact, it was in Kanepi that one of the torches to be taken to the nation's capital was lighted. There was a high-level conference on economics. It was dedicated to the future of Kanepi and attended by Raimond Hagelberg, a native of the locality. There were all the signs that society was changing.

The next 'Days' were postponed for the distant future – the political contretemps and the 'identity condition', underlying the success of the Days had alleviated. The economic situation got worse and there were fears that the 'singing revolution' might turn into a 'singing occupation'. Instead of the common expression of general collective interests, one set about searching for a strategy for individual adjustment in conditions of increasing social-economic involution.

The Restoration of the Monument to the Heroes of the War for Independence

The year of 1988 was an apogee in restoring the monuments to the War for Independence. If it had not been for the restoration of the monument, the activities of the local support group for the Estonian Heritage Society would have been limited to reminiscences. However, the restoration of the monument turned out an immense and pivotal undertaking. Actually, Kanepi was the sixth municipality to again erect the stele; there were 28 steles restored in Estonia in 1988. The success of residents of Kanepi was also explained by the fact that the explosives originally used to tear it down did not fully fragment the stele, and some remnants failed to fall into the lake. Those four to five months when the people were busy with the stele (from June to November) were an important epoch in dismantling the Soviet power in Kanepi.

The first half of 1988 was largely a mental preparation for the change in official attitudes to the War for Independence. The War was usually presented as the suppression of the people's revolution by British imperialism and Finnish butchers. The remnants of the stele had been lying face down beside the church for 40 years. It was a silent monument to the terror of the Communists, a taboo too dangerous to be named; one dared not mention it for fear of even those few fragments being destroyed. In addition, there was a personal fear about the future. Although *perestroika* vouched *glasnost* (openness) and democracy, they were allowed only within the framework of the so-called socialist *Rechtstaat* (rule of law). The chairman of the village soviet intimated that the mood of the people was under vigilant surveillance:

> The KGB men never failed to remind you of them. They did not directly interfere but they were observing what was going on. They tried to find out what was underway and how the erection of the monument stood. They also wanted to know what the village soviet's stance to all this was. They tried to leave the impression that our activities were likely to bring about conflicts and public unrest.

The interest displayed by the secret police was a warning in itself. The secret police was primarily trying to intimidate the local public servants.

The status of the monument in Kanepi changed as early as in 1987, when people unobtrusively started to lay flowers at its site. As a teacher in Kanepi said, for many families the stele was "a monument to slain relatives, whose names were carved onto the stone slab. Now, the candles were no longer taken away like they used to be, but the [local] KGB functionaries tried to find out the identity of those having brought the candles, even by interrogating the schoolchildren."

Celebrating Independence Day[2] on February 24 in Kanepi, and throughout the whole of Estonia, in 1988 turned out to be a breakthrough because the people overcame their prevalent fear. The memory of the chairman of the support group for the Estonian Heritage Society shows how that memorable night developed:

> On the evening of February 23, I was in the workshop. We had a glass or two in honour of the coming independence day and thought about how it should be celebrated. It was in the air; we couldn't go on like this any longer. With searching minds, our group of men listened to the Voice of America. Rammo Andres and Kuke Ats were there. Kuke Ats said 'Look here! I will go and sweep the place round the monument and lay some fir branches and put up candles'. We agreed that 3–4 men should go. The head of the workshop heard what was up and warned us, saying 'You'd better not go, lest something happen'. I was a bit late and at seven there was a phone call saying that Kuke Ats had been apprehended. Ats had been sweeping the snow near the memorial stone. He had been arrested by a Major in the KGB. It seemed that first Ülo Leib had come up and asked, 'What are you pottering about here, Ats?' Ats had remonstrated that he had swept the snow there on earlier occasions and set the candles, too. After that the Major had approached him and had ordered Ats to get into his car. Ats had been taken to the next crossroads and released. The KGB man had asked Ats

---

2   The first republic of Estonia was declared independent on February 24, 1918.

when Parek would come. They knew that Parek had visited here and he sounded Ats out whether they had met.

Lagle Parek was staying in Tartu at that time. She had been threatened that if she dared turn up in the street, she would be physically harmed (Laar, Ott and Endre, 1996, 269).

The attempt by the KGB and ECP to force the members of Voluntary People's Patrol (Rahvamalev) to prevent candles being set was abortive. However, the above action was not the brainchild of the Party Committee in Põlva, but a part of the scheme of activities elaborated under a confidential resolution by the ECP. The leader of the Estonian Heritage Society in Kanepi saw "the chairman of the village soviet with a stranger on the lookout in the square facing the church, all day long the next day." The intimidation continued as the main means for psychological terror. "The brother of Ats, Kalmer Kukk was a member of the militia. He warned us that it would be wise for us to stop because the KGB already has a file on us. He warned us that the times might change and then we would be packed off to Siberia. Ats, however, retorted that the times *were* different, as they were."

Perhaps the winter intimidation accounts for why the people, when establishing the support group for the Estonian Heritage Society in Kanepi in the summer 1988, were still extremely cautious and, "at the meeting nobody dared say outright that the monument must be restored. The older men did not dare undertake anything, Vijard with his friends set it up again," said a local amateur historian. However, the head of the Estonian Heritage Society rated the role of veterans highly:

> The veterans of the War for Independence kept the matter close to heart. A man named Maiste had a picture of the monument on him at the meeting. The honouring of the then recumbent monument became an essential part of the 'Days of Kanepi'. There were flowers set at the stele, with the women's choir singing. There was the [practical] problem of locating the means and equipment for the work. The job called for powerful equipment and machines.

In summer 1988, the 'official attitude' towards the War for Independence underwent a drastic change. The Põlva Rayon Committee of the ECP, finding itself under the criticism of the Popular Front, conceded in public that "the destruction of monuments was an act of vandalism." Only four months after the events in Kanepi, it was announced that "the leadership of the rayon will support the restoration of monuments and consider it natural that such activities will be supported by local soviets, institutions, collective farms, enterprises, and all those inclined to engage in such acts" (Aas, 1988). In July, Kanepi was visited by the chairman of the Executive Committee for Põlva Rayon. He allegedly had a look at the recumbent stele and said to the leader of the Estonian Heritage Society support group: "This is such a beautiful stele. It is a shame that it should be left lying here." He advised it be set up in the centre of Kanepi, just where it stands today.

The contribution of the local residents was needed to restore the half-destroyed stele to the War for Independence (KMS, 1988). Later, the help of construction units in Võru and Põlva came in handy. The re-consecration of the stele on August 1988, as originally planned, failed – there were not enough machines, nor were there sufficient up-and-going people. The then headmaster of the secondary school remembered that the chairman of the collective farm was not against the restoring the stele: "We visited the chairman and discussed where it [the stele] should be set up, in front of the school maybe. I think that was a good place because several school ceremonies could be held near the stone. I also heard that the collective farm financially supported the initiative." The local leader of the Estonian Heritage Society said that donations were also collected. The work started like bees in a hive; in August they started digging a hole – without an official permit. "We got the machines and started to dig. Nobody left when the rain poured." The hamlet followed developments, holding its breath. "Nobody moved in the streets; people stayed at home during the time when we were digging. We decided that come what may we must be ready with the hole by daybreak." The men were not discouraged by the fidgety approach by the village soviet to this civic activity that was not only politically flammable but also lacked legal coverage. However, as the work progressed during September the people joined in wholeheartedly:

> The largest problem was how to get six cubic meters of mortar quickly. There were only a couple of men available when the invitation was circulated but quite a few people arrived, everybody who had tools. There were construction workers carrying boards; everybody did their best and everything was a success.

The leader of the restoration remembered that the head of construction on the collective farm charged the Põlva office of the Joint Construction Company of the Kolkhozes (Kolhooside Ehituskontor), the Road Construction Team of Võru and the collective farms for the materials (mortar, stone, the use of cranes, etc.). The stone was set in the centre of Kanepi in its proper place with a powerful tractor by Kuke Ats, whose fingers the KGB had twisted in the winter. The crane was procured by Järg, the Party Organiser at the Põlva office of the Joint Construction Company of the Kolkhozes. He was a member of the Estonian Heritage Society of Kanepi.

The monument to those slain in the War for Independence was reinaugurated in Kanepi on September 25, 1988. The Master of Ceremonies was Georg Pelisaar, the head of Popular Front of Põlva rayon. He made the event a public occasion. There was a performance by the Union for the Blind of Tallinn Choir and the Põlva Brass Band. There were also five veterans of the War for Independence. They had survived deportation and had succeeded in hiding their involvement in the fight against the Russians. One of them had attended the first dedication of the monument in 1926. He was too overwhelmed with emotions to speak at the ceremony.

At the same time, it was clear that the people were still in the grip of fear; the ECP still strove to stay in control. The leader of the Kanepi support group for the Heritage Society was still angry when he recollected that the "chairman of the village soviet said, 'you'd better keep two flags ready on the flagpole – one blue-black-white and the second red, just in case. If there's trouble, we'll hoist the red one'. I remonstrated, 'Look, we can get the flagpole ready, but I will never hoist that flag'. If I had done that, the people would have lynched me."

The absurd proposition of the chairman of the village soviet was not his own concoction; it was part of the plan prescribed by the Central Committee of the ECP, to 'ennoble' the Soviet symbols. A similar plan was also proposed in Põlva, when, at the official commemoration of the day of deportation, the red and the blue-black-white flags where set side by side. The manoeuvres by the henchmen of the ECP aroused deep indignation (Pärnaste and Niitsoo, 1998, 508, 596). The ECP did not give up its struggle for the symbolic world and it even ordered the red flag hoisted to honour of those who had fallen in battle fighting against it! The leader of the Estonian Heritage Society in Kanepi estimated that about 20 KGB men had infiltrated among those gathered.

The last largest undertaking by the Estonian Heritage Society in Kanepi was in the spring 1989. It was a conference to commemorated the March Deportation (1949); like all other occasions, the KGB monitored that function, too. The local leader of the Estonian Heritage Society said:

> On March 25, there was a big meeting in the house of culture. Professor Aadu Must and an elderly man whose name I don't recall attended. Olev Pärna, who knew all the local KGB men by sight, came and said that one of them had arrived

in Kanepi and had left his car at the church. When he [the KGB man] had noticed that he was being followed, he disappeared among the houses.

By 1989, the role of the notorious 'organ' (KGB) was on the decline. At the same time, the public and honest commemoration of the March Deportation had dotted the 'I's and crossed the 'T's in recalling the 'bloody patches' in history to their originator and perpetrator – the Communist Party of Estonia.

The Collapse of the Estonian Communist Party; Political Reorganisation and Reforms

Besides the coercion, there are references to a mythical 'collectively charismatic' authority in several works dealing with the heart of the power in the ECP (Jowitt, 1992). Actually, the best part of the Estonian rural population only became reconciled to the system of collective farms as late as the 1960s. Hence, the 'charisma' of the power of the ECP in the Estonian village is questionable.

Over the years the Communist Party changed. The party, which used to organise and supervise the mass terror against the peasantry in 1949, was clearly regarded as something very different from the Estonian Communist Party that did not actually block the restoration of the monument to those who fell in the War for Independence in Kanepi in 1988. Deplorably, the transfiguration of the ECP has not been studied in any detail. By tracing the transformation of the power machinery in the ECP and the collapse of its might on micro-level (by the example of the 'primary Party organisation' of the collective farm of Kanepi) we would be able to elucidate the changes in the proportions of coercion, routine and belief in the acts and practises of the occupying power.

The Enforcement of Power by the ECP in the Estonian Village; the Opportunism of the Particular Policy Pursued (suaviter in modo)

The initiative of the people in Kanepi was also paralysed because of the pervasive scheme of power. The secretary of the primary ECP organisation was also the vice-chairman of the collective farm in Kanepi (actually the Commissar). In addition, there was a Party cell in every department of the collective farm. The workers were faced with a predicament from which they were unable to extricate themselves and actually amounted to a violation of human rights. "You had to join the Party on the collective farm and at school, otherwise you wouldn't have been given a chance to develop your talents and abilities" explained the former chairman of the village soviet, giving his reasons for joining the Party. The collective farm accountant stated that he kept his convictions and did not yield to pressure. The vice-chairman of the collective farm also faced a Catch 22: "They repeatedly wanted to recruit me into the Party. I told Comrade Madisson [the Secretary of Põlva Rayon Committee of ECP] that if I could not keep the job of the vice-chairman, I was quite willing to quit. And this was how it [the pressure] actually ended." It was not easy for the ECP to find a cadre in the rural districts. For instance, in the years following the 'Thaw' of the sixties (1963–1974) the chairman of the village soviet of Kanepi was a non-party member. However, he was later dismissed. When he joined the ECP, he was restored to his office.

According to some retrospective estimates, the beliefs and convictions of the Communists totally lacked support in the Estonian village. "I think the number of Estonians with Communist views and outlook was negligible. The majority of people were just keen on winning their daily bread. So was I," explained a man who for decades used to be in the ECP *nomenklatura*. It was known that the former chairman of the village soviet had been convicted to hard labour in the mines in Siberia and that later he had converted to "an active proponent of the Soviet power, being now an advocate for the Republic of Estonia." His Soviet-period zeal was frowned upon, and he was considered rather an opportunist, not a dedicated Communist.

The former headmaster, a man that had belonged to the power apparatus, now stressed his background – something he had earlier denied:

> I come from a family of farm owners, a close relative of mine used to be an officer of the Estonian Army, my uncle served 12 years hard labour in Karaganda, and another relative of mine was executed. My father was wanted by the police for years after the war. I couldn't finish secondary school because I was not a Komsomol member. Later I joined the Party and I was then offered the headmaster's job. I was elected to the Local Council of People's Deputies [i.e., the village soviet], then to the ECP Rayon Committee.

He did not mourn the downfall of the ECP, although he was bitterly critical about the economic reform. He left the Party at the first opportune moment. However, the people did not trust this chameleon; he was fickle, lacking steadfastness. The loss in confidence, a vital component of social capital, and the decline in mutual respect were the destructive results of the Soviet system.

The distribution of the so-called 'short supply goods' also fell within the domain of the ECP, so people were goaded into the Party with the helpings of food and manufactured goods. "The Party Committee distributed the goods delivered to the village soviet. You then called your friends telling them to come and buy them," said a resident of Kanepi when explaining how the system of privileges worked.

In the 1980s, the Party cell on the collective farm in Kanepi started to wither away. The former vice-chairman of the collective farm estimated that it had 40–50 members, including old-age pensioners. The ECP primary organisation in the school had a dozen members. The activities of the ECP in the village were becoming a formality, a mere playacting. "The Party work at school was carried out mainly on paper," explained a teacher. The former assistant headmaster at the school said their Party cell anticipated and forestalled conflicts instead of exposing them or 'laying them bare', as the common jargon went. "Politically, we had no problems with students. When something happened, no one created a hullabaloo, which would have triggered a problem."

The salaried Party secretaries, the 'spongers, the pests of society', as they were later described by the former accountant of the collective farm, were not respected. "Actually the Party organiser did nothing but collect the monthly fees", said the lady. The Party secretary was respected by whether and how he interfered with the rational organisation of life. This explains why the leader of nationalists in Kanepi did not hold anything against the local head of the ECP:

> When I came to work on the Kanepi collective farm on September 10, 1981, the Party organiser was Arno Tamm, an engineer by training. He was also the vice-chairman. His roots were in Kanepi. He understood being a Party man in a very Estonian way. He never harmed anybody. He just happened to have the appropriate background. His mother had been associated with the Reds, and his father was killed by local servicemen during the German occupation. He thought that the official Party line was to be kept apart from real life, so policy had to be twisted to meet the people's interests.

The former vice-chairman of the collective farm thought the same: "In general, the Party members understood the rank and file of the people and their wishes. At least they understood the problems of the rural economy." Nobody expected them to embark on creative business-like Party activity.

The period of Perestroika ('realignment') was decisive for the village Party organisers. The last of these organisers, who was assigned the task of banishing Lagle Parek (the future Minister for the Interior of the Republic of Estonia) from Kanepi, gave his motives to the chairman of the village soviet as follows: "Power has been vested in the workers and the peasants, who have established their dictatorship." The chairman of the village soviet suggested, on his part, that "the man has been educated at the Leningrad Party School and is therefore just stupid." The prevailing belief was that the roots to this primitive line of thought were to be sought in Russia.

The survey of Kanepi proves that the ECP also held on to power during the Perestroika, relying on the 'production' of fear and not on the newly created beliefs in the Party, as claimed by the ECP (Väljas, 1989). The failure to display power, which was also designed to be displayed in Kanepi, on the orders of the ECP Central Committee on February 24, 1988 (the arrest of Kuke Ats) showed that the Party was deeply isolated in the countryside and its capacity was permanently impaired. Political initiative was seized by the militarised KGB, which used the Party as its legal extension (cf. the Days of Kanepi – the Restoration of the Monument to the War for Independence). In the summer 1988, the local apparatus of ECP in Kanepi was already manoeuvring to evade a collision with public opinion. "Comrade Paisnik was a Member of the Party Bureau. I asked Paisnik about developments. However, he said that he had no opinion on the subject. Nevertheless, he never interfered. The Party Secretary, Comrade Mölder, replied that he was not a local resident and he knew nothing about the matter, nor did he want to get involved," recalled an activist for the restoration of the monument. However, the Party organiser in the construction team was a Heritage Society activist who supported the restoration of the monument.

In the second half of 1988, the disintegration of the ECP became an open secret. The Chief of the Põlva KGB, Comrade Tereste, voiced his concern in November 1988 in the rayon daily newspaper: "the best Communists are quitting the Party." The ECP must have been quite weak for its members to desert it without any fear of reprisals. The peripheral rural areas witnessed the Party crumble even earlier.

However, people also tried to make use of the Party. In 1989, the Party organisations in the rayon of Põlva openly opposed the policy of the CPSU. The Party cell in Kanepi school sent (with the local Komsomol group) a letter of protest against the Intermovement (the movement of pro-Russia activists), which was hostile to Estonia. Also, in an open letter to the ECP, the primary organisation on Kanepi's neighbouring collective farm, Rand vehemently denounced a campaign of terror spearheaded against the youth of the Baltic States serving in the Soviet Army (Ranna, 1989).

The ECP went to great lengths to stave off the exodus of Estonians from the Party. By the spring 1989, it reneged its principles and established an ECP independent from the CPSU. The chairman of the village soviet recalled:

> The Party organiser on the collective farm held another special meeting. Mr Palmaru from Tallinn attended. He represented the Estonian-minded ECP. We were nonplussed. The speeches suggested independence, a market economy and private property were in store in the future. First the people were reluctant to speak up, mistrusting the visitors. I took the floor. A couple of men supported me. A man from Palmaru's team assured us that we were moving in the right direction, reiterating that the direction was the only one to be followed. Whereupon everybody laughed, and our fears were dispelled.

However, by sanctifying and legalising 'nationalism' and private property, the ECP eroded its *raison d'être*. What it was promising now, was just the same as all other parties were promising.

Here is a description of the collapse of the so-called Estonian-minded ECP in Kanepi by an ECP activist: "Everything proceeded simply. As far as I remember, the letter from the ECP was signed by [Vaino] Väljas [Secretary General of the ECP]. The letter said that those willing were free to quit the Party. Consequently, nobody wanted to stay in the Party. Membership cards were handed over to the Rayon Committee, the school organisation was also wound up." The vice-chairman of the collective farm said, "you never noticed that the Party was no longer there." The ECP organisation on the Kanepi collective farm ended. It was among the first in the county. As the school headmaster said, the ECP primary organisation in the school was liquidated earlier than that on the collective farm. The reason was the simplicity of the process – a small organisation was easier to dissolve than a large one. The collective farms had already 'dismissed and forgotten' the party. Hence, the ECP did not breath its last breath in a struggle of political *programmes*, and it did not collapse as a political association failing to stand its own in an ideological competition. It evaporated into thin air as a stigmatised, useless and discarded structure.

The Väljas-minded local apparatus in Põlva attempted to keep the disintegration of the ECP at bay by infusing fear into the hearts of men. "There was a call from the personnel department of the ECP Rayon Committee warning us that we would be brought to account for the forced liquidation of the Party." There was intimidation, "you will be very sorry and will acknowledge your guilt, and you'll soon be asking for your papers [ECP membership card] back." The people of Kanepi held that they just tried to safeguard their convenient featherbedded jobs and not the Party interests.

Nevertheless, not everybody found it easy to make such drastic decisions, to expose their ideas and make their frame of mind public. The local vet and head of the Defence League (Kaitseliit, or *Schutzkorps*, as it used to be translated under the Soviets) said people had 'two flags ready in the cellar'. The same view was reiterated by another founder of the Defence League; the people were "of the opinion that the destiny of the country would be moulded in the capital [and not in the countryside]." Furthermore, they failed to understand the local issues within the context of the so-called 'wider policy'. This prevented many Estonians from leaving the ECP for fear of its being overwhelmed by the pro-Moscow oriented Party members. The people of Kanepi reported that for the Moscow-minded people did attempt to set up an ECP organisation in Põlva.

The Lines of Force in the Political Life of Kanepi

Public political life in Kanepi in the 1990s was somnolent. Those surveyed had political preferences but there were few people actively involved in party work. The extent and importance of political organisation were reflected by political rivalry – primarily related to elections. This rivalry was seen in the local elections in 1989, 1993 and 1996 and in national elections in 1990, 1992 and 1995, as well as in 1999.

The political struggle of the parties was clearly visible in Kanepi during the 1990 elections to the Supreme Council. This culminated at the 1992 elections to Riigikogu (the Estonian Parliament) and 1993 municipal elections. The local leader of the Estonian Heritage Society suggested that the "movements [the Estonian Popular Front, the Estonian Congress and the Estonian Heritage Society] had no impact on the elections and no role to play in them." All basic political directions looked for sustenance elsewhere and several interest groups turned into political parties. The efforts of the chairman of the municipal council to develop the 'Memento' (Eesti Oigusvastaselt Represseeritute Liit, Estonian Union for Illegally Repressed People) movement into a political force was abortive. The 'Estonian Party for Illegally Repressed People' (founded December 24, 1991) failed to become an actor either in Kanepi or nation-wide. "We imagined that the political prisoners had an important role to play in Estonian policy. Now, however, the movement seemed to founder. Heino Ainso had it right when he said that we would hardly influence policy by relying on the elderly." Neither did the party round the pastor, representing the Christian Union, succeed.

The Rural Union also had its representatives in Kanepi but there was no local association. The attempts by the chairman of the municipal council to restore the old liberal rural party, the Agriculturists' Assembly, failed to rally support. The economic and socio-cultural structures, which would have provided the content for 'historical' ideology, were no longer there. Pensioners came out at the 1993 municipal elections with their own slate – they were the only group with a clear link to the central party organisations in Tallinn.

At the beginning of the decade, the politicians from the cities eagerly agitated in the countryside. In 1989, the municipality was visited by the leaders of several movements and parties – Marju Lauristin, Indrek Toome, Arnold Rüütel, Jüri Toomepuu, Kaido Kama, Mart Laar, etc. The visits were organised by the municipal government. One can colourfully recall the apogee of party-political activity – the 1992 elections to Riigikogu. In Kanepi, this was the only occasion when party-politics had a significant role in parliamentary elections, which primarily are elections of individuals. Several parties had zealous proponents in the municipality. An activist from Isamaa Party said: "We had very close contacts with the headquarters in Tallinn. Everything we needed was delivered without delay – paper, publications, and advertisements." Since the activist was the [later] chairman of the collective farm, he was able to use the resources of his workplace in the election campaign. "I never wanted money from them [Isamaa Party] for organising the election campaign. I was the chairman of the collective farm; I could use the farm buses to arrange tours and so on. Isamaa paid for the brass band we used for the election campaign. We travelled over the whole district in one week. Each member of the orchestra was paid 100 kroon per night, plus free meals and drinks." When Mart Laar and (Kaido) Kama visited here, "a grand party was held in their honour near the lake." The number of participants at the election events, however, never exceeded 20–30. The Reform Party also enjoyed active support, mainly among businessmen and other educated people, such as the local vet.

Although the same isolated activists were available, more permanent political structures never formed in Kanepi. The local people said that the Reform Party had its county organisation in Võru and the Isamaa Party and the Social Democrats had their county organisations in Põlva. The headmaster suggested that central issues in political preferences were the exchange of opinions on jobs and the circle of one's acquaintances. The librarian thought the same. "I think everybody had his preferences. The campaign affected only

20–30 per cent of people. In the countryside, it is also important what your neighbour thinks. People actively discussed the elections." However, "they found it hard to decide between the parties, so individuals were elected and not parties. This explains why [Arnold] Rüütel won here." The repute and image of individuals came to the fore against the abstract nature of the background to party programmes (Rüütel was chairman of the Supreme Council and Toomepuu emphasised that he was a retired US Army officer).

At the 1993 municipal elections in Kanepi, the main controversy was the national election slogan of Isamaa Party – 'Make a Clean Sweep'. Although dismantling the Communist system in Kanepi was much less painful than in the towns, the rancour towards the former regime was sufficient to be used. "People were fooled with slogans and catchwords, nobody was familiar with the actual programmes," said the former chairman of the municipal council. The group that won the municipal elections in the wake of Isamaa did not see any cardinal difference between their programme and those of other parties. In their opinion, "any group having won the elections would have acted in the same way, the question was just who would be wielding power." The very limited economic options of the municipalities set rigid restrictions on any plans and programmes – there were no means for pressing ahead with large reorganisation or for promoting active economic policy. The electorate also considered the problem as:

> The people were indifferent to who would eventually be elected because the promises of the candidates were no longer taken seriously. The important thing was whether a new man would be elected or the old leader of the municipality would remain in office. The people were glad because a new man was elected. He would have new ideas. The former municipal director would not have been likely to embrace any new ideas.

One activist gave the opinion that power in the municipality provided a number of lucrative economic opportunities, "either a forest felling contract, or some other job, like access to the levers of power." Hence, underlying the formation of groups were also direct economic interests.

However, at the 1993 municipal elections the opposition between the 'former figures' (from the Brezhnev era of stagnation) and the 'new figures' (the anti-Communists) had also the programme-related content. The 'former figures' consolidated round the Association of Rural Population and, with the pensioners, supported the social programmes and protective customs tariffs of the rural economy. The candidates from Isamaa Party were supported by the church and the Defence League. In the municipal council, Isamaa and the associated Deputies won a narrow victory (7 seats out of 15).

With the economic decline in the rural municipalities, by 1996 the municipal government became ever more important. In the 1996 municipal elections the number of lists of candidates decreased from seven to three. The candidates were expected to show greater expertise, responsibility and ethical behaviour. The antagonism between the Past and the Present in the village receded. To win the elections, the former chairman of the village soviet, the later chairman of the collective farm Kalev and the pastor, an activist from Isamaa all decided to co-operate. Subsequently, the candidates of the 'Association of the People of the Municipality' overwhelmingly won the elections. "The people were content, the municipal director did not get involved politically [in the elections] in any way, although his views were right wing," explained one prominent figure in Kanepi.

Hence, at the level of political organisation in the municipality, the Soviet-period corporate relations (which relied on the life of the collective farm, the membership in the CPSU, and the administrative position) were insignificant and did not have the pivotal social capital to promote the formation of groups. The poverty of the rural district provided a potentially greater power for the entrepreneurs than the parties had. However, in the opinion of residents of Kanepi there was no such economic power to effectively influence the election results. The main type of social capital was the capacity for co-operation. This was based on responsibility and it took practical needs into account. A knowledgeable and businesslike attitude was considered of primary importance for the local leader.

The Church as a Source of Social Capital

In the Soviet society, the church was an off-system, a non-Soviet phenomenon. Nonetheless, it was not eliminated. Unlike all other Soviet organisations, the church had no primary Party organisation to direct it. However, the church was prevented from operating within society because of its total infiltration by the KGB (Jürjo, 1996).

The pressure on the church depended largely on the local leaders (Hart, 1993). In Kanepi, that pressure was rather strong. The pastor's mansion, which was associated with the memory of Baron Philip von Roth, was the oldest construction in Kanepi. It dated from the beginning of the 19th century and it was pulled down on orders from the ECP. The pastor of Kanepi recalled that "the roof over the massive cellar vaults and the walls were demolished. They built the collective farm offices on the site." The fate of the Erastvere cemetery was also sad. "In the fifties, the cemetery of landlords, the burial ground of some of the most renowned German noblemen of Estonia was destroyed with the chapel of German landlords." Both those atrocities are remembered in Kanepi with bitterness, and the blueprints of a plan to convert the old church building into a storehouse have been preserved for posterity.

In the 1980s, the role of church in the public life of Kanepi, as well as throughout Estonia, was nearly non-existent. The pastor of Kanepi was almost 80 years of age. He was not substituted by a younger pastor. As it was, the school situated next to the church was the centre of anticlerical propaganda. The young pastor taking office at the beginning of the 1990s described his predecessor as "the last of the Mohicans, who was going under in the struggle for existence." The village soviet also made its utmost to deter the people, mainly the young and the intelligentsia, away from the church. In the Soviet era, "one did not dare go to church . . . It could be that someone would report you for having been there," admitted the young librarian ruefully. The non-verbal law closed the doors to the university for believers and made it hard to find a decent job. The residents of Kanepi remembered the chairman of the village soviet stood by the church door on Christmas Eve and eyed everyone who entered.

The church had a congregation of about five hundred. However, on Sundays there were only a dozen churchgoers listening to the sermon. To save electricity, the service was sometimes held in the dark (the state charged the church for electricity at an exorbitant rate – five times higher than normal). Even the clerical ceremonies were banned. "The pastor dared hold only burial services in public, baptism was at home. For burial, the pastor visited the house of mourning the preceding day; the next day the lay preacher took the deceased to the cemetery," said the new pastor when describing the customs during the Soviet era.

Lutheran church did not play as drastic a role in the Estonian anti-Communist revolution as did the church in Germany for example, which was much more liberal towards religion. However, the pastors still supported the national radical movements (Paul, 1991). The new pastor of Kanepi was mystified that his predecessor had altogether taken part in the renewed consecration of the monument to those fallen in the War of Independence. He said that, "the old pastor Peiker had regarded the Estonian struggle for independence with scepticism. Peiker had low expectations for the Estonian

Heritage Society and the Popular Front and he was convinced that it was unlikely that anything good would come of it all." Notwithstanding, he participated in the restoration of independence by infusing boldness into the activists. "Pastor Peiker had a crucial role in the creation of the support groups for the Estonian Heritage Society and the Popular Front in Kanepi. He attended their meetings. He had lived here since 1945 and he knew the local situation. He was often consulted." The founder of the Kanepi support group for the Estonian Heritage Society also supported this new pastor's vision of the hidden role played by Peiker.

The 'Days of Kanepi' ushered in the restoration of the church in public life. The clerical ceremonies – commemorative church services, consecrations, inaugurations, etc. – were given an important status. More often than not, this reflected an anti-Communist approach rather than religious rebirth. The same tendency manifested itself in private life, where prominence was given to church ceremonies. The impact of church was also enhanced when a young new pastor was ordained in Kanepi (1990). The new pastor turned out to be a radical, active nationalist politician. According to the pastor, the number of church ceremonies (burials, weddings, baptisms, etc.) grew 7–8 times in a couple of years. The congregation increased to one thousand. An added benefit to ending the Soviet tax terror was the economic help the church received from the West – from Germany and Finland. The family of Philip von Roth from Germany supported the church. A society was established there to take care of his burial ground. Võru deanery even started its own newspaper – 'The Word of Võru Deanery' (Võru Praostkonna Sõna).

The church also attempted to act as the social service provider, which used to be strictly forbidden under the Soviets. The collective farm returned the real estate (ten plots) belonging to the church in Kanepi earlier than in the other municipalities in the Põlva County. The church gave the land in the centre of Kanepi (50 hectares) for free use of the members of congregation. This land was cultivated, also for free, by a tractor from Germany. The tractor was a gift. However, the church lacked funds for wider social work. "In the latter years chocolate was distributed, five bars per child. That was all. Families with five or more children got a turkey and some smaller gifts for Christmas. There are two such families in Põlgaste." The financial means of the church were severely limited by the poverty of the elderly members of the congregation. However Dean Jürjo considered the decline in willingness to sacrifice as the main reason (Jürjo, 1995a). "Under the Church Law, you had to contribute 1% of your income to the church. In Kanepi, we turned a blind eye to it, paying only what the Consistory demanded from our proper means," explained the pastor of Kanepi. Those "proper means" evidently came from the gifts from the West, suggesting the direct dependence of the church on fraternal congregations.

In the following years, 1994–1998, the church lost its influence. The congregation (1,300 at its highest in 1991) dropped to 1,000, according to the information from the pastor (in the official records there were 800 nominal donators). However, the pastor thought that, "30–40 people on Sundays in church was satisfactory for a municipality this small. Secular burial ceremonies have almost ceased." The records of the church from 1993–1994 show that 101 people were baptised, 6 couples married, and 84 people were buried by church in Kanepi (Jürjo, 1995b). At its all time low at the end of 1970s, *in the whole of Estonia*, and with a birth rate twice as high as present, the Lutheran church baptised as few as 500–600 children per year (Paul, 1991). However, it is difficult to re-establish old ways and traditions disrupted during the Soviet period. The requirement for confirmation before marriage and the requirement that church taxes be paid before burial entangled communication with the church. "The arrangements for a secular burial ceremony are simpler," admitted a schoolteacher.

Neither has the work with children, restarted in 1993 (in the Soviet period it used to be a criminal offence) born fruit. This situation is the same throughout Estonia. The headmaster of Kanepi Secondary School said: "The church started with religious instruction (at school, with 30 students), attendance was optional. More pupils were interested in the junior grades, in the senior grades there were fewer. However, the class closed this past year because nobody showed any more interest. Only the Sunday school was preserved for of those genuinely interested." The pastor thought the students were just too tired to go to the afternoon religion classes. There had been no active support for religious instruction at school, which used to be the bastion for anti-religious activities.

The pastor's wife has been conspicuous in pushing the church to the forefront and making it prominent. She teaches in the Sunday school, plays the organ, and directs the joint choir of the house of culture and church. At the same time, secular and clerical cultures are fusing. The pastor said:

> The choir participates at family events and birthdays. You can also have a drink there. In Kanepi, nobody is scorned for that trifling sin. Some places are very strict but the Kanepi choir sings both clerical and secular songs and the parties are in perfect accord. A spin off from the choir is the youth choir. It is a quartet of two teachers and two businessmen. It gets the youth interested in the church.

The tolerance of church to 'worldliness' is indispensable and so it does not become isolated from its largely secularised environment.

The headmaster of Kanepi Secondary School said that various religious sects were actively involved in the so-called 'awakening activities', however the preachers of the sects were not the best possible. "Three years ago several villages were visited by a man from Vastseliina but his behaviour and manners, far from attracting the students to the religion, pushed them away." In Põlgaste, another preacher seemed to have found some support and extended his influence to Kanepi. The pastor was very negative about both of them. "There are no sectarians here, I have packed all of them off. The evangelists have their place in the larger towns. Let them save the drug addicts and drunks there." Hence, the Lutheran church has found itself under the pressure of the freedoms of a liberal society.

The Kanepi study supports the conclusions from another study of Estonian municipalities (Granquist, 1993) – that among social factors the church has the least important status, sharing it with the political parties and the former *nomenklatura*. The root cause is the secularisation of society. The rather prominent place of the church in the life of Kanepi during the transition resulted from a certain strengthening of its public role and from the generally poor situation in civic initiative. With the feeling of mission among the rural *literati*, the pastor became the factor in social impact. He was elected to the municipal council in Kanepi.

The church will make its final exit with the departure of the elder generation. Even now, its role as mediator in the permanent values of society is questionable. In unison, the young people of Kanepi answered that they did not participate in religious movements and church life and considered it the concern of the older generation. However, the pastor of Kanepi was optimistic: "The church is currently the pivotal centre of life. It has been separated from the state and politics. However, no one can bypass the Kanepi church. People not only refer to the priest for religious matters – they also ask about their everyday problems." The pastor is contemplating renovating the church buildings. He plans to have the old school building renovated to house the rectory.

The Associations for Civic Initiative

The associations that were unrelated to any institutions (the school, the church, and the house of culture) were a separate group. Unlike the Estonian

Heritage Society and other organisations, they were concerned with environmental issues, the problems of public services and utilities, working conditions, professions, and so on. They did not set any general political objectives.

The attitude to associations during the Soviet era was ambiguous. It ranged from outright rejection to admitting that there was something positive in them. The former chairman of the village soviet suggested that the Voluntary People's Patrol, the nature protection activity, and the voluntary traffic control were necessary, underpinning the grassroots contribution to maintaining law and order. "Now, nature protection is defunct. The situation in the fishing industry is especially worrisome. In the period of the collective farms, you managed to preserve some balance in the lake, now nobody gives a damn. Everyone uses the lake for their own purposes." However, the trade unions were held in unanimous contempt:

> Trade unions were a real joke in the village. The union was like an old granny, wishing well for everybody, but disposing of a budget so meagre as to be out of comparison even with that of the village soviet. The union distributed tourist and rest home vouchers and spun demagogic yarns. Lenin called the trade unions the school of Communism; God preserve you from such a school! The union was cunningly engineered to set the people against one another, to incite them to trample on one another grabbing for the vouchers.

One respondent explained his frequent trips abroad by saying he used to be supported by the trade union. However, other interviewees said that his son used to be employed by the KGB and that accounted for his privileges. The school teacher was also critical: "At our school a young teacher was illegally dismissed but the trade union never raised a finger to help him. At the time, it was impossible to quit the old trade union."[3] By 1989, the old trade unions had lost their privileges of allocating benefits for the simple reason that there were no benefits to hand out.

The advocates of the 'perestroika' in Moscow saw civic associations as devices to put brakes on the disintegration of the society. In 1986, the temperance society, the soviets of work collectives, the women's associations, etc. were all established in the Soviet-bureaucratic way by a directive. They left their stamp on life in Kanepi. The Women's Association was active in Põlva; there were also active women's councils Kanepi and Põlgaste. A division of the Estonia's Women Union was established in Põlva, effectively

---

3   By law it was possible to resign one's membership in a socialist trade union, but in practice it was difficult since the trade unions were the main providers of social security, seaside vacations, children's summer camps and some out-of-the-way commodities.

doing away with the above associations (Vill, 1988). By raising issues related to families and homes, the women's organisations stood out against the terror reigning in the Soviet Army, and conscription of Estonians (Vill, 1989). The local people recalled that the temperance society, created in 1986 under the leadership of Gorbachev, turned out to be a tremendous fiasco and became a laughing stock (Jõgiaas, 1988). There was hope that the new society would better organise leisure time but its activities amounted to no more than the forced collection of membership fees. It was on this foundation that local initiative was used to create associations like the Põlva Union of Engineers, the Foresters' Union, and the Põlva Cultural Foundation. The numerous societies in the County of Põlva were used as examples. In the pre-W.W.II period, these societies had united into the influential Convent of Kanepi (Toomet, 1989). There was even the idea of building a House of Societies in Põlva (Reimer, 1988). The Cultural Foundation of Põlva was established to promote and invigorate life in the county (Luiga, 1989). The society was created to keep the burial ground of Philip von Roth in good repair. He was a prominent figure in the 19th century and, since he was a von Roth, his name currently draws support from Germany.

The most important thing, from the point of view of Kanepi, was to get agriculture organised. The Farm Law created a category of 'independent producers' in January 1989 and the new farmers set up the 'Põlva Region Farmers'. It was a grassroots union, whose umbrella organisation was yet to be created. In 1997, the chairman of the union said:

> In Põlva County, the union rallied 1,000 members; there were about 350 active members contributing EEK 120 in membership fees each year. In turn the union gave them support. We set up the union because at the collapse of the Soviet system brought a shortage of everything. The task of the union was to help the farmers by supplying agricultural hardware, fertilisers, fuel, etc. By now, we have evolved into a union of producers, with the goal of developing private ownership and counselling. A member of the union must be a producer, not just a landowner. The form of ownership is not important but the collective-farm type of ownership will make a farmer ineligible for membership.

In the County of Põlva, the union was organised by municipalities, had representatives on the management bodies of Põlva County and co-operated with the Farmers' Union of South Estonia. The head of the Põlva Region Farmers' Union said their goal was to negotiate "the contracts for sales and supply, the establishment of protective customs tariffs, and the subvention for production and export." The Põlva Region Farmers' Union had a stake in the company Põlva Piim (Põlva Dairy), which provided the income necessary for operation. The daily newspaper in Põlva reported that the union had helped to create dairy, grain, and flax co-operatives, and it had established six agricultural machinery co-operatives (Põlva Talupidajate Liit, 1994; Koit, October 20). However, also the leaders of the union found themselves on the 'winning' end. As reported in Kanepi, "the chairman of the Võru Region Farmers' Union stocked himself well with agricultural materiel delivered as donations from Finland and Sweden."

The union played a major role in liquidating the collective farms; its representative was the secretary of the reform committee in Kanepi. The Rural Union was founded on May 7, 1989. It embraced the leaders of the collective and state farms. The collective farms of Kanepi and Kalev were also represented. March 23, 1991 witnessed the creation of a political party based on the union and bearing an identical name.

The second large source of civic initiative came from marginalised groups – the former victims of Communist reprisals and pensioners. In January 1988, deportation was officially pronounced a criminal offence in Estonia and in September 1988, the 1949 court judgements on the deportation of kulaks (prosperous peasant-proprietors) were declared null and void. The victims of the reprisals rallied with due circumspection into 'Memento', the 'Estonian Union for Illegally Repressed People'.

The professed goal of the movement was the restitution of rights and obtaining indemnification. In Kanepi, the first gathering that was attended by the victims of the reprisals was held clandestinely in Jüri Street, Võru. An activist in Kanepi said: "Many former dissidents had gathered there, and there were also some future leading figures of the Popular Front present. We discussed how we could contribute to the restoration of independence in Estonia. The meeting was promoted by the Popular Front of Võru. Some 50–60 people from Võru and Põlva counties attended."

A division of 'Memento' was founded in Põlva County in the spring 1989. An activist present at the meeting reported that " 'Memento' originally had a couple hundred members but soon the senior citizens of 70–80 years of age tended to slacken off." In March 1989, a 'Memento' group was also created in Kanepi. According to a former inmate of Kolyma, it had a mottled composition: "Memento was very ill assorted. It included former political prisoners, deportees and people who had been maltreated by, for example, the Party organiser, and those who vocally claimed that they had been persecuted."

The movement of former political prisoners got new impetus after the Supreme Soviet of the ESSR declared the annexation of Estonia to the Soviet Union in 1940 illegal in its resolution of November 12, 1989 – hence, the former political prisoners were no longer 'transgressors'. The 'Estonian Alliance of Former Political Prisoners' set the goal to achieve the restitution of rights for imprisoned students and 'forest brothers' (Estonian patriotic partisans), etc. "Originally there were about 20 such people in Kanepi, but now there are only 8." One former Kolyma inmate recalled: "there were three to four large rallies in Põlva County and one of them was held on the initiative of Andres Reimer in House of Culture of Kanepi (see Reimer, 1989). We sent an official appeal to Arnold Rüütel, Edgar Savisaar and newspapers." However, the 'National Party of the Victims of Illegal Reprisals', set up by the victims of reprisals (founded on 24 October 1991), never became a political force.

There were other cases of setting up job and profession-related associations. The people of Kanepi were involved (through the mediation of Põlva) in new associations like the Teachers' Union, the Union of Veterinary Surgeons, the Union of Physicians, and the Foresters' Union. The only union that operated on local initiative was the Hunters' Union and it met in Põlva, too.

Trade unions operated only in municipal governments or governmental agencies. The reorganisation of the school trade union took place because the old union continued in the time-honoured tradition of being the headmaster's henchman. A teacher from Kanepi said: "I was elected a trustee. When I looked into the matter, it turned out that we did not even have so much as a contract of employment. The people having no idea of its need." The trade union had the headmaster dismissed. Although the leaders of the new trade union supported the strikes organised by TALO (Teenistujate Ametiliitude Organisatsiooni, the Organisation of Employees' Professional Unions), it focused mainly on local gatherings and providing economic support. A businessman of Kanepi thought that the trade unions had no rationale because "they have no money to support the strikers for the lost working time."

The pensioners were also very active, and they were a very large slice of the population. They had their own club in Piglets and Kanepi. The club functioned both as a community centre to pass the time and as a political club. The club had close links with pensioner clubs in neighbouring municipalities. The pensioners also had good relations with the parish administration, which channelled help to the needy. The token financial support obtained from the parish was pivotal in keeping the club going and in maintaining relations with national organisations, including the Union of Pensioners founded on October 3, 1990.

The apogee for the civic initiative of the associations was the period of 'perestroika', which released social energy. Kanepi is far too small for an active and rich civic life. After the restoration of independence, the role of associations in protecting public interests dwindled and the promoters of corporate professional or elitist hobbies (like hunters) stepped to the fore.

Summary: Civic Associations and Reforms in Kanepi

Civic initiative in reforming life in the Municipality of Kanepi worked like a tsunami; the eruption in 1988–1990 was followed by a rapid recession, leaving in its wake a greater void than there was earlier. The results of civic initiative in the reformation of the villages did not depend only on the social capital of the past (both pre-W.W.II and in the Estonia under occupation), which could be transformed, actualised and mobilised to open "the structures of new opportunities and options." Quite understandably, the links to one's neighbourhood, etc. were of central importance in the relations with the nationally integrated network (Woolcock, 1998). However, the main factor was the rate and sequence in the process of transformation.

In the second half of the 1980s, the power machinery of the *ancient regime* lost the best part of its automatic and mechanical character, particularly in the countryside. The study showed that the official associations and institutions, including the ECP, assumed the features of real collectives, including national collectives in the village. Therefore the novel treatment of the Stalinist past in Gorbachev's 'glasnost' put the village society under stress. However, it did not block co-operative relations. A network of co-operation and trust based on nationalist and human values evolved in the village within the framework of official associations. These networks of communication, autonomous to the machinery of power, had a significant place in the anti-system movements and the preparation of actions in the 'period of awakening'. Authentic civic initiative was triggered in cultural life, which evolved into political mobilisation. Civic initiative drew its energy primarily on historical-cultural identity for its mental capital. Based on the common activities of national culture and the rediscovery of symbolic capital, a new social capital evolved. However, the organisational capital that accumulated in repressive social relations could be converted into creative activity in a novel rule-of-law and world outlook only under certain conditions.

The transfer of the pragmatic-constructive modes of employment of intellect at the end of 1980s from the private sphere to the area of public usage rendered the official-rhetoric discursive environment more rational. *Trust* as social capital focussing on human co-operation became ever more prevalent. The traditional symbolic capital (in the form of flags, signs, songs, etc.) was sufficient for the organisation of mass rallies and popular actions. However, it failed to evolve into the capital for ideas and the relations of co-operation that are indispensable for rejuvenating common activities. The ECP had made a great job at eradicating the capital of the ideas of the past epoch from the social memory, and new ideologies take some time to develop and institutionalise.

The past decade in the Estonian society has been paradoxical in the evolution of political parties and the new political system. When confronted with sudden and deep changes, rural life was in dire need for political openness, the instruments for social dialogue, and the organisational capital to verbalise problems to render society more transparent, and to spark public dialog on the options to solve those problems. The ECP capital of ideas and policy, particularly as represented by the former collective farm party organisers, had been reduced to an ossified 'solid mandala' or 'mantra'; each and every communal initiative was grabbed by the kolkhoz economic elite. The organisational show of pretension in party-political life did not allow the ECP to become a forum of any significance in independent Estonia. The social capital consolidating and holding the Soviet system together (norms, system of values, corporate networks) progressively rarefied. The 'black and grey markets', the so-called relief production (the production of alimentaries, sanctioned by the authorities to relieve the pressure on short-supply foodstuffs), the alternative cultural life, the 'social memory' of those subjected to repression, etc., gained ever increasing ground and colonised public life.

Notwithstanding the ideological opportunism of the ECP, the Party disintegrated. The inability of the ECP to transform into a significant left-wing political party and the fundamentalist features of the subsequent party-political organisation has had serious and inhibitory consequences on the fate of the Estonian countryside. The political development had shattered all earlier economic structures and the creation of new ones was a time consuming and slow process; the new social capital was slow to appear. In conceptualising and organising the future of Kanepi, sectarian and group interests pushed to the fore. The blatant onslaught of public opinion by groups striving to grasp power at the beginning of the 1990s also ideologically polarised the countryside. The bottom-up approach to the creation of interfaces (a technique used to change the culture of an organisation that depends on the involvement of group members in the process), which would have enabled the problems to be channelled upwards from the grass-roots level, was stalled. The rural interest groups (economic) failed to comply with the power groups, 'designed and downloaded' from above. The relationship between the state and the society turned out to be a dead-end street for rural society. The links between the local population and the political parties were, in many respects, *ad hoc* (the Rural Union, the Isamaa Party, the Estonian Conservative People's Party, and the Estonian Citizens' Union). They slackened or became a matter of tertiary interest. The institutions that could offer a counterbalance to the anomie (the lack, in a society or individual, of moral or social standards of conduct and belief) and deprivation were weak. Neither the school nor society and its civic activities, nor the civic defence or the church (as testified by the low willingness to make sacrifices) were adequate supporters of up-to-date social capital, the mediators of permanent values and the partisans or promoters of solidarity.

The social capital based on individuals, families, kinship, and the traditional 'solidarity relations of the neighbourhood' in the near future will underpin local life and co-operation in Kanepi and, to all appearances, in general throughout the countryside.

References

Aas, P. (1988), 'Kas üksi või hulgakesi?', *Koit*, no. 88 (5798), 28 July 1988.
Allik, J. and Raelo, A. (1996), 'On the Relationship Between Personality and Totalitarian Regimes: A Critique of Western Stereotypes', *Journal of Baltic Studies*, vol. XXVII, no. 4, pp. 331–336.
Beyme, K. (1996), *Transition to Democracy in Eastern Europe*, MacMillan Press, London.
Gill, G. (1994), *The Collapse of the Single-Party System: The Disintegration of the Communist Party of the Soviet Union*, Cambridge University Press, Cambridge.
Granqvist, N. (1993), 'Vallavanemad ja demokraatia', in K. Strahlberg, (ed) *Omavalitsuste areng Eestis*, Soome Linnade Liit, Helsinki, pp. 53–68.
Grigorjev, K. (1988), 'Sõnavõttudest mõne kandi pealt', *Koit*, no. 134 (5844), 17 November 1988.
Hart, A. R. (1993), 'The Role of the Lutheran Church in Estonian Nationalism', *Religion in East Europe*, vol. 13, no. 3, pp. 6–12.
Jõgiaas, A. (1988), 'Mõtteid karskusühingu konverentsilt', *Koit*, no. 42 (5905), 27 April 1988.

Jowitt, K. (1992), *New World Disorder: The Leninist Extinction*, University of California Press, Berkeley, Los Angeles, and Oxford.

Jürjo, I. (1996), *Pagulus ja nõukogude Eesti. Vaateid KGB, EKP ja VEKSA arhiividokumentide põhjal*, Umara, Tallinn.

Jürjo, V. (1995a), 'EEKL Võru praostkond 1993', *Võru Praostkonna Sõna*, no. 1–2. (92–93), January-February 1995.

Jürjo, V. (1995b), 'EEKL Võru praostkonna aruanne. EEKL Võru praostkonna arvutabel 1994/93', *Võru Praostkonna Sõna*, no. 5–6 (96–97), May-June 1995.

'Keda valida?' (1990), *Koit*, no. 22 (5997), 22 February 1990.

Kermas, K. (1978), 'Põlva', in V. Tarmisto (ed), *Põlva rajoonis*, Eesti NSV TA, Tallinn.

KMS (1988), 'Mööduja, seisata siin ja mäleta', *Koit*, no. 88 (5798), 28 July 1988.

Konn, A. (1989), 'Muinsuskaitse Selts Võrumaal', *Koit*, no. 5987, 12 October 1989.

Laar, M., Ott, U. and Endre, S. (1996), *Teine Eesti. Eesti iseseisvuse taassünd 1986–1991*, EE & JS, Tallinn.

Lane, D. (1996), *The Rise and Fall of State Socialism*, Polity Press, Cambridge.

Lehestik, P. (1988), 'Kodu-uurimisest ja muinsuskaitsest', *Koit*, 1988, no. 80 (5790), 30 June 1988.

Luiga, H. (1989), 'Põlvamaa kultuurifondi põhikiri', *Koit*, no. 76 (5939), 13 June 1989.

Pärna, O. (1988), 'Arutati valupunkte', *Koit*, no. 132 (5842), 12 November 1988.

Pärnaste, E. and Niitsoo, V. (1998), *MRP-AEG infobülletään 1987–1988*, SE & JS, Tallinn.

Paul, T. (1991), 'Eesti Kirik 80. Aastatel', *Vikerkaar*, no. 6, pp. 59–64.

'Põlva Maaliidu Maapäeva Resolutsioon' (1989), *Koit*, no. 48 (5911), 27 April 1989.

Põlva Talupidajate Liit (1994), *Koit*, no 89 (6432), 20 October 1994.

Rahvarinne (1989), 'Võim vabale rahvale', *Koit*, no. 141 (6004), 2 December 1989.

'Ranna kolhoosi parteialgorganisatsiooni ja volinike koosolek. Eesti NSV Ülemnõukogu presiidiumile', *Koit*, no. 48 (5911), 27 April 1989.

Reimer Andres (1988), 'Seltidele oma maja', *Koit*, 13 (5785), 31 January 1988.

Reimer, Andres (1989), ' "Memento" Kanepis', *Koit* 46 (5909), 20 April 1989.

Rigby, T. H. (1990), *The Changing of Soviet System: Mono-Organizational Socialism from its Origins to Gorbachev's Restructuring*, Edward Elgar, Aldershot.

Saar, A. (1998), *Aktsioonide aeg*, Võru.

Toomet, O. (1989), 'Põlvamaal tegutsenud seltsid ja organisatsioonid Eesti Vabariigi päevil', *Koit*, no. 5999, 16 November 1989.

'Täiesti salajane' (1993), *Sirp*, 19 February 1993.

Vaht, V. (1988), 'Eesti NSV Ülemnõukogu Presiidiumi otsuse, "Kodanike algatusel korraldatavate koosolekute, miitingute, tänavarongkäikude, demonstratsioonide ja muude ürituste kohta rakendamise kord" ', *Koit*, no. 17 (5727), 11 February 1988.

Väljas, V. (1989), 'EKP ülesannetest poliitilise situatsiooni stabiliseerimisel vabariigis', in *Eestimaa Kommunistliku Partei Keskkomitee XIV Pleenumi materjalid 1989*, Eesti Raamat, Tallinn.

Vananurm, I. (1989a), 'Kuidas, keda?', *Koit*, no. 160 (5941), 31 August 1989.

Vananurm, I. (1989b), 'Ümbervaatavalt: Enne uusi samme', *Koit*, no. 112 (5939), 6 June 1989.

Vijard, L. (1988), 'Kanepis muinsuskaitse selts', *Koit*, no. 161 (5902), 25 June 1988.

Vill, S. (1988), 'Pidupäeval Põlgastes', *Koit*, 31 (5889), 2 March 1988.

Võrumaa EKK (1990), 'Eesti Kongressi valimiste ringkonnakomisjonid Põhja-Võrumaal', *Koit*, no. 4 (6043), 16 January 1990.

Waller, J. M. (1994), *Secret Empire: The KGB in Russia Today*, Westview Press, Boulder, San Francisco, and Oxford.

Woolcock, M. (1998), 'Social Capital and Economic Development: Toward a theoretical synthesis and policy framework', *Society and Theory*, vol. 27, no. 2, pp. 152–181.

7 The Significance of the Kanepi Study

ILKKA ALANEN, JOUKO NIKULA AND REIN RUUTSOO

All social processes are simultaneously unique and general by nature. Hence, the transition from a state socialist system to a capitalistic one always creates relations of production characteristic of capitalism, i.e., a prevalently commodity economy, which can only exist under the conditions of private ownership, and with a reserve army of wage-workers detached from the means of production.

Viewing any issue from this perspective makes it less necessary to assess how close to the 'average' the case under study is. Besides, two average outcomes of decollectivisation may not necessarily be the result of the same mechanism. Those who prefer averages should use other, more appropriate, approaches, such as a survey method based on random sampling. However, in such a case, the research data would consist of individual people and households or other similar separate units, while the object of decollectivisation was something quite different – an organic entirety such as a kolkhoz or a sovkhoz. This entirety has its own social and natural conditions, characteristics, and mechanisms of operation. Thus, if you set out to ascertain and examine the transition mechanisms in decollectivisation, a case study involving a collective farm is much more practical and often the only applicable method. Furthermore, it offers the opportunity to pay closer attention to small but strategically important groups, such as kolkhoz chairmen, and to follow step-by-step processes of political importance such as changes in the climate of opinion, changes in the relative internal strengths in the kolkhoz, or changes in the organisation of production. This enables you to discover the intersections of the alternative lines of action, the underlying causes behind the selection of a particular operations model, the key figures in the decision-making process, and the transfer of national policies to the local level.

Above all, the Kanepi study is an analysis of the disintegration of a specific organic whole and of the special character of the creation of structures. Naturally, it would have been better if we could have examined more than one community in detail to enrich the overall picture, but even that would not have helped us to detect a 'typical' case in the sense of a statistical average. A case study is not an alternative to a survey: rather such methods are complementary to each other.

A kolkhoz as a unit of analysis is only natural, since the collective farm was the definite focus of rural transition problematics. Collective farms were responsible for most of the production in the countryside, as well as numerous other functions, particularly in the fields of social services and cultural activities. They were also local centres of political power. Kolkhoz chairmen were the power elite of the countryside and only collective farms had full-time party organisers. In time, the collective farm became the most important social institution in the countryside, much more important than the village soviet, which was formally the basic local administrative unit in Soviet rural areas.

The kolkhozes and sovkhozes were also important because of their communal nature. The patrimonial formation of communities typical of socialist work collectives was also characteristic of collective farms. The decollectivisation of kolkhozes and sovkhozes alone had a greater effect on the future development possibilities of rural industries than any other part of the transition process. It also had a wider influence on the restructuring of the entire rural way of life, local administration, and civil society, including other informal social relations. The disintegration of the community spirit as it had existed under the collective farm system was also the unavoidable reverse side of the (re)creation of capitalist production relations in Estonia. However, the remains of the community spirit continue to influence people's behaviour even today.

In the following pages, we will discuss the overall significance of the Kanepi case based on our findings and within the framework of overall transition problematics. Although we attempt to contextualise our findings on a more general level, unfortunately space does not permit systematic comparison with other studies.

Rural Areas as the Driving Force in Estonia's Struggle for Independence

Although the forced collectivisation of Estonian private farms in the 1940s and the formation of kolkhozes and sovkhozes was a highly traumatic experience, the new socialist system of production – once it had been established –

provided the rural population with opportunities for higher education and relatively high incomes. The arts and other cultural activities prospered even in the smallest rural communities, albeit they were under careful control and subject to the inherent constraints set by the Soviet state and predominantly directed from the top to the bottom.

The new nationalist movement born in the largest Estonian cities soon received support in the rural areas that are predominantly ethnically Estonian. This was particularly true in communities such as Kanepi with its strong cultural heritage from the period of Estonia's first independence and even earlier. The support arose largely from the middle-class of the kolkhozes, but it is a fact that rural areas were generally more nationalistically inclined. Even the collective farms often supported the nationalist movement. In Kanepi, the two kolkhozes gave mainly material support to the nationalist associations.

Undoubtedly the kolkhoz system also bred inefficiency and negligence, which were mixed with a pervasive fear of the Communist Party and the KGB, the secret service, in particular. However, ignoring the positive aspects would be a serious mistake in view of ensuing historical developments. The collective farms not only created fertile spiritual soil to the nationalist movement of the middle-class, but they also provided the material and mental building blocks necessary for the creation of entrepreneurship and the unfolding of a new civil society. These building blocks were not always the most appropriate for the new purposes and often they had to be complemented, but at least the local people did not have to begin from nothing.

The Agricultural System of Estonia and the Preconditions for the Success of the Kanepi Reform

The state socialist system also left a negative imprint on the pattern of thought in the Estonian rural population. The patrimonial approach characteristic of collective farms had the advantage of personal care and the disadvantage of making the employees more passive. The lack of initiative and a low work ethic (new entrepreneurs frequently raise the topic of their workers' lack of discipline), as well as the critical attitude towards the new 'kulaks' and private employers in general may indeed be partly attributed to Estonia's Soviet past. However, this is not the whole truth, hardly even the gist of the truth.

In the nationalist atmosphere of the transition period such an explanation functions primarily as an all-encompassing defence against unfavourable criticism, i.e., if you criticise any aspect of the transition process or the new owners you are labelled as a 'Soviet citizen'. Based on this type of reasoning, the critic himself is guilty of all his problems, lazy and passive, yet envious of the enterprising few that carry the main burden in the local community. However, passivity, a lack of work discipline, criticism of present ownership relations, and a number of other phenomena treated in more detail in our study may also be interpreted as a protest against glaring cases of abuse of public funds, other grievances, and the nation-wide (or local) way of executing the decollectivisation process – in other words, an attempt to challenge the legitimacy of those people who had acquired their wealth by morally questionable means. The idea of decollectivisation in itself was not challenged by any of our interviewees in Kanepi.

Both post-socialist entrepreneurship and civic initiative were in an embryonic state, even before the era of perestroika, but they were burdened by the 'pathological' characteristics created under and fed by the non-modern circumstances of the long Soviet occupation. Civic initiative and entrepreneurship came into being and developed within the Soviet system as clandestine or semi-tolerated 'deformations'. The experience thus acquired – albeit limited – played an important role in post-socialist society in promoting civic initiative, organisational skills, entrepreneurship, and market-oriented thinking. Unfortunately, that mentality also fostered a sub-culture and an attitude of mind foreign to the businesslike and competitive attitude considered 'normal' in a market economy.

Under an economy of simultaneous shortage and wastage, circumventing the law, thieving, falsifying accounts and other formally illegal activities became standard practice in the new enterprises. They became an integral part of the people's everyday way of life. Thus, the pathological mentality also shaped the prevailing concepts of honesty, obedience to the law, career building, etc. In addition, other pre or non-capitalist forms of social interaction, such as the emphasised role of social relationships in the procurement of daily necessities and services, influenced the transition in, for example, the way existing resources were redivided among the people. Undoubtedly this influence on the accumulation of economic and social capital will continue for a long time.

The main strategy employed in privatising agriculture was contrary to the wishes of the agrarian population, as they did not want to give up large-scale production. This became the most poignant issue of conflict in the Estonian agricultural transition: the 'dialogue' between the proponents of large-scale farming based on the kolkhoz tradition and the nationalist-minded proponents of family farming by restitution. Nowhere else do these two alternative models of social organisation have such deep social and emotional roots, dimensions and differences. In terms of 'path dependency', both options had heavy interest based and personalised references and roots, whilst 'bifurcational' condition helps to explain the dramatic behaviour of elite groups.

The Estonian agricultural population was largely unable to influence the making of laws pertaining to privatisation. National policies and consequently the agricultural reform were controlled by the urban leadership of the nationalist movement that had a background in the humanities. The anti-Communist and national-romantic attitudes of the urban elite had much more in common with the small-scale peasant farming tradition of the 1920s and 1930s than with the 40 year tradition of Soviet large-scale agriculture led by 'red barons'.

Nowhere else in Eastern Central Europe was the historical interruption between the pre-World War II independence and the new order imposed by a foreign power (including deportations and forced collectivisation according to the Soviet model) so abrupt. Moreover, Estonia – more than any other nation in Eastern Central Europe – was historically a predominantly peasant state of independent small-scale producers with their accompanying individualistic way of thinking and types of social organisation characterised by strong agrarian parties, co-operative organisations, and civil guards, etc. Since the only frame of reference considered legitimate was the time of former independence, a serious conflict arose between the restitutionalist approach and the more practical approach that would have taken the social structures that had come into being under Soviet rule into account.

The conflict between the restitutionalist-legitimist and economic-pragmatic tendencies already came to a head during the relatively good economic situation. However, it was only after the deterioration of the economic situation, as the 'division of labour' ties with the Soviet Union were broken, as the painful process of transforming collective enterprises into independent businesses began, and as the domestic and export markets collapsed and hyperinflation broke loose, that this conflict became the decisive factor in shaping future agricultural policies. Consequently, Estonian history and the prevailing conditions during the transition created a different social basis and circumstances that are more difficult for this period of exceptional politics compared with other countries. This situation diverted the attention of the nationalist elite from pragmatic issues and heightened purely ideological, i.e. dogmatic, thinking.

The Middle-class of the Collective Farms and the Decollectivisation

Specialists and professional employees – the middle-class of the collective farms – were the most fervent opponents of the restitution of small-scale farming. They realised that their employment and professional status in the future would only be secured by the Tayloristic specialisation of large-scale organisations. In Estonia, the middle-class of the agricultural collectives was exceptionally well off compared with the agricultural population in other Soviet Republics and the urban population in Estonia, and probably exceptionally well educated, too.

In the 1970s, agriculture in the Soviet Union was already entering a period of stagnation, but in Estonia the period of growth in the best collectives continued through the 1980s until the very end of Soviet rule. This can largely be explained by the experimental agricultural programme initiated on Estonian farms that allowed collective farms much more leeway in independent expenditure than previously.

At the start of decollectivisation, neither of the rival factions of the nationalist movement was able to create a concrete reform plan – not the more pragmatic Estonian Popular Front that had governed at the end of the Soviet era nor the highly dogmatic Estonian Congress that came into power after Estonia regained independence. Although the political elite did not intentionally set out to destroy the technological units that formed the backbone of large-scale production units, priority was given to the abstract attempt to restore land tenure as it had existed during the first independence of Estonia.

It was believed that large-scale production units could be preserved as subordinate units to small-scale farmers, as a type of 'partnership farm' (see Tamm, Chapter 8). More generally, it was believed that the material and mental resources of the large-scale farms could be detached from kolkhozes and sovkhozes, and successfully transferred to the new small-scale producers. In practice this turned out to be an impossibility – the machinery and buildings of the collective farms, not to mention the basic infrastructure of agricultural industry and rural settlements, and the local non-material resources (well-educated and highly specialised professional employees) were even in principle non-transferrable to the small family farms dating back to the era of Estonia's first independence. The agricultural population themselves were largely unwilling to set up new family farms. In retrospect – even considering the nationalist sentiments detailed above – it is hard to explain why these obvious facts were ignored as there was reliable information on the people's reluctance to set up small-farms.

Moreover, the premise of the reform in itself was impracticable. The Estonians also failed badly in synchronising the restitution of former agricultural ownership relations with the privatisation of other sectors of agriculture. Based on the agricultural policies drawn up by the first governments, the farms were the first to be returned to the former owners: later to be followed by the privatisation of the remaining collective assets. The process of land restitution, however, turned out to be so complicated legally that the re-establishment of former farms *en masse* was carried out only after the privatisation of other collective assets. Consequently, many people had to acquire machinery and implements for maintaining farms that legally did not yet exist.

In spite of all these problems, a number of thriving agricultural enterprises were established. The cream of the crop was usually the handful of collective farms that had remained largely undivided. There were also some technically advanced family farms. However, it must be noted that the most successful family farms were established based on the Farm Law of 1989, well before the dissolution of the kolkhozes or sovkhozes was decreed and not as a result of the restitution model. Most of these early family farms benefited from the generous support of the state and the large-scale collectives during the last years of the Soviet era. These support measures (price subsidies, loans that eventually became virtually free due to hyperinflation, and the basic infrastructure constructed by the state) were entirely abandoned when the first farms under restitution laws were *de facto* set up. The resources available to the government were drastically reduced, but just as important was the change of cabinet as the Estonian Congress took power and the consequent shift in ideological orientation toward ultra-liberal economic doctrines.

The attempts to save enterprises and technological units appropriate for large-scale production may be regarded principally as indications of the aspirations of the kolkhoz middle-class. To the extent that these aspirations were successful, the results may be attributed to efforts on the local level and not to government policy. In addition, the encouraging experiences gained in Eastern Central Europe spoke in favour of the preservation of large-scale production. Many representatives of Estonian enterprises toured other post-socialist countries; besides this, agricultural consultants from the former GDR also visited Estonia and advocated the keeping large production units as intact as possible.

Despite all the economic and political problems (heightened by the attacks on the 'new kolkhozes' by the media), some of the large-scale enterprises or production units of the Soviet era were successfully adapted to the market-economy environment. From the techno-agricultural and economic perspectives, the relatively prosperous large-scale enterprises are concrete proof of the high level of production achieved in Estonia under Soviet rule, since these enterprises immediately faced tough competition with heavily subsidised foreign foodstuffs imported on to the Estonian domestic market without the protection of customs duties.

The Possibilities of Kolkhozes and Sovkhozes for Transforming into Large-scale Enterprises in a Market Economy

The decollectivisation of the Kanepi kolkhoz did not result in the creation of feasible large-scale enterprises. In fact, would the creation of successful large-scale enterprises have been possible there at all?

Although the Kanepi kolkhoz was top of its class in the County of Põlva, by Estonian national standards it was only average. In addition, the quality of kolkhoz soil was poor, but the current large-scale farms do not cultivate their own land, instead they rent it. Since it is likely that ultimately poor soil quality will be compensated by lower rents (today, land in Kanepi is often rented against the payment of the land tax), the quality of soil should not impede profitable production. Furthermore, one of the best agricultural enterprises in present day Estonia is operating in the neighbouring municipality, therefore geographical location should not be an obstacle to successful farming. Today, there is a rapid reconcentration of agricultural production and land use taking place in Kanepi as an industrious (former) family farmer is buying up production units that once belonged to the Kalev kolkhoz. Simultaneously, he is rapidly increasing the acreage of rented land. Also, the two large-scale units (the only ones that had a business plan) remaining from the six larger enterprises set up on the basis of the Kanepi kolkhoz, have managed to secure their position. Therefore, in principle, large-scale production units should also have a chance of prospering in Kanepi.

The same principle is also applicable at the national level. The large-scale production of the Estonian SSR with its well-educated employees must have been far more capable of transferring to effective market-based production than the political leadership of Estonia gave them credit for. However, the government was unable to realise this potential.

The better the results of the reforms, the faster the successor enterprise or enterprises could intensify their production and modernise their machine stock by purchasing western equipment. It was a definitive advantage – if the enterprise being decollectivised had prospered at the end of the Soviet era. However, the success story of the collective farm in the neighbouring municipality – ranked only a little higher than the Kanepi kolkhoz – demonstrates the potential of more or less 'average' kolkhozes. On the other hand, if the reform process failed, a new enterprise established on the ashes of the best of collective farms was usually doomed to rapid and complete failure (there are several examples of this). The optimum size of an enterprise and the model of decollectivisation undoubtedly depended to a large degree on local circumstances, but the most crucial precondition was undoubtedly keeping the technological units (cowsheds, piggeries, etc.) from the Soviet era as intact as possible.

The reformers at the Kanepi kolkhoz failed to keep the technological units intact. The demoralisation of the kolkhoz leadership together with the auction strategy it promoted led to such an outcome that even the best newly formed agricultural enterprises started out with inadequate equipment. The fact that kolkhoz and sovkhoz general assemblies were required to give their approval to the chosen privatisation strategy opened up the possibility for struggle between the various interest groups. Hence, the privatisation strategy finally adopted was the result of severe internal struggles between the workers, specialists, and managers of kolkhozes and sovkhozes. This conflict assumed a highly politicised character since the nationalist movement trained and created a name for new social organisers especially from the middle-class of the collective farms. These new activists were soon able to challenge the Soviet-era elite of the collective farms in a battle for power. In this battle, they were able to rely on the new elite networks created within the nationalist movement (just as the former leadership relied on their well-established networks).

This is how the social and political division into the old guard and new guard was born. The old guard could be labelled as 'communists' or at least 'tarnished' by the Soviet era, while the struggle for independence gilded the heroic efforts of the new guard, pure and untarnished by the foul play of Soviet times. From the perspective of the new enterprises, it was unclear whether the old or the new guard would be more recommendable. Limited as it may be, our information suggests that undivided technological units were preserved both in kolkhozes where the old guard selected the method of privatisation and where it was chosen by the new guard. Moreover, the members of both elite groups founded more or less similar types of enterprises.

Of course, the result of the local power struggle determined the individuals that received the wealth divided in decollectivisation – particularly as managers and owners of new enterprises. The power struggle between the guards contributed somewhat to the preservation of large-scale production, as the rival groups may have had to rely on the middle-class that was most interested in maintaining it. Thus, the middle-class of the agricultural enterprises became the most significant counterforce to the urban leadership of the nationalist movement. Our research in Kanepi proved the validity of this train of thought.

In international comparison, the rivalry between the new and the old guard was based on two special characteristics of the Estonian agrarian reform: that it was simultaneously both heavily decentralised and formally democratic. If either of these two preconditions had been missing the power struggle would have failed to arise or it would have come about in a significantly weaker form. This might be why the villages did not put up a fight for collective resources (as in Hungary), despite the fact that there were often several traditional villages within the confines of a kolkhoz or a sovkhoz, and even though large cowsheds and other technologically advanced production units had been constructed in some of the more remote villages.

When the old guard communicated its plan on the division of the kolkhoz at the general assembly, it was confronted by the opposition, which was led by the new guard that had gained valuable experience in the nationalist movement. The opposition relied on the support of the middle-class, which wanted the kolkhoz to remain as a unified whole whilst also accusing the kolkhoz leadership of taking advantage of their position, and in so doing it also profited from the highly anti-Communist atmosphere.

Once they gained power, the new guard rather quickly gave up the goal of preserving the kolkhoz and reverted to the reform plan of the old guard. Their objective appeared to be preserving kolkhoz resources by transferring them outside agricultural production, since agriculture had become entirely unprofitable by the time kolkhoz assets were privatised. The line of action chosen by the new guard led to a privatisation process that was highly anarchic and even destructive to collective resources, and to the collapse of public morale. Consequently, every large-scale enterprise set up was more or less technologically impaired and the majority of new owners lacked a viable business plan.

The Estonian agricultural reform was executed in very unstable circumstances, and the selection of the best possible method of reform was not an uncomplicated issue for anyone. Consequently, debate was intense everywhere and emotions were often overheated. The deterioration of the overall economic situation lowered public morale throughout the country, but as common as misconduct was the leaders of all collective farms about to be privatised did not succumb to temptation.

The Effects of the Failed Decollectivisation outside Agriculture

The demise of technologically well equipped large-scale production units also had catastrophic effects on non-agricultural enterprises since the majority of them relied on local consumer demand. In Kanepi, the decline in consumer demand became sharper as four newly established large-scale enterprises ceased operation. The two remaining large-scale farms, let alone the small-farms set up during the restitution, only manage to provide their employees and owners with a meagre income. For the same reason, a significant portion of the non-agricultural enterprises also went out of business fairly shortly after they were established, and the majority of other enterprises remaining are barely surviving.

The majority of former kolkhoz employees were either impoverished or forced to leave the municipality, which was stricken by massive unemployment. The position of the people remaining in the local employment market grew weaker. When it became apparent that the core of the new kolkhoz leadership had initiated the widespread thievery that followed the approval of the kolkhoz dissolution plan against the wishes of the majority of the employees and members, it is no wonder that former kolkhoz employees and members often became embittered and viewed the new owners of local enterprises with cynicism. As the position of the employees worsened over time, they generally reacted by withdrawal, self-destructive behaviour (heavy drinking increased) and they adopted primarily indirect and anonymous measures of protest, such as refusal to work or dropping out from work without so much as an excuse. In addition, thieving, destruction of property, and anonymous threats with violence were common. This partly explains the cynical and passive attitude towards politics and other social activities. The lack of a civil society in turn has resulted in the transformation of municipal politics into a forum for the pursuit of private interests.

The Estonian government is barely capable of collecting taxes from enterprises and individuals. Many people's official wages from their regular employment are low and the remainder of the true wages is often paid by bypassing the tax authorities. In some areas of the economy, such as forestry, the evasion of taxes and felling license fees has become the norm, since legislation is rapidly changing and for the most part unpredictable. Furthermore, law enforcement is inadequate and there are too many loopholes enabling the evasion of taxes and fees. Small enterprises in particular consider taxes and fees unrealistically high in relation to their business-making abilities.

It is difficult for the impoverished state to escape the vicious circle of deterioration and its closely associated corruption. There were also signs of corruption in Kanepi. Besides the economic precariousness of the state, the causes of inefficiency may be traced to the inadequacy of the government's regional and industrial policies and to the fact that there is no overall nation-wide policy at governmental level to support regional development in agriculture, services, and industry.

One remedy, which would increase trust (and subsequently efficiency) in other actors and local administrative organs, would be the revitalisation of various club activities thereby strengthening the sphere of civil society. However, the lack of this same trust is currently the largest obstacle to revitalising such activities.

Future Prospects

The present conditions of existence in the Estonian countryside essentially depend on the degree the decollectivisation process succeeds. About seven years have passed since the execution of the reform, although there was wide variation in the local schedules. Considering Estonia's liberal external trade policy, it is quite remarkable that so many agricultural enterprises were capable of strengthening their positions in 1995–1998. In the autumn 1998, this positive development was halted by the repercussions of the Russian crisis in the Estonian food processing industry, dairies, and slaughterhouses. In the summer of 1999, the entire agricultural sector in Estonia was still under threat. Many first-rate enterprises had already shut down operations and many of the remaining ones were forced into freezing all their investment plans.

On the other hand, these harsh conditions have speeded up the adaptation of Estonian agriculture to the realities of a market economy. The best enterprises in the Estonian agricultural sector have specialised and modified their internal division of labour, which had been too rigid before. In addition, marketing has greatly developed, but employees have been discharged, wages have been cut and seasonal workers (e.g., tractor drivers) have frequently been laid off. The crisis has taken a particularly heavy toll on family farms and plot farms, since their produce has been deprived of a market. Descriptive of the situation in 1999 was that many minor milk producers let the dairies take their milk without remuneration – the only other alternative was simply to throw the milk away.

The opportunities for developing and operating non-agricultural enterprises have radically changed since the introduction of the Business Law in 1995. Individual people no longer have the same chances of setting up enterprises based on their own savings as a few years ago. Today, establishing an enterprise requires a business plan and outside capital in order to succeed. In Kanepi, the only growth industry has been the retail trade, while the activities of other businesses have been curtailed due to insufficient consumer demand, a lack of competitive ability, and the lack of markets. The most successful entrepreneurs both in agriculture and outside agriculture are persons with sufficient education and working relationships with the local political leadership and fellow entrepreneurs outside the locality.

One of the weaknesses of the agricultural reform, and more generally the rural policy, has its roots in the local administration reform. The goal of the administrative reform was to restore the local municipal governments of the inter-war years. The reform has never fully been carried through and this has hindered economic development. As yet, the municipal administrations have not been able to contribute to the creation of a modern public sphere and non-governmental organisation to replace the collective activities of the kolkhoz era.

Furthermore, the current average size of municipalities is often prohibitively small and the lack of economic resources in many places has rendered any larger investments impossible. The latter half of the 1990s has shown that the future development of rural areas may well depend on whether small municipalities are successfully merged and, of course, on the determined support measures by the government.

At the beginning of the transition period, the people of Kanepi were able to utilise both the historic resources in the struggle for independence and the forms of Soviet era collectivism to effectuate strong identity-based protest and mobilisation. However, once the formal institutions, new enterprises, and local administration had been set up, the institutions of the informal sphere were unable to keep up with the changes. A modern civil society typical of a capitalist society only evolves in a dialogue between political powers, private enterprises, and institutions producing and disseminating information. Apparently, it is impossible to reconstruct the everyday moral norms of a modern civil society from the elements of Soviet community spirit – except perhaps in extremely small and careful steps.

People's ability to organise associational activities has proved to be very weak now that social development has moved to the stage of interest based articulation. Also, the lack of material, economic, mental, and information resources channelled through civil society, and the limited possibilities to exert their influence have sharply diminished the readiness to become organised.

The local administrations are operating under difficult circumstances. Their efficiency and sensitivity to local issues have greatly suffered from the underdevelopment of civil society, e.g., problems in the creation of local political organisations, interest groups, and the third sector in general. Activities organised by the citizens are chiefly limited to recreational oriented club activities, the distribution of foreign humanitarian aid, and some leisure activities. There is little civic initiative oriented to the public sphere, which has resulted in social isolation in people's everyday lives, thus limiting the amount of social capital available. Family relations, neighbourly relations, and loyalties established during the Soviet era still form the basis of the social network of interaction and activity for the people of Kanepi.

The Terms of Sustainable Development

Our case study focusing on the Municipality of Kanepi enabled us to observe the most decisive stages in the agricultural decollectivisation and the formation of a new enterprise structure. In a very concrete manner, it demonstrated the way and extent to which each new turn in the national economic policy has affected the enterprises and farmers working on them. Rural people have been continuously forced to find new economic strategies and to utilise all available non-material resources. The mental capital required by the new agricultural enterprises did not suddenly come into existence the moment these businesses were set up, instead it – higher education in particular – was passed on from the kolkhoz era. Many new initiatives were not thwarted due to a lack of enthusiasm for work or the lack of work experience. Instead of inadequate skills or laziness, the cause of the failures should be sought in e.g. inadequate lending arrangements, which in turn resulted from difficult economic circumstances. This is why the majority of new enterprises did not come up with sufficient working capital, and they were unable to make even the most imperative investments to secure the high quality of their products or to amend the technological shortcomings that resulted from the decollectivisation process, such as acquiring a vitally important piece of machinery. The new enterprises were also plagued by undeveloped legislation and a changeful national economic policy. Some of these problems may well be regarded as problems almost unavoidably linked to transition. These, just as a part of the organisational problems and the lack of co-operation between farmers, the low participation in interest groups, and the limited scope of informal social networks, are only temporary by nature.

The majority of problems can be traced back to the very deliberate economic policy by the government of Estonia – a policy that is based on ultra-liberal economic doctrines. Due to its intrinsic nature, agriculture, perhaps more than any other sector of the economy has suffered from the government's policy decisions. The circulation of capital is very slow in agriculture, which is why special lending arrangements to meet the needs of farmers have been developed around the world. Furthermore, individual agricultural enterprises are too small and weak when compared with the more concentrated, partly monopolistic agricultural trade and processing industries (e.g., the dairy and meat processing industries).

On the international market, the prices of agricultural produce are heavily subsidised by the exporting countries. In addition to this, exceptionally cheap lots that are large enough to collapse the entire agricultural market of a small nation are frequently offered for sale on the international market. In Estonia, these problems have befallen most violently on such enterprises where the reconstruction after decollectivisation is yet not entirely complete.

On the strength of the Kanepi study, we may also add that the development potential of the small enterprises certainly exceeds what has been realised so far. The few technologically advanced family farms in Estonia have suffered more than the large-scale farms from these circumstances over the past few years.

It may well be that the agricultural industry in Estonia is in better condition and that it is endowed with better development potential than agriculture in the neighbouring countries of Latvia and Lithuania. However, these positive aspects may not be attributed to the government of Estonia, but to the exceptionally high level of Estonian agriculture in the Soviet era and the employees who struggled to keep the former collective production units intact.

All in all, the social cost of the agricultural reform has been enormous and it is certain that the entire bill is to be paid in full. The Estonians have yet to realise all the consequences of the reform in economic equality, public morale, structural unemployment with all its social consequences, the demographic structure of the population, the balance of payments, the business community as a whole, and even the stability of the political system. The basic structures of rural communities continue to decay, the former kolkhoz based community spirit has dissolved and it has not been replaced by an active civil society with a decent set of norms. Moreover, civic associations and the dialogue with the organs of power have not evolved beyond the embryonic state.

No qualitative changes to the situation are in sight for the majority of the population. Instead, what they witness is the uninhibited self-interest of one segment of the population, while the rest, the losers and the powerless have been isolated into islets of family relationships. The extent of abject poverty in rural areas relates directly to how successful the decollectivisation process is. Hence, in small municipalities such as Kanepi, the demands set on the municipal social services and other administrative branches far exceed their economic resources to manage the problems. Falling back on a largely unmechanised plot or a smallholding to provide sustenance for the family and closest relatives is a common manifestation of poverty. Despite its primitive nature, plot farming forms a significant part of the overall foodstuff production in Estonia even today. Instead of sustainable development, the Estonian countryside is trapped in a vicious circle. Breaking free from the circle requires a new kind of social vision and a new political approach.

As a process for creating capitalist social relationships, the transition resembles in theory, the process Marx labelled as the 'so-called original accumulation'. It is not a question of the creation of new social wealth but rather the redistribution of existing wealth. The classic realisation of this process in England and Scotland was everything but an 'idyll' and indeed it cannot be described as 'idyllic' in Estonia either, no matter what the final outcome (at the level of national economy the transition was one of the most successful of the post-socialist countries). Besides, in agriculture and in the countryside, the end result of the so-called original accumulation has been as a rule poor considering all its economic, social, and psychological consequences.

Even more serious than the economic consequences is the deep state of normlessness, i.e. anomie, which is widely observable in Kanepi and the Estonian countryside. The disappointments and insurmountable financial problems people have met have resulted in withdrawal from public life. The efforts of far too many people are focused on everyday survival and this struggle displays no sign whatsoever of hopes for a better life.

The further development of a given community or society in general presupposes mutual trust between individuals and the means to anticipate the future. There have been relatively few problems in the development of formal institutions in Estonia, but the social glue that cements people together, the shared values and norms that ultimately provide formal institutions with their efficiency and legitimacy, are precariously weak. The commitment to ultra-liberal policies by consecutive Estonian governments and the faith in the 'true spirit of capitalism' – where an industrious and capable individual has all the chances of prospering without government patronage or support – have not served to consolidate the trust of the peripheral rural population in the vision of Estonia that the political elite has embodied and offered to the people as the common home country of every citizen.

In many respects, the road to the future presented by Estonia's governing elite is in conflict with the interests of peripheral and predominantly agricultural municipalities such as Kanepi. The precarious state of agriculture calls for the introduction of customs duties and more effective support measures and not free competition. Meanwhile the further development of rural areas requires decided and functional regional and industrial policies and not the current policy of the 'survival of the fittest'.

8 Appendix:
Agricultural Reform in Estonia

MATI TAMM

The restructuring of Estonian agriculture in the reforms of recent years was a mixture of many different ideas and approaches that had their roots in specific group interests. The ideology behind the transition was discussed in several reference groups, but not all discussions were highlighted to the same extent in newspapers or by the electronic media, nor was anybody able to participate in all the meetings and evaluate all the ideas expressed. This paper presents some of the decisive events and early concepts in which the author participated as the co-author of drafts on the Farm Law and the Law on Agricultural Reform. The transition process is described briefly and some results and conclusions are also presented.

The Pre-reform Situation and Ideas

The pre-reform situation in Estonian agriculture was complicated. Over the past decades, Estonian agriculture had the highest level of productivity in the USSR and the increasing production resulted in a rising level of wages. The wages were higher than in most other industries in Estonia and in the entire USSR. People in regions with poorer soil specialised in growing potatoes and vegetables (cucumbers, tomatoes, onions, etc.) which were sold at high prices on the markets of large industrial centres, such as Leningrad, all over the USSR. Rural people also increased their income by selling the milk, cattle and hogs they produced on auxiliary homesteads and plots.

Cheap imported grain, purchased with "oil dollars," fuel, machinery, fertilisers and building materials, supported by the subsidised prices of agricultural products, created a picture of successful farming. Agricultural economists, such as Professor Mikhail Bronstein, pointed out that the growth in production was achieved by increasing farming inputs by up to five times. Soviet large-scale farm chairmen gave illustrative examples of the wasteful usage of farming inputs and work. For example, rural people bought cheap bread called "cow's cake" in local shops for their cows and pigs because bread was cheaper and easier to obtain than cattle fodder. They sold pigs and bulls at relatively high live-weight prices and enjoyed lower prices for meat and sausages, but somehow there was always a shortage of these commodities.

The Stalin regime, in the early days of collectivisation when restrictions on auxiliary households[1] were strictly controlled, was a thing of the past. In the late 1980s, three cows were enough to meet the living expenses for one family. In this situation, a mirage of wealthy family farming was created in the political debates on independence. The first so-called private farmers emerged at the end of the 1980s. At first, they used a variety of new legal ways of renting assets, such as the machinery and buildings of a sovkhoz or kolkhoz, and sometimes they stayed on the kolkhoz payroll.

The period of political and economic transition in Estonia started with Gorbachev's "perestroika." The first political turning point was the Declaration of Independence, passed by the Supreme Soviet of the Estonian SSR (Estonian Parliament) on 16 November 1988. Two years later, on 20 December 1990, Soviet collectivisation of Estonian agriculture was declared an unlawful act and the Supreme Council voted for land reform by the restitution of ownership of land. In 1940, when the Soviet Union annexed Estonia, all land was nationalised and the private ownership of land was abolished. This caused more complications for land reform here than in Central European countries, where the ownership of most land was never interrupted.

Kolkhoz or Joint-Stock Company?

Under the concept of "market socialism," some managers developed the idea of transforming a kolkhoz into a joint-stock company. The best-known proponent for this principle was Tenno Teets, the chairman of Valtu kolkhoz in the County of Rapla. In 1989, he proposed this idea in the general meeting of the kolkhoz. Instead of issuing stocks, they decided to calculate every member's share (osak). The members had two possible choices: to take their

---

1   Auxiliary holdings are sometimes called private plots. This is not correct. In Estonia, it was permissible to farm 0.5 hectares of land around the house, and keep one cow, a heifer, up to 10 sheep, one pig or sow with litter, 15 hens, and 10 swarms of bees. Those figures were sometimes amended in the by-laws of an individual kolkhoz.

share with dividends in cash over a period of some years or to reinvest it and claim dividends in the future. Some kolkhozes followed this example, which was recommended by the board of the Kolkhoz Union. The issues that required further clarification were establishing the value of collectivised assets, including the value of land, and the conditions on the approval of former members and employees as shareholders. This approach was widely criticised as a method of preserving the kolkhozes.

Profit Centres and Rental Agreements in Kolkhozes and Sovkhozes

Soviet agricultural scientists were continually searching for new models to motivate the workers. After collectivisation, the kolkhozes were not able to pay wages or salaries because Stalin had established such low prices on government purchases that they could not even cover transport costs. In reality, the farmers were denied a yield on the legal basis of planned state procurements.

Khrushchev raised the prices of agricultural produce significantly, and in the late 1950s and early 1960s, Estonian kolkhozes switched from Stalin's "workday quotas" to roubles and more or less stable wages. Brezhnev continued the development of agriculture and raised prices every five years. This was the basis for wage increases and the introduction of various new bonuses. However, the lack of efficiency was a real problem. Workers and foremen had no interest in efficiency and the effective use of farming inputs. Agriculture is based on the use of land; agricultural workers are dispersed over a large territory and their control is complicated.

The advantages of private farming become manifest when individual interest in the results creates the motivation for effective work and the effective use of resources. There were various examples of this in the USSR, where the results of good farming in work groups were sometimes rewarded by the farm management. This was the cornerstone of Gorbachev's agricultural policy when he held the leading position in the Kremlin. In the 1980s, teamwork and production cost calculations were propagated and leasing assets was permitted. However, it must be pointed out that renting land was not allowed.

My experience of working in different positions and twenty years of research into the management of kolkhozes and sovkhozes told me that large-scale farming was burdened by the high cost of management and transport as well as the wasteful and ineffective use of farming inputs due to the lack of the motivation of the labourers (Tamm, 1988 and 1989). More careful control of production costs, the establishment of profit departments and the legalisation of rental agreements at the level of the family appeared to offer a possibility for the decentralisation of management and increased responsibility based on property rights as well as increased production and revenue. Furthermore, these revenues were supposed to finance purchasing further new or existing assets for group or individual ownership.

Later, these minor reforms were viewed as a good source of experimental knowledge enabling people to adjust to a market economy. However, the protected "greenhouse" conditions of the Soviet times briefly described above were not a favourable environment for any major changes. There was no obvious crisis forcing people to change their mindsets and behaviour. If top kolkhoz executives attempted to initiate real changes their activities met with opposition from the middle management and specialists. Accountants refused to file the costs, production amounts, and revenues of the production units. The main reason for this was that most managers understood that radical decentralisation would mean the loss of their authority and positions, and that independent units could function without higher managers. To summarise, there was a lot of debate and paperwork, but few real changes or experiments.

Private Farming and Co-operatives

Gorbachev's "perestroika" opened the door for individual entrepreneurship through licensing from the rayon administration and the Law on Co-operatives. Some Russian authors have confirmed that this law was initiated and pushed through Soviet legislation by the leaders of powerful groups whose interest was to legalise their underground businesses. This might be true, and it appears to be the result of the efforts of a corporate network of criminals, local and top-level administrators interested in having legal incomes and funds without "laundering" it. It is worth remembering that substantial force was needed to bring about such concrete changes in the huge Soviet administrative system.

In Estonia, the new opportunities offered by the legal system were used by people who wished to gain a higher income through individual or group businesses rather than through their salaries. However, they were met with resistance. The directors of large enterprises were afraid of losing their employees to the private sector and hence refused to rent rooms and equipment. However, some managers saw the opportunity "to do business" by selling materials, production inputs and finished products at low prices (and often at a loss for the enterprise) to co-operatives for resale. These directors and managers often received large dividends as members or heads of the said co-operatives. In agriculture, the number of workers' co-operatives was relatively small and they did not play any significant role.

In the late 1980s, the myth of prosperous family farming sprouted from auxiliary homesteads and the nostalgia of pre-war independent farming. In his published studies, Ivar Raig statistically confirmed the efficiency of production on auxiliary homesteads (Raig, 1987 and 1988). An open discussion about small-scale family farming started in 1988, when permission was granted to the workers of kolkhozes and sovkhozes to lease assets and livestock. Most kolkhoz chairmen and managers were convinced that people would not enjoy small-scale farming because of the high personal responsibility and hard work, and because it could never become as efficient as large-scale farming. However, the ratio of agricultural producer prices to input prices in the Soviet economy were so favourable that it encouraged small-scale farming.

In 1988, the first 100 farmers applied for a total of 2,400 hectares of land. Approximately 25 farmers took up farming. It must be remembered that private ownership or the rent of land was not permitted at that time and land was provided under the Soviet Land Code for permanent use. The first applicants to start small-scale farming were mostly people who disliked working under managerial control; some preferred self-employment to team-work whilst others just had "conflicting personalities." Many of the first farmers had agricultural school diplomas or degrees from the Estonian Agricultural University.

In the following year, 1989, the government passed legislation permitting individual farming and 21,096 hectares were granted to 828 farms that same year. However, there still remained a social demand for family farms. The first draft of the Farm Law was prepared by officials and made public in August 1989 (Rahva Hääl, 1989). It stated that rayon land commissions should make the decisions on land tenure with the participation of representatives of the former land user, i.e. a kolkhoz or a sovkhoz. As a positive decision was only possible for non-contested cases, the representative of a collective farm had the right of *veto*. Following the Soviet example, the draft had a declarative content and most details remained unspecified. When the draft was published, discussion became rather more heated. Assistant Professor Heldur Peterson organised workshops with the participation of several people from the countryside, the Estonian Agricultural University and

Tartu University at the headquarters of the Estonian Agricultural University in Tartu.

The discussion mainly revolved around the alternative ways applicants could acquire farming land. One alternative would have been to form new farms (this was suggested in the official draft) with up to a hundred hectares of arable land using modern technology. The other alternative was to restore the pre-collectivisation family farms. These would have had approximately 25 hectares of land each, including 8–9 hectares of arable land. It was clear that this would not be enough for the investments in modern machinery in a free market. However, the experience of people was that three cows were enough to provide a livelihood for an entire family – and ten cows would have appeared as large-scale farming in Estonia.

Another problem was that many people, especially those with an agricultural education, no longer lived on the farms of their parents or grandparents. A large part of the population had left the countryside and sold their houses but, of course, they could not sell the land because they had no ownership of that land. Many people did not leave their homes voluntarily and their houses were requisitioned and given to kolkhozes. Sometimes, people bought back their houses (usually at minimum prices) after returning from Siberia, but often the houses had been sold to other people. The question was, who had the right to land: the present owners of dwellings and other buildings (who sometimes had restored the buildings from ruins, set up gardens, and lived there for a long time) or the heirs of the former owners living somewhere in the city?

Preference was given to the rightful owners and their heirs and in most cases, people had the opportunity to redeem the buildings through voluntary purchase. However, buildings on many farms remained unclaimed and the people currently living there, who maintained the homesteads and were fond of rural life, were indeed often more successful farmers than the heirs of the original owners would have been.

After some quite heated debates, I spent two or three nights at my typewriter and completed the first text for a draft on the Farm Law on the anniversary of the Molotov-Ribbentrop pact. Professor of Law Vilma Kelder and Assistant Professor Paul Varul (who later became Minister of Justice) formulated the draft based on my text.

In order to eliminate the possibility of officials misusing (e.g., for their country homes) the government funds appropriated to finance the construction of roads, electric lines and dwellings for family farmers, it was decided that only a person who would work full-time on his farm could have the rights of a farmer. For the first time, it became legal for a farmer to detach his share from a collective farm in kind. This law made no reference to the private ownership of land and it included only an allusion to the original size and borders of the land owned in 1940. As in the Soviet legislation, where the employment of other individuals was strictly prohibited, only three paid workers were permitted, but this rule was never enforced. In the draft, family farm ownership was the exclusive right of kolkhoz members.

An alternative draft was prepared by Assistant Professor Lembit Saarnits. Both drafts were presented at a meeting of the restored Tartumaa Taluliit (Tartu Region Farmers' Union) and preference was given to our draft. It was released for public debate and passed without significant changes by the Supreme Soviet of Estonia on 6 December 1989.

The restoration and establishment of family farms began mainly through auxiliary homesteads, where the former farm buildings remained or new ones were built. Officially, the number of cattle was restricted but some families kept as many as five cows. The Farm Law stated that a person's share of the collective property was to be calculated based on the value of collectivised assets and the time of membership (or employment) in a kolkhoz. A farmer who left a kolkhoz was permitted to claim his share in kind: a tractor, cattle, or other assets, for example. This was rarely used in practice as the kolkhoz management saw a danger of the disintegration of large-scale farming and the loss of their positions. In addition, the workers saw that family farming as an alternative would eliminate their jobs and they did not agree to vote for the reform at meetings. The socialist ideology opposing private ownership as a tool for exploitation had a certain role. However, in many cases, aspiring farmers had conflicted with kolkhoz chairmen and managers and in setting up their own farm they saw the possibility of leaving the collective farm and the influence of the management.

While writing the draft, we assumed that only a few new farms would be established and that only a few people would wish to restore the farms on their former private or parent-owned land. As the government gave significant financial benefits to family farmers, many people in possession of buildings applied for land without former ownership. In many cases, these new farmers were more experienced and committed to farming than the average citizen was. Besides, they had often already acquired machinery and equipment and were fervent advocates of restoring small-scale farming. An official practice was established to demand that the applicant provide a written denouncement of ownership by the former owner. This measure restrained the establishment of new farms. In many cases, farming was viewed as a prospective subsidiary enterprise, while the individual made his living from another type of business, such as wholesale or cutting and selling timber from his father's forests.

The Farm Law of 1989 was in force until the Land Reform Law was passed on 17 October 1991. The Land Reform Law was based on restitutional ideology, though it recognised the rights of the farmers who were allocated land under the Farm Law. By the end of 1992, there were 8,555 small farms with a total area of 218,867 hectares. The average size of a farm was 25.6 hectares, of which 11.1 hectares was arable land, 2.7 hectares natural meadows and pastures, 8.3 hectares forest and 3.5 hectares other land. These farms amounted to only 6.8% of the hectarage that small farms had covered up to 1940. At that time, however, the average area of a private farm had been smaller than 3 hectares.

Furthermore, there are two points that must be mentioned. I had forecast that the managers of the collective farms would be alarmed about the disturbance of large-scale farming by family farmers when the private farmers' share of land tenure reached about one tenth. However, this already happened when farmers took possession of 3% of the arable land. Secondly, the new farms on the land of other persons consist of just one third of the total number of farms and delivered land. The area of the land allotted to non-owners (with no history of legitimate former ownership) is not more than 1–2% of the total agricultural land.

Table 8.1 The number of family farms in Estonia

Total area, ha	1991	1992	1993	1994	1995
0–5	164	576	659	818	1,634
5.1–10	244	894	1,040	2,298	1,827
10.1–20	581	1,881	2,269	2,823	3,750
20.1–30	539	1,499	1,804	2,191	2,721
30.1–50	581	1,511	1,811	2,090	2,488
50.1–100	213	631	784	879	1,027
Over 100	17	37	45	54	66
Total	2,339	7,029	8,412	10,153	13,513
Average area	26.6	25.1	25.4	24.8	23.1

Source: Statistical Office of Estonia

The first farmers received significant aid from the government and the kolkhozes, including financial support. This encouraged people to restore small family farms and also encouraged naive expectations for the feasibility of those farms in a market economy. Afterwards, these expectations turned into a demand for an agricultural support policy, which is practised in most developed economies, e.g. the Common Agricultural Policy of the European Union. Thus, the initial financial support for small-scale farmers caused new problems, including a steep government policy towards small-scale farming and the splitting-up of kolkhozes and sovkhozes during the agricultural reform process.

The Ideology of Restitution and The Law on the Principles of Property Reform

The first agrarian political parties were organised in 1989. Taluliit, the Estonian Farmers' Federation (established on 22 January 1989) was not declared as a political party but it was an interest group defending the rights of private farmers. The Rural Union (established on 7 May 1989) united people who held top managerial positions in kolkhozes and sovkhozes. As a follow-up, the Estonian Central Rural Party was established to support the most radical changes toward restoring small-scale farming, a free market economy, and privatisation. The leaders of this party, Ivar Raig, Liia Hänni, and Jaan Leetsaar were very active politicians who supported the privatisation of kolkhozes and sovkhozes through a system of common vouchers following the example of industrial enterprises. The Land Union held a more conservative line and was against this model of reform as vouchers would have equalised the shares of rich and poor kolkhoz members. However, the conservatism of the land unionists did not allow them to propose any active plan for the transition reform and they rapidly lost their positions to restitutionists.

On 20 December 1990, the Supreme Council of the Estonian SSR declared the collectivisation of agriculture by Soviet authorities an unlawful act and voted for a land reform by the restitution of land ownership. This meant that collective farms would lose land tenure. The underlying idea was that the rapid privatisation of assets and the establishment of new enterprises owned by employees would create an interest group that would support the principle of "land to the ploughman." Obviously most managers of collective farms did not realise the inevitability of radical changes. Their former experience of Soviet planned improvements was that after some disputes no real changes took place. However, this time their experience did not help them.

On 13 June 1991, the Supreme Council passed the Law on the Principles of Property Reform (Omandireformi aluste seadus), which proclaimed the restitution of previous owners' rights to their property and land. A week later, on 20 June, a resolution prohibiting any reorganisation or changes to kolkhozes and all transactions in the capital assets of kolkhozes and sovkhozes was passed by the Supreme Council. The main idea of the law was that privatisation should be performed according to unified rules in all sectors and the first priority would be given to the restoration of the previous owners' properties. The law defined the rightful owners and their heirs, but only one article (number 14) referred to the possibility of returning or compensating collectivised assets under a special law.

As we will see later, a draft on agricultural reform had already been prepared but the conservative agrarian politicians missed the chance for the transition of agriculture based on large-scale production units. The radical restitution ideology emerged as the victor in the struggle and the Land Reform Law was applied to the restoration of pre-war small farms. However, as often happens, the results were just the opposite of rapid restitution. Due to complex procedures and the lack of sufficient regulations on land reform, this law halted the process of restoring the former family farms and establishing new ones.

Changes in the Economic Environment and a Pessimistic Forecast for 1992–1994

The stable and quiet Soviet system collapsed before most people became fully aware of the unavoidable transition and changes, including the reorganisation of the collective structures in agriculture. The political decision for independence meant that the eastern market for agricultural and other products was largely lost. Estonians had learned from history that their eastern neighbours used foreign trade to apply political pressure and this pattern of behaviour had not changed. Hence, after gaining independence, Estonia lost the eastern market as Russia closed its borders to trade.

However, the principal problem was not in the market for produce but in the supply of farming inputs, as Estonian agriculture was 90% dependent on supplies from Russia and other regions of the USSR. In 1991, the Ministry of Agriculture decided to prepare a forecast for 1992–94. Experts from different institutions were invited to prepare the forecast and it was proposed that I would provide a paper for the government (A short version of this paper was later published in Tamm, 1992). Later I had to present this paper at a meeting of the government. It was the first issue on the agenda but at the beginning of this government meeting, the Minister of Foreign Affairs, Lennart Meri, introduced two extra issues for consideration. Then the Prime Minister, Edgar Savisaar, informed the cabinet that he had to leave in 15 minutes. The Ministers discussed the colour of the Estonian passport for more than half an hour and then the Minister of Economy, Jaak Leiman, the stand-in for the Prime Minister, said that only 5 minutes remained to discuss agriculture. He is a good friend of mine, so he did not interrupt me, and after my brief 5 to 7 minute presentation there was open discussion. Answering some questions on the issue took another 15 minutes. However, nothing was really resolved. Government officials prepared the text of the minutes (Eesti Vabariigi Valitsuse Istungi Protokoll, 1991) and that was all. The most crucial proposal in the forecast paper concerning the rapid ownership reform and transition in agriculture was not mentioned at all.

Experts saw the main problem was the changing prices of imported inputs. According to the estimates by the Ministry of Agriculture, the import of farming inputs in 1990 was approximately USD one billion at world market prices (except for one million tons of fodder grain). The sales of agricultural products were only about one half of this sum and export (including timber) was only USD 30 million. Experts and managers regarded the diminishing supplies of fodder grain and the rising prices of fuel as the main problems. In particular, the effects of the destabilisation of the fuel supply were considered potentially disastrous. The forecast included three scenarios. The basic scenario was based on a 70% decrease in the former supplies from the USSR and a 10–15% decrease in agricultural production. The "optimistic" scenario was based on the presumption that there would be the possibility of importing half a million tons of fodder grain and fuel by barter agreements. Meanwhile, the "crisis" scenario prognosticated a 30–40% decrease in production in 1992 and the continued deterioration of machinery due to a lack of fuel and spare parts.

However, this was only the beginning of the changes. We were inexperienced and unaware of the pressure of market forces, where markets could be lost. Furthermore, the USSR distribution organisations that received our production no longer paid for it. In the summer of 1991, the government made a decision to free prices. After this, consumer prices rose, but producer prices lagged far behind. Food processing plants got into debt because they were not able to find buyers for butter and meat.

The deficit in working capital and high current debts to fuel and electricity suppliers caused a collapse in ineffective agricultural production. In 1992, fuel loans had an interest rate of 38%. Most agricultural enterprises lost their ability to pay wages on time. The worsening situation made reform unavoidable and the politicians and the management of the collective farms used this as a weapon against the "reformers." The management of the collective farms sold cattle and hogs to get revenue for the current needs. Employees lost their motivation and more and more often produce, cattle feed, equipment and machinery were stolen for use on auxiliary homesteads and farms, or for sale.

Finally, the currency reform on 20 June 1992 set the rate of exchange at one Estonian kroon (EEK) to 10 roubles and swept away the working capital of enterprises as well as the people's savings. The fixed exchange rate, EEK 8 for one DEM, was vital to stabilise the economy but agricultural producers were unexpectedly pushed into the harsh environment of the market economy. The shock that Estonia experienced during 1990–1993 could be characterised as "price scissors;" the costs for farming inputs rose an average of 55 times compared with an increase of approximately 1.5 times in the prices for agricultural products. Estonian agricultural producers lost their protection and subsidies as the market was opened for subsidised export from other countries – in many cases, surpluses, which had been stored for years, were sold to Estonia at low (dumping) prices.

The Main Ideas of Agricultural Property Reform

Main Goals and Preconditions

The main goal and problem in the transition from a socialist to a market economy was establishing private ownership. This far-reaching reform was necessary, but serious, theoretical concepts or the experience for doing it without a sharp fall in production was not available. On the other hand, there was no immediate crisis or social pressure forcing the politicians to pass the Law on Agricultural Reform (finally enacted in 1992). Nobody had well-founded arguments or a clear image of its social consequences.

The Land Reform Law (1991) pursued the rights of landowners or their heirs. These had principally been outlined in the Property Reform Law (1990). In those days, the prevailing opinion was that most landowners would be returned their land, which they would then use themselves. Thus, the former Soviet large-scale farms would lose their tenure to land use. Political parties played on the differences of group interests. Most radical parties demanded the restitution of family farming. The conservatives warned about the destruction of large-scale farms, the decrease in agricultural production, and that it would cause a remarkable increase in rural unemployment.

The fellows of the Higher School of Agrarian Management (reorganised as the Institute of Rural Development, Maaelu Arengu Instituut, in 1993) organised a workshop on 9–11 August 1990, near Põlva. Here, agrarian economists, farmers, the chairmen, and managers of collective farms and other officials, journalists and members of parliament from the Supreme Council of Estonia discussed the main points and goals of the reform. After three days of discussions, there were no clear conclusions or concrete ideas. However, my experience in preparing the Farm Law (1989) helped me to propose some ideas for small group discussion. On 15 August 1990, I finished the first text of the draft. A team consisting of Jüri Ginter (Ph.D. in sociology and a lawyer), Mati Tamm (Ph.D. in agricultural economics), Tõnu Ivask (Ph.D. in agricultural economics) and Mati Meeliste (lawyer) did further work. One of the researchers took up many of the ideas in private discussions with his father, who was the chairman of Kanepi kolkhoz, but our attempt to test the ideology of the law in Kanepi was rejected by the kolkhoz general meeting. (In Chapter 3, Ilkka Alanen's colourful description sheds light on the background of the events in Kanepi. At that time, we had no knowledge of the developments leading to the defeat of the proposal). There was no financing for the project. In fact, we worked voluntarily and signed our texts as a temporary work group at the Extension Centre of the Agricultural University.

The team was unanimous that the only way to avoid a collapse of agriculture was rapid privatisation and that this would give the owners a better chance to decide on the other problems related to adjusting to the market system. After the closure of the eastern market and the diminishing demand on the internal market, it was clear that production could not be maintained at previous levels. Agricultural machinery and equipment needed modernisation, but was usable for some years. We laid our hope on department managers and the specialists of collective farms as the potential entrepreneurs that would establish new enterprises based on former collective farm units – such as cowsheds, pig houses or repair shops. We believed that this would give birth to an interest group that would be able to form a political party that would pursue land reform based on the traditional idea of "land to the ploughman."

Another point that we agreed on was the decentralisation of the reform. The Estonian government and administrative system were in transition, and the legal system and courts did not really function. There were no officials available to oversee a centralised reform under the rule of the government. In the Soviet system, local administration had been reduced to a minimum and low salaries did not allow active and educated personnel to be employed. In rural communities, the most educated people, who presumably were interested in the reform, were the managers and specialists on the collective farms. The members of kolkhozes firmly knew that they were the owners of kolkhoz assets. Nobody would have been able to convince kolkhoz members that they should acquire kolkhoz assets through purchase – for them, buying their own assets would be nonsense. If such a law were enacted, they would simply have taken what they wanted. Armed guards were in some places posted in an attempt to avoid destruction, but as agricultural assets were scattered throughout the whole country, such action was unrealistic and ineffective. Sovkhozes were state-owned, but in reality they were a reorganised form of kolkhozes and people did not perceive much difference between the two.

We worked hard on the problem of how to ensure the right of every entitled subject to claim his share in kind or in cash. The idea was that only in this way would people with an entrepreneurial attitude be interested in the reform; the more passive majority of employees could be forced into it. However, all the proposed ideas presupposed complicated rules and they were left out because they would hardly work.

The team also compiled a list of the main principles of the agrarian reform on which various groups and political parties could reach an agreement. These ideas were:

1) The restitution of the rights of the previous legitimate owners and their heirs to the land and other property;
2) The compensation of collectivised assets by the existing tangible assets of kolkhozes and sovkhozes, whilst the rest of the assets would be divided into "workshares";
3) As the sovkhozes had been reorganised from kolkhozes, both large-scale farm types would be privatised according to the same principles and regulations;
4) The prevention of a rapid decrease in agricultural production, as well as prevention of the destabilisation of the market and a lack of food and unemployment.

In the beginning, we naively believed that the politicians as well as kolkhoz chairmen and municipal officials would support the draft for the reform, and we included the privatisation of agricultural production processing plants in the draft. However, when we analysed the character of the interests of the directors of those enterprises, it was clear that this strategy would not have been successful. The draft on agricultural property reform was published in November 1990 (Maaleht, 1990). There was little discussion about it. The Minister of Agriculture, Vello Lind, was interested in this project and invited us to meet him and two emigrant experts of Estonian descent. Those experts considered it ridiculous to conduct the reform with the participation of the current collective farm management. We explained that in fact all educated people available for this work had worked in the Soviet structures. They offered no alternative proposal.

The Deputy Minister of Agriculture, Maido Pajo, participated in the further work on the draft and made an official proposal to the government. However, the official procedure was that all drafts had to be approved by an expert commission. During the next winter and spring, Maido Pajo repeatedly applied for approval and we met with the commission three times. As the members of the commission were officials with little knowledge of agriculture, they hardly understood the underlying concept of the draft. On the other hand, we did not understand the behaviour of the commission. I was informed in private conversations that our draft was not approved because it did not appear to fully satisfy the interests of the former owners.

As a reaction to the criticism, I composed the text for a new draft on 30 August 1991, in which the former owners were given a key role. This happened after the coup attempt in Moscow and the declaration of independence in Estonia (20 August 1991). After the return or compensation of collectivised assets and the municipalisation of social services, the remaining assets of collective farms were regarded as a profit on collectivised assets, and the proposal was to deal out 30–70% of it as dividends to the former owners. The rest would have been divided between the employees according to their participation in the reform and from the viewpoint of the continuity of the production process. In this proposal, the concept of workshares was eliminated. The idea was for this to be adopted as a softer alternative. I presented the text to Maido Pajo and he distributed some copies. Some days later, the new draft was sharply criticised in a leading article in the "Rahva Hääl" newspaper and compared with Stalin's repression during collectivisation. The restitutionist politicians did not react but the media worked against the reform under the slogan "demolishing of collective farms is inadmissible."

The drafts by our team aimed at establishing large-scale farming. Of course, they did not openly specify that collective farms would remain as a whole. As mentioned above, the Estonian parliament declared the collectivisation of agriculture an unlawful act on 20 December 1990 and the decision to execute the land reform by restitution was passed. However, the second draft proposed the privatisation of technological units as whole units and would have granted them the privilege of land tenure.[2] To maintain those units, a so-called partnership farm model was proposed (Tamm, 1991b), and there were no obstacles to further mergers of technological units into larger enterprises on the scale of the former collective farms.

I can only guess at why this draft was not supported by the chairmen of collective farms and politicians. The chairmen, who had made their careers as the members of the ruling Communist Party, were not ripe for political divergence and criticism. I remember a meeting of all the chairmen of the kolkhozes and sovkhozes at the Estonia Theatre in Tallinn at the beginning of Gorbachev's "perestroika." They demanded that the Communist Party should defend collective farm management against any public criticism and that such criticism ought to be banned in the media. To me this was reminiscent of Estonia's history of German landlords, who had full power over their tenants without any responsibility for their well being. I am far from denying the positive role of the kolkhoz chairmen in developing Estonian rural life, social services, and recreational activities. The restoration of architecturally notable landlords' manors surely indicated care for cultural heritage. However, I remember a case, when in conversation, where a sovkhoz chairman planning to retire had asked the rayon party secretary to appoint his son as his successor. Supposedly, hundreds of years ago a similar type of behaviour had helped dependent vassals obtain the hereditary title of "baron." There were other examples of where a son of a kolkhoz chairman followed in his father's footsteps. This matter is not only morally unacceptable, but it also explains the roots of the workers' attitude to kolkhoz chairmen as "red barons."

Usually the question of why many chairmen of collective farms were passive and did not support the reform is explained by political attacks, such as the common usage of "red baron" as an abusive ideological label. This seems to be less than half the truth, but maybe the kolkhoz chairmen were afraid of facing the real reasons. When losing the powerful party umbrella,

---

2   A "technological unit" was later defined in the Law on Agricultural Reform (1992) as "things aggregated as a whole, where separating any part of the whole would render the remaining part technologically useless for its original purposes."

they lost their courage. They had been bosses, not entrepreneurs and leaders. They had no heart to hand over the right of decision to entitled subjects and to support the reform plan. They feared the risk of changes and democracy and hung on to their former authority because they did not regard the new alternatives attractive or even satisfactory. Of course, there were a number of cases where chairmen actively participated in the reform process, but not always successfully. In addition, other places in Estonia went through events similar to those in Kanepi. The reasons were identical but the scenarios were different.

While working on the drafts and discussing the interests of different groups, including the chairmen and managers of the collective farms, we found that there had to be some leadership or key positions available for them to alleviate their fears.

The passing of the Land Reform Law on 17 October 1991 decreed the restitution of land ownership. For the technological units, there was a possibility to reserve land tenure through the decision of the municipal council but I know of no example where this rule was applied. The most complicated and crucial problem of the agrarian reform was how to restore real estate proprietorship, and to harmonise the separate ownership of fixed assets and land. There was also the problem of what should be privatised first: land or assets. The political decision prioritising the restitution of land property caused about a two-year delay in the privatisation of agricultural assets. Furthermore, the constraints imposed by the interests of different social groups led to a political compromise as a basis for legislation, consequently those laws did not fully satisfy any group. This again caused debate and conflict between social groups and delays in the reform process. As most economists and politicians later agreed, the delay to agricultural reform resulted in the essential losses of assets and cattle, a rapid decrease in production, jobs and incomes, and a fall in the standard of living.

The Law on Agricultural Reform

The Law on Agricultural Reform and Structural Transition

The decision was made to privatise the assets of the Soviet large-scale farms (kolkhozes and sovkhozes) when the Law on Agricultural Reform was passed on 11 March 1992. It itemised the following principles:

1. Collectivised (mostly in 1949–1950) assets would be returned if they remained (buildings), or compensated by other assets of equivalent value or by a share of assets in kind or by payment in cash.
2. Both kolkhozes and sovkhozes would be reformed according to the same rules. Only buildings financed by the government would be treated as the property of the Estonian Republic and could be used, leased or privatised by the government.
3. The land would be improved with drainage and other constructions.
4. Public buildings and other public assets would be transferred to municipal ownership. Buildings constructed with government funding would be transferred to state ownership and later municipalised or privatised.
5. Long-term loans, once borrowed from the Soviet State Bank, could be paid off through the government budget at a sum equal to the value of the municipalised assets.
6. Other loans and unpaid accounts would be settled or transferred to the newly established enterprises as debts on received assets.
7. The remainder of kolkhoz or sovkhoz property would be privatised based on "workshares" calculated by the number of years worked. The law would define a list of "entitled subjects", which would include persons employed at the time of the reform, pensioners, persons who had worked five or more years or were elected to local administration.
8. Compensation for collectivised assets in the form of shares and workshares could be used (1) for privatising assets for farming, or (2) for joining the shares to receive the assets for partnerships, joint-stock companies or co-operatives, and (3) shares could be freely given or sold to other shareholders of a kolkhoz or sovkhoz.
9. Buildings, equipment, machinery, and implements would be privatised as integrated technological units (building, cattle, machinery, etc. together in one package). The goal of this rule was to avoid parcelling and breaking down functional production units, causing a collapse in production and unemployment.
10. The reform would be organised by a commission approved by the local municipal council. The commission would consist of three representatives elected in a kolkhoz or sovkhoz general meeting; three representatives elected in a meeting of local small-scale farmers; three representatives from the local municipal council, and one or two government officials. The election of kolkhoz or sovkhoz chairmen and chief accountants as members of the commission was prohibited.

11. The execution of the reform would be delegated to different bodies. Initially, the chairmen of collective farms would be responsible for working out the reform plan that would be submitted for approval at a kolkhoz general meeting and endorsed by the reform commission. The municipal council was responsible for settling complaints.

12. Five percent of the book value of the assets were to be transferred to a reserve fund that would be used to cover the expenses of the reform and was also reserved for claims up to three years after the completion of the reform.

The law did not establish any date for the completion of the reform; it was later decided that the reform plans had to be finished by the end of 1993. All decision-making was decentralised at local level. The task of government representatives was to ensure the correct appraisal of public property and the legitimacy of the decisions made by the reform commission. Discussion and sometimes intrigue delayed the reform and caused various problems. These will be discussed later.

In practise, delays to the reform were caused by the fact that the review and decision-making process on the applications for the restitution or compensation of unlawfully collectivised property went more slowly than had been presumed in the Property Reform Law. At first, the term for applications (27 January 1991) was postponed for six months, and in certain conditions for even longer. The special commissions in the district administrations were unable to review all the documents in such a short period. The number of applicants claiming land was one and a half times more than the actual number of farms in 1940. Furthermore, the officials had no clear rules for or experience in matters such as this. Usually the applications were reviewed by the reform commission. The commission used the former farmers' applications and old inventory lists from kolkhozes that had been released by the records officers, to calculate the value of collectivised assets. The rayon commission made the final decision.

The Supreme Council did not solve the main problem: how to determine the value of collectivised assets. In the kolkhozes, where the first experiments in calculating shares as described above took place, it was relatively simple as the rouble was still a stable currency at that time. In 1991–1992, the rouble was devalued and the monetary reform of 20 June 1992 signified the change from roubles to Estonian kroons. The real market values of assets deviated significantly from their book values in both directions. It was impossible to compare the market or book values of existing and collectivised assets used in an era of horses, since most collective farms no longer had any horses. Nobody proposed a working solution. When the draft was first composed, we assumed that this problem would be solved in the meeting of entitled subjects. However, finding a solution for the problem was very important from the viewpoint of the different interest groups. The former owners were interested in a higher value while the kolkhoz employees were interested in a lower one, as an individual's share of the total assets would thus be bigger. It was clear that the employees would form a majority among the entitled subjects.

The politicians supporting restitution gained another victory and the resolution on the application of the Law on Agricultural Reform stated that the rules for determining the value of collectivised assets would be enacted by law. It seems that this delay in the reform also satisfied the conservative politicians. However, some kind of a solution was necessary. I found that the only assets with a more or less comparable value at the time of the forced collectivisation and the current reform, which could therefore be used as a measure, were cows. It seemed sensible, as the "cow unit" was commonly used for calculations in cattle feeding. When I presented this idea to my colleagues, it was taken as a joke. Next, I presented the idea in a discussion with a small group of officials in the office of the Deputy Minister for Agriculture, Maido Pajo, where Kaido Kama, a Member of Parliament, advocated the rights of former owners. I am not quite sure what happened after that, but at the beginning of the following year (27 January 1993), the Estonian Parliament passed a Law on the Evaluation of Collectivised Assets, which was later nicknamed the "Cow Price Law." The law set the value of a collectivised cow at 700 kroons and the other assets were appraised by various coefficients. The "cow unit" coefficients were also used for other types of cattle, horses, pigs, poultry, etc. The general meetings on the collective farms, where the reform process was initiated immediately after the Reform Law came into force, were already using the cow as the uniform yardstick although it had not yet been decreed by law. Usually, a relatively low price was established for the assets. The law legitimated those decisions, if the value of a collectivised cow was not established below the average of the current book value.

To summarise, by using the "collectivised cow value" as a uniform measure, the commissions divided the value of the assets of collective farms between two interest groups: 1) compensation for the collectivised assets for the aged former owners and, 2) workshares for the middle-aged employees.

The heirs of the former owners also had the right to claim compensation in kind on the condition that they would start their own farms.

The Reform in Action

Training the Reform Commissions and Chairmen of the Collective Farms

After the ratification of the law, additional regulations were elaborated, such as the article on the reform commission, the procedure of calculating shares, the instructions for determining state ownership, etc. The government confirmed these regulations on 24 March 1992 and soon afterwards, the Central Reform Commission was set up at the Ministry of Agriculture. It was headed by Deputy Minister of Agriculture, Maido Pajo, and the members of the team that had prepared the draft as well as ministry officials participated in it. The task of the commission was to share experiences and to consult with the Ministry of Agriculture as well as with the local reform commissions of other bodies.

After adopting the regulations in April 1992, the team that had prepared the draft and some officials from the Ministry of Agriculture held three regional seminars for the chairmen of collective farms and local administrators. The seminars were mostly intended for preparing for the formation of reform commissions. A few weeks later, the next step was training offered to the chairmen of the reform commissions. The participants at those seminars represented the different, sometimes contradictory views of various interest groups. Moreover, a number of seminars were held, mostly to introduce alternative procedures for the reform plan.

As mentioned earlier, transactions with capital assets had been prohibited but now they were permitted with the consent of the reform commissions. Some chairmen did not follow this rule or were dissatisfied with the restrictions on their freedom of action. At the same time production fell due to a diminishing supply of inputs and the loss of motivation in the unclear situation. A rapid rise in the prices of farming inputs, inflation and delays with payments for production at the processing enterprises "ate" into the working capital of the collective farms. In the spring of 1992, the government arranged sales of fuel on credit, but the interest rate was 38%. Most kolkhoz chairmen, accustomed to Soviet interest levels of 0.2–0.7%, did not believe that this interest rate would really have to be paid and put their collective farms into heavy debt. Later, the debts increased due to unpaid social services expenses and sometimes income taxes, because bookkeeping now showed good profits as a result of *the revaluation of capital assets (goodwill)*. To balance cash flow, chairmen often attempted to get money for wages, fuel, purchases and other immediate needs by selling cattle, tractors or other assets in demand. This was, in many cases, the first step towards the demolition or bankruptcy of a collective farm.

Main Models for Transition, Procedures for Privatisation

According to the Law on Agricultural Reform, the following actions for the transition process were enacted: assets were inventoried, values were fixed to technological units, a list of entitled subjects was drawn up, share values were calculated, the reform plan was prepared and confirmed, the privatisation applications were drawn up, assets were transferred and the collective farms were liquidated as legal entities. *Not all this was dictated by law*, but the reform plan was mostly prepared by the managers of the collective farms themselves. This document regulated the terms and preconditions for submitting applications, and the procedures for decision-making. The reform plans were confirmed at the general meetings of the kolkhoz employees and if the reform commission subsequently passed the plan, it was put into force. If a case was opposed, the municipal government counsel decided whether the plan would come into force or if it was to be rejected. In the latter case, the plan would be modified and the procedure of confirmation repeated.

The entitled subjects (the former owners and their heirs, current and former employees) received shares with a total sum equal to the book value of the assets after the values already paid to extant former owners (restitution), state and municipal assets, debts and reserve fund (5%) had been subtracted. The former owners or their heirs had three possibilities to realise their share: 1) substitution by other assets to the same value (compensation in kind, for example in cattle), 2) a share of collective farm assets (compensation vouchers) and 3) a cash payment.

The performance of these rights was restricted by the rule on how terms would be decided by the reform commission, according to the reform plan. In practice, this meant that a meeting of present kolkhoz employees approved the reform plan with little regard to the former owners and their desire for compensation in kind. Due to the lack of cash reserves, compensation in cash was also rather exceptional. At this point, the prevailing form of compensation in shares (compensation vouchers) was in the same pot as the compensation in the workshares according to working years. Every entitled subject could apply for any asset. Privatisation meant the trading of shares to assets, which then became the property of the applicant. For the privatisation of technological units or assets with a large value, the combined applications of several persons and the free of charge or paid transfers of shares between entitled subjects were permitted.

It was submitted that after privatisation, assets could be joined into different types of business, such as a private or family farm, a co-operative, a partnership, or a joint-stock company. The Law on Agricultural Reform did not control the establishment of new businesses because this was regulated by other laws and regulations. Of course, interested persons had the possibility of an earlier agreement to a joint application for assets with the goal of later using it in their business. However, this matter was not within the scope of the reform plan. The law enacted the preference for co-operatives to privatise units particularly in the service industry (flour mills, etc.). Hence, new forms of business were to be established after privatisation based on the owners' free choice to combine their assets.

Problems, Conflicting Interests, and Shortcomings

At a time when most politicians were talking about speeding up the reforms, especially privatisation, to create private ownership as the basis for a market economy, dragging by both the main interest groups became obvious. No serious studies on the reasons behind this attitude have been made, hence the conclusions presented here are based on a generalisation of the information received during the training courses and numerous formal and informal meetings with the representatives of different interest groups in negotiations and consultations, the discussions at the meetings of the Central Reform Commission, the complaints to the Ministry of Agriculture, articles in the press, and my personal findings.

The chairmen, managers, and employees of the collective farms delayed the process, obviously hoping that large farms would somehow remain and everybody could enjoy their former jobs, incomes, and positions. Some started their own farms or businesses, which offered contracting services that had previously been available from the collective farms. Usually those services proved unprofitable, even though the machinery was often purchased at its book value, which was significantly below the market price. Sometimes there was thieving in the strict sense of the word. In many cases, the kolkhoz leaders needed more time to give their grey businesses a legal status. They were not ready for equality and democratic decision-making. In the beginning, they used manipulation to defend their interests in the kolkhoz general meetings by exploiting the uncertainty of the less-informed employees and pensioners.

As an interest group, the former owners were not organised to the same degree as the previous group. The declarations on restitution promised them more than they received. For example, the land reform was only at an initial stage. The former owners entitled to restitution had other more urgent problems than the privatisation of collective farm assets. The former owner's share was defined in kind and a decrease in total assets or the demolition of collective farms meant no change (or an increase in their relative share). They had no reason to hurry – quite the opposite; they needed time for reorientation to establish their farms or some other type of business. Some heirs of former farm owners worked as collective farm employees but in many cases they lived in a different part of the country.

It seems that politicians were not interested in rapid reform – the opposite appeared to be true. Every transitional change obviously causes some destruction, something will be lost, and people are under stress and uncertainty. This is a good environment for political games such as "fishing in muddy water" – promising people (the voters) that things will get better if they support a certain political party. In this rapidly changing situation, the lack of information was total and people's naive expectations were exploited to meet this deficit. Rural people, a privileged group in the former Soviet Estonia, lost their high standard of living and dissatisfaction was fertile ground for political ambitions. Rapid reform would have clarified the situation and the people, no longer busy with the business of satisfying their most basic needs, would then have been less influenced by political leaders.

Shortcomings in the reform process began with the formation of local reform commissions. Unqualified people were often appointed as members. Moreover, farmers' representatives were sometimes on bad terms with the representatives or chairmen of the collective farms. There were fewer problems and shortcomings in those collective farms where the chairmen were more co-operative. Often it was a great help if they proposed qualified candidates for election to the commission at the kolkhoz general meeting.

The next round of problems was the inventory of assets and the calculation of shares. Sometimes, in the earlier years of the kolkhozes, accounting had not been kept up to date and some documents on collectivised assets were destroyed or lost. Also, the data for calculating workshares was sometimes incomplete and the entire procedure was time consuming as the calculations (with few exceptions) were made by hand. Many debates arose over the technological units. Farmers wanted to divide tractors and other machines among themselves but the chairmen of the collective farms insisted on putting them on the inventory of assets for technological units.

The reform plan was the most important document regulating the execution of the reform. Many people were not fully aware of the importance of the careful preparation of this document. Therefore, most cases of the misfortunes and bad outcomes of the reform had their roots in a poor reform plan. Following the decentralisation of agricultural reform, the future destiny of each parish or village was determined by the people who had been given the task of drawing up the reform plan, and Kanepi was one of the more unfortunate cases. An even worse situation arose when there was no real plan at all, and the assets were divided without rules. To some extent, this happened on most collective farms. Sometimes the heirs to the former owners claimed their fathers' cows and sent them to the slaughterer. Tractors were given out to farmers or farmers' co-operatives with no regard to the functionality of larger technological units. However, a cowshed without cows is useless, just like a dairy farm with 200 or 400 cows is impossible to maintain without tractors. Today, the fact is that the Estonian countryside is full of empty buildings with equipment, windows and doors all broken and scattered.

There were no clear reasons for the chairmen, managers, and specialists not trying to maintain the technological units. The usual explanation was political pressure and the fact that the chairmen were called "red barons." The real reasons are obviously something else. It was mentioned earlier that some kolkhoz chairmen did not agree to the loss of their position.

I tried to propagate the establishment of Savings and Loan Associations as financial centres based on the facilities and employees from the collective farms in the hope that this would create a new role for former chairmen and top managers (Tamm, 1991a). However, it was obviously too different from their previous experience and knowledge. However, some people followed this path. The Bank of Estonia established strict rules for Savings and Loan Associations. The evident but undeclared reason for this was the division of the financial market and the elimination of competitors to the urban banks. The moment was lost and the result was that the savings of the rural people were deposited in bank accounts in the larger towns and local loan institutions did not come into existence. The Savings Bank closed many rural branches and people had to waste their time going to towns for the simplest transactions.

Another visible reason was that chairmen, managers, and specialists felt uncertain about doing business and managing under new and unknown market conditions. As they saw how the situation was worsening, the cost of farming inputs rising and production declining, they preferred their own small farms or businesses outside the field of agriculture. Most managers and specialists had grown up in farming families, but as they did not work near their parents, many of them left the collective farm and "returned home." Before this, they tried to acquire as many collective assets for themselves as possible.

On some collective farms, the management drew up a reform plan that featured few changes to the existing collective farm. In the central part of Estonia, Adavere sovkhoz was one of the farms where the reform plan included an article on a producers' co-operative. Later, their example was followed by the other collective farms in the Jõgeva County, thus performing the reform without dividing the assets or dividing the large farm organisation. In the County of Järva, the three largest and richest collective farms in Estonia (Aravete, Estonia and Väätsa) adopted the same model and they were reorganised into partnerships. The decisions were made by a majority vote in kolkhoz general meetings. To some extent, this was a restriction of the rights of the subjects entitled to compensation in kind, but their claims were more or less satisfied by giving out cows, tractors and other assets, and sometimes pay-offs in cash.

In Kanepi, the kolkhoz chairman that proposed the first reform plan was outvoted when the division of the collective farm was foreseen. Usually, the middle managers were behind this, since they were worried about their positions and jobs. They were supported by privileged groups of workers, such as lorry drivers – middle-aged men who were highly paid and highly respected. The division of the large farm was a threat to their jobs because smaller units had no need for in-house transport capacity. These groups easily found support among older people. These retired persons evidently believed that after the division of assets and the closure of the collective farm, nobody would offer affordable services (usually paid by a bottle of vodka) for their auxiliary homesteads.

The reform was delayed because of suspicions that the management "was grabbing the best pieces." There were cases where the chairman and managers tried to use their privileged position to privatise the more profitable or modern assets.

In general, the decision whether to break up the collective farm or not was the crucial question. This inevitably needed a solution and was a matter of vehement discussion. However, when people consulted authorities and experts, time flew, the value of assets decreased, the technological units lost their capacity, equipment deteriorated, and cows were sent to the slaughterer. The above-mentioned large farms did not suffer a significant decrease in production. This was because they maintained themselves as a whole and were able to make fast decisions. A radical decision was usually needed, but where it was made, farms continued production at almost their former levels. When the decision was delayed, the situation destabilised and usually resulted in a breakdown. This was the case in Kanepi.

In practice, deliberate obstructions to the reform process took place at the stages of preparing and approving the reform plan. The representatives of different groups, e.g. collective farm employees and the members of the reform commission, did not agree on decisions. Sometimes, the reform was suddenly accelerated after the chairman or the members of the commission, or the managers of the collective farms, had obtained the assets they wanted.

The next type of confrontation was also very common. It arose when managers reorganised a collective farm or its departments into a partnership and continued production. In other words, they took over the assets without any legal privatisation under the Law on Agricultural Reform. Thus, they bypassed the legal procedure of privatising the assets to entitled subjects. Again, the managers were obviously afraid that if individual people became owners they would not agree on combining their assets to form a joint enterprise. Some managers also attempted to get the assets into the hands of a select small group. Some entitled subjects remained without any possibility of getting their share in kind if they did not want to allow the managers to allocate their share as a partial payment for a partnership. The problem was that these people did not want to be members of a given partnership, or the reverse, and that the managers of the partnership did not like to see them as such. The people who intended to set up a farm were dissatisfied, as they could not get any assets necessary for their farm.

There were complicated lawsuits on issues of possession. However, as the process of privatisation dragged on, it became impossible to privatise the assets that were in the possession of a partnership. Those partnerships used the assets without any rent or other payment, and sometimes sold the assets to get money for wages and other current expenses. As the assets were not formally transferred, there was no real responsibility. These cases were usually quite complex and difficult to solve because the parties involved usually disagreed on most aspects of the issue. The situation became even more complex due to changes in legislation. For example, the amendment to the article on the evaluation of collectivised assets established excessively high coefficients for buildings (due to a decimal mistake in the calculations).

As this significantly increased the value of collectivised assets, there were cases where workshares were recalculated and some complaints had to be solved in the courts.

In the autumn of 1993, the Central Reform Commission compiled a summary of the information on the shortcomings of the agricultural reform. Connected to this, I wrote and published some commission recommendations demonstrating various possible models for the execution of the reform (Tamm, 1993). In these recommendations, I stressed the rights of entitled subjects and demonstrated ways for using the rights. However, people usually did not organise themselves sufficiently to defend their rights.

The following year, 1994, it became clear that some reform commissions were not able to fulfil their duties and the idea of reform trustees was decreed by adopting amendments to the Law on Agricultural Reform. It was decided that a reform trustee would be appointed by the Minister of Agriculture on the proposal of the county governor in the event that the reform commission was unable to complete its tasks. After the appointment, all the tasks and powers of the commission were passed to the reform trustee. The trustee had to find a solution to controversies, prepare changes to the reform plans, and organise the sales of assets to compensate collectivised assets in cash. About twenty reform trustees, mostly lawyers, were certified after a four-day training course. This measure did not significantly affect the reform as a whole but in some cases, it helped to bring an end to the reform.

Conclusions and Outcomes

By 1 January 1995, about half the Soviet large-scale farms had been privatised and restructured or reorganised into smaller partnerships, joint-stock companies, or co-operatives. The number of different enterprises in agriculture reached 3,392, which was 11 times the number of kolkhozes and sovkhozes in 1990. Some, less than 2–3% of the large-scale farms remained undivided and they were only reformed. Officially, about half the large-scale farms were still undergoing the reform process, but in reality most of the assets had already been divided or leased to new enterprises.

One by-product of the Law on Agricultural Reform was the emergence of a great number of co-operatives. The underlying cause for this was that the law supported the re-establishment of the farmers' co-operative movement. The author surveyed over 120 of the approximately 600 agricultural co-operatives by sending out a questionnaire in 1995. Most of these co-operatives provided jobs rather than services for their members. They would obviously qualify as "employee-owned" enterprises, but in reality, it was the managers who suggested forming a co-operative to the employees of a collective farm as a whole or one of its departments (Adavere and others; see above). Thus, the idea of a co-operative was often used for opposite purposes: to prevent the division of assets to farmers. On the other hand, the positive side was saving production and workers' jobs. If these co-operatives had not been transformed into other types of enterprises they would most likely have been liquidated or gone bankrupt.

Many times, I have had to answer the following question: What were the crucial things that the authors of the draft for the agricultural reform did not foresee, and what really did happen? First, we hoped for a more active role from the managers of the collective farms, especially on the privatisation of technological units. The inactivity and timidity of the managers of the kolkhoz departments was unexpected. Secondly, we forecast that there would be some intentional delays, as well as conflicting interests and thieving, but what happened exceeded our expectations.

The land reform had no direct legal links to the agricultural reform but it did have a significant influence on the privatisation process. As it became clear that the land reform would be performed through the restitution of land ownership, people understood that the technological units could not continue the tenure of former collective farm land. This was one of the more concrete reasons why the managers were inactive in carrying out the privatisation. They were psychologically not ready to start making rental agreements with the owners who sometimes threatened to deny the former managers the use of their lands. Of course, in reality, most of the former owners who received their land back were not able to farm – they lacked the necessary equipment and capital. However, they often agreed to rent land, but only after they had attempted to farm it by themselves.

In 1995, the politicians demanded that the agricultural reform be accelerated, as the lack of clarity in the ownership of assets was leading to significant losses. Moreover, continuous quarrels about the division of assets upset rural society as a whole. In 1995, experts estimated that one third of the collective farms had already successfully completed the reform and these were usually transformed into partnerships – even if mostly by departments. Another third was in the final stages of the reform. However, approximately one third of the collective farms fell into very complicated and unclear situations and the local reform commissions were unable to complete the reform or were incapacitated in one way or another.

Based on various sources of information, the Central Reform Commission concluded that the main problem hindering the completion of the reform was that the partnerships possessed and used assets in excess of the individual partners' combined shares, thus preventing the privatisation of said assets to other entitled subjects. However, both parties were in fact delaying the reform. Partnerships were using assets that did not belong to them without any rent or responsibility. Others were hoping to get their shares in kind, or even get them in cash, which was the last legal option. In other words, the entitled subjects had not allocated their shares to partnerships as suggested in the reform plan, and the partnerships were illegally using the assets covering the shares of the other beneficiaries. In many cases, entitled subjects were not allowed to become partners, neither were they paid off in cash.

To accelerate the execution of the agricultural reform, the Commission proposed to set a date (in 3–5 years) by which time the assets in the possession of partnerships but not covered with shares should be nationalised and settled in cash. The unused shares would be compensated with EVP vouchers to entitled subjects. The idea was that after adopting such measures both sides would be interested in clarifying the ownership relations and completing the process of privatisation. A draft was prepared at a three-day workshop. The workshop included participants from the county administrations responsible for the management of reforms. Subsequently, the draft was presented to the Ministry of Agriculture. However, it took another year before it was passed by the Parliament (Riigikogu) in June 1996. Some details of the draft were modified, but the principal model remained unchanged. The legal deadline for the agricultural reform was set for 1 December 1996. After this, the county governor was to make a proposal for the compulsory close of the reform.

By that date, the 361 former collective farms were transformed into 710 co-operatives, 600 partnerships, 1,411 joint-stock companies, and 13,513 private farms. The agricultural reform was completed on 171 collective farms – in 91 cases, it was closed by an act of law, and in 80 cases, it was practically closed. However, documentation was not fully implemented (Eesti riigi hetkeseis ja arenguprobleemid, 1996). In general, the main obstacles for completing the reform were debts and pecuniary objections, as the assets delivered for covering debts could not be sold or had to be sold at book value.

Of the total value of collectivised assets, 365.5 million kroons were compensated in kind or cash and 235.5 million kroons (64.4%) were restituted. Of the total sum of 942.9 million kroons in workshares, 797.2 million kroons (84.6%) were realised through privatisation. Municipal councils had taken over 6,470 different items and 730 items were given to state-owned farms, enterprises, or institutions.

Bankruptcy procedures were initiated for 19 collective farms and reform trustees were appointed in eight cases. During 1995, the Ministry of Agriculture received 200 complaints concerning the execution of the agricultural reform and there were illegalities in more than half the cases (ibid. 65).

There are no usable statistics on the economic results and losses of the reform. It is simply impossible to calculate the influence of the collapsed markets, the dumping of imported foodstuffs, all the privatisation games around processing plants, agricultural reform, and the transformation of large-scale farms into smaller units or family farms. The "grand old man" of Estonian agrarian economists, Johannes Kaubi presented the main factors for the decreasing agricultural production in a descending order of significance in June 1996 as follows (Kaubi, 1996):

"At first the economic conditions substantially changed, then followed the agrarian reform with its concrete troubles and thirdly, weakened by those factors, agriculture fell victim to the ideological strife which concentrated around agricultural policy." I agree with his conclusions, since it appears reasonable to pay attention to the market situation, to macro-level economic conditions, and maybe to the government's agricultural policy, too.

Against the background of restructuring agriculture in all the Central and East European countries, the results of the Estonian agricultural reform look quite promising. In Bulgaria, priority was given to land reform by restitution. The local Land Reform Law determined the destiny of the large-scale farms that were liquidated. The result was chaotic, as a huge number of really small farms, approximately from a half to two hectares, were established. Obviously, this aggravated the difficult situation and caused the collapse of the entire economy.

The opposite example is Hungary, where agricultural reform went very smoothly. According to the law of March 1992, collective farms were transformed into co-operatives by changing the pertaining articles only. However, the subsequent collapse of the market and "price scissors" caused a loss in revenue and a mass of bankruptcies. As the situation worsened, people grew increasingly disapproving of transition. It seemed that the magic moment was lost, and true transition was delayed. In most Central and East European countries, restored family farms have less land than in Estonia. However, in the near future it is obvious that many Estonian partnership enterprises will have to be transformed into family or partnership farms and enlarged to the scale suitable for modern machinery and technologies by renting land.

The Estonian agricultural reform was decentralised and in every village it was implemented by local leaders. This also applied to Kanepi, and what happened there was quite typical for more than one third of all collective farms in Estonia.

References

Eesti riigi hetkeseis ja arenguprobleemid, [The Current Situation of Estonia and Problems of Development], Tallinn, June 1996, p. 65.

Eesti Vabariigi Valitsuse Istungi Protokoll (1991), [The Minutes of the Government of Estonia], 30 September 1991, article no. 52. päevakorrapunkt 3.

Kaubi, J. (1996), 'Põllumajandust on raputanud kolm tormihoogu' [Three Surges That Shook Agriculture], *Sõnumileht*, 12 June 1996.

Maaleht (1990), *Maaleht*, 8 November 1990.

Rahva Hääl (1989), *Rahva Hääl*, 1 August 1989.

Raig, I. (1987), *Teie pere majapidamine: sotsiaalmajanduslikud ja õiguslikud aspektid*, [The Household of Your Family: Social, Economic and Legal Aspects],Valgus, Tallinn.

Raig, I. (ed) (1988), *Maaelu: Sotsiaalse arengu probleeme Eesti külas*, Valgus, Tallinn.

Tamm, M. (1988 and 1989), 'Suurmajandite juhtimise raskused' [Difficulties in the Management of the Collective Farms], *Sotsialistlik Põllumajandus*, no. 24/88, pp.17–18, no. 1/89, pp. 24–26, no. 2/89, pp.21–23.

Tamm, M. (1991a), 'Majandijuht – tulevane pankur' [The Executive Manager of a Farm – Future Banker], *Põllumajandus*, no. 3. pp. 26–28.

Tamm, M. (1991b), 'Omandireform. Tervikvara ja suurtalu – alternatiiv popsitaludele' [Property Reform and Partnership Farms], *Põllumajandus*, no. 1. pp. 1–3.

Tamm, M. (1992), 'Situation and Forecast of Rural Life and Agriculture of Estonia in 1992–1994', *Development of Rural Life and Agriculture of Estonia*, Estonian Association of Agricultural Economists, no. 1/1992, pp. 29–33.

Tamm, M. (1993), 'Kui reform ei edene' [Why the Reform Does Not Progress], *Maaleht*, 18 November 1993.